Huston Smith: Wisdomkeeper

# Huston Smith: Wisdomkeeper

Living the World's Religions

The Authorized Biography
of a 21st Century Spiritual Giant

By
Dana Sawyer

FONS VITAE

First published in 2014 by
Fons Vitae
49 Mockingbird Valley Drive
Louisville, KY 40207
http://www.fonsvitae.com
Email: fonsvitaeky@aol.com

Copyright Fons Vitae 2014

Library of Congress Control Number: 2014939305
ISBN 978-1891785-290

Printed in Canada

To Stephani

With profound gratitude
to
Dean and Lois Griffith,
James E. and Sarah Haynes,
Jill Haden Cooper,
Anne Brewer Ogden,
Nana Lampton,
Cornelia W. Bonnie
Rowland Antoine Dumesnil Miller,
and
Benjamin Worth Bingham Miller
for
their generous support.

# Table of Contents

My soul is from elsewhere, I'm sure of that, and I intend to end up there.

Jalal ad Deen Rumi


It's hard to see how modern man can survive on what he now gets from his conscious life—now that there is a kind of veto against impermissible thoughts, the most impermissible being the notion that man might have a spiritual life he is not conscious of which reaches out for transcendence.

Saul Bellow, at his Nobel Prize ceremony in 1976

# Foreword

In the fall of 1969, I began my first year of college at Western Connecticut State University. It was a trying time in American society, with the Vietnam War raging and several cultural and social revolutions brewing simultaneously, including the civil rights movement and the women's rights movement. There were significant pressures on young people trying to find themselves. Like my contemporaries, I was trying to navigate those pressures and looking for answers. But I never expected to find them where I did, in a philosophy class.

I had not, in my eighteen years, had any interest in philosophy until we read Aldous Huxley's *Brave New World*, as part of our course on "The Nature of Man." The professor, Dr. Robert Rice, had a talent for engaging students in the material and opening their minds. One day, at the beginning of the term, a young man in our class blurted out that philosophy was a waste of time, and he didn't understand why he, a history major, should have to take it. "Are you saying that philosophy is *entirely* a waste of time?" Rice asked. To which the student answered that it was. "Then you're making a truth claim. In fact, it's an absolutist truth claim. Aren't you actually saying that philosophy is a waste of time *in your philosophy*?" The student scratched his head. Rice had worked his magic.

Professor Rice had pointed out that we don't escape philosophy by ignoring it. Reading other of Huxley's books, I came across a passage in *Ends and Means* that perfectly made Rice's point:

> To the "practical man" the [philosophical questions] may seem irrelevant. But in fact they are not. It is in the light of our beliefs about the ultimate nature of reality that we formulate our conceptions of right and wrong; and it is in the light of our conceptions of right and wrong that we frame our conduct, not only in the relations of private life, but also in the sphere of politics and economics. So far from being irrelevant, our metaphysical beliefs are the finally determining factor in all our actions.

*****

I was hooked. This was the first of two epiphanies I had that year, and the beginning of my interest in philosophy.

My goal was to find a meaningful and defensible foundation for my values and actions. I didn't only want to understand what renowned thinkers of the past had said about the nature of reality, but weigh their positions to frame my own. Pouring through scores books over the next year, I did, like many people in my generation, look for answers in Asian texts, including the *Bhagavad-Gita*, the Upanishads and the *Tibetan Book of the Dead*. Studying these texts triggered my second epiphany that year, an epiphany that came as a question: what if the Western philosophical tradition had been wrong to believe that Truth (capitalized here to signify the variety of truth that brings ultimate meaning and purpose) is an idea? What if Truth cannot be captured in a framework of concepts anymore than a rhinoceros can be captured in a butterfly net? What if, as Hindus and Buddhists believe, Truth is experiential and dependent upon an enhanced state of consciousness? This idea haunted me, and still does.

During the following years, and as I studied philosophy further at other universities (in Hawaii, Toronto and Iowa), I kept coming back to Hinduism and Buddhism, and their notion of Truth as a state of mind and a condition of consciousness. I grew interested also in the work of Westerners who had been attracted to Asian thought, and who had sought Truth as an experiential insight, including Ralph Waldo Emerson and Henry David Thoreau. This led me back to Aldous Huxley, and his book *The Perennial Philosophy*, which I had read my second year of college.

Since this book deals with the perennial philosophy in depth, we won't look into it now, except to say that it is what led me to Huston Smith. Huxley's viewpoint had urged him to learn meditation (as it did me), but it also led him to study the world's religions for clues to the primordial spirituality he believed resides in each of them. Wishing to do the same, I purchased a copy of Huston Smith's *The Religions of Man* in a used bookshop, and delighted in how succinctly and sympathetically he described each tradition. Huston seemed to emphasize elements of the religions that were useful to me as a perennialist, and I was bowled over backwards when I learned he had been a friend of Huxley's. I would later discover that Huston had a different perspective on organized religion than Huxley, valuing it where Huxley did not, but both men were perennialists and offered good arguments for the position. During the 1970s, there were no two books I read more often than *The Perennial Philosophy* and *The Religions of Man*, viewing them as primary resources for my own journey.

In 1977, I met Huston for the first time. I was a graduate student studying Asian religions at the University of Hawaii and Huston had been invited to give a lecture. After the lecture, I went up to the podium and waited patiently to thank Huston for insights I had gleaned from his recent book, *Forgotten Truth*. We talked for a moment, and I was struck by his poise and presence. His demeanor was something I had encountered with the yogis and swamis who had taught me meditation, but unusual in a necktie-wearing professor.

What, if anything, is attractive about the perennial philosophy? What are its philosophical virtues? And related to this, why do Westerners seem increasingly drawn to it? As one way of answering these questions, and after I had become a professor, I began to research why Huxley and Huston Smith had been attracted to Asian thought, which, in 2000, led me to write a biography of Aldous Huxley focused on his philosophical development. To my delight, Huston endorsed the book and invited me to visit him in California when I came there to promote it. I did so. And that's what led me to write the book you're holding.

In 2002, when I met Huston for the second time, we formed an instant bond and fell easily into conversation about mutual interests. Later that evening, after having dinner at a Thai restaurant near his home in Berkeley, Huston gave me a new copy of *Forgotten Truth*. When I opened it, I saw that he had written, "For Dana. Kindred spirit. Huston Smith." I was moved and flattered. An author I had admired for nearly thirty years had suddenly become a friend.

Huston asked me who I would write about next.

"How about you?" I answered.

"No, not me!" Huston replied curtly.

"Why not?" I wanted to know.

"Because I'm not really worthy of a biography," Huston answered, expressing his characteristic humility.

"Not true," I said, knowing a good deal about Huston Smith's significance. But I could see he had made up his mind. I thought to myself, "Well, that's it."

But it wasn't. Huston, my wife and I had dinner that night with Jon and Anna Monday, two of Huston's close friends, who had admired my Huxley bio. Two years later, Jon contacted me to say that he had re-pitched my idea of a biography to Huston. To his surprise, and mine, Huston had finally agreed. When I called Huston to ask what had changed his mind, he said, "I thought I might be expressing too much ego by acting so humble. You and Jon think it's a good idea, so why should I object? I decided to be like the tree that just lets the wind blow through! Do you still want to do it?"

I had recovered sufficiently from writing my last book to say 'yes,' and that's how I came to write this biography, or I should say, that is how I got permission to write it. Once permission came, I began working in earnest, reading everything in print by and about Huston Smith, including his early works of which I hadn't been aware. Then I started talking with Huston himself, spending many hours in his home, interviewing him and his wife, Kendra. The next step was a visit to the Huston Smith archives at Syracuse University, where Larry Smeed, one of the curators, helped me copy many pertinent documents and resources. Also, I am grateful for interviews (in person or by phone) with many important figures from Huston's life, including Michael Murphy, Ram Dass, Michael Horowitz, Deepak Chopra, Seyyed Hossein Nasr, Gray Henry, Phil Cousineau, Pico Iyer, Jeffrey Kripal, Ralph Metzner, Robert Thurman, John Roger Barrie, Walter Nowick, Stanislav Grof, Paul Lee, Robert Forte, Mary Beaton, Joan Halifax Roshi, Khen Rinpoche Lobzang Tsetan, Arvind Sharma, Laura Huxley, Phil Novak, Hilary Putnam, Tim Cassady, James Cutsinger and many others. Meanwhile, I also began several correspondences with figures from Huston's life, including his daughters, Gael and Kim, with whom I'm still in touch.

It took me nearly seven years to complete this biography, with lots of stolen moments from summer vacations, weekends, evenings and holidays, and through all of this my extraordinary wife, Stephani, was rock solid in her support of the project, having grown fond of Huston during our many visits with him in California (I have a photo of them hugging and laughing on my bookshelves as I write this). I want to thank her for that, while also thanking all the people who welcomed me into their homes or took the time to write or speak with me on the phone. I take it as a testimony to Huston's presence and personality that everyone I contacted was not only willing but eager to talk about him, giving me the time I needed to get things right.

Thanks also go to Julian Piras, Jeffrey Kripal, Eric Reinders, Jon Monday, Anna Monday and Philip Goldberg for reading all or most of the manuscript, and to Huston and Kendra Smith for working with me every step of the way. Thanks also to Stanislav Grof and Michael Murphy for reading the chapters pertinent to their involvement with Huston. Cathrine Duclos and Eileen Ringel transcribed some of the interviews, and my book agent, Lynn Franklin, gave me excellent feedback on the initial drafts. Lynn worked hard to find the manuscript a good home, which it finally did, at Fons Vitae, where Gray Henry, the director, and my editor, Cindy Castleman, did everything to give Huston's story its due. Jon and Anna Monday deserve a special thank you, for reading the many drafts, correcting my understanding of the Vedanta Society, conducting emergency interviews with Huston when I was stuck on a particular point and putting together most of the photographs that appear in this book. Further thanks to the team of Fons Vitae proofreaders—Anne Ogden, Elena Lloyd-Sidle, Christopher Tate, Steven Johnson, and Graeme Vanderstoel—for their valuable input and suggestions.

To conclude, I only wish to add that I struggled with how to refer to Huston in his biography. Formally and academically, it made sense to call him "Smith," but subjects of biographies are often identified by their first names. Huston is a friend of mine, so in the end "Huston" won out. I hope the reader looks forward to learning about Huston, that rare philosopher who not only wished to describe the human condition but improve it.

Dana Sawyer
New Year's Day, 2014
Portland, Maine

# Preface:
# The Man Who Wrote the Book
# on the World's Religions

No philosophical realist was ever more vigorous in insisting upon the existence of truth, nor was any skeptic ever more cautious in citing the human difficulties in reaching truth, particularly any account of it for which he has little sympathy, than is Huston Smith. . . . Huston Smith has won his way into the most elevated philosophical circles of our day.

> James B Wiggins
> Professor Emeritus of Religion at Syracuse University,
> former chair of the American Academy of Religion

In November of 2007, in San Diego, Huston Smith was honored at the annual meeting of the American Academy of Religion (AAR), the largest organization of scholars of religion in the United States. There was thundering applause as this frail, eighty-eight year old man, cane in hand, took the stage to accept appreciation for his many years of explicating the world's religions, including a richer, less culturally biased, exploration of their roots in mystical experience. Arguably, he was the best-known advocate for religious tolerance since Mahatma Gandhi. Huston, with a twinkle in his eye, accepted the tribute humbly, as he had accepted so many other honors in recent years, including the "Man of Conscience Award" from San Francisco's Grace Cathedral in 2007, an award whose previous recipients include Martin Luther King Jr., Rosa Parks, and the Dalai Lama. But this tribute from the AAR was especially moving because it came from his academic peers, colleagues he had worked with and sometimes fought with for more than five decades.

Huston braced himself with his long arms at the podium, his back bent with osteoporosis, and then smiled. Prior to Huston Smith, the academic view of religion had been that it was either a waste of time or something much worse. Freud had said that religion is a delusion we create to comfort ourselves in an uncertain world; we, based on an "infantile model," project a cosmic father or mother onto an indifferent universe in order to have someone to plead to for help when matters get beyond our control. Marx, another modernist who theorized against religion, had argued that religion is the opiate of the masses, a drug fed to us by our oppressors, placating us with a series of pretty lies so we won't launch revolutions against them.

Attendance at churches was at an all-time high in America in the late 1950s when Huston wrote his landmark book on religion, *The Religions of Man*; however, in contrast with popular opinion, the job of a majority of professors, in a majority of colleges, was to explain religion away as something quaint and outdated—something we'd be better off without. It was the fifties after all. The Russians had just launched the world's first satellite and the United States was trying to catch up in the "Space Race." In short, it was high time we outgrew our non-scientific ways of making sense of the world. Modern society, using scientific advances in technology, medicine, and engineering, would lasso heaven out of the sky and pull it down to earth, disposing of religion and its superstitions in the process. But Huston Smith had warned that there might be a baby in the bathwater we were throwing out, and that religion should not be indiscriminately discarded. There should be attention given to the benefits it had delivered for millennia, including that it gives purpose to human existence, a benefit that science still seemed ill equipped to replace.

Huston had hoped for an assessment of religion that was less one-sided. While modernists and existentialists in the 1950s were telling us that the ultimate truth is that there is no ultimate truth, Huston urged us to keep our minds open, taking care not to discard the world's traditional platforms of meaning just because some philosophers of the time found them suspect. Academic conferences on religion are now much more tolerant of the value of religion than they were in the 1950s and we have Huston Smith in large part to thank for that shift in acceptance. No small accomplishment, and yet it is only one of his many achievements.

Huston Smith was the first person to describe the mechanics of Tibetan harmonic chanting, an important practice in Tantric Buddhism. While staying for three weeks in a Tibetan monastery in India in 1964, Huston heard in the monk's voices something that scientists of acoustics later verified as having been unknown to the West, bringing a new word into the musicological lexicon, "multiphonic chanting." Huston was also a pioneer in research with psychedelic drugs, studying them for their spiritual potential. In 1964, he published a definitive essay on their import for religion that became the most reprinted article in the history of *The Journal of Philosophy*. Huston taught groundbreaking workshops on the value of mysticism and religion at the Esalen Institute in Big Sur, California (and his friend, the mythologist Joseph Campbell, sometimes taught with him). He testified in 1993 before the United States Congress on behalf of the Native American Church, in support of their sacramental use of the peyote cactus, and this effort helped them to win a landmark decision in the cause of religious freedom. In 1996, Bill Moyers, having interviewed Huston for a five-part program on public television, deemed him the "wisest man in America." Huston inspired contemporary writers on religion and spirituality such as Deepak Chopra, Karen Armstrong, Andrew Weil, Stanislav Grof, Joan Halifax Roshi, Ken Wilber (whose first book Huston helped get published), Andrew Harvey, Pico Iyer and a host of others. In summary, Huston was for more than fifty years the most celebrated advocate of world religions, interfaith dialogue and comparative religion in the world.

Perhaps above all, Huston helped to reclaim the significance of metaphysics in the study of philosophy, even challenging his colleagues to consider that the highest Truth of human existence is not known with the rational mind but by other aspects of our being. Truth is an experience, an existential enhancement of what we are and how we apprehend things in consciousness. It is the experience of something noetic (from the Greek word, *nous*), spiritual 'other,' that can fill our awareness with *gnosis* ('spiritual knowledge'), connection, meaning, hope and purpose. What the advocates of many religions termed "enlightenment," Huston urged his colleagues to take seriously as a possibility of the human potential, and many of them did.

Many of the scholars in the audience at the AAR that night in San Diego knew Huston best as the primary champion of Aldous Huxley's "perennial philosophy," a perspective that had, at one time or another, drawn Huston into debate with several of those who were present, including Steven Katz of Boston University. Huxley had argued that beyond disagreements among the religions on points of beliefs and values, there is a shared mystical experience of what Meister Eckhart had termed the "Divine Ground of Being." The apprehension of this state is the highest truth we can know, and causes a transfiguration of what we *are*. Huston, having studied the perennial philosophy with Huxley himself, became its primary spokesperson during the 1960s, 1970s and 1980s, and in the 1980s, this position led him into academic disputes. After his heated and high profile debate with Katz, regarding the viability of the perennial philosophy and its practicability as a theory of the origin of religion, it was demonstrated to most scholars that whether or not Huston was right, the perennial philosophy was certainly a rational and viable position. With such debates in mind, Huston was deeply touched by the applause of his colleagues, for whether they agreed with him or not, it was clear he had been regarded seriously.

Huston held a realistic view of his own place in history. He had not unlocked the DNA code, nor had he discovered the cure for cancer. What he had done was defend the world's religions as viewpoints more valuable than grist for one academic theory or the other. That was his unique contribution. He had not formulated any breakthrough theories but he *had* supported the breakthrough theories of others, sitting, as he often put it, at the "elbow of greatness" in his friendships with Aldous Huxley, Joseph Campbell, Thomas Merton, the Dalai Lama and others. Huston had been the religions' champion and a gadfly against the strictly materialistic view of the universe that had become entrenched in academia, and in that he had been effective—as this tribute in San Diego demonstrated.

To cap the evening, Harper San Francisco, the publisher of several of Huston's most important books, announced they had established an annual "Huston Smith Award" for scholars who worked in the same vein. Smiling broadly, Huston was reminded of a quote from Socrates that he had once observed on a moonlit night in Athens, inscribed on a temple near the Parthenon, "no wasted journey, that." Acknowledging the applause, he nodded his head in gratitude and thought back on his childhood, eight decades earlier, to a time when, as the son of Christian missionaries, he had grown up in China, a boy never imagining where his journey would lead him.

# Chapter One:
# A Middle Child of the Middle Kingdom

If anything characterizes modernity it is the loss of the sense of transcendence—of a reality that exceeds and encompasses our everyday affairs.

Peter Berger, sociologist

Nothing has changed the nature of man so much as the loss of silence.

Max Picard, Swiss philosopher

Huston Smith was born on May 31, 1919, in Soochow, China, fifty miles west of Shanghai and thirty miles from Changshu (in Mandarin, Dzang Zok), the village where he actually grew up. Huston's father, Wesley Moreland Smith, a graduate of Vanderbilt's Methodist seminary, came to Soochow a decade earlier to teach English at the local university, and to learn Chinese in preparation for starting a mission in the countryside. Huston's mother, Alice, had grown up in China (which still referred to itself as the "Middle Kingdom," based on its belief that it was surrounded by less civilized countries) as the Methodist daughter of missionaries from Fredonia, New York. Fluent in Chinese, Alice had left China only long enough to attend Knox College in Galesburg, Illinois, where she mastered the piano in preparation for teaching the instrument to Chinese girls back home.

By the time Huston arrived, his parents, who married in 1910, had long since moved to Changshu, returning to Soochow only for holidays or to buy supplies—or to see the doctor, as they had when Alice was about to give birth. Huston was to be a middle son, arriving between his brother Robert, born in 1917, and Walter, the youngest, born in 1921. Unlike his fair-haired brothers, he came into this world with dark hair and even darker eyes—so much so that his parents' friends sometimes joked that there must have been a mix-up at the hospital. "The older and younger boys, we'll give you," they told to his parents, "but we're not too sure about this middle one. Are you certain he's yours?"[1]

As an infant Huston was sickly, once nearly dying of dysentery, but as he grew older he gained strength—a relief to his parents who had lost their first child. Wesley Jr. had died in his father's arms on his second Christmas Eve, collapsing while he was in the process of reaching for an ornament on the Christmas tree.[2]

The Smiths' church in Changshu, which Huston and his brothers would attend every Sunday, attracted a fairly large congregation of seventy or eighty, and Huston attributes this success to his father's emphasis on Christian charity rather than conversion. World War I had ended the November before Huston was born, and China was then, despite its growing antipathy to the West, moving away from its traditional folkways, including those of religion. Wesley, drawing on a Midwestern sensibility rich in community spirit, established a school for girls in Changshu even before he built his church, and he and Alice soon added a medical clinic and an orphanage to their enterprises. In short, Huston's parents were pious but they were not dogmatic, and this deeply appealed to the Chinese. The Methodist Board of Missions often sent Huston's father shipments of medicines, and whenever these were distributed, he was careful not to show special favor to his parishioners. Everyone who came to him was treated with equal respect, and this came to matter a great deal to the Chinese' perception of him—as it would later matter a great deal to Huston. "My father inoculated almost everyone in the area against smallpox when I was a child and I was very proud of him for that."

Huston lived with his family in a compound near the center of town, in a small house his father had built, humble and without the convenience of a flush toilet. "Each morning a man came around and left coins for the privilege of composting our 'night-soil,'" Huston related. But hardships didn't matter to the Smiths because they were such a close-knit family, "living," as Huston once put it, "like millionaires without money."[3] For Wesley and Alice, it had never been about getting rich; it was about living a righteous life, and Huston respected them for their commitment, and he remembers his childhood in general as a happy time. Several memories stand out and in particular he remembers the family's Christmases together: "In daytime during Advent, my two brothers and I would accompany our father to houses of church members to deliver red lanterns. They had 'Jesus Christ' painted in large black characters on one side, and the character for 'birthday' on the other. The lanterns were large and we boys had to hold our arms almost straight out to carry them all."[4]

Other memories suggested how deeply Huston was affected by his early, idyllic years in China: "The stillness of the night in a town that had no engines, the brilliance of the stars in a town without street lamps, the sound of the night watchman waking me with a gong that he carried on the end of a bamboo pole, riding on barges up and down the Yangtze, cormorants lining the sides of small boats with strands of straw tied around their necks to keep them from swallowing the fish they had caught. It was a place where the modern world just didn't exist."

Rickshaws moved the common people around town while the wealthy traveled in sedan chairs carried by two men with long poles on their shoulders. A range of small mountains crowded up to the walls of the city on one side and the river ran along the other, flowing into the Yangtze, twelve miles away. Changshu was densely populated in those days, as it is now, with the houses usually sharing a common wall between them, and with the lanes so narrow that when Huston stretched out his little-boy's arms, his hands touched both sides. Each morning, the single-page daily newspaper was plastered to the walls in various parts of the city to be read by the 20 percent of the population who were literate.[5] "It was primitive in many ways," Huston explained, "but for a boy it was paradise. Besides, in many other ways, including culturally, it was complex and sophisticated."

Huston remembers that life in China, though pleasant, had its particular set of challenges. "China's central government was weak," Huston wrote in his book, *And Live Rejoicing*, "and War Lords battled one another for power and control. Twice in

18

my childhood the American Consulate in Shanghai sent word that for safety's sake we must leave our town as soon as possible and go to Shanghai, taking only what we ourselves could carry in our hands, but only on the second of these evacuations was I old enough to understand what was happening. . . . [When] my father handed over the key to the house to Tsai Kung, our cook, not knowing if we would ever see him or our house again, I saw a tear drop from our cook's eye onto the key, and we departed."

A happier memory of that time involves a beautiful tea set decorated with Chinese characters that Huston recalls his parents bought from a traveling merchant who came to their door. Some months after the purchase, the presiding bishop of the area, a very formal Chinese gentleman, arrived to check up on Wesley's mission. Huston's parents, wanting to afford the bishop every possible hospitality, served him with their special tea set. But when the bishop scrutinized his teacup he found that it read, 'Tinsin-Pukow Railway.' "My parents hadn't paid much attention to the calligraphy," Huston told me, "assuming it was a snippet of classical poetry, but as it turned out, they were serving the bishop tea in purloined cups!"

*****

Huston's first lesson in a religion other than his own came because of a vacant lot across the street from his parents' back gate. The spot was generally reserved for public festivals and other events, and even as a boy he often took note of what happened there, including a vivid memory of a funeral:

> [A] life-size paper house was constructed that contained real tables, chairs, and beds (on which I saw genuine silk coverlets spread). Sheaves of rice straw were propped against the house, and at the appointed moment (while Buddhist priests processed around the house playing flutes and chanting) the makeshift structure was consigned to flames. The obvious point of the ritual . . . was to ensure a comfortable hereafter for the deceased. In the last such rite that I witnessed, a *papier-mâché* replica of a Model-T Ford was parked by the front door, presumably on the assumption that whereas the deceased had only *lived* in this world, he would *really* live in the next.[6]

Huston's parents taught him that these practices were based on Chinese superstition, but Huston noted that, "The only accurate definition of *superstition* is 'what you don't believe,'" and made clear to him that even as a child he had kept an open mind. "It is just how I was for some reason," he stated, and then, looking for a cause, noted that his parents, though unshakable in their faith, were never overly judgmental of their neighbors. "They sometimes saw what they took to be superstition but they were far more liberal than most other missionaries and I prized them for that. They respected the culture, and even employed a Chinese scholar to come in for an hour, three days a week, to teach my brothers and me how to write Chinese characters. I still have my Chinese primer and I can still recite those lessons. It was a great gift from my parents, as I came to realize later."

Huston's mother was especially tolerant, having been exposed as a child to several of the native religions, and with a fairly sophisticated understanding of the functional value of those religions. She taught her sons not only to respect the Chinese people but to appreciate their history and values, and she never suggested that the Smiths were somehow superior to the people around them. In fact, it was she who had hired the

19

Chinese tutor, an elderly Confucian scholar, to help establish in her sons' minds that the Chinese were their equals. In the years ahead, she would keep her boys on track with their language lessons and use her knowledge of Chinese culture to keep her husband from stepping on the toes of his parishioners. Huston reminisced that an American bishop had once visited their church to give a sermon and a disaster had nearly ensued. Having no knowledge of the Chinese, the bishop began to make a joke to the packed hall, saying something about how one's ancestors are like potatoes, "since the best part of them is underground." For members of a society steeped in ancestor worship, this would have been a tremendous insult; however, the day was saved when Alice made eye contact with the Chinese translator, who was red-faced with embarrassment, and cued him that it would be best to edit out the embarrassing punch line. The joke flopped but the day was saved.

When talking about his childhood, Huston saved a special smile for his mother. It was clear that she had been the deepest source of emotional comfort in his early life, and he related fondly how she had read to him and his brothers every night before bed, and gave special care to them when they were sick. His mother had also been their schoolteacher until they finished the eighth grade. One part of her lessons that Huston especially cherished was her teaching of music to them. Huston often heard his mother play the piano, in church and at home, and she had instilled in him a love for singing. "Every Sunday we sang hymns," he said. "Typically the hymns had four verses, and I would sing the soprano line in the first verse, alto in the second, tenor in the third, and bass in the fourth. This was something special that I got from my mother, a love of music."

*****

In 1932, at the age of thirteen and having finished eighth grade, Huston was obliged to leave home and attend the American High School in Shanghai, a move that he accepted as the first step in his journey toward becoming a missionary like his father but that also put an abrupt end to childhood. Most of his memories of high school are pleasant if uneventful, having to do with making new friends, learning new subjects, and transitioning from boyhood to young adulthood. His first weeks in Shanghai, however, were quite traumatic. Having been so close to his mother, and having lived an insular life for the most part, he admitted to me that he had spent his first three weekends at school crying his eyes out. "However," he added with a chuckle, "after that it was all over and I was fine."

Huston stayed in Shanghai for most school vacations, since they were so short, but Christmas vacations were long enough for him and his brothers to return to Changshu. "I looked forward immensely to going back home, but the trip was an ordeal. The three-hour train ride wasn't so bad, for at least we were out of the wind; but the five hours on the launch going up-river were torture. We kept wiggling our toes and thinly-gloved fingers to try to keep the circulation going. When we arrived, our cook, Tsai Kung, would always be on the dock waiting for us, to help with our luggage. But even when we arrived home the ordeal wasn't over, for we would have to plunge our bare feet into a pail of almost freezing water in the hope of preventing chilblains. Still, we were happy. A warm supper was awaiting, and then we would tumble into our warm beds—spent, but infinitely happy."

# A Middle Child of the Middle Kingdom

## WHAT HE CARRIED FORWARD

What did Huston take away from those childhood years? He points out that people often assume, "plausibly though inaccurately," that he inherited a deep Christian piety from his missionary parents, or that he, having been surrounded by exotic religions, became inspired to study them. "Not true on either count," he confided. As a member of a minister's household, he accepted the presence of Christianity as a fact of life, and he had taken it in, as he often later remarked, "*cum lacte*, with my mother's milk," but hadn't been either particularly devout or overly interested in salvation. Furthermore, regarding the religions outside his door, they were also taken for granted, as part of life's window dressing, to be ignored for the deeper boyhood concerns of fishing, tree climbing, kite flying, biking along the town wall, and other such pastimes. But what generally *did* come across from his boyhood was an unequivocal faith in life's inherent goodness, and Huston came to see that as no small inheritance.

Huston explained in 2001, in an interview with journalist Richard Gazadayka, the difference between the faith in life he had been given as a child and faith in a specific religion:

> I think that faith is a character structure, and therefore if it's present, it's present more deeply than the specifics one has faith in. . . . I think faith is deeply ingrained in my stance toward the world rather than in any specific belief. I can give you an anecdote. When I was in college, I had a summer job and had to get out of bed at 5:30 A.M. Fortunately there was another fellow who had an alarm clock. So all summer long he would come to my room and shake me to wake me up. At the end of the summer, he said, "In the thirty-nine mornings that I woke you, when you roused, even before your eyes opened, your first word was 'good.'" I think that says something about faith, because who likes to be awakened, especially at that age? Faith is an affirmative stance toward life.[7]

Huston attributes this ingrained optimism to growing up in a house where he learned there are dimensions of life that transcend the merely physical. He has spent an entire career arguing that what our lives mean at street level is not the whole story; there is a God's-eye-view of their significance. In an interview with Bill Moyers, Huston once tried to make this point by using an analogy of a child who has dropped his ice cream cone on the ground: "For the child the entire world has been lost and he refuses to be comforted, but the parent has a broader perspective that sets the event into a context. We need to understand that there is a broader context for our existence, for our lives." But Huston quickly added that this is not to say that profound suffering doesn't exist in the world. Indeed it does, he told Moyers. Reality is hierarchical, and as one moves to higher levels of spiritual understanding, suffering becomes more bearable. One gains perspective on life and death as one matures spiritually, and this is a truism that Huston first experienced as part of his upbringing.

For Huston, the rewards of this broader perspective reach beyond our individual concern, offering benefits to society as a whole, and this also was instilled in him by his parents. "We are in good hands," was the message from them, "and in gratitude for that fact it would be good if we bore one another's burdens."[8] Wesley and Alice worked to be good citizens of their community, and their desire to be of service would echo in Huston's actions again and again. When I first met Huston and his wife Kendra in

2002, I noticed they had installed solar panels on their roof, had a hybrid-electric car in their driveway and an organic vegetable garden in the backyard. Tibetan refugees lived in their in-laws cottage and they had two dogs rescued from the local pound. Living modestly and with concern for the earth, Huston commented on the general need for those who are well-off to help those who are not, and he has written that, "It is easy to forget, not the 'third world' but the two-thirds world, where hunger and epidemic disease are the rule of life."[9]  Thanks to the lessons of his parents, throughout his life Huston would work for noble causes.

In terms of his own service, his efforts to create tolerance towards the world's religions and among them stands out sharply, and this is also part of what he carried forward from China. On "New Dimensions" radio with Michael Toms, in 1994, Huston explained that he had had many early lessons in tolerance: "We were in a foreign land—foreign to us. We were the only Westerners in our town, which meant that every contact outside the immediate family was with Chinese. Being a boy I wasn't overly aware of or alert to anthropological issues, nevertheless, the experience of living in an alien land while being welcomed by our associates as friends, that was an experience that I rejoice in." People, he had learned from childhood, could recognize their differences without hating each other.

As an adult, Huston would come to delight in the differences between cultures. Because his parents had taught him that beneath the differences lies a common humanity that binds us all, or that should, Huston developed his generous nature and his general disdain for discrimination, racism, and other forms of bigotry. Huston spent more than five decades in the public eye, working to convince us that we live in one world and must therefore work to live in harmony with each other, and also with our planet. "The sooner we realize that we're all in this together," Huston said, his arms spread wide, seemingly to embrace everyone, "the better our chances for survival are going to be."

## ONE FOOT IN EACH CULTURE

Huston is in many ways quintessentially—and even iconically—American. Lean, tall (standing six-feet-two before his back failed him), bright-eyed, confident and inventive, friendly and sociable, square-shouldered and eager to smile, he enjoys eye contact and gives a firm handshake to whomever he meets. Though well educated, Huston speaks in anecdotes and everyday language, his delivery containing more of an 'aw-shucks' Midwestern tone than a propensity for Ivy-League clipped sentences. But those who know Huston best say he has another side as well—one that is decidedly more Chinese than American. In 1983, when Huston retired from Syracuse University, Philip Novak, one of the only students ever to receive a Ph.D. under Huston's direct supervision, pointed this out in the alumni bulletin:

> Open the pages of the *Analects* to Confucius's description of the *chun-tzu* (ideal gentleman) and you touch Huston's fiber. Chun-tzu [is] one who possesses a truly human heart, who cherishes the arts of learning and teaching, and who is as concerned to teach by moral example as by intellectual knack.[10]

Joan Halifax Roshi, a contemporary Zen master and a close friend of Huston's for many years, agrees, noting in his demeanor "a kind of equanimity associated with someone coming from the East." Kendra, Huston's wife, cites his tendency to be diplomatic and deferential in conversations as part of his Chinese inheritance, while Jon Monday, a filmmaker and friend, finds something "Oriental" in Huston's "graciousness and civility." In *Rational Mysticism* (2003), author John Horgan refers to Huston's bearing as "both gentle and regal,"[11] adding that he has "a slight stoop, perhaps the result of his habit of leaning intently toward anyone speaking to him." This last comment speaks to Huston's general tendency to be self-effacing, almost bowing when he meets someone for the first time. Though he has been a revered professor for most of his life, he somehow still manages to see himself as "no big deal," and when I asked about this, he quoted a line from the *Tao te Ching*: "The axe falls first on the tallest tree."

Huston is a cultural hybrid and proud of it, telling me once that he "relishes every identity with my upbringing in China," and many events of his life serve to illuminate that fact. I offer you one that I find particularly poignant. There is a well-known characteristic of Chinese society called *hsiao*, 'filial piety' or respect for elders, including gratitude toward one's parents. Certainly it was part of Huston's Christian upbringing to "honor thy father and mother," but in his particular case that reverence took on a distinctly Chinese tone. And so in 1958, when he published his first major book, *The Religions of Man*, it included a special dedication to his parents. Written in Chinese, and quoting a Chinese classic, the dedication included the following translation:

> When I behold the sacred *liao wo* [a species of grass symbolizing parenthood]
>     my thoughts return,
> To those who begot me, raised me, and now are tired.
> I would repay the bounty they have given me,
> But it is as the sky: it can never be approached.

Huston's offering of a Confucian dedication to parents who were Methodist missionaries says everything about what he took away from his first seventeen years. He was a young man with one foot in each of two cultures as China itself soon would be (when it mixed Marx's philosophy from the West with its own Asian pragmatism). With his core values now firmly in place, Huston was ready to board a steamship for America to begin college. "Eighteen days on the Pacific, with overnight stops in Nagasaki, Yokohama, and Honolulu, was an exciting prospect," he told me, "and I could hardly wait to get started."

# Chapter Two:
# The Night of Fire

If we take in our hand any volume, of divinity or school metaphysics, for instance; let us ask, Does it contain any abstract reasoning concerning quantity or number? No. Does it contain any experimental reasoning concerning matter of fact or evidence? No. Commit it then to the flames; for it can contain nothing but sophistry and illusion.

David Hume

Literalism is the sin of idolatry—mistaking words for the things they represent.

Aldous Huxley

Huston came to America in 1936, just two weeks after Jesse Owens, the American track star, demonstrated to Hitler at the Berlin Olympics that the "master race" could be defeated in a fair fight. One of the highlights of Huston's overseas voyage was a brief shipboard romance with a young lady named Hilda Benson, who was herself headed off to college in Minnesota. Though there wasn't any hugging or kissing—or even hand-holding ("shuffleboard and ping-pong was about as far as it went"), Huston called it a true romance for both of them.

In California, he bought a train ticket east, arriving eventually in Fayette, Missouri, exhausted but eager to start work on his bachelor's degree. Don Lattin has commented that Huston's college was "chosen by his father,"[1] but it's perhaps more accurate to say his choice had been a forgone conclusion. Huston had accepted since childhood and without much thought that he would become a missionary. "Because we were the only Americans in our small town," he wrote later, "my parents were my only role models, so I grew up assuming that missionaries were what Westerners grew up to be."[2] Furthermore, the Methodist Mission guaranteed that all children of missionaries could receive a tuition-free education from the denominational college nearest to where a given missionary had originally departed, and since Huston's father was poor and from Missouri, Central College (now Central Methodist College) in Fayette, was in Huston's future essentially the moment his father first went abroad.

The prospect of living in a small, mid-western town might not have seemed very exotic or attractive to other young Americans at the time, but for Huston it was both. "I was totally unprepared for the dynamism of the West," he has said. "It was only a little Methodist college in a town of 3,000 in Missouri. But compared to 'Podunk,' China, in those days, it was bright lights and the Big Apple!"[3] The United States was still recovering from the worst of the Great Depression, which had put more than 25 percent of the work force into the bread lines, but Huston felt a deep vibrancy in the air and wanted very much to be part of it. In a radio interview with Michael Toms in 1999, he remarked: "I didn't pay a whit of attention to the rest of the world; I was just scrambling to prove myself a red-blooded American. And, of course, my teachers didn't pay much attention to the rest of the world either."

Huston, a lanky teen with big ears, was trying to cram in as much excitement as possible, given that "It was the settled expectation that I would be back [in China] as soon as I had my theological credentials in hand."[4] During his teen years in Shanghai, Huston had been a quiet boy working on his social skills, but at Central he really came out of his shell, joining the staff and later becoming editor of the college newspaper, and also becoming class president for each of his four years. And as he learned of a bigger world, it wasn't long before he determined that he wouldn't be returning to China when his degree was finished. China was fading into a happy memory that would not be part of his future. He decided that instead of becoming a missionary he would make a "minor occupational shift" and become a minister instead.[5] Actually, his goal was to have his cake and eat it too: by switching his major he would receive the free education of other missionary children but get to stay in America where the real action was taking place.

Despite a fondness for tennis, jazz and American girls, Huston found that what most excited him about America were the new ideas he was being exposed to. He was particularly interested in science, a fondness that would stay with him all his life, and philosophy, and especially philosophical theories of religion, including disparate views on his own faith. Huston's parents weren't without intellectual curiosity and they had encouraged him to scrutinize his faith, to find his own way in his religion, never considering that he might actually leave it. Huston, for his part, learned early on that Christians come in many different stripes, and that not all Christians were as liberal as his parents. Every seven years the family had enjoyed a furlough from China, and when Huston was six years old he had attended first grade in Fayette; at fourteen he had also taken his junior year of high school there. During those visits he had gone with his parents to Pentecostal tent-revivals in Missouri and Arkansas, and learned about fundamentalist Christians who interpreted every word of the Bible literally.[6]

It is a well-established fact of religious studies, beginning with the work of Bronislaw Malinowski (1925), that people become increasingly devout when circumstances are such that their own efforts are unable to improve their lives. During the economic hardships of The Great Depression, as families landed upon harder and harder times, and in many cases were driven from their land by poverty or failed crops, a religious fervor swept through parts of the country, especially the Midwest and the Dust Bowl, and Huston had witnessed this phenomenon firsthand. Evangelicals touted Biblical literalism, preaching in tents large enough to hold a circus. Though Huston's parents enjoyed the Christian fellowship at these events, and certainly understood the comfort of religion, they strongly disagreed with the fundamentalists' position on the Bible. In fact, Huston's father believed literalism was actually a form of heresy, and Huston rejected it for the same reason, seeing it also as untenable, misleading, overly judgmental of other faiths, and, at times dangerously insular in its thinking.

## THE DANGERS OF LITERALISM

*Parabola* magazine celebrated its thirtieth anniversary in 2005—four years after the tragedies of 9/11—with an issue devoted to the dangers of religious extremism. In that issue Huston, who also had been featured in the magazine's first issue in 1976, reminisced about a time when he was fourteen, when his whole clan had gathered on a lake in Michigan for a three-week vacation. His father had gotten into a series of arguments about fundamentalism with one of his uncles, and another uncle, who was also a pastor, had agreed with Huston's father. However, the first uncle, an insurance salesman, had argued vehemently for the literal accuracy of the Bible's every word, and he wouldn't budge on the matter—that night or any other. "As far as I can remember, the heated debate about the inerrancy of the Bible was the centerpiece of their conversation every evening in those three weeks."[7]

Huston pointed out in the *Parabola* interview that fundamentalists often claim they are going back to the religion of Jesus, admonishing other Christians that, "You can interpret the Bible in your way, but I'll interpret it in *His* way," but, Huston added that, "they don't know their history." Elsewhere he has explained that the present form of Christian fundamentalism is barely more than a century old, begun by Charles Hodge, a Calvinist theologian.[8] "Two things," Huston explained in the *Parabola* article, "were ticking the Protestant Church off at the time. . . . One was Darwinism—the idea of human beings created by natural selection working on random mutation, rather than as a supernatural act of God's conscious will, since Darwin had given a plausible, alternative explanation to the origin of mankind that required no supernatural agency. The second thing that aggravated Protestants is what came to be called the 'Higher Criticism' of the Bible, which focused on knowing the actual history of biblical times and understanding the languages involved." Fundamentalists worried that these secular approaches would not afford, or not allow, an interpretation of the Bible's deeper intent, and they might even cause people to question the Bible's validity. For instance, linguistic analysis of the text makes it clear that it was sometimes pieced together from fragments, and that books of the Bible such as *Isaiah* were written over a period of centuries, negating the possibility of there having been, for example, just one Isaiah. In short, science and secularism seemed to be threatening not only the Bible's authority but also its authenticity.

One response to this threat, Huston explained, was to read the Bible in such a way that one's interpretation didn't demand a contradiction of scientific or historical facts. Did it really matter that there might have been more than one author of *Isaiah,* or any other book of the Bible for that matter? With reference to scientific facts, Galileo, a devout Catholic, had argued as early as the seventeenth century that the Church should change its dogma to accommodate new and irrefutable scientific and historical discoveries, and in the nineteenth century, the mainline Protestant Churches (Congregationalist, Methodist, Lutheran, Episcopalian, Baptist, Presbyterian, etc.) had generally agreed with him. One should be able to be a Christian and still advocate for science.

Huston pointed out that it really wasn't much of a stretch for Christians to agree with Galileo, since biblical literalism had never been an aspect of Christianity. In fact, St. Augustine, Bishop of Hippo (354-430), whose views strongly shaped later Christian doctrine, had actually written a pamphlet against literalism, arguing that such a perspective would have to be challenged from page one, given that the Bible begins with

26

two incompatible creation myths. For instance, in the first chapter of Genesis it is said that man was the last creature God set upon the earth, whereas in the second chapter, relating what is often called the "Eden Story," Adam is the first creature put on the earth. Also, in the first creation story, the first man and woman are created simultaneously, "male and female, created he them," but in the Eden Story, Adam is created first and Eve is taken later from his side. "So which is it?" Huston asked with a twinkle in his eye. "Augustine was right, literalism just doesn't work, and there are thousands of examples why."

To resolve contradictions, which occur in the Bible with great regularity, fundamentalists are forced to rely on various pretzel logics that contradict even common sense—not to mention historical and scientific facts, so Huston defends, and has defended for sixty years, the non-literal approach to the Bible endemic to traditional Christianity. In one of his most recent books, *The Soul of Christianity,* he explains that Augustine coached the pious to "reference the spirit of the text," and that that spirit is often communicated symbolically, metaphorically and allegorically. The New Testament makes clear that Jesus taught his disciples "in parables."[9] However, some Christian groups of the nineteenth century felt so threatened they decided to nail a few things down for certain, to form what they believed would be a more solid platform for their faith. However, Huston believes their fear caused them to go too far, or as he once explained it to the writer Phil Cousineau, "the fundamental cause of Fundamentalism is the sense of being threatened."

Huston's thinking on the dangers of religious fundamentalism appears later, but his general pronouncement is that any form of extremism represents a "hijacking of religion" by those who have become too polarized in their thinking, creating an 'us versus them' mentality based on their fear of something, including science, secularism, or even different forms of their own religion. This is the error Huston believes fundamentalists have made—and are still making—not only separating themselves from those of other religions but also from their own Christian brethren.

The liberal Christian viewpoint with which Huston grew up made it easier for him to question the tenets of his faith—and even to explore philosophical ideas outside that faith, but it also bred respect *for* his faith, since his religion included room to test his own beliefs and values. Investigations of new ideas and new interpretations of scripture were part of the curriculum at Central College, and Huston jumped in with both feet, excited about his newfound love of ideas.

## Becoming a Naturalistic Theologian

Huston became a truth seeker his very first year at Central College and today he calls this deep thirst for insight into the nature of reality the "big hunger," in line with the San People of the Kalahari, who contrast it with the "little hunger" for food.[10] One result was that his theology soon became more complex—mostly because of the influence of a brilliant and charismatic young professor named Edwin Ruthven Walker. "I was fresh to a new world," Huston has stated, "and by comparison this teacher seemed omniscient. My life was unformed, and I needed a pattern, a mold to pour my life into, and at the time he provided it."[11]

Walker advocated *naturalistic theology*, a perspective that holds this world is all that exists and that God is the most important entity in it. Relying on scientific facts, naturalistic theology, championed most prominently in those days by Henry Nelson Wieman with help from John Dewey, taught that the processes of God are simultaneous with the processes of nature, and that those processes are natural rather than supernatural, physical rather than metaphysical. And so God is manifest in the Red Sea, as he is manifest in all creation, but he did not miraculously help Moses to part the sea. God's ways are extraordinary but not miraculous. In this view, evolution by natural selection is simply the process by which God created the various species, and with regards to 'God' himself, there is no exception to natural principles; God is a force existing within those principles. Huston has written that from the position of a naturalistic theologian, "God is not omnipotent, but like everything in this world is limited. 'God the semipotent' is the way Annie Dillard speaks of this God." [12]

This transition in theology formed a radical shift in Huston's viewpoint, from the "something more" perspective of his parents to the semipotent-God perspective of Walker and Wieman, but Huston seems to have accepted this move without the blink of an eye, and he would write later: "As I think back on the matter, I am surprised that the collapse of my youthful supernaturalism seems to have caused no trauma." [13] In his youth, he had become part of a religious movement that was actually somewhat anti-religious, in that naturalism denounced all metaphysics—including the postulate of a soul or a heaven beyond this world. Huston had aligned himself with what was then *the* major theological outcome in the war between science and religion that had been raging for more than two centuries, but that outcome had its roots in the eighteenth century.

Naturalistic theology grew out of the work of the Scottish philosopher David Hume (1711-1776), who maintained that all explanations, whether of the cosmos or of the human mind, must be based exclusively on observations taken from the natural world, with no consideration for anything supernatural, since 'supernatural' for him was a term synonymous with 'false' or 'non-existence.' Naturalists of the nineteenth century, building off of Hume, argued that nothing—no phenomenon of any kind—can resist explanation by the sciences, and no explanation beyond science is feasible.

In line with this viewpoint, they argued, and continue to argue today (Daniel Dennett and Stephen Pinker are examples), that the mind is synonymous with the brain; that there are no absolute moral duties or absolute human values; and there are no phenomena for which science cannot account. Of course, this raises philosophical problems, since naturalism has not yet found adequate or agreed-upon explanations for a wide range of everyday human experiences, including the nature of love, aesthetic beauty, or consciousness. And with regards to the latter, we all are currently awake, but what does 'awake' mean and why does it exist? One's body may be currently digesting lunch, but one is not mindful of the process; it happens on its own. So why don't all of one's actions, and reactions, happen on their own? Why must one be awake for some of them? And why must we know that we're awake? What use, evolutionarily speaking, is there in our *knowing* we're awake? What survival value does it have? These things continue to boggle the minds of naturalistic philosophers, escaping both quantification and exclusive explanation—though, and this is the important note here, it would be absurd to deny the existence of these phenomena. They *do* exist and we must deal with them whether they are explicable by science or not.

Given the tone of Huston's later work, most readers will be surprised to learn that he started out as a fundamentalist of naturalistic theology, but naturalism was in vogue on college campuses at that time, supported by the work of Alfred Ayer, who had published *Language, Truth and Logic* in 1936, the same year that Huston arrived in Fayette. Naturalistic theology was about the only 'religious' position that could gain traction in philosophical circles, and this helps make clear Huston's choice; he was under the spell of a brilliant professor who gave him compelling reasons for embracing a new perspective—heady stuff for a young newcomer.

## THE NIGHT OF FIRE

Of course, not all of Huston's concerns were philosophical and not all of his worries were theological in nature. There were practical problems to solve, including what to do during summer vacations. China was too far from Missouri to even think of going home, and travel was too costly. His college expenses were covered by his scholarship but he had no financial support during his vacations, so he had to find other means of making it through the long, hot summers—and this was especially challenging during a time when so many were out of work. Fortunately, he had a few options. "My father grew up on a farm three-and-a-half miles south of Marshall, Missouri," he recalled. "And so the first summer I went to that farm. Two maiden aunts lived there. I would milk the cows and do unskilled labor. And then the second summer was the same except that I had four little, country churches." In the Methodist Church there was a structure whereby a district superintendent matched ministers with congregations, and since the superintendent in Fayette knew of Huston's plight, he assigned him to preach at four churches in the cornfields.

Over the three months that followed his sophomore year, Huston hitchhiked among these churches, dividing his time in such a way that he could visit each of them three times during the summer break, and after only two years of college, Huston was already preaching. His pay consisted of the coins put into the collection plate so needless to say, he barely got by. Regarding his credentials, Huston once explained: "In order to preach, why there are two echelons of ordination: an 'elder,' which is more modest, and a 'deacon,' which is higher than that. I had become an 'elder,' so I could officiate. I rather wince now that I was pontificating at my age [barely nineteen] but with the hubris of youth, I did it."

Once back at school for his junior year, Huston was reunited with his friends—including his first real girlfriend, Mabel Martin, who stayed in a relationship with him for more than two years, separating immediately after graduation. On the recommendation of Walker, he also joined an honors society that year, called The Philosophy and Religion Club, formally listed in the college directory by its Greek name, "Phi Rho Kappa." Many topics were discussed in the club, including the social and moral ramifications of philosophy and ideology, along with the possibility of America's entrance into the new war with Germany, and this storm of ideas had an enormous effect on Huston, so much so that one night it reached a kind of crescendo. After strolling back to his dormitory from one of the club's meetings, his stomach full of cherry pie *à la mode*, Huston lingered with some friends in the corridor of his dormitory to discuss ideas that had come up. What happened next became one of the major events of his life. "My excitement had been mounting all evening, and around midnight it exploded, shattering mental stockades. It was as if a fourth dimension of space had opened, and ideas—now palpable—were unrolling like carpets before me. And I had an entire life to explore those endless, awesome, portentous ideas! Unhappiness might return, but I knew that I would never again be bored."[14]

This was the first of three great epiphanies that occurred in Huston's early life, exerting so much force on his psyche that he came to refer to it by the name Pascal had given his own mental breakthrough, the "night of fire." Huston has said that philosophical ideas had been taking him over for some time, but on this particular night, "with the force of a conversion experience, I watched them preempt my life."[15] The first consequence was another change of career. Having shifted his earlier vocational intent from missionary to minister, now he decided to move farther down the block, opting for a career in teaching rather than ministry. He would become, as he has put it, "a teacher, not a preacher," believing that as a professor he would have maximum time to explore ideas.[16]

## GRADUATION

Regarding the practical concerns of Huston's life, the summers following his junior and senior years were mostly about getting by and marking time. Jobs were still tight and he had to take whatever he could find. After his junior year he worked at a conference center in Estes Park, Colorado, busing tables for room and board and one dollar per day. The next summer, after his graduation in 1940, he landed a work/study fellowship for a seven-week seminar on the Synoptic Gospels in Algonquin Park, Canada, 200 miles north of Toronto. He greatly enjoyed the Canadian wilderness but took little inspiration from the seminar because his attention had been drawn away from such superstitions as were found in so-called 'revealed' scriptures. Naturalistic theology had precipitated his "night of fire" and he was now red hot to explore it further. "Through naturalistic theism, the two most powerful forces in history—science and religion—were about to be aligned," he has commented on his thinking at the time, "and it would be my life's mission to help effect the splice."[17] It would seem he wasn't quite finished with the hubris of youth.

# Chapter Three:
# Deepening the Search

The justification for the privileges of universities is not to be found in their capacity to take the sons of the rich and render them harmless to society or to take the sons of the poor and teach them how to make money.

Robert Maynard Hutchins

Huston's mentor, Edwin Walker, was a protégé of Henry Nelson Wieman—then the most famous naturalistic theologian in America—and so Walker urged Huston to apply to the University of Chicago where Wieman was teaching. To his delight, Huston was accepted into the Ph.D. program, and soon had the opportunity to hear ideas straight from the horse's mouth. Surprises awaited, and Chicago would show him what bright lights and big city were all about.

In the fall of 1940, barely more than a year before the Japanese would bomb Pearl Harbor, Huston moved north from Fayette to Chicago, where he remained for the next four years despite the outbreak of World War II—staying free of the draft (though he supported the war on moral grounds) because of a ministerial deferment. On paper Huston was still headed for the chaplaincy though he secretly wished to become a professor. He had been accepted into the Divinity School of the University of Chicago to study philosophy of religion, and he was chomping at the bit to meet Wieman.[1]

Huston has called John Dewey the "Jesus figure" of naturalism and Alfred North Whitehead its "Saint Paul,"[2] but it was Wieman who brought their views into the study of theology, and he was at the height of his success. Wieman, along with Teilhard de Chardin, was working overtime to reconcile Christianity with science and modernity, placing himself with Reinhold Niebuhr for the position of primary influence on the Protestant mind. Wieman was trying to affect a new dispensation by defining *religion* specifically as an effort to make society more compassionate and egalitarian. 'God' for Wieman was a verb, a living force in the world that flows through all of us when we act benevolently. Huston explains Wieman's position in his memoir: "God, so he taught us in his graduate classes, is not a Creator but a creative process, superhuman but not supernatural. . . . Since God enters our lives when, through our creative interchanges, we make history more just"—and Huston adds that for this reason, "Wieman became a socialist, active even in his old age, opposing the Vietnam War and campaigning for civil rights."[3]

Based on his parents' conviction that religion should serve humanity, Huston found Wieman's theology easy to like. If Huston set aside the supernatural elements of his parents' perspective (and he was doing just that), then what remained was the desire to affect positive change, which was exactly what Wieman was teaching. Moreover, Huston was swayed further by Wieman because Wieman was so convincing: "When he spoke, people listened—even those who disagreed with him. For here was a passionately religious spirit who seemed to be marching with the truth. If the old found the combination impressive, to the young it was intoxicating."[4]

Huston thought himself part of a grand and timely ideological movement, extending the light of reason into all areas of human endeavor, including those of theology and religion that had mostly resisted it. He hoped to help elevate the ideology of the West to a place where it was no longer compartmentalized into various incompatible fields—for instance, the duel and duality of science and religion—and in this way help intensify its beacon light for all humankind. Robert Maynard Hutchins was president of the University of Chicago at that time, and he had chosen as the school's motto Walt Whitman's "Solitary, alone in the West, I strike up for the new world." This concept of the university as something much richer and more valuable than either a country club or a job-training facility had Huston glowing with pride, enthusiasm and resolve. Science and naturalism would help the West to reach its zenith, and Huston would help make that happen.

*****

Despite the intellectual ferment, and though Huston was studying six or eight hours per day, he somehow still managed to find a love life—for which Wieman unexpectedly, and inadvertently, played Cupid.

Huston met his future wife Kendra, who was Weiman's daughter, at a lecture by Gregory Vlastos, a scholar of Greek philosophy. After the lecture, which was hosted by Wieman, Kendra was introduced to two or three of her father's graduate students. including a young man from China. For whatever reason no sparks flew between them that night. "He impressed me," Kendra wrote in a letter, "but apparently I didn't impress him." And so it wasn't until their second meeting, again at a lecture, that she showed up on Huston's radar. He had been turned away from a capacity crowd for Norman Thomas, a socialist and ardent pacifist who was then arguing against America's involvement in war, and found himself standing outside the hall with nothing to do. By chance he bumped into Wieman's son, Robert, who was also turned away, and the two men shook hands, striking up a conversation. The next thing that Huston knew Robert called his sister over and introduced her. After a shy moment on both sides, they began to chat, since, having been keyed up by the prospect of hearing a popular speaker, none of them wanted to go home just yet. Robert decided he had other places to be and was about to take his sister off with him, but "Providence struck," Huston said, "and I was able to get Kendra to stay behind. I'm not usually this bold but I looked at her and said, 'Would you like to go around the corner for a lemonade or something at Walgreen's Drug Store?' She accepted, so for the better part of an hour, sipping on lemonade or whatever it was, we discussed Thomas's views."

During their conversation, which quickly turned into a debate, Huston argued that sometimes war is justified and that with Hitler conquering Europe, this was one of those times. Thus, he made clear he disagreed with Thomas' viewpoint. But Kendra didn't back down. Though four years younger than Huston and still only a teenager, she was adamant in her pacifism, with Quakerism and Buddhism having influenced her views. The two of them went at things hammer and tongs for nearly an hour with neither of them giving way before they decided to part company. Saying goodbye and returning to his dormitory, Huston realized that he was somehow smitten with this girl, and the next morning he telephoned her brother, got her number, and asked Kendra out on date. "For two years," Huston once explained in an interview for *Yoga International*, "under his [Wieman's] aura I wouldn't have believed that anything on earth could have topped his philosophy, but then I discovered his daughter and realized I was mistaken."[5]

## JOINING WIEMAN'S FAMILY

Kendra Wieman Smith was born on July 17, 1923, in Eagle Rock, California, a suburb of Los Angeles, as the youngest of five children. Her birth name was Eleanor and she was still using that name when she met Huston, changing it to 'Kendra' thirty years later. The name change occurred in a sense by accident. She had registered to participate in an advanced training session on group dynamics and when she received a letter instructing her not to use her real name or reveal her occupation to other participants, she was stymied about what to call herself. Discussing the situation over dinner one night, Kim, her youngest daughter, suggested she use "Kendra." Huston liked the name, and later, in 1969, while she was helping him lead a round-the-world trip for the International Honors Program, she used it again. After nine months of being called "Kendra," she decided to stick with it.

Her childhood, in many ways the opposite of Huston's, was charactered by parental abuse and neglect—which perhaps fueled her determination later to be a devoted mother to her three daughters. When she was four years old, her father, then teaching at Occidental College, accepted an appointment at the University of Chicago and consequently packed up his family and moved east. But Kendra's mother, Anna, soon became ill with stomach cancer and had to undertake a series of debilitating treatments, causing the three youngest children, including Kendra (just before her sixth birthday), to be parceled out to sisters who lived on farms in Michigan. A few months later, with her condition worsening, Kendra's mother returned to California for an experimental treatment program while Wieman's unmarried sister, Lois, was called to Chicago to take care of the children. The cancer went into remission for about a year, giving Kendra and her two youngest siblings a chance to go to California and spend time with their mother, but she relapsed and died in 1931. Wieman was now not only without a wife but without a mother for his children, a situation made worse by the fact that Lois, who had devoted two years of her life to nieces and nephews, wanted to pursue a career. The result was that Wieman moved hastily into a second marriage, this time to an attractive and ambitious California woman drawn to the role of socialite. What followed for Kendra was a period of misery not unlike something out of a Dickens' novel.

Kendra said in an interview that her father had "made a disastrous second marriage to someone he didn't really know," and as a result "horrible things happened." Regina Hanson Westcott, the stepmother, who, like Wieman, had been married before, moved to Chicago with her two sons, aged 18 and 20, to live with Wieman and his two oldest children, a son and a daughter, both teenagers. Kendra and the two other younger children stayed in California with family friends and, in Kendra's case, two aunts. In the fall of 1933, Kendra and her brother Robert moved back to Chicago, leaving their fourteen-year-old sister behind to finish high school.

After reaching Chicago, Kendra learned that her oldest sister had supposedly eloped, which precipitated a third loss of a motherly influence in Kendra's life, following that of her actual mother and her Aunt Lois. Kendra was put into the university lab school founded by John Dewey and for the most part enjoyed that experience, at least more than she did her life at home. According to Kendra, her stepmother proved to be both narcissistic and dictatorial, and Huston has gone on record saying that Regina was "self-centered, melodramatic, manipulative, and imperious," with her influence on Kendra, "toxic."[6] Kendra received little attention from her father, who, she said, was mostly emotionally inept and unavailable. "My father," Kendra wrote in a letter, "can rightly be called neglectful and failing to protect," but she then added, somewhat sympathetically, "But he was [even] unable to protect himself." Though a strong personality at the lectern, Wieman was no match for his headstrong wife, and the upshot of this for Kendra was that, "I became a social isolate. I read, I drew, I walked long distances, and was so emotionally shut down that I was like a zombie."

When Kendra was twelve years old, Regina called her into her office, "a grandiose affair with an oversized desk," sat her down and explained that Kendra was too unattractive to catch a husband and lacked the necessary intelligence to attend college. She would therefore be best suited to the life of a domestic servant, a vocation that Regina, magnanimously, would help her to secure.[7] Kendra was saved from that fate by a sympathetic male teacher who recognized both her plight and intelligence, and who helped her to find the family support that she needed. At thirteen years old, Kendra returned to her father's sisters in California for high school, leaving Wieman and the dictatorial Regina behind.

Following graduation, Kendra set her sights on matriculating at Stanford University, but Regina, still controlling Wieman's purse strings and his choices, pushed her toward Grinnell College in Iowa. Kendra attended Grinnell for a year but then, unhappy with Regina's constant complaints about how much it was costing, decided "it would be easier if I waited for a year or two." After returning to Chicago, she found an apartment and started working to support herself. During the next year she rethought her options and applied to the " 'Great Books' program" at the University of Chicago, where she was accepted without her father's help. Deprived of a childhood, Kendra began, in the spirit of Buddhism, to which she was attracted, to work out her own salvation. "Bitter childhood experience destroys some," Huston wrote later, "while others triumph in spite of it. It's hard to avoid the trite metaphor of caterpillar /butterfly, but Kendra slowly unspun the cocoon of her early pain and numbness, and she emerged."[8]

It was at this point in Kendra's life—while living on her own and finishing her education—that Huston invited her to Walgreen's Drug Store. After two years of courtship, Huston and Kendra were married on September 15, 1943, in the Hilton Chapel of the University of Chicago. Huston, having learned music from his mother, composed a prelude for the ceremony and his father acted as the officiant, while Wieman looked on, hitching his daughter to one of his most promising students.

Since their wedding day, Huston and Kendra have been, as he called it, "honing each other," forming not only a marriage but also a professional partnership. "I make it a point," he remarked, explaining how Kendra has been an asset to his work, "never to have a meal with her without a pen and paper beside me because of how much she funnels into my thinking. The rooster crows but the hen lays the eggs. That's not a bad description of our relationship. Every book I have written has been influenced by her. She's a marvelous editor and she corrects my memory, and so, if I were honest, I should put on all my books, 'Huston Smith with the assistance of Kendra Smith.' But I don't do that, I just crow."

## KENDRA AND HER FATHER

Kendra might have born a grudge against Wieman, since she had essentially been left to 'twist in the wind' after the death of her mother and given little emotional support by Wieman, who seemed to be a textbook case of a professor so wrapped up in his career that he had forgotten the everyday world. But Kendra asserted, "There was no critical anger toward him," and she "never felt there was any breach that needed healing." In a long letter she discussed her views of her father. First she pointed out that, "Typically WASP (White Anglo-Saxon Protestant) families are not emotionally close, and additionally ours was scattered over the states after my mother's illness, so I saw little of him while I was growing up and after. Until my mother's terminal illness when I was six I doubt that he was any more inept as a father than other WASP fathers of his era, who regarded child rearing as women's work." In that era it was Wieman's job to be a breadwinner, something he did very well. Also, he had been more emotionally available before her mother's death and she had happy memories of him from that time. The problem in Kendra's mind was entirely Regina.

Regina was a manipulator and there didn't seem to be anybody capable of putting her in her place. After Kendra had returned from Grinnell, during her student days at the University of Chicago, she sometimes dropped in on her father at his office. She recalled that she "always got a very warm welcome from someone very different from the zombie standing stiffly near Regina when they were together." Unfortunately, she mostly saw him with Regina, who then dictated the tone of their relationship. Neither daughter nor father, she would find out later, wanted it that way but that's the way it was. Wieman, in Kendra's words, was "Regina's thrall" and as much a victim of her influence as was Kendra.

One result of this lack of nurturing in childhood was that Kendra lacked self-confidence, which intensified her general sense of feeling uprooted. After her mother's death she had been bounced among relatives. When she graduated from high school her aunts had told her that they were selling their house in California and she should take everything with her to college. "So I was on my own, carrying what I could carry, with no home I could return to." She depended on her father for college expenses but little else. Consequently, when she met Huston she was in a phase where she was "as desperate to belong to somebody as a stray dog." And when Huston sometimes seemed to waffle in his affections toward her, Kendra grasped at him "like someone drowning." She needed someone to want her and, no matter what, she wanted it to be Huston. She would have to wait many years to overcome her lack of self-esteem, but in the meantime, she was a new bride at nineteen years old.

## STARTING A FAMILY

Huston finished the course work for his Ph.D. in the spring of 1944, and, almost as if it were a graduation present, his first daughter Karen was born on July 1st. The baby was healthy and everything in the couple's life was running along smoothly, but there was one problem they still wrestled with; Huston couldn't receive his degree until he wrote a dissertation and he now lacked an advisor. Having married into Wieman's family, he couldn't receive guidance from Wieman, which would have been viewed by the University as a conflict of interest. Wieman asked Bernard Loomer, a staunch Wiemanite and a newly appointed instructor, to take over the job. Loomer accepted, but Wieman still pulled the strings—even to the point of suggesting Huston's dissertation topic.

Out west, at the University of California at Berkeley, there was a professor named Stephen Pepper who had written a breakthrough book called *World Hypotheses* (1942); that book, and Pepper's other work, was focused on *pragmatism* (or *contextualism*, as Pepper called it), and since pragmatism was at the root of Wieman's theology, Wieman wanted someone to explore the fit between Pepper's work and his own. Wieman convinced Loomer to push Huston toward that project, and so, with wife and child in tow, Huston was sent off for a year at Berkeley, to write his doctoral thesis. Titled "The Metaphysical Foundations of Contextualistic Philosophy of Religion," the thesis was the source of his first academic article, "The Operational View of God," which won Huston the Colver-Rosenberger Award, his first academic prize.

During work on his dissertation, Huston's living expenses were no longer covered by scholarships, and for nine months he took a job as pastor of the Seaside Community Church on the north side of the Monterey peninsula, about two hours south of Berkeley. Taking this job created a challenge to Huston's living arrangement. He had to be in Berkeley during the week to do research at the library and also to meet with Dr. Pepper, but on the weekends he needed to be in Seaside to preach. The way he and Kendra worked it out, Huston stayed in a rooming house during the week and then on Friday afternoons caught a city bus out of Berkeley to highway 101 where he then hitchhiked to Kendra at Seaside. "On Sundays," he recalled, "I conducted this funky little church service and Kendra had sandwiches made, and we'd go to the sand dunes. We'd spread out a blanket; I'd take off my shirt in the sunshine; and, we would have a picnic lunch. But then came the agonizing moment at 3PM, when I had to leave the two loves of my life and hitchhike back to Berkeley."

This was a difficult arrangement, since the young couple didn't want to be apart and they were barely getting by financially. Furthermore, in between stints of library research and heady intellectual discussions, Huston had to write sermons for the weekend. This was at times an awkward assignment, since his theological views didn't always mesh with those of his congregants. How much of his natural theology could he actually share with them? In Huston's first professional article,[9] he outlined what he was working with in those days, *process theology* or "operationalism," which defined entities (including God) "by their operations without postulating them as substances." The hiccough in this for his parishioners would have been that this position denied the traditional view of God as an entity with an essence independent of the physical world, someone who existed in his own being even before he created the universe. In short, naturalism was a view that denied at least some of their beliefs.

Huston laughed while recalling this disconnect between his theology and his role as minister, and acknowledged that he rarely tried to blend the two in any complex way. "The congregation, mainly made up of Cannery Row workers, had no background in theology, only a familiarity with the Bible," he said. "They were simple folk, but good. I liked and respected them, and they liked me." Consequently, his general maneuver on any given Sunday was to emphasize his parents' ideal of Christian charity and compassionate action, which agreed with Wieman's perspective, keeping his sermons focused on God's love and how we should respond to it by helping others, and simply leaving out the parts that didn't fit.

Another challenge of that time was that during the week it was Kendra's job to interact with the parishioners, which was not always easy for her, having never been a minister's wife. Sometimes one of the parishioners would invite her for dinner and, not wanting to be rude, she would wrap up the baby and take her along. The first time this happened, as Huston related the story, the man of the house asked Kendra if she would begin the meal by saying grace. "She was terrified," Huston said, "but she managed to dredge up a few things, like 'Give us this day our daily bread.' But she could only remember fragments and that presented a problem. How do you end? She knew there was an ending but her mind was inexplicably blanked. The suspense was mounting in the room. Everybody at the table was waiting. Finally she blurted out, 'Goodbye.' When she picked her head up to see the reaction of those around the table, her face was beet red. The man, who had been a sea captain, was seated at the other end of the table. He was perplexed for an instant but then he smiled at her and said, 'Would you like a beer?' And she knew she had been accepted."

## The Second Great Epiphany

During their first few months in California things proceeded uneventfully for the most part; however, Huston did manage to get over the Bay Bridge in April, 1945, to witness the founding ceremony of the United Nations, which took place in San Francisco. With the German army defeated, and Berlin having just been taken over by the allied forces, the war was nearly at its end. Though the horrible bombings of Hiroshima and Nagasaki were yet to happen, there was a general attitude of optimism rising in America; things would be better now, and perhaps the U.N. could promote a more stable and informed global awareness. Huston hoped so, and witnessing the birth of the UN that day buttressed his hopes. There was another event that spring that became even more influential on his life: while working in the library one night, he made a discovery that changed his philosophy forever.

Huston had been writing his dissertation when the idea came into his head that he should research the topic of pain, in all its manifestations, to see if it had any pertinent connections to his thesis. Rummaging under the word 'pain' in the library's card catalogue, he found four titles that seemed somewhat relevant, and one of them, Gerald Heard's *Pain, Sex and Time*, had such an intriguing title he decided to check it out first. By the time he reached page two it was clear the book had nothing to do with his dissertation, but Huston couldn't manage to put it down, which marked the first time in his life that he stayed up all night to read. The book took hold of him in a profound way.

# Chapter Four:
# The Best Kept Secret of the Twentieth Century

The hypothesis of this essay is that evolution is seeking its only possible continuation along this path of enlarged consciousness, and that those who have grasped this fact can not only co-operate with it, but that only by their co-operation will further evolution be possible.

Gerald Heard, from *Pain, Sex and Time*

The mystics are channels through which a little knowledge of reality filters down into our human universe of ignorance and illusion. A totally unmystical world would be a world totally blind and insane.

Aldous Huxley

What kept Huston up that night was Heard's startling and compelling endorsement of mysticism as the critical means of gaining insight into life's essential mysteries. Heard wasn't arguing that science and rational thought have no value, he was suggesting that science's particular tools cannot access the full spectrum of what we are, or of what the world is. He argued that we have a noetic, experiential capacity for accessing knowledge, a mystical function of our being that directly accesses a truth unattainable by scientific or analytical means. There are methods, Heard argued, whereby we can expand our minds, expand our consciousnesses, to the point where we apprehend metaphysical dimensions of what we are (and of what the world is) that escape an exclusively rational or quantitative approach. Heard further argued, awakening to these noetic dimensions, as had been achieved in earlier generations by mystics in all cultures, is not only our innate human capacity but also a necessary step in our evolution as a species.

Huston wasn't so sure about this last claim of Heard's, but he couldn't keep his mind off the basic premise—i.e., that consciousness could be expanded to the point where a deeply meaningful breakthrough into a more authentic state of consciousness was achieved. Maybe people were assuming that their consciousness was fixed by its very nature when in reality it was only fixed by nurture, based on social conditioning and the momentum of everyday habits; maybe there is a wide band of possible experiences that we shut out daily because of that conditioning and the weight of our personal assumptions. In short, maybe Heard was right! To accept Heard's theory, Huston would have to revisit from his past the idea that human existence has a metaphysical aspect, like a soul, which would take him beyond Wieman's naturalism. For the first time in his life, even after eight years of studying religion, mysticism had been presented to him sympathetically, and when it was, to his surprise, Huston found it deeply convincing. Later he would comment in a radio interview with Michael Toms that, "It wouldn't be too strong a word to say I was *converted*."

What would this conversion mean for his study with Wieman, Loomer and Pepper? Huston understood that he had to be somewhat cautious since they all considered mysticism to be a kind of intellectual pornography focussed on illicit material. However, Huston had certainly been won over and had to face up to that, at least with reference to his own viewpoint. And what was the result? "The naturalistic world I had loved and lived in since my mind's arousal was, with a single stroke relativized. It was but part of the whole. An island—lush to be sure, but rimmed round about by an endless shining sea."[1] Huston made two vows that night before he finished the book: "The first was that I would not read another line this man wrote until I had my degree firmly in hand; I was obviously afraid that I would just peel off from academia. My second vow, once I had my meal ticket in hand, was to read everything this man had written."[2] Huston, as it turned out, kept both promises. After receiving his Ph.D. (the "meal ticket," which he has also sometimes called a "union card") later that same year, he immediately began poring over Heard's other fourteen books, filling in what he believed was a blind spot in his—and most people's—education.

## GERALD HEARD

Few people today know the name Gerald Heard, but his influence on popular philosophy in the last seventy years has been considerable in that he was a major bridge-builder between Eastern and Western thought; in fact, several writers, including Huston, have called him the "best kept secret of the twentieth century."

Heard was born in London to an Irish family on October 6, 1889, and later received a degree in history from Cambridge, graduating in 1911. He briefly studied theology in preparation for the Anglican clergy but in 1916, following a crisis of faith, took a job as secretary to a wealthy aristocrat, in which capacity he met and befriended the Irish poet, George Russell. Russell convinced Heard that mysticism is neither folly nor bunk, encouraging his young friend to study especially the Vedanta philosophy of Hinduism, which he considered the supreme example of a philosophy that valued mystical experience. Heard was drawn to this viewpoint from the moment he began studying it (as Huston was drawn to Heard's), deeply influenced, as it was, by Vedanta.

After 1926, Heard changed occupations several times. He lectured for Oxford's Board of Extra Mural Studies; he became an editor of a short-lived journal on "scientific humanism"; he published a book on the philosophy of history called *The Ascent of Humanity,* which won a British Academy of Science Award; and soon afterwards, in 1930, he became the first science commentator for BBC Radio. During this last period, in the early and mid-thirties, Heard gained a wide range of knowledge about scientific principles that formed a primary source for his later work. Meanwhile, because of his popularity on the radio, he moved in a circle of British intellectuals including E.M. Forster, Somerset Maugham, W.H. Auden, H.G. Wells (who once said that Heard was "the only person I listen to on the wireless"), and most significantly for Huston's biography, the novelist and essayist, Aldous Huxley. In 1934, Huxley and Heard began a friendship that Huston would later term one of the most fruitful philosophical partnerships in history.

Gerald was instrumental in arousing Huxley's interest in mysticism (a subject that would make Huxley both famous and infamous) and together they studied all the works on mysticism—and especially Vedanta—that were available in translation at the time. A few years later their professional partnership extended to giving lectures on the prospects for peace in Europe, with World War II looming on the horizon, and in 1937 they sailed from Southampton, with Huxley's first wife, Maria, to begin a pacifist tour of American colleges. As it turned out, the tour of colleges resulted in full immigration to the United States, and Heard and Huxley settled in Los Angeles, having driven cross-country from New York in a new Ford with Maria, barely five feet tall, behind the wheel.

In Los Angeles, Heard decided it would be useful to have some formal training in a traditional school of mysticism, so he made contact with Swami Prabhavananda, the head of the Vedanta Society of Southern California located in Hollywood, and set up lessons for himself and Huxley. Prabhavananda, an Indian immigrant who spoke perfect English, was a proponent of the very school of Indian philosophy George Russell had first recommended, and so the two Brits began studying with him in 1939. Articulate and convincing, Prabhavananda so impressed both men that they brought others to meet him, including the novelist Christopher Isherwood, whose characters and narratives in the *Berlin Stories* became the basis for the play, *Cabaret.* Isherwood would go on to become one of the swami's most ardent disciples, collaborating with him on several books.[3]

Heard found tremendous insights in the swami's teachings that formed the foundation for most of his later philosophical writings, including *Pain, Sex and Time.* Huston thus inadvertently became a fan of Vedanta because he had read the works of Heard, but what ideas had he actually accepted?

## What the Swami Said

Prabhavananda taught Heard and Huxley a specific level of Hinduism called Advaita Vedanta, an interpretation of the ancient religion that was first introduced to America at the World Parliament of Religions in Chicago, in 1893, by Swami Vivekananda, a charismatic personality who took America by storm. 'Vedanta' relates to a set of teachings drawn from the Upanishads, a group of texts forming the last section of the Vedas, Hinduism's most sacred scriptures, and 'Advaita' refers to a "nondual" interpretation of those teachings. Advaita Vedanta then is a philosophy maintaining that the physical and metaphysical aspects of reality form a seamless unity. Prabhavananda explained that the physical universe and everything in it is a manifestation of a underlying metaphysical reality that is infinite, timeless, unmanifest. This metaphysical or spiritual source of all existence is called *Brahman* (commonly capitalized to signify its absolute nature) and it is the realization of this Brahman, the experience of this wellspring of all reality, that defines the 'enlightenment' achieved by swamis, yogis and adepts.

According to the Vedantic viewpoint, everything in the universe arises from Brahman in the way that waves arise from the ocean, and some of the 'things' that arise from It are us. As physical beings, we take form out of this one eternal, limitless reservoir of all Being. This Brahman is not a *thing* in the usual sense, since it has no form or mass, nor duration (in this sense, it is nothing—*no thing*—with reference to the world of time and space and matter), but it is also not a vacuum or void like empty space. It is a reservoir of pure potentiality out of which all reality emerges from nanosecond to nanosecond; it is The Being that flowers into all forms of being. And so it is in some sense both an Everything and a Nothing, defying the relative terminology of physical existence. According to Vedanta, the import of this is that we are, in our essence, non-different from this underlying Being or Brahman. Returning to the ocean analogy, each wave on the surface of the ocean can be perceived as an individual entity (so a surfer might say to her friend, "I'll catch *this* wave and you catch *that* one"), but at their root, and in their essence, each wave is one with the ocean from which it comes. In this same way, Swami Prabhavananda explained to Heard and Huxley, we have two sides to our nature: here in this physical world, we are characterized by the relative features of our body and mind, but beyond these relativities, at the root of our being, we are synonymous with Brahman, since it is the absolute substrate of all existence. Our essential being is non-different from *the* essential Being. In Sanskrit, the word for 'self' is *atman*, but at the highest and deepest level, our 'self' transcends our discrete individuality and this *atman* is synonymous with Brahman, in the same way that the water of the wave is at its root one with the water of the ocean.

Huxley and Heard learned from Prabhavananda that this does not mean the individual somehow becomes God. Brahman is not considered by Vedantists to be the same sort of 'thing' as the Judeo-Christian-Islamic entity called God, a sentient being who answers prayers or has any sort of form or gender. Brahman is the source of all relative existences but it is not the Creator in the usual sense, a personality that Hinduism also speaks of and acknowledges. It is more accurate, when we speak of Brahman, to use the term *Godhead* than God, for this identifies it as the absolute wellspring of existence, including God's own existence, without pushing onto it any anthropomorphic tendencies. And so, though the enlightened person does not become God, she *does* awaken to that dimension of her own being that is synonymous with the essence of God's own being.

Huxley and Heard also learned from the swami that the *atman*, the aspect of self that is one with Brahman, is not what is usually referred to as the 'soul.' It is the individual's spiritual essence, but in this case that essence transcends all personality and individuality and can not be distinguished from the essence of anything else, whether plants, planktons or planets. If spoken of as a 'soul,' one would have to call it a *world soul*, or, as Emerson and the Transcendentalists (who were also deeply influenced by Vedanta) termed it, "Oversoul." In Advaita Vedanta, only the subtlest aspect of the physical self, a sort of subtle body called the *jiva,* takes rebirth lifetime after lifetime. To use an analogy, the jiva is like the SIM chip in a cell phone; when one phone is kaput, the chip retains all the important information about that phone's 'life' (as the jiva retains all karmic information inherited from the person's physical self) and can be moved to a new phone body. In most sects of Hinduism, it is this jiva that reincarnates, while the absolute atman, as the *Bhagavad-Gita* relates, is "never born and never dies."

But Heard and Huxley had a question about all this: if the true nature of existence—our own and the world's—is configured in such a way, why don't we experience it in this way? Why do we only experience the relative side of who we are, with no awareness of the Absolute Brahman underlying it? Why are we only aware of our wave aspect and not our ocean-ness? Prabhavananda explained to them that we are, unfortunately, prevented from realizing our 'ocean side' because without the proper expansion of consciousness, we mistake the realm of change, time and multiplicity for the whole story of our existence. And because of this ignorance about our complete nature, we experience problems. For instance, without knowing ourselves as 'ocean,' the realization of which Vedantists see as the ultimate goal of our existence, the 'wave' lacks perspective on life and so we flounder in our appreciation of it. As Huxley once put it: "It is because we don't know who we are, because we are unaware that the Kingdom of Heaven is within us, that we behave in the generally silly, the often insane, the sometimes criminal ways that are so characteristically human."[4]

Huston would come to see this viewpoint as the true explanation for how life can contain terrible suffering and yet, from a larger perspective, also be experienced as perfect. The 'ice cream cone' of our relative lives gets dropped into the dirt but there is, via the mystical apprehension of our higher selves, a broader spiritual context in which to set that tragedy.

Thinking ourselves to be nothing more than our physical bodies, we have a neurotic fear of death, for to lose our body (which includes, from the perspective of naturalistic philosophy, our mind also) is to lose everything that we are. But Prabhavananda maintained that when the body is dropped, we experience something analogous to the wave falling back into the ocean after the wind dies; individuality is sacrificed, since the wave can no longer be discerned as something separate from the sea, but the wave's essence as water remains.

This idea, as an intellectual datum, was interesting to both Heard and Huxley, but what intrigued them more, and what came also to intrigue Huston, was the notion that a person could get beyond these ideas—in fact, beyond *all* ideas—to actually experience reality in this unitive way, from the ground of our being out to the tips of our fingers.

To experience our 'ocean' side, our absolute essence, while still functioning in the world, Prabhavananda explained, consciousness must be purified and expanded, enlivened and enriched, and this was the traditional significance of practicing yoga and meditation. The Sanskrit term *buddha* literally means "awakened." But could a person wake up in the way that Indian tradition claimed the Buddha, the "Awakened One," had done? Prabhavananda assured the two men that it was not only possible but had happened many times. It had happened to Sri Ramakrishna, Vivekananda's guru, and it had happened to Vivekananda and other of Ramakrishna's disciples—and it was still happening. The enlightenment breakthrough might be as rare as seeing a double rainbow during a hike through Death Valley, but with the proper training and the proper effort it could happen and sometimes *did*: moreover, any amount of growth in that direction was beneficial to one's psychological health, so there were also rewards along the way.

Heard and Huxley were eager to cultivate the enlightened state, and after reading Heard, Huston was too. In 1945, the world was making a new beginning, and Huston was off in a new direction too.

# Chapter Five:
# Hitchhiking to California

I believe that God is in me as the sun is in the color and fragrance of a flower—
the Light in my darkness, the Voice in my silence.

Helen Keller

You could not discover the limits of the soul, even if you traveled by every path
in order to do so; such is the depth of its meaning.

Heraclitus

After receiving his Ph.D., Huston, at twenty-six years old, took his first job as a college professor, accepting a one-year appointment at the University of Denver to teach philosophy half-time while also acting as Director of Religious Activities. For the next two years he would remain in Colorado, first teaching at Denver and then, in the fall of 1946, at the University of Colorado, while also lecturing part-time at the Iliff School of Theology.[1] To save money and work on paying off his student loans, Huston and Kendra first lived for about six months in a small trailer without running water, and then moved into subsidized campus housing. Part of Huston's responsibility at the University of Denver was to bring dignitaries and performers to campus. One of his first guests was a banjo player he had heard in a downtown church. The man's name was Pete Seeger and he would later become a major influence on songwriters across America, including Bob Dylan, Arlo Guthrie, Joni Mitchell and Bruce Springsteen. When the big night arrived, Huston was standing backstage and realized immediately that he was, as he put it, "listening to a winner." Pete and Huston, both at the very beginning of their careers, actually looked somewhat alike (they still do) and by coincidence were both born in May of the same year. More significantly, they shared the same values and were deeply interested in the plight of the underdog, which quickly became the basis for a friendship.

Pete Seeger became a fixture on national radio during the late 1940s, and soon had a string of hits with a group called The Weavers, including the songs "If I Had a Hammer" and "Turn, Turn, Turn," both penned by Seeger, the latter based in part on the Book of Ecclesiastes. Several members of The Weavers were banned from performing in the 1950s, during the McCarthy crackdown on "un-American activities," but this further galvanized Seeger's desire to sing about political and social injustice. Sometimes he even got himself arrested, earning further respect from Huston, who, like Seeger, worried that America, in its pride after the war, was losing track of the Jeffersonian principles that made it great. The civil rights movement hadn't yet come along, nor had Cesar Chavez arrived on the scene, and so Seeger, like Woody Guthrie before him, took on the role of America's conscience, becoming a leading advocate for workers' rights and the need to extend brotherhood across the racial divide. Huston admired Seeger's efforts, and given his love of music he relished every chance he had to hear Seeger perform—and sometimes sing along. For several years, whenever Seeger played near where the Smiths were living, he stayed with them.

*****

In 1947, after two and a half years in Colorado, Huston was offered a tenure-track position at Washington University in St. Louis, Missouri, at the beck of its chancellor, Arthur Compton. "He somehow heard of me through Wieman," Huston later wrote, "whom he had come to respect while the two of them were at The University of Chicago."[2] Huston was glad of Compton's support, and later Compton would also help him publish one of his early books, an honor of some significance in that Compton had won the Nobel Prize for physics in 1927 (for his discovery of the "particle" concept of electromagnetic radiation). But before Huston packed up his family and left Denver, he decided to set off in the opposite direction, heading west on a journey that became something of a spiritual pilgrimage.

Huston and Kendra didn't have a car, though Gael, a second daughter, had arrived on July 12, 1947; if Huston was going anywhere he still had to hitchhike. After reading all of Heard's books, Huston determined that he had to meet the man, and he reasoned that this break between jobs gave him the best chance he would have to do this, for a while at least. During the preceding winter, he had mailed off a letter to Heard by way of his publisher Harper & Row, asking if he and Gerald could somehow meet. Heard answered promptly, saying that he'd be happy to get together with the young professor but warning that he was hard to find, living as he did in the Laguna Hills on a remote estate in southern California. Huston answered Heard's letter gleefully, saying he was willing to give it a try. On July 12th, Kendra gave birth to a second daughter, Gael, and soon afterwards, and once Kendra had recovered, Huston made ready to leave. He set off in the summer heat with a duffle bag in his hand and his thumb out, hitchhiking his way to the Pacific.

## PILGRIM'S PROGRESS

What had captured Huston's attention in Heard's books was not simply the premise that there is a metaphysical reality underlying our physical existence, or that that reality could be experienced directly in human consciousness, but the idea that this experience could be of tremendous benefit to the world. Based on the teachings of Vedanta, Heard believed that social conflict, whether within a particular society or between societies, arises out of individual conflict; given that society is fundamentally a collection of individuals, its actions and institutions reflect the sum of those individuals' neuroses, fears, angers, and jealousies, as well as their strengths. Today's national behaviors are large-scale, collective projections of individual behaviors. But, Heard argued that this situation, when negative, could be remedied if individuals would wake up to their full potential. To use an analogy, a forest is only as green as the trees in the forest are green; so if we want a green 'forest' of civil society, we need to 'green' our individual trees. If we want world peace, we should begin with inner peace—and with helping others to find their inner peace. This aspect of mysticism appealed to Huston because it resonated with what he had inherited from both his parents and Wieman, the call to be of service to humanity. And Gerald gave this specific teaching of Vedanta some new and exciting twists.

Heard had argued in *Pain, Sex and Time* that the human species, unlike most other species, is still evolving, and that mysticism is destined to move humanity up the ladder to our next stage of development. Furthermore, Heard had no doubt about the direction of that growth: the first great stage of human advancement had been in terms of the physical domain, the second had been in the technological domain (think 'Industrial Revolution') and the third, he contended, "must be psychical."[3] This last stage would be into enlightenment, the realization of our oneness with Brahman, and Heard argued that evidence of our taking this next step was already clear to the discerning eye. Our evolution on the level of the human body was complete but the body contains two properties that suggest our minds can evolve even further. One is the mind's inordinate sensitivity to pain (which Heard considered a warning sign that we're misusing an accumulating store of energy that could better be used to evolve). The other is the enormity of its sex drive (a misapplying of that energy to the pleasure principle), which, unlike the sex drive of other species, is available to us without "periodicity," i.e., we can 'do it' whenever we want. Later Huston would describe the pertinence of these ideas to Heard's theory in a foreword he wrote for a re-issue of *Pain, Sex and Time*:

> The surplus vitality that these properties token suggests that in humanity the life force is pressing like a jack-in-the-box for the release that mental evolution could afford. Rudiments of such evolution can be spotted in historical times in the increasing acuity of human vision and its ability to distinguish more bands in the color spectrum. But the real evolution will be in the ability of consciousness to break out of individual pockets . . . and merge into God's infinite consciousness. This is more than a theoretical possibility [according to Heard]. Mystics are the advance scouts of mankind; they have transcended their egos, and in exceptional cases, merged with God completely.[4]

Heard had wanted to help effect this grand evolutionary leap, not only by formulating a set of spiritual practices that individuals could use to upgrade their consciousnesses but also by establishing centers where they could study and work together to reach that goal. Ideally, people would live at these training centers, given that, as Heard explained in *Pain*: "The continuation of evolution consciously to higher consciousness needs complete devotion, complete knowledge and a complete way of life, so as to give the psyche those conditions under which all its efforts at growth will not be thwarted by its circumstances."[5] Heard wished to nourish a cadre of spiritual adepts, who, he reasoned, would become the evolutionary vanguard, an engine driving humanity into the light of a brighter day. Referencing Brahmin priests, the highest caste in Hindu society, Heard wrote that such adepts would be "Neo-Brahmins" and a "New Doctorate" to "salvage civilization."[6] Six years after publishing *Pain*, Heard moved deeply into his project, creating the hybrid institute/monastery in the Laguna Hills where Huston was now headed.

As Huston hitchhiked toward the Pacific, he speculated that maybe the true 'brave new world' mankind was destined to achieve was not, as he had once speculated, the world that science would create, but something even more fantastic. Maybe Western intellectuals were thinking too small. Furthermore, he was happy that Heard had couched his metaphysical speculations in ways that weren't culture specific. Heard's books made a strong case for the Vedanta perspective but he wasn't talking about conversion to Hinduism, and that attracted Huston. Heard and Huxley both believed that the enlightenment experience had happened to mystics in all religions—and even outside of religion *per se*, since the essential nature of man could not be different from place to place or era to era—and with this in mind Heard and Huxley had searched the world's mystical literature for evidence of that fact. Huxley then argued in his book *The Perennial Philosophy* (1945), an anthology of what he had found, that this breakthrough into a direct experience of the Sacred or the Oversoul, is "the Highest Common Factor underlying all the great religions and metaphysical systems of the world." Heard not only agreed with the viewpoint but helped Huxley work out the details of what became their shared perspective, publishing his own views in *The Eternal Gospel* (1946). These two books had a tremendous impact on Huston, who was, in fact, carrying Huxley's *Perennial Philosophy* under his arm like a sort of Bible as he hitchhiked to California.[7]

## A VISIT TO TRABUCO COLLEGE

Heard had built his institute in the lonely hills east of the Pacific and south of Los Angeles, naming the place 'Trabuco College' after Trabuco Canyon, where it was situated. It was rather a "college" mostly in the earlier sense of "monastery," and it was so remote that it took Huston most of an afternoon to find it after he arrived in the general area. Winding his way up through a series of switchbacks to the top of a small, rock-strewn mountain, Huston, weary from his travels, finally arrived and was greeted—to his delight—by Heard himself. Heard was then living the life of an ascetic, meditating for six hours a day in a windowless, dark, stone building with a domed ceiling, specially built for meditation. He was also eating simple food, avoiding bourgeois entertainments, and completely abstaining from sex. (Heard had been a homosexual and when he first arrived in California was in a relationship with the writer Christopher Wood—best known today for his screen adaptations of James Bond novels.) Gerald had piercing blue eyes, very red hair, and a pointed goatee, all of which contributed to his striking appearance. When he greeted Huston at the gates of Trabuco, he was neatly dressed in an unbuttoned, starched shirt and pleated trousers, his hair closely clipped and carefully groomed. Before he opened his mouth, he struck Huston as compelling, as someone who knew what he was talking about, as someone who by his very presence conveyed that he was having the experience he espoused.

After showing Huston to a simple room in the main building, Heard lead the young professor around the grounds on a tour of the college. He had modeled the layout on that of a medieval Italian monastery, and Huston found himself impressed with the results; the brownstone buildings, with their red-tiled roofs, were situated dramatically on a rocky outcropping with an expansive view that stretched all the way to the sea. Today, Trabuco College remains mostly as it was then, having later been donated by Heard to the Vedanta Society of Southern California, which maintains it as a monastery. In its beautiful small library, containing a lovely brick fireplace, Huxley outlined most of *The Perennial Philosophy* and one still finds many signed, first editions of books by Heard, Huxley, Christopher Isherwood and other writers who studied there.

# Hitchhiking to California

After dinner on Huston's first evening he and Heard walked out onto the cliffs in front of the dining hall to sit under the stars and have a chat; however, as it turned out, that chat never happened. "After I had hitchhiked all that distance," Huston later related in a magazine interview, "when we were face-to-face, I found I didn't have any questions to ask him, which was fine. I didn't go there because I had burning questions. I just wanted his *darshan* [a Hindu term for being in someone's presence]. After supper, we sat on the brown hills and looked out, sitting in silence."[8]

Gerald seemed to be a sage of the twentieth century, which reinforced Huston's belief that people *can* actually grow into higher states of consciousness. Heard had woken himself up, and was waking up others also; his facility was filled with young people eager to increase their spiritual growth. Fifty years after meeting Heard, Huston recalled that evening as one of the most memorable and positive events of his life.

The next morning Heard asked Huston if he'd like to meet Aldous Huxley, quickly adding, as if Huston somehow needed further convincing, that "He's very knowledgeable about Vedanta and likes to meet people who share our interests." In actuality, Huston could have been knocked over with a feather at the prospect, and he immediately jumped at the chance. After spending another day with Heard, and after securing a letter of introduction from him, Huston set off to meet the famous novelist.

## A STROLL IN THE DESERT

Aldous Huxley, the author of fifty books, and one of the most prominent intellectuals of the twentieth century, was born in Godalming, Surrey, on July 26, 1894. He was from a family of British intellectuals, including his grandfather, Thomas Henry Huxley, a physiologist and close associate of Charles Darwin, and his granduncle, Matthew Arnold, the celebrated Victorian poet. Leonard Huxley, Aldous' father, was the editor of a distinguished literary magazine, *The Cornhill*, and his mother, Julia Arnold, had founded a girls' school that is still operating today. Aldous Huxley became a renowned essayist and novelist; Julian, his elder brother, became an influential biologist, knighted by the Queen; and Andrew Huxley, Aldous' half brother, won the Nobel Prize for Physiology in 1963. Altogether, the family presented a formidable bloodline.

Huxley attended Eton and then Oxford, where he had hoped to study biology in preparation for becoming a doctor; however, after a severe eye infection robbed him of half his eyesight, he settled on a literary career. In 1919 (the year that Huston was born), Huxley took a job as columnist for the London *Athenaeum*, but soon after, in 1921, he published a short novel, *Crome Yellow*, that cast him into the spotlight and established his name as an author.

Once able to support himself with his writing, Huxley traveled the world, composing collections of essays and several cynical and satirical novels, including *Point Counterpoint* (1928), still widely considered his literary masterpiece. During the time he was writing that particular novel, he made friends with D.H. Lawrence, and the two men thereafter kept up a close friendship (Huxley's wife Maria actually typed the manuscript of *Lady Chatterly's Lover* while they were on vacation together) until Lawrence's death from tuberculosis in 1930. Huxley and Lawrence complained of the moral and spiritual bankruptcy of the Western world—especially after World War I—and together they had hoped to find new foundations of meaning to replace those eroded by the Scientific and Industrial Revolutions. Huxley, who often made fun of organized religion, and religion in general, nonetheless worried that if the grounds of human purpose and meaning were reduced to only what science could prove was valuable, humanity would be herded toward nothing more than a search for physical comfort and pleasure. The West would degenerate into abject consumerism, materialism and superficiality. Lawrence believed it already had. Huxley, like Lawrence, found this trajectory decadent, and in *Brave New World* (1931) he presented a cautionary tale warning against it, offering a thinly disguised satire of what he believed society had already become.

Huxley is remembered today primarily as a novelist, often studied in conjunction with his contemporaries Virginia Woolf and James Joyce, but of his fifty books only eleven are novels. For the most part Huxley's focus, and this is true even in the novels, was on the problems that plagued humankind and discussions of how those problems might be solved. He was, in the final analysis, a moral philosopher and social critic, and in the mid-twentieth century few intellectuals commanded as much public respect.

Huxley and Maria, his Belgian wife, were keeping an apartment in Los Angeles, but since 1942 they also maintained a small ranch in the desert at Llano del Rio, about fifty miles northeast of the city. This is where Huston met them. When Huston telephoned Huxley, Huxley invited him over immediately, explaining which bus Huston should catch and saying that their cabin would be the only one in sight from where the bus would leave him off. A couple of hours later Huston reached Llano and Huxley, tall and lean (at six-foot-four he was two inches taller than Huston) with a majestic head and regal bearing, greeted him with a smile and handshake. Close up, Huston could see that Huxley's right eye was clouded, the result of his childhood eye-infection. Huxley was dressed in work clothes, which Huston somehow hadn't expected of a great novelist, but his posture and manners were entirely those of the British aristocracy from a bygone era.

Huxley, still smiling, suggested the two men take a walk in the desert, but before setting off, he brought Huston into the cabin to meet his wife. Huston reminisced about his first meeting with Maria: "Later that day I ended up helping her sweep the sand out of their cabin and make their bed, and I remember thinking that life could only go downhill after that. She was very sweet and kind."

Once out in the wasteland of the desert, Huxley immediately began talking about the Hindu concept of Brahman, the Buddhist Void, Jakob Boehme's *urgrund*, Tillich's "God-above-God" and Meister Eckhart's "Divine Ground of Being," which he believed were all synonyms for each other. When, on the twenty-fifth anniversary of Huxley's death, the *L.A. Times* asked Huston to write a commemorative piece to be titled "Remembering Aldous Huxley," he included some of what Huxley had said during that walk:

> He loved the desert, he told me, for its symbolic power. Its emptiness emptied his mind. "The boundlessness of its sands (I paraphrase) spreads a mantle of sameness—hence unity—over the world's multiplicity in something of the way snow does. The Nothingness to which the Desert Fathers were drawn is not a blank negation. It is a no-thing-ness in which everything is so interfused that divisions are transcended. Pure light contains all the frequencies of the rainbow but undemarcated. The Void is the vacuum-plenum complex [the Oneness of Reality in both its forms, as the transcendent 'nothing' as well as the 'something' of the physical universe], grasped by its vacuum pole."[9]

Huxley also spoke directly about the perennial philosophy, explaining his belief that

Advaita Vedanta (in its many iterations, and not just that espoused by the Vedanta Society) was a clear revelation of that truth, but that he, like the Vedantists themselves, didn't believe Vedanta was the only revelation. Using Vedanta as a launch pad, Huxley had pulled free of any specific form of perennialism, showing that its core could be found in all mystical traditions—including that of Christianity. (Heard once pointed out that Augustine himself had written: "That which is called the Christian Religion existed among the Ancients, and never did not exist, from the beginning of the Human Race until Christ came in the flesh, at which time the true religion, which already existed, began to be called Christianity.") In *Vedanta for the Western World* (1945), Huxley had outlined this core idea in terms of what he called "the minimum working hypothesis":

> THAT there is a Godhead or Ground, which is the unmanifested principle of all manifestation.
> THAT the Ground is transcendent and immanent.
> THAT it is possible for human beings to love, know and, from virtually, to become actually identified with the Ground.
> THAT to achieve this unitive knowledge, to realize this supreme identity, is the final end and purpose of human existence.

In the two years after *The Perennial Philosophy* was published, Huston had accepted this four-point premise as gospel. Heard had introduced him to the idea that mystical experience is real and valuable, but Huxley's specific privileging of mysticism as the root of all religion, supported by the testimonies of such adepts as Meister Eckhart, St. John of the Cross, Rumi, St. Teresa of Avila, the Buddha, Kabir and Shankara, is now what held his attention. If the world was ever to live in peace, it would have to learn to distinguish this deepest core of Truth from the various ways it is packaged in the traditional religions.

Huston then quizzed Huxley about the specifics of his apprenticeship with Prabhavananda in Hollywood, and Huxley spoke positively about it—though there had been bumps along the way. Huxley explained that he wasn't prone to the devotional services towards God(s) that Prabhavananda generally recommended (it might be the right path for some people but not for him), nor did he approve of the guru-worship he often observed around Prabhavananda at the Vedanta Center, seeing it as too Hindu-specific. But he explained that these problems were mostly matters of cultural relativity and personal taste, and he didn't hesitate to recommend Prabhavananda and his teachings. Upon arrival back at the cabin, Huston told Huxley that he had just taken a teaching post in St. Louis, after which Huxley, still on the topic of Vedanta, remarked, "Oh, there's a very good swami there!"[10]

"Swami?" Huston asked, not completely sure what a swami was.

"Yes," said Huxley, fetching paper and pen to jot down the name 'Swami Satprakashananda.' "You should visit him."

The next morning, after a simple breakfast, and after thanking Aldous and Maria for their hospitality, Huston headed off down the road, making a promise to himself that one of the first things he'd do when he reached St. Louis was look up Satprakashananda. This resolve lead Huston Smith, the future authority on world religions, to undertake his first full immersion in a religion outside his own. In China, he had observed other religious traditions, but now he would become an actual participant.

# Chapter Six:
# The Journey Within

The soul's answer to the problem of time is the experience of timeless being.
There is no other answer.

Jacob Needleman

What is soundless, untouchable, formless, imperishable,
Likewise tasteless, constant, odorless,
Without beginning, without end, higher than the great, stable—
By discerning That, one is liberated from the mouth of Death.

Katha Upanishad

After embracing his new perspective, Huston knew that he had to keep his cards close to his chest when dealing with academic colleagues. To admit that he was taking the contents of religion seriously, including claims of mysticism and metaphysics, could have impeded his career, since it would be taken as evidence of a compromise in his scholarly 'objectivity' and his allegiance to naturalism. If Huston was going to argue against strict materialism, he first had to delve much more deeply into the theory he had accepted. At the moment he had little more to go on than the testimonies of Huxley and Heard, as well as a deep intuitive hunch that he was onto something. These components weren't nearly enough. To complicate the matter, he was moving up in the academic ranks mainly because he was in Wieman's camp, so what would happen if he revealed himself to be a turncoat? Not a wise move, at least not before getting tenure—and Kendra agreed. She too had accepted the perennialist viewpoint but understood that they should stay mum about it when talking with her father, or, for that matter, most of Huston's colleagues. Huston would speak up when he was ready to fully defend the position; in the meantime, he liked to try ideas out on his students.

Huston sometimes talked about perennialism in his classes, pointing out its virtues as a theory for the origin of religion, though it appeared in no textbooks—and still doesn't. Furthermore, its central claim (that there is a transcendent source of all Being that can be directly experienced) had been the foundation of Indian philosophy for nearly three thousand years, and why shouldn't it be taken seriously as, at least, one possibility? What if the viewpoint were true? What if the world that meets our senses really is only part of the story of life? What if William James was right and there *are* modes of consciousness beyond and above those we usually experience? To make a point about the possible repercussions, Huston often referenced Plato's "Allegory of the Cave."

In the seventh book of *The Republic*, Plato gives a story of prisoners chained inside a cave in such a way that they are forced to look at only one wall. Behind these prisoners, who have never seen anything except that wall, their captors perform puppet shows that the prisoners see only as shadows projected across the wall in front of them. Since they don't see the puppets, they have no understanding of how the shadows are made—or even of the fact that they *are* shadows. All of this leaves the prisoners thinking that the entire world takes place in black and white and two dimensions. But making these assumptions, based on no knowledge of the world beyond their dim existence, has grave consequences for their view of reality and the quality of their judgments, as Huston once explained in an interview:

Plato then says, what would happen if one of those prisoners were to be unchained and turned around and led toward the opening of the cave? What does he see?

First he sees not just black and white, but Technicolor. Hey, there's color, color in this world! And not just shadows but light! Light? What's that? Then he goes out into the enchanted garden of the world, and he understands that this light is coming from a source—the sun that fills the world with light.

"Would he not be astonished?" Plato asks.

Fair question, I would say. But now suppose he is led back, and he wants above all to share this world with his fellow prisoners.

"This isn't it at all," he says to them. "It's out there!"

Plato winds down the story by asking, what would they think? They would think he was crazy, and if he persisted in his opinions they would *kill* him. Plato was not imagining this because that's exactly what they had done to [his teacher] Socrates.[1]

Huston pointed out to his students that a mystic who tries to convey the unseen world to non-mystics probably experiences a conundrum like that of the returned prisoner—or like that of a musician trying to explain the beauty of music to people who have been deaf since birth. The deaf people would laugh at the musician and call him delusional, not because music doesn't exist but because *they can't hear it.* So, Huston wondered, isn't it possible that the theories of Asian religions or the postulate of mystical insight were being wrongly dismissed because modern man, too focused on physical reality, mistook his lack of transcendental experience for proof that it doesn't exist? Huston managed to get more than a few students to wonder if he didn't have a point. Following the premise of Evelyn Underhill, the best-known authority on mysticism of the time, Huston was asking young people to consider if there couldn't be "another world to live in," outside the darkness of Plato's Cave.

## A HALL FULL OF DOORS

When Huston arrived in St. Louis, true to his promise he promptly went to the phone book and looked up the name 'Satprakashananda.' To no surprise, the swami was the only person listed under that name. Huston gave him a call and the swami immediately invited him to a study session a few days later, which Huston agreed to attend in the hope of improving his knowledge of Vedanta.

Satprakashananda had explained that every week, on Tuesday and Thursday evenings from seven to eight o'clock, he held a discussion group focused on the Upanishads, and on Sunday mornings he also gave a general lecture. The next Tuesday evening Huston took a streetcar from University City down Delmar Ave. and began looking for the swami's apartment, eventually finding it on the second floor of an old building. After walking down a long hallway to what turned out to be the last apartment on the left, he discovered the door was ajar and went in to find four rows of eight chairs. Five or six people had already arrived and were sitting in the front seats, but Huston, not knowing what to expect, stayed in the back row, near the door, in case he wanted an early exit. Incense was burning and a large photograph of Sri Ramakrishna (the guru of Satprakashananda's guru) hung on the wall at the front of the room, creating a sort of eerie mood for Huston. After several more people arrived, a dark-skinned fellow in saffron robes came flowing out of a bedroom, sat down crossed-legged and pronounced, "I will begin with a Sanskrit chant." The group, who were evidently accustomed to this, lowered their eyes, and began to listen attentively. Huston thought to himself, "Could all this be happening in St. Louis?"

After the chanting, and just before Huston decided the proceedings were just too strange, the swami lifted his eyes and said, "We are working on chapter three of the Katha Upanishad, so let's take a look at the first few verses and then we can discuss what they say." This helped to put Huston's mind at rest. "I was very familiar with Bible study, so after the spooky part at the beginning, I began to relax. I thought, 'I know this procedure!'"

During the rest of the evening the swami remained very matter-of-fact, doing nothing to draw attention to himself as some sort of great man, and this impressed Huston. "He simply was who he was. He was not self-aggrandizing in the least." After the discussion, as everyone made ready to leave, Huston noticed that there were ochre bound copies of the Katha Upanishad on a table by the door. He picked one up, dropped money to cover the cost in a jar on the table and left, making his way back down the hallway.

Huston decided to have a quick look at the book before bed, and this proved fortuitous. "I opened the text," he said, "and by the second page I was hooked. I could not believe that so much truth could be communicated in so few words. As I read, I kept saying to myself over and over, with a rush of conviction, 'This is it!'" In fact, Huston was reminded that Schopenhauer had once judged the Upanishads to be "the product of the highest human wisdom,"[2] and he thought the German might be correct. The next morning he made plans to revisit the swami.

## TUESDAYS WITH SATPRAKASHANANDA

Once Huston and his family were set up in their new home and Huston had settled into his office, he began taking a weekly tutorial with the swami. Over the next decade, from 1947 to 1958, Huston rarely missed a meeting, relishing the opportunity to study with a real Indian holy man. Satprakashananda proved to be as congenial and considerate a person as he was a patient and inspiring teacher. Kendra, for her part, was too busy with the girls and projects of her own to attend the tutorials but she came to visit the swami whenever there was a special event and found him totally charming. "On special occasions he would make the most wonderful rice pudding that had to be stirred on the stove for three hours while chanting special mantras, and it was completely delicious" she recalled. "He knew I enjoyed it, so he went out of his way to make sure I knew whenever he made it. I liked him very much, and I also liked the followers that gathered around him. They were an exceptional and interesting group of people."

Swami Satprakashananda, who became Huston's first tutor in an Asian religion, was born in Dacca, Bengal (later to become the capital of Bangladesh), in 1888, and at the age of thirteen heard a lecture by Swami Vivekananda, who had made such a splash at the World Parliament of Religions in Chicago, in 1893. The lecture affected him so deeply that it set the direction for the rest of his life.

After joining the Ramakrishna Mission in 1908, and after completing graduate studies in philosophy at Calcutta University, he took vows as a monk of the Rama-krishna order, giving up his householder name of Harish Chandra Das and gaining the monastic name Satprakashananda, "Bliss of the Light of Truth." In due course, he took charge of the Vedanta Center in New Delhi for six years, but in 1937, the same year that Huxley and Heard first arrived in America, and one year after Huston reached college in Fayette, he was sent to Providence, Rhode Island, to establish a center there. Once successful, he moved along to St. Louis to set up something else farther west, and ac-cording to Huston, "He told me that when he first arrived, in 1938, he had zero money and lived for the first few weeks on popcorn!" The swami was able to gain a following and would remain in St. Louis until his death more than forty years later, in 1979.

When Huston met each week with the swami, he accepted the swami's teachings as effortlessly as he had once accepted naturalistic theology—and as with that first awakening, he was again embracing a perspective that his parents would find alien. Where Christianity posits a God who created all things, including souls, and whose es-sential personhood remains separate from his creation, Vedanta's perspective is that God's "soul" and our soul are one. Our deepest essence, like His, has always existed and always will, since by nature it transcends time and space. The swami explained, this mutual essence, this Absolute that we share with God, is not only the source of all creation but manifest *as creation*.

In Vedanta, the Absolute is described as having two aspects: one of them, *nirguna* ("without qualities") Brahman, lying beyond time and space, is the unmanifest essence of all things, while the other aspect, *saguna* ("with qualities") Brahman, is that essence as it extends into the world of forms and relativities—in the way that waves of the ocean are extensions of the ocean itself. Though God is more than creation, He (or She or It, as is also appropriate in Vedanta) is not separate from the universe; He extends His being into it. He *is* it and it *is* Him. And so Vedanta teaches a strict nondualism, with all Reality not only interconnected but ultimately a Oneness, as Chandogya Upa-nishad proclaims: "I am That [Brahman], you are That, all this [world] is That, and That alone is." Consequently, Huston was accepting a theological perspective that consid-ered his essence to be non-different from God's, which for his parents, as Methodists, would have been a strange and heretical notion. However, the swami argued that it *wasn't* heretical, and in support of this he cited the testimony of Christian mystics who had made a similar claim. For example, Meister Eckhart had once written: "Where God is, there is the soul and where the soul is, there is God."[3]

Another tenet that Huston readily accepted though it contradicted his parents' religion was the tendency to privilege God's essence over God Himself. In Vedanta, it is the *nirguna* aspect of Brahman that adepts most want to understand and experience, and on that level God is not God as a discrete personality but rather a formless, pure potentiality, a 'world soul' or 'Godhead' from which all forms rise—including God's own form. And so "nondual" Vedantists, seeking their mutual essence with God rather than a personal relationship with Him, are sometimes denigrated by other Hindus as "impersonalists." However, Advaitins have also criticized personalists (both Hindu and otherwise) for elevating their gods and goddesses to so high a position that they forget about the Oneness from which all gods come, compromising reality into a dualism of "I and Thou." Huxley, who also focused on the impersonal level of God's being (and, for that matter, of all being), once explained the distinction between personalists and Advaitins by observing that "The religiously minded dualist calls homemade spirits from the vasty deep; the nondualist calls the vasty deep into his spirit, or, to be more accurate, he finds that the vasty deep is already there."[4]

Huston was now, with the swami's encouragement, interpreting Christianity in a Vedantist and impersonalist light, and he found no problem with doing so. Vedanta, like the perennialism of Huxley and Heard, allowed him to keep his Christianity but stay open to other religions also, since it forwarded a theology broad enough to accommodate all of them. As the swami explained, in Vedanta the different religions are considered various trails up the same holy mountain of insight. The 'mountain' can be approached from different sides, which afford different views, yet adepts of all religions have found their way to the same summit. The swami further explained, even within Vedanta there are different pathways to awakening, each prescribed according to a particular person's personality and inclination, and no path is thought better than the others, since all lead to the same goal.

"He explained to me that there were four main pathways one could take," Huston said. "And these could be found in all religions." The swami outlined the basics of this notion and Huston learned the specifics by reading the Upanishads, the *Bhagavad-Gita* and other Hindu scriptures. There is the path of *jnana yoga* for those who seek to experience the Godhead through the intellect, discriminating between truth and non-truth; *bhakti yoga* for those who make their way to It via devotion to God(s); *karma yoga* for those inclined towards dedicated service to others; and *raja yoga,* the path of meditation, for those with the proper discipline. For both Huston and Satprakashananda, this viewpoint made room for the 'personalists,' including Huston's parents, who relate to the Sacred more easily if it has a face, while also honoring 'impersonalists' like Huxley and Heard who prefer to deal with 'god' as Godhead alone.

Satprakashananda persuaded Huston that there was no conflict between these four pathways because they are only the relative means of reaching the Absolute summit. As Huston would later put it, there is no conflict between them because each can be "sufficient unto salvation." The best approach to follow then is that path to which one is most suited. True to the swami's claim that these pathways are inside every religion, Huston found them in Christianity, summarized for him in the biblical verse: "Thou shall love the lord with all thy heart [*bhakti*], thy soul [*raja*], thy mind [*jnana*], thy strength [*karma*]."

In summary, Huston came to believe that Vedanta completed and complemented his parents' religion and he found tremendous meaning in it. Though he never took formal initiation into the Vedanta Society, there was a time for about five or six years when Huston Smith was both the President of the St. Louis Vedanta Society and a minister of his local Church (though he rarely preached). This might have disappointed his parents and confused some people in his congregation (actually, *lots* of people) but nobody seems to have ever found out, perhaps because the Vedanta Society was not well known in St. Louis and Huston didn't broadcast the situation. For his own part, he saw no problem. Was he a Methodist or a Vedantist? His answer at that time was "Yes."

## LESSONS IN MEDITATION

Another aspect of Vedanta accepted outright by Huston was the view that concepts, even when they are accurate, ultimately count for nothing. What really matters in terms of apprehending Truth is the mystical breakthrough into the Divine Ground of Being. Reading the Upanishads had strengthened Huston's conviction that there is a Divine Ground or Oversoul, but now he wanted to experience that as something more than a concept. Sufi mystics have a way of describing this relationship between idea and experience, concept and percept, that Huston came to accept and sometimes used in interviews: "They speak of the lore of certainty, the eye of certainty, and the truth of certainty. The lore of certainty they liken to hearing about fire, the eye of certainty to seeing fire, and the truth of certainty to being burned by fire."[5] He had heard about "fire" from Heard and Huxley; he had studied the truth of fire while reading the Katha Upanishad; but now he wanted to be burned by fire.

Satprakashananda, who meditated for four hours each morning, told Huston that meditation was the best practice for reaching the inner flame. He taught Huston a common form of Hindu meditation, instructing him first to sit comfortably: "Your trunk, the neck, and the head should be in one vertical line," he wrote in one of his books. "The body will then offer the least resistance to the practice of meditation, because all the important organs function rightly, and physical resistance is minimized."[6] Next, Huston should close his eyes and turn his thoughts inward, into the innermost depth of his being, allowing himself to free-fall into his center while also letting go of all thoughts, allowing himself to dissipate into silence. Pico Iyer, an essayist and longtime admirer of Huston's work, once wrote about the value of this inner silence for a Vedanta Society publication: "In silence, we often say, we can hear ourselves think; but what is truer to say is that in silence we can hear ourselves not think, and so sink beneath our daily selves into a place deeper than mere thought allows."[7]

To effectively sink below the surface of thought into what Satprakashananda called "Samadhi," he recommended that Huston use a particular thought or image as a vehicle. By concentrating on the object Huston would be able to free his mind of other objects and concerns. But what object should he use? If he had been devotionally oriented or drawn to effigies of God, the swami would have prescribed an image, perhaps of Jesus, but he explained that other objects would work just as well. "You can practice on anything that is uplifting," Satprakashananda makes clear in *Vedanta for All*, "a flower, the sun, even beautiful scenery, or the character of a great personality."[8] He pointed out to Huston that he could use either an "interior object," for instance a *mantra* (a syllable or set of syllables), or an "exterior" object such as something set before his eyes, for instance a photo. Huston decided to follow the most common approach in Hinduism of using a mantra, specifically the syllable "om";[9] however, he didn't have much luck at first. "It's very difficult to empty a mind crowded with thoughts," he once said. "But I was willing to be patient and keep trying. I began meditating every day." He knew the experience of the Divine Ground wasn't likely to come overnight, let alone complete enlightenment (as Jack

Kerouac had once aptly remarked, "Walking on water wasn't built in a day"), but he had started up the mountain, taking the raja yoga path of awakening.

## AN UNEXPECTED VISITOR

Huston, now in his early thirties, was settled into a new home and job and had an inspiring teacher to work with, but on December 23, 1949, barely over a year after his arrival in St. Louis, his life became fuller when Kendra gave birth to their third and last child, Kimberly Robin.

To give a sense of the Smiths' family life in those years, Kendra related many wonderful stories about the girls. Karen and Gael, the two oldest, shared a bedroom and once a cousin who was visiting came out of their room and said to Kendra, "Karen is cooking." Kendra remarked, "Oh, that's nice, dear." But the cousin seemed confused by her remark, and repeated, "No, Karen's *cooking*." Kendra, not understanding what she meant but sensing some urgency, went in and found Karen closed tightly inside a cardboard box, broiling in the afternoon heat and needing immediate rescue. "She *was* cooking," Kendra told me with a chuckle, "I had to get her out of there at once."

Another time Kendra overheard Karen playing with her cousin Jane. "Jane said, 'My daddy's bald,' and Karen echoed 'My daddy's bald, too.' Then, all of a sudden I heard, 'I'm bald, you're bald, and the whole world is bald.' When I looked in, they had cut their hair off with scissors!" Then Kendra added, "And there is more to that story. We were on our summer vacation and lived near a lake where we went swimming every afternoon. A boy, seeing Jane with her hair chopped off, came up and said, 'Are you a boy or a girl?' And Jane told him, 'Half boy and half girl.' The boy thought for a moment and then asked, 'What's your name?' She answered, 'Jane.' Then he smirked and said, 'You're a girl.'"

*****

One highlight of the Smiths' early years in St. Louis came in the fall of 1951 when Gerald Heard visited from California. Heard had come down from his mountaintop at Trabuco after realizing, according to Huston, that he had neither the taste nor the talent for running an organization. Others have argued that Heard grew discouraged by finding out that many of his celibate pupils were actually sleeping with each other, but whatever the cause, he had left and put himself back on the lecture circuit.

Huston, still keeping his Vedanta and perennialism to himself, had nonetheless been seeking ways to introduce the subject into academic circles; he hit upon the idea of having Heard give a series of lectures at Washington University. There was no department of religion at the university but the philosophy department gave Huston five hundred dollars to slip a bit of religion into the curriculum. This was just after World War II and there was a tremendous interest in understanding the 'Asian mind' as a way of helping to prevent future wars, and religion was viewed as one gateway to that goal. Huston, who was eager to spend more time with Heard, saw this as an opportunity and decided to play a long shot. He wrote to Heard saying that he could offer only a pittance but would he be willing to give some lectures in St. Louis for five hundred dollars? To Huston's surprise, Heard wrote back and said he would.

Heard's lectures that fall were greatly anticipated by everyone, and the buzz only intensified when Julia Watson, a reporter for the campus newspaper, *Student Life*, wrote on October 26, 1951: "Perhaps in the hurry of crossing campus, you have encountered a slight figure with piercing blue eyes and distinctive brown beard, and perhaps you have wondered idly who this man is. . . . This man is a philosopher, a man of world renown, considered by some to be the best-informed man alive today." It was a heady claim, but when the lectures took place, Heard seemed to deliver on the hype.

"He took St. Louis by storm!" Huston exclaimed. "When I say that, I mean Gerald was a master orator. It just flowed. He never prepared his lectures; it was all there. He had a real gift. Huxley, of course, was the better writer, but Heard was the better speaker. People just wanted to hear him. He would fill the largest auditorium on campus—about eight hundred people—every time he spoke."

Heard was invited to return in the fall of 1952, and this time so many students signed up for "The Philosophies and Religions of Asia," a course he would teach with Huston, that they had to split it into two sections. Heard arrived with a stenographer, a middle-aged woman who was one of his followers, of which there were many, and she was assigned the task of taking down his lectures. Heard's pubic lecture series was titled, "The Crises of Meaning in the Modern World," and the hope was that he could turn the transcript into another book.

Heard's lectures were offered as part of the celebration for the university's centenary year, which meant that there was a tremendous amount of publicity. In article after article that fall in the student newspaper, there occurs praise for Heard, and as the semester progressed the momentum increased. Heard spoke on a wide range of topics: from our need to reconcile ourselves with nature to the need to develop our "latent human potentialities"; from the wisdom of working to understand other cultures to the dangers of nuclear holocaust. In every instance Heard made his way back to the same point, that compassionate action must follow from philosophical insight, as a kind of proof that the insight was legitimate. "A person must have an interest in others," he explained to a student reporter that fall. "If he does not have this faith, he becomes a fanatic stuffing his ideas down the throats of others." Huston not only agreed but it was one of the few principles he still carried with him from childhood. Even enlightenment couldn't be very 'enlightening' if it didn't result in service to others. Heard was describing Huston's bottom-line as well as his own.

Because Heard's public events drew such large crowds, Huston, as a junior faculty member, was allowed to introduce him only at the first few talks, and as the series reached its crescendo, the higher-ups at the university wanted in on the action, including the chancellor himself, Arthur Compton. The last lecture was promoted as something of a gala, so those on the stage committee were required to wear tuxedoes. Heard was nonplused by the formality and didn't own a tux, but there was little he could do about it. Luckily, he soon learned that there was a vice-president of the university who was a true fan and therefore willing to buy him one. "So there was Gerald decked out in a tuxedo when I drove him to the auditorium," Huston recounted. "When we got there, however, we discovered there was a new problem: this vice-president greeted us backstage and saw that Gerald was wearing brown shoes with a black tuxedo. He knew that would never do but the lecture was about to begin. Then the vice-president had a bright idea. They traded shoes and the day was saved."

*****

During Heard's visits to St. Louis, he and Huston had become quite friendly, sharing myriad viewpoints in common and enjoying each other's company. During their classes for the religion course, Dr. Smith had proven himself no slouch as either a communicator or intellectual, and so it happened one evening just before Heard left town that he made a proposal: why didn't he and Huston work together on the book he hoped to create from the stenographer's notes? Huston was dumbstruck. "It seemed," Huston recalled, "to be the opportunity of a lifetime, so I accepted." When Gerald left the next day, Huston and Kendra quickly began making plans to load up the kids for a drive to sunny California that summer, to work with Heard on his next book. Unfortunately, once they got there things would not go quite as Huston hoped.

# Chapter Seven:
# The Human Venture

This time, like all times, is a very good one, if we but know what to do with it.

Ralph Waldo Emerson

Be not simply good—be good for something.

Henry David Thoreau

Things were rolling along for Huston at home and work, and his tutorials with Sat-prakashananda were particularly productive, creating a deep source of inspiration for his life and encouraging him to take his meditation sessions seriously. His belief in enlightenment had deepened for the simple reason that the swami seemed to be experiencing that state. "Satprakashananda," he would write years later, "was perhaps the only person I know who was truly a saint."[1] But even with all of these blessings his life was poised to become even better now that he would be working with Heard.

Gerald's stenographer had produced a large ream of notes from Heard's St. Louis lectures, including lectures from the religion class, and this was a real chance for Huston to get a book published, albeit as the co-writer with a well-known author. The two men didn't see eye-to-eye on all matters related to the perennial philosophy, and Huston was working out his own interpretation of Huxley's "minimum hypothesis," but the young professor kept his disagreements to himself. At this point in his career he had published exactly one professional article, so who was he to tell Heard what to do—especially with his own project? Gerald was giving Huston a rare chance and Huston couldn't be more pleased. "To think that I would be co-authoring a book with Gerald Heard," he reminisced one evening over Thai food. "Greater fame no one could want."

## A BONE OF CONTENTION

One example of where Huston disagreed with Heard stemmed from Huston's unwillingness to accept that mystics were in the vanguard of an evolutionary leap for mankind. Huston considered that belief tangential to the main body of the perennial philosophy. He had held that perspective briefly (dovetailing the evolutionary bit with his notion that the West was becoming a beacon to the world) but changed his mind after meeting Huxley in the desert. For Heard, it was unconditional that we wake up to the next stage of our development: we would either soon have "fulfilled the purpose of our Being, the meaning of evolution," or we would "capsize" as a civilization.[2] Huxley, on the other hand, believed that waking up was a good idea but disagreed that our demise was inevitable if we didn't. Huston found himself agreeing with Huxley.[3]

By the time Heard visited St. Louis, Huston had reverted to the Taoist perspective regarding the future that he had first learned from his Chinese tutor (a perspective that coincided with Huxley's), that there is nothing new in the dynamics of the world; we either live in balance with nature or we do not. Period. For the most part there will always be those who strive for balance and those who won't, and the ratio between these two groups tends to stay consistent across time. Looking at world events in the 1950s, Huston didn't see any convincing reasons to believe humanity was either on the Eve of Destruction or the doorstep of something like Harmonic Convergence. There were reasons to worry, of course, since the Cold War with the Soviets was heating up, but there were, on the other hand, new technologies like television that had everyone cheering loudly. Was there any evidence of an imminent, dramatic shift in human circumstances for either good or bad? Huston didn't see any.

Regarding the notion of 'progress,' which had become the be-all and end-all of Western utopianism, Huston had let go of the idea, settling into the position that the French had it right according to their adage that "the more things change, the more they stay the same." He saw this perspective as consistent with the Taoist view. Only a few years later, he interviewed the theologian Reinhold Niebuhr on television and had a chance to inquire what Niebuhr thought of progress in history. When Huston asked if he saw any, Niebuhr answered flatly, "No"—but then corrected himself, adding: "Oh well, in certain areas." "Like what?" Huston asked. To which Niebuhr responded, "Like plumbing—or dentistry. But overall progress? No. We split the atom and thought we had solved our energy problems, and then along come nuclear missiles and waste. And we develop pesticides and then in thirty-five years we have a 'silent spring.' So it's a trade off. We think we've done it but then comes the full picture that we've not progressed." Niebuhr, it turned out, also held the French/Taoist position.

Huston's disagreement with Heard about a possible evolutionary upgrade in humanity's destiny didn't, however, imply that he had no hope for the future. Huston simply believed he was making a realistic appraisal of the human condition based on a long look at human history; his outlook did not include the assumption that our efforts to improve our lot in life, either as individuals or a society, are futile—at least not entirely, for even if utopia isn't right around the corner, neither is the apocalypse. Something beneficial *can* be accomplished and efforts in that direction should be made. The U.S. was right to stop the invasion of South Korea, and doctors should try to stop disease, but being overly utopian can set people up for discouragement if their dreams don't come true. And being overly cynical keeps people from trying to improve their lives. Huston advised his students to stay away from either extreme, as he avoided those who preached the extremes. Later he would write:

> I myself regularly receive letters both from doomsday prophets who see us going down the drain like Rome and from their opposite numbers—bright-eyed, bushy-tailed New Agers who sound as if they expect a mutation of consciousness to re-open the gates of Eden for two-way traffic any day now. I wish I could readdress each letter, unopened, to one of its opposite number. Let them fight it out while I hold their jackets.[4]

In summary of his disagreement with Heard, Huston had accepted the Vedantist view that whether or not we are progressing or devolving as a society, it is possible for the individual to attain a level of consciousness in which life is, universally and always, perfect. Trusting in life's ultimate goodness, as Huston had always done, and the theory that in enlightenment one could gain perspective on life's trials, Huston believed that an inner utopia is always possible. Inner peace can come even in the midst of suffering and turmoil, as the lives of St. Francis, the Buddha, Mother Teresa and Ramakrishna had demonstrated. "And then there is the sense that in spite of everything," Huxley once observed in an interview with John Chandos for the BBC, "[and] I suppose this is the Ultimate Mystical conviction—in spite of pain, in spite of death, in spite of horror, the universe is in some way All Right, capital A, capital R. . . ." This was the view Huston accepted, at the time and throughout his life, but it did not negate the fact that life can be trying, as Huston was about to find out yet again.

## THE LONG, HOT SUMMER

After the spring semester of 1953,[5] Huston and Kendra drove their recently purchased used car out to Southern California to spend the summer with Gerald. (Kendra remembers that along the way they stopped to give the kids a rest somewhere in Nevada, and Huston, dressed in jeans and a work shirt, was asked if he'd like a job as a muleskinner.) Heard was living at that time in a one-story guesthouse in Santa Monica Canyon, on a property covered with eucalyptus trees owned by a wealthy patron of his whose name was Margaret Gage. Upon arrival, Huston and Kendra rented a small house in Pacific Palisades, where Kendra could take the girls—now ranging in age from nine to three— to the beach while Huston worked with Gerald. "But here," Huston recalled, shaking his head sadly, "is where the story goes sour."

At his first meeting with Heard, Gerald handed Huston a thick manuscript and, according to Huston, stated matter-of-factly: "Here. It's all done. Compile an index and we'll send it off to the publisher." Huston stood stock-still, dumbstruck by Gerald's comment; he and Kendra had scraped together all of their meager savings to rent a house, and he believed there had been a clear agreement about writing the book together ("Anyone could write an index!"), so what was Gerald talking about? Speechless, he took the manuscript out of Heard's hands, turned around and walked out of the house in silence, not knowing what to say; however, once back at the cottage, and after reading the manuscript, he realized the project might still be saved. "The manuscript was terrible," he said. "It had no punch. I mean, this guy was so eloquent and wrote such wonderful books, but this was incoherent and desperately needed rewriting."

After working up a list of comments about where the manuscript was particularly weak, Huston delivered it to Gerald. Heard then read it over quite quickly but seemed to agree with Huston on many points, telling him to get busy on the rewrite; they could discuss the specifics later as Huston moved along. So Huston, believing the partnership was back on, rolled up his sleeves and got to work; however, in the weeks ahead his frustration returned when he couldn't manage to get a moment alone with his mentor. Heard always seemed to be off doing a lecture or meeting with his group of followers, who called themselves the "Wayfarers," and whenever Huston was sure Gerald was at home, he found himself running a gauntlet of devotees who seemed determined to get in his way. "Oh, not now, Gerald's resting," or "He's very busy with his agent right now," or some other such excuse would be proffered.

Toward the end of summer, and after a memorable visit for tea with Aldous Huxley, Huston was called upon by one of Heard's senior devotees, a woman who helped with his book projects. "And it was so disappointing," Huston reported. "You could see that her commission was to mollify me and get me to go along. I wanted to say to her, 'Have you read this manuscript? Do you think that it's publishable?' But she was not up to hearing anything from me, so I gave her the chapters I had rewritten and then just gave up. It was over."

During the next couple of weeks, as he and Kendra prepared to return home, Huston wasn't able to find out whether Heard was intentionally dodging him or too busy to bother, but either way it seemed rude not to acknowledge that his collaborator and friend was leaving.

Arriving in St. Louis in mid-August, Huston felt more frustrated than angry about the turn of events, unable to make sense of why Heard had called him to California only to ignore him. But when the book eventually came out, he was even more deeply bothered. The book, entitled *The Human Venture*, appeared with its first three chapters almost exactly as Huston had rewritten them but without the name 'Huston Smith' appearing anywhere in it, including the 'Acknowledgments' page. And so Huston wrote to Heard, expressing his disappointment that he had not received even a nod for his work. A few weeks later, in a postcard, Heard wrote back that he believed there might have been copyright issues if he had mentioned Huston's help. How had he reacted to that comment? He dropped his head, his tone changing abruptly from sadness to incredulity. "Nonsense. Nonsense! He knew what was going on. Gerald always made the final decisions about his books and he knew what he was doing. So what began as a love affair ended very sour."

Out of his tendency to search for the bigger picture, Huston later put things into a perspective, claiming he had gotten more from Heard than he had given—despite the slight in California—and even today he has a strong sense of gratitude toward the man. It was, after all, Heard who first introduced him to the worldview he carried for the rest of his life, and discussions with Heard about how the world's religions might fit together not only showed up in *The Human Venture* but in Huston's own work, including, "Accents of the World's Philosophies," an essay he published in *Philosophy East and West*, in 1957.[6] To Huston's credit he was able, over time, to separate his personal disappointment about California from Heard's general importance in his life, and as proof of that he would lend his credentials and support to several of Heard's later projects. In fact, John Roger Barrie, the director of Heard's archives, speaks with pride about Huston's collaborations with Heard,[7] and acknowledged his influence on *The Human Venture* in a phone conversation. And when Gerald's *Pain, Sex and Time* was re-released by Barrie in 2004, after being out of print for sixty years, it included a foreword by Huston. However, in 1953 the bloom was off the rose, and never again would Huston feel the same warmth toward Gerald that had marked their early friendship. Furthermore, Huston would never again place his heroes on so high a pedestal. "Even a very good man can make mistakes," he told me, "and I've made my share. Gerald was an important voice for the perennial philosophy and I've never forgotten that he introduced me to it, but he had his faults after all."

## A DETOUR TO MEXICO

Back at school for the fall semester, Huston found some comfort in how successful he was becoming as a professor. He was having no trouble attracting new students to his courses, even without Heard's help, and this was something to celebrate. Word had gotten around that Dr. Smith had a keen sense of humor and a real knack for making philosophical issues come to life. From his side, Huston loved to interact with students and threw himself into his work, invigorated by a new focus on World Religions that had resulted from the class on Asian Religions he had taught with Heard.

In the meantime, and after the beautiful weather of California, Kendra was interested in where the family might spend their next summer vacation. She had become determined to get the girls out of the sweltering heat and humidity of St. Louis again, and this time set her sights on Mexico, which would not only be cooler but cheaper. Then, almost by divine providence, there arose a chance to head south of the border.

In 1952, Washington University had appointed a new Dean of Arts and Sciences, Tom Hall, who the year after that had received a grant for $18,000 from the Carnegie Foundation to study how best to teach the humanities. Hall was a biologist by training and knew very little about the humanities, so he decided to host an every-other-week discussion with members of the liberal arts faculty to hammer out the possibilities. The group, which included Huston, started by reading Cardinal Newman's *The Idea of the University*, Alfred North Whitehead's *The Aims of Education*, and other books that might give them clues about how to proceed, and then they worked on their own assessments. Huston commented that toward the end of spring, which was most likely 1954,[8] Hall pulled him aside and said: "You're scheduled to teach summer school. I'm going to cancel that but here's a bushel basket of all the notes I kept during our meetings. Huston, you're a bright young punk. Turn this bushel basket into a coherent report I can send to the Carnegie Foundation to tell them what I did with the $18,000 they gave me." When Huston came home and told Kendra about the offer, she was thrilled, exclaiming: "Good, you can write that report *anywhere*, so let's go to Mexico!"[9]

In the 1950s it was especially inexpensive to live in Mexico, but they had to get down there first. Huston and Kendra rationed themselves to a budget of twenty dollars per day, for each of the six days they had calculated it would take them to drive to San Miguel de Allende. Huston was the early riser of the family, so every morning it was his job to get their VW bus packed up, shovel the kids inside, and drive until late afternoon when Kendra took over, driving until late evening. This system worked quite well, except that one night Kendra, who had stayed at the wheel until Huston fell asleep, became too exhausted to keep driving and started looking for a motel, spotting one on the other side of the road. The consequence of this was that when Huston got up the next day and made his usual right-hand turn out of the motel to head south, it was two o'clock in the afternoon before they realized the sun was setting in the wrong part of the sky. They had been driving north instead of south! By stepping on the gas Huston had just enough time to get back to the motel where they stayed the night before.

After arriving in San Miguel, they experienced the summer proceeding pleasantly and without incident; Huston put his time to good use on the report, while Kendra worked on her Spanish and enjoyed the agreeable weather with their girls. When the summer was over and the family, after another long drive, arrived back home in Missouri, the dean passed out mimeographed copies of Huston's report to the other members of the committee, which led to a second moment of providence.

Walking across campus one day, Huston bumped into a speech professor, Dan Smith, who had also been on the committee. "Oh Huston," the prof said, "I've been meaning to contact you. Remember that report that Tom circulated? We're reading three paragraphs from it in a choral reading course I'm teaching. They begin with the last paragraph on page 18, in case you're interested." "Well," Huston commented, "I *was* interested. I pulled out the report from my desk drawer and started reading it, discovering it was better than I had thought. 'Not bad,' I found myself saying, and then, 'This is really good!' And so on impulse I slipped it into an envelope and sent it out to a publisher. When the response reached me by return mail, it said that the report had to be expanded tenfold, but a contract was enclosed!" In his memoir *Tales of Wonder,* Huston adds to this story, "I had fantasized about writing a book, but that's what it was—a fantasy, like of climbing Mount Everest or swimming the English Channel. Now here was a contract in my hand." [10]

## HUSTON'S FIRST BOOK

The book appeared as *The Purposes of Higher Education* (1955), and it is a well written if overly dry little tome reinforcing the educational theories of Alfred North Whitehead and John Dewey. The volume's central position can be summed up in the common sense aphorism (often ignored) that, "Students should be taught how to think rather than what to think," a key point of Whitehead's. However, this is not to discredit Huston's effort, for as he explained in the preface, his goal was mostly to outline the objectives of liberal education so that his university could perform a curriculum review, not to knock someone's socks off with cutting-edge philosophical theories.

The book begins with an endorsement of liberal education, Huston explaining that students should be taught to distinguish "between authorities which provide floors on which freedom can build and those which constitute ceilings keeping it down." [11] To reinforce and protect this approach, he tells us that universities "should not grant charters to particular philosophical perspectives" or instruct students to blindly respect academic authority. [12] Next, using this as a yardstick for establishing a balance between freedom and authority, Huston makes clear that special care should be taken when investigating the world's religions. Specifically, the religions are best described historically, in terms of facts regarding their importance for a particular culture at a particular time, rather than in the judgmental terms of evaluation. It is not the job of academics, he wrote, to condemn the various religions out of hand—for instance, on the basis of a naturalistic predisposition towards materialist explanations. He coaches the reader not to assume that the answers to all life's questions are available in science books, and we should not become dogmatic about the materialist perspective that the physical parameters of the world contain the whole story of reality—given that this offers a very biased view of religion.

With regards to this specific danger, Huston quoted Albert Einstein, who considered himself an agnostic rather than an atheist, and who observed that, "Most 'free thinkers' are so satisfied with their refutation of the benevolent Father in Heaven that they content themselves with a very shallow conception [of Him]." [13] Today one could cite Richard Dawkins and Daniel Dennett among those guilty of that same contentment Huston advised against. Agreeing with Einstein and paraphrasing Shakespeare, Huston offered a note of caution to those inclined toward any form of dogmatism, reminding them that, "It is no sign of superstition or credulity to believe that there are more things in heaven and earth than our philosophy has dreamed of." [14]

Huston points out in *Purposes* that we cannot deny that there have been times when religion acted as an opiate of the masses and an instigator to atrocities, but he denied that it *always* and *only* functioned in those ways. Religion has exhibited both sides of human nature, illustrating both our weaknesses and strengths, and one side of the matter shouldn't be taken as the whole story of faith: "Millions have used religion as a curtain to draw across aspects of reality they could not stand. But millions of others have used it to push the curtain the other way to reveal more of being than would otherwise have been disclosed. For these, to borrow Whitehead's words, 'The worship of God is not a rule of safety: it is an adventure of the spirit.'" [15]

Almost to prove his point, the civil rights movement, which was led mostly by a cadre of black ministers from the south, was gaining steam at that very moment, demonstrating to the world that religion can function as a positive force for social change. Later, Liberation Theology in South America would make the same point, with Catholic clergy fighting effectively for justice and equality. So, while secular materialists pointed out the dangers of religion, they seemed oblivious to the fact that any ideology—including their own—taken to an extreme could turn destructive. "In the twentieth century," Huston said, "the ideologies that produced the greatest loss of human life—Nazism, Maoism and Stalin's communism—were all secular in nature, not religious. People forget that secularists can be as dogmatic as religionists, and when they are, they can be equally dangerous." In 1955, Huston was sharply aware of how dangerous dogmatic secularism could be, for his parents, who had lived in China for more than forty years, had been rounded up by the communists and then, after living under house arrest for more than two years, were kicked out of the country on the grounds that they were imperialists breeding superstition as a means of gaining control of the people. Brokenhearted, they had left China to start a new life in America, while their parishioners were, "forced to wear dunce caps and kneel for two hours on broken glass in front of jeering mobs, and the like." [16]

Huston's bottom line in *Purposes* was that we should understand how different societies view the world through different cultural lenses, based on divergent viewpoints on the nature of reality. And when societies do not grasp the relative nature of their assumptions they can turn dogmatic, dictatorial and violent. He acknowledged that our psychological and social conditioning has value, for it provides a foundation for culture and social exchange, creating a strong sense of community and a profound sense of personal identity and meaning. But when we set our training in cement, we can become robotic, sclerotic and blind. In *Purposes* he tells us to avoid absolutist judgments against religion to avoid the possibility of throwing the baby out with the bathwater. "Religion is," Huston reminded his readers, borrowing an analogy of Ramakrishna's that he had learned from Swami Satprakashananda, "a cow that kicks but also gives milk."

## BEING GOOD FOR SOMETHING

During the conservative 1950s, with the "House Committee on Un-American Activities" trying to skew the American mind into ultra paranoia, Huston taught tolerance for others and an open-minded attitude toward their viewpoints, not only in the classroom but in his daily life also. When the St. Louis Vedanta Center had grown to a point where the swami's apartment could no longer serve as a meeting place, the group decided to buy a house located at 205 South Skinker Boulevard, but nobody would sell a house to a dark-skinned Hindu, prejudiced as they were to both the swami's race and religion. "In those days," Huston explained, "the St. Louis papers would not even accept paid announcements of religious services other than those of Christians. Jewish synagogues were acceptable but newspapers wouldn't accept Vedanta Society announcements, even if they were paid for. Vedanta was a 'heathen' faith—that was the actual word people used." Agreeing with her husband, Kendra added, "St. Louis was a Jim Crow town and a segregated city. Even the Methodist ministers would make racist jokes during their sermons." Since nobody would sell to the swami's group, Huston bought the house incognito in 1952 and then turned it over to the Vedanta Society the next day.[17] And so Huston was acting on the convictions he was teaching in the classroom—and not only in this regard.

In 1949 he and Kendra joined a group called The Congress on Racial Equality (CORE) to help end prejudice and segregation in St. Louis. CORE had begun in Chicago in 1942 as an early precursor of the civil rights movement, and soon afterwards it had spread to St. Louis. Huston, who had grown up as a member of a racial minority in China, knew what it was like to feel different, and his parents had just been discriminated against, so he was eager to participate.

The St. Louis chapter met on Monday evenings to plan strategies for the coming week, and often those meetings dealt with the logistics of sit-ins they were holding at local restaurants. One inspiration for these activities had been Shridharani's famous book *War Without Violence* (1939), based on Gandhi's specific tactics for civil disobedience. CORE had targeted lunch counters as good places to try out these tactics. All department stores had lunch counters in those days, but blacks were not allowed to eat at them—or even to sit on the stools, and so the strategy was to have a white person (in St. Louis it was often Kendra) sit at the counter and then, when a black woman appeared, then he or she would invite that person to join them, after what appeared to be a chance meeting. Sometimes this worked and sometimes it didn't (and sometimes even if the black friend was allowed to stay, she was served garbage on her plate). But even if it didn't work, some good often came from the effort, since the white person would complain to the store manager, appealing to that person's better nature, and sometimes write a letter to the newspaper.

"It was an uphill battle all the way," Huston observed, since St. Louis had been famous for its opposition to racial integration. To give a notorious example, when Jackie Robinson joined the Brooklyn Dodgers in 1947, as the first black baseball player ever to join the big leagues, the St. Louis Cardinals came out against him, pledging they that would strike if he tried to play. When the president of the National Baseball League threatened to fine any player who refused to take the field that day, the Cardinals did so but then flagrantly roughed up Robinson during the game—and in every game they played with the Dodgers over the next two years. Robinson's sweet revenge came soon after, in 1949, when he won the Most Valuable Player award for the National League. Huston and Kendra were working with CORE at a time when St. Louis was hardly amenable to desegregation.

After a few successes at lunch counters, and then at municipal swimming pools (where they held "swim-ins"), and with intolerance for intolerance finally starting to budge in America, CORE looked around for more ambitious projects in St. Louis. Someone in the group suggested they target Washington University, since it was still not fully integrated (limited desegregation had begun in 1947, when the School of Medicine and the School of Social Work began accepting blacks into their programs), and since Huston was the only academic in the group, they asked him to lead the project. As a first step, Huston and CORE affiliated themselves with a student organization called the Student Committee for the Admission of Negroes (SCAN), and together they played a significant role in the board of trustees' eventual resolution against all forms of segregation, which came in May of 1952.

Huston recalled that a highlight of those days with CORE occurred in 1957, when Martin Luther King Jr. visited St. Louis to speak at Washington University. Huston, who was a member of the faculty committee that invited King, remembered that, "When he arrived, I went to meet him by taxi and acted as his host for the event. While we were in the taxi headed to the university from the railway station, we talked only very briefly, and he learned that I had also studied theology. But there was a surprise for me too." The surprise was that King, who had recently finished his doctoral degree from Boston University, told Huston that he had written his dissertation on the theology of Henry Nelson Wieman, whose emphasis on working as God's agents in the world greatly appealed to him. "Sadly," Huston added, "I was too shy—and I didn't want to disturb his thoughts—to tell him that I was actually Wieman's son-in-law!"

It was raining when Huston and King arrived at the hall but a huge crowd had gathered. "He gave this stunning address," Huston recounted, "and you could just tell the tide had really turned in his favor. The crowd was ready to hear his message." Huston added to this in his memoir that, "King's southern mellifluousness, biblical cadences and moral argument left that overflowing crowd stirred and steeled."[18] A major leap in our biological evolution might not have resulted that day, as Heard was hoping for, but King's visit gave definite encouragement to Huston's view that positive change *can and does* occur, so we must do what we can to be of use in the world. King would remain an inspiration to Huston all his life, and especially for his ability to arouse the American people to embrace racial equality and individual freedom as fundamental human rights. Perhaps one day the Chinese would also shift away from their newly formed dogmatism, including their hatred of all religion, and allow his parents to return home to their beloved village. In the 1950s, the House Committee on Un-American Activities was terrified of communism at the same time Chinese communists were terrified of religion and the Russians were terrified of capitalism (and everyone was terrified of the A-Bomb). When would it be, Huston wondered, that people would simply try to understand each other and get along? Given the tendencies of the world, Huston was careful to hope but not let his hopes get too high.

# Chapter Eight:
# Finding His Niche as a Philosopher

What is that which gleams through me and smites my heart without wounding it? I am both a-shudder and a-glow.

St. Augustine

Jejune and barren speculations may unfold the plicatures of Truth's garment, but they cannot discover her lovely face.

John Smith, the Platonist

All that the imagination can imagine and the reason conceive and understand in this life is not, and cannot be, a proximate means of union with God.

St. John of the Cross

With so many young men attending college on the G.I. Bill, enrollment at Washington University was at an all-time-high at the very moment when Huston Smith was one of its most popular professors. After receiving an increase in salary, mostly due to the publication of his first book, along with a loan from his parents (who were now living in the United States and had stayed with Huston and Kendra for more than a year), Huston could afford a mortgage—not only on his first home but also a summer get-away in Luddington, Michigan. Before air conditioning was available, it was advisable to get out of St. Louis in the summertime, so Kendra and Huston bought a cottage overlooking Lake Michigan, dubbed "Eagle's Nest" by its previous owner for its high purchase on the sand dunes. This getaway situated on pilings set them back only $2,500, and the Smiths instantly fell in love with the place, holding onto it for nearly ten years.

Family life for the Smiths at this time was typical for middle class Americans in the 1950s. Huston was the breadwinner, Kendra worked at home as a wife and mother, sometimes also taking part time jobs in town, and the girls were free to enjoy childhood—with each exhibiting her own distinct personality along the way. Karen, just eleven years old in 1955, was fiery and independent, and later, as a teen, she would speak her own mind—for instance, refusing to go to the youth group at church and preferring to attend a Hebrew Youth group with her friends. Gael, the middle child, who looked the most like Huston, was sweet, intuitive and creative. Huston would later write that as a teen she would excel "in sports, dance and relationships."[1] Kim, the baby of the family, who looked the most like Kendra, had just begun school. As

Kim grew up, she would prove to be, according to both parents, the most practical, steady and dependable of the three girls. "I would trust her with anything," Kendra once reflected.

Huston, unlike his father, was very affectionate and forthcoming about his love for his children, never hesitating to give them a hug or say, "I love you." He looked forward to playing with the girls whenever he had the chance, sneaking through the house with a little gong that signaled it was time to play. In 2006, Gael reflected on those playtimes and what they meant to her in an interview with filmmaker Jon Monday:

> Huston's career was beginning to get interesting, but I didn't know anything about that. He was my 'Daddy Long-legs' and I was proud of him for other reasons. It really was a different America in the 1950s. In the evenings after dinner, a gaggle of neighborhood kids would gather for one last game. It was usually hide and seek or a jerry-rigged game of softball with three on a team, or some other game of our own invention. My father was the only adult who ever joined our games. Ordinarily we kids spent an inordinate amount of time discussing the finer points of the rules and quibbling about fair or foul, safe or out. But when we had my father in the feathering dusk, before we were called home to bed, we settled in to play.
>
> The game suddenly was more exciting. He taught us all to count to ten in Chinese—Shanghai dialect. There he would be with his eyes cradled in the crook of his arm, counting to twenty while we ran to hide. Somehow the competition always seemed to be neck-and-neck, but I often won. I could feel, even back then, that his exuberant participation was adding a missing nutrient for all the children, not just his own, and that's why I was proud of him.
>
> Years later, when I was one of only a few women on a teaching faculty and the politics and power-plays of the environment were less than pretty, I reflected on the hidden influence of this play with my father. In conversations with other women I learned that either they never played with their fathers or they were trounced in all competition. My assumption [as a child] that I had had a neck-and-neck chance on the field, and that I just might win my point, had stayed with me.[2]

In terms of Huston's professional life, his ongoing tutorials with Satprakashananda were still the primary engines of his spiritual growth and philosophical inquiry. The swami had recommended several books that stirred his thoughts, including and especially, *The Gospel of Sri Ramakrishna*. "I remember that during the first summer we were on Lake Michigan," Huston reminisced one morning, sitting in his living room, "I read *The Gospel of Sri Ramakrishna*. I was reading through the unabridged *Gospel* and I rationed myself to ten pages per day. I wanted to digest it slowly and it lasted the whole summer vacation." In particular, he was struck by the presentation of Ramakrishna as a person, for in his everydayness he made the idea of an enlightened master seem so much more possible and down-to-earth. Later, Huston would credit this effective tone of the book to his friend Joseph Campbell, who had helped Swami Nikhilananda translate the *Gospel* into English from Bengali. Campbell was another Western intellectual whose views had been deeply influenced by Ramakrishna's Vedanta. In his early career he often promoted the viewpoint, though later, after suffering something like a crisis of faith while visiting India with his guru, whose integrity he came to question, he became more circumspect.

## EMBRACING THE WORLD RELIGIONS

By 1955, Huston was fully settled at work with a book just published. This pleasant state of affairs was something of a surprise to him because only a few years earlier, around the time of Heard's first visit, things had not looked so great. Huston's teaching credentials and academic expertise were in the philosophy of religion with an emphasis on naturalistic theology, but his actual interests had drifted far from there. In the 1950s, there was no room for courses on metaphysics or mysticism in philosophy departments, *any* philosophy departments, though that's what now interested him most. He considered leaving philosophy altogether to study for a new degree in psychology, a discipline that, due to the efforts of C. G. Jung, Erich Fromm and others (all of whom opposed the trend toward Behaviorism), still allowed for a wide range of theories concerning the nature of the psyche, some of which had metaphysical components. When Heard visited him in the autumn of 1951, Huston was looking at the University of Michigan as the most likely place to finish this second Ph.D. But Heard's visit helped to change his mind, getting him excited again about philosophy, at least if he could focus on issues related to religion and spirituality.

Heard had studied Asian religions as a dilettante for many years and had accumulated a good deal of expertise; consequently, when he visited Washington University during the second visit, Huston was able to make a plausible petition to his department that he and Gerald teach a course on those religions. After co-teaching with Gerald, Huston was deemed competent enough to teach the course on his own. Huston was then able—given his own background in Judeo-Christian tradition—to offer a course on World Religions, which not only became his niche at Washington University but a real door-opener for his career. While teaching World Religions, he was able to openly discuss metaphysical issues (inherent in world traditions) without having to admit to his colleagues in the philosophy department that he took them seriously. And while talking about Hinduism and Buddhism specifically, he could outline the theory of enlightenment for his students, defending it as an Asian perspective rather than his own. In this way, World Religions became the focus and pivot of his work, while also the context that allowed him to stay inside the discipline of philosophy, which is partially why he had defended the study of religion so strongly in *The Purposes of Higher Education*. Religion was not only a focus of inquiry, it gave him a job.

Huston was also encouraged to create classes on religion because he found so many of the students hungry to study it, looking, as they often did, for some form of spiritual life. While growing up in China, Huston absorbed from religion that we are "in good hands" and that life is ultimately positive, but his students had generally developed a different view. Later, he would explain this in a radio interview: "I find that many of my students look to me like wounded Christians, or wounded Jews, in that what came across to them was dogmatism—we have the truth and everybody else is going to hell—or moralism—don't do this, that or the other."[3] Huston argued back that religion could have a very positive side that might help them find meaning in their lives, especially if they were willing to entertain metaphysical theories. He saw wisdom in religion and told them so, quoting William James, author of *The Varieties of Religious Experience*: "There is an unseen order, and our supreme good lies in harmoniously adjusting ourselves thereto."[4] "By 'adjusting thereto,'" Huston explained, "we gain forbearance, so that, as the saying goes, 'what can not be cured, can be endured.'" For more students than Huston's colleagues would have expected, this made a great deal of sense.

## AN UNOBSERVED DISAGREEMENT WITH HIS MENTOR, HUXLEY

Based on what has been covered so far, it's clear that Huston owed Gerald Heard a debt for making credible Huston's ability to teach World Religions, but this same debt was, to an even larger extent, owed to Swami Satprakashananda. Huston would write later, in 1958, that the swami had "taught me almost everything I know about Hinduism,"[5] and it was also from the swami that he borrowed his specific theory of religion as a phenomenon. Of interest here is the fact that those views disagreed with Heard's, but even more significantly that they disagreed with Aldous Huxley, Huston's primary mentor.

From the swami's perspective, every religion is a separate manifestation of the one "Eternal Dharma," and each leads, if diligently followed, to the same Buddha-like awakening, a position summarized in Hindu scripture (Rig Veda 1.164.46) as, "one truth, many paths." Huxley didn't see the connection that way, believing instead that the Eternal Dharma is often found in the world's religions *in spite of their teachings rather than because of them*. Adepts in every tradition, according to Huxley, have found their way into the breakthrough experience of oneness with the Divine Ground but rarely by following the paths of orthodoxy. More often than not (as was the case for the Fourteenth century Christian mystic Meister Eckhart and a Sufi master in Islam), their allegiance to a mystical perspective was considered heresy and grounds for persecution. (Eckhart was put under house arrest and the Sufi mystic al-Hallaj was executed.) Only a few religions, Hinduism and Buddhism topping the list, have as their stated goal an enlightened state of consciousness, and even these religions perpetuate their caste systems, institutional hierarchies and rigid doctrines as obstacles to waking up. Huxley damned religion when it got in the way of man's growth toward truth, and he believed religion got in the way more often than not.

Huxley argued that even if religion originated from an "Eternal Dharma," which he termed the "perennial philosophy," it tended to degenerate quickly into vacuous and counter-productive doctrines. He championed an experiential spirituality in which people found their own way to the "unitive knowledge," and never at any point did he suggest they stay within their traditional religions. "People ought to take their religion warm from the cow," he wrote in his last novel, *Island*, "not skimmed or pasteurized or homogenized. Above all not canned in any kind of theological or liturgical container."[6] Aspirants might find useful suggestions and signposts for their own journeys by studying the world's religions, which is why he wrote his anthology of mysticism, but he wasn't advocating piety or church attendance.

Huston seems to have been unaware that he had accepted Vedanta's summation of religion over Huxley's (or Heard's, for that matter, who agreed with Huxley). What the swami described as a collection of tried and true pathways up the spiritual mountain, Huxley and Heard saw mainly as a collection of roadblocks. Why Huston didn't, at this time, catch this difference isn't clear; however, many of today's thinkers, including Stephen Prothero, author of *God is Not One*, continue to make the same wrong assumption about Huxley's views on religion.[7] Perhaps the reason Huston had missed this point is that it didn't affect his general agreement with Huxley's position. As noted much earlier, Huxley had outlined the "minimum working hypothesis" in his landmark book on perennialism, and Huston still agreed with that position ten years after reading it. Furthermore, since Vedanta's idea of an Eternal Dharma agreed with Huxley's four-point hypothesis, perhaps Huston assumed the two perspectives ran parallel in all respects, including their assessments of the traditional faiths. The result was that Huston continued to see himself as a perennialist in Huxley's camp, and in most ways he did still fit there.

This raises an issue that Huston would later remark on many times. He observed that scholars too often refer to the perennial philosophy as if it were a monolithic position, a dogma offering no room for variety in either theory or outcome. This is indeed not the case. Huxley didn't try to create a systematic philosophy (or a universal religion, as others, including Harry Oldmeadow, have mistakenly claimed).[8] Rather, Huxley described a general tendency or sub-routine that he saw running across and between the religions, mostly hidden in the writings of their persecuted mystics. This tendency falls broadly within what is called in the formal discipline of philosophy, "Transcendental Idealism." *Idealists* generally postulate that there is a metaphysical foundation to reality that informs our existence with absolute meaning and purpose, and they position this view against "Realism," if the latter is based, as it generally is, on the belief that only the physical world exists and provides sources of knowledge. But Huxley was not attempting to advance an exclusive and systematic version of Idealism, as Schelling, Fichte, Fuerbach and others had, or even a systematic version of the perennial philosophy, as Ken Wilber has tried to do today. He was postulating that there is a distinct pattern within many systems of Idealism—including many of the world's religions and viewpoints such as Emerson's Transcendentalism. Huston believed Huxley's four-point 'hypothesis' that broadly described the perennial philosophy but felt free, as Huxley himself would wish, to disagree with his mentor about specifics such as the place of religion. Again, Huxley had been describing a general pattern, not a system, so there was leeway under that umbrella for rival viewpoints.

## AN OBSERVED DISAGREEMENT WITH HIS FATHER-IN-LAW

By 1956, Kendra Smith's father, Henry Nelson Wieman, had experienced a host of challenges, both personal and professional, that kept him in turmoil for nearly ten years. His twenty-year stay in Chicago had ended with a scandal in 1947; Regina was now long gone from his life; and Wieman had married a third wife, Laura Wolcott Matlack of Grinnell, Iowa, a recently retired school teacher who also happened to be the sister of Wieman's daughter-in-law.

One of Wieman's most important books, *The Source of Human Good*, had come out in 1946, while Huston was still studying with him in Chicago, but before Wieman had a chance to enjoy the success of that, all hell broke loose. "Regina, his second wife, was decidedly ambitious," Kendra wrote to me. "She persuaded my father to do some very unethical things that he knew were wrong, but he was weak. She convinced him to sign up to teach a summer class at the University of Chicago, which she, true to her original intention, actually taught. Also, she persuaded him to co-write a book with her, which then somehow became mostly her book and which he did not feel good about." That book, *The Normative Psychology of Religion* (1935), written ostensibly by "Regina Hanson Westcott," was put together under Wieman's guidance and featured an essay by him. However, these actions of Regina weren't what caused Wieman the most distress. In 1946, she had also accused him of having a love affair, and though it never became clear whether or not that affair took place, Wieman resigned from his post, believing he had caused the University some embarrassment. Thinking his career was now over, he decided to retire at the age of 63.

After Wieman's resignation from Chicago, he divorced Regina and married Laura that same year, 1947. He spent the next eight years or so bouncing from one institution to another as a visiting professor, and never staying in one place more than two years. Wieman came close to settling down in 1951 when he accepted a position at the University of Houston, but after arriving he became caught up in a controversy between the Houston and Wichita Conferences of the Unitarian Church (Wieman had become a Unitarian in 1949, joining his wife's Church). The Houston Conference was hosting the 1952 annual convention of Southwest Unitarians but had prevented a number of African American delegates from Wichita from attending. This caused Wieman to write an editorial for the local newspaper in which he attempted to reconcile the two Conferences. The result was that he alienated both. His detractors in Houston took quotes from his letter that suggested he supported segregation (he didn't) and published them nationally in *The Humanist*. Before he could fully clear his name on this issue, the Wichita Conference accepted the allegation as true. And while his head was still spinning, he became involved in yet another controversy.

Like his father before him, Wieman held socialist leanings and consequently had signed a letter against the rearming of Germany, and that letter was then published in the premier socialist paper of the time, *The Daily Worker*. This action branded Wieman a communist, which, during the Cold War, was about as dirty a word as there was, especially in Texas; consequently, Wieman was forced by the university to resign his post and move along.

Eventually, in 1956, after brief stints at three other universities, Wieman was invited to accept a distinguished position at Southern Illinois University, a few hours away from Huston and Kendra in St. Louis, and at 72 years old finally found a home. He would remain in Carbondale for the next ten years and do some of his best work there, living a quiet and happy life with Laura. "During the years that I was tied down with young children, he and Laura, his third wife, visited quite regularly, or he came by himself," Kendra said. "It was nice to see him finally happy, and both Huston and I liked Laura very much."

During these visits in the late 1950s, Huston and his old advisor enjoyed their many moments together, but they knew they would bump heads if they discussed philosophy or theology, so they tended to avoid the subjects. In public Huston was still a naturalistic theologian but his views had long since shifted, and when he revealed them to Wieman sparks flew between them. The result was that they settled into an accommodating *détente*, something analogous to 'don't ask, don't tell,' in order to protect their familial relationship. However, what might have begun as a series of friendly disputes over tea or coffee became a professional debate, with each of them taking pot shots in academic journals at the other's viewpoint.

Wieman believed that God operates in the world as the creative force that urges us to be of service to each other. For Wieman, only in the world of actions, and only when we act with compassion and justice toward each other, can the so-called 'Divine' be either experienced or understood. But the good news, from that perspective, is that this world of actions, and the world in which those actions take place, can be explored fully with the tools of science and reason, i.e., science can give support to this kind of 'religion.' Huston, for his part, agreed that the tools of science are useful but he disagreed that only these tools could be used, especially in matters of theology. He argued that Huxley's "unitive knowledge" about the Ground of Being could also give valuable insights, even helping us to serve each other, if we could, as James had wished, "adjust ourselves thereto."

Wieman turned his nose up at such an idea, arguing back in an article of his own that no such experience of a Ground of Being is possible; later, in 1963, he would state this point clearly in an essay for the book *The Empirical Theology of Henry Nelson Wieman*. We can almost hear him shouting directly at Huston when he writes:

> It is impossible to gain knowledge of the total cosmos or to have any understanding of the infinity transcending the cosmos. Consequently, beliefs about these matters are illusions, cherished for their utility in producing desired states of mind.... Nothing can transform man unless it operates [directly and exclusively] in human life.[9]

By the time Wieman wrote this, Huston had achieved his first great success, having published *The Religions of Man* in 1958, and was much better known to the general public than Wieman, which may have precipitated some professional jealousy on Wieman's part. Huston, in his own essay for that same book, supposedly a tribute volume to Wieman, felt empowered to retaliate, announcing that he was no longer under Wieman's wing. In "Empiricism Revisited," he explained that he agreed with Wieman that it's impossible to have any knowledge "of the infinity transcending the cosmos" *if we rely exclusively on the tools of empiricism*, but this did not prove that knowledge couldn't come from elsewhere or that other sources of knowledge don't exist.

Huston wrote that he didn't repudiate naturalism, however when it claimed itself to be the exclusive approach to studying reality, he felt it was going too far. He then accused Wieman of "incipient positivism," though he knew "Wieman will recoil at the appellation,"[10] on the grounds that Wieman had said only empirical methods were viable for studying all aspects of reality. Furthermore, Huston added that doing so was commiting the academic sin of 'reductionism,' reducing analysis of a topic to what can be understood about it only from a particular angle; for instance, reducing the whole story of religion to what can be grasped about it from the discipline of sociology. Huston argued back that the 'true empiricist' would have to wonder beyond his assumptions and accept that mystical experiences may also help us to understand the universe and our place in it.

The following year, in 1964, Huston published, "The Death and Rebirth of Metaphysics,"[11] a landmark essay in which he finally laid his cards on the table, admitting not only his interest in metaphysics but also the sort of metaphysics that had caught his attention. This essay came as something of a broadside hit to Wieman because it not only signaled Huston's decisive split from naturalism but also his interest in the work of Tillich and Niebuhr, Wieman's primary rivals in theology at that time.

The debate between Wieman and Huston over the viability of metaphsyics would reach a crescendo a few years later, in 1969, in a book of essays that Huston contributed to entitled *Transcendence*.[12] Huston was by then a well-known scholar and the primary defender of what he termed "Ontological Transcendence" (since he was describing transcendence from one state of being to another), and consequently was given the lead essay. In it he explained that to entertain the possibility of experiencing such a profound transcendence as that of enlightenment was "to fly in the face of recent 'secular theology.'" (We can hear him between the lines saying, "Wieman's for instance!") He added a few lines later, "[But] we need not approach the question apologetically, as if Ontological Transcendence were a crutch for the maimed." [13] In fact, Huston argued, there is a profound value in transcendence, which is why Buddhists traditionally use it to clarify their minds from the various attachments and negative patterns that come up in everyday lives.

Wieman, to no one's surprise, disagreed. In his own essay for that book he admitted it was possible that, "transcendent being is beyond the reach of scientific research," [14] but quickly added that this only means we can never know whether 'transcendent being' exists or not. Furthermore, even if it did exist and even if we could experience it (which Wieman didn't believe), this is still no reason to abandon the exclusive use of empiricism when seeking to answer life's questions. Whatever insight we might gain from transcendence would still have to be proven useful here in the world of actions. [15]

Huston agreed that it is in the world of actions that the rubber meets the road (seconding Huxley's position that, "Even if the kingdom of heaven lies within, we must still try to create it on earth"), but this was no proof against transcendence or its potential usefulness. He agreed that the proof of the pudding was in the tasting but disagreed that only empirical methods could be used in the preparation. The Ground of Being exists and it can be experienced. In fact, to say otherwise was to imply that Buddhism and Hinduism, or any other religion that involved transcendent experience, was a waste of time—which, for Huston, was not only a hubristic claim but, given his interest in world cultures, too Western and provincial for his taste.

As a late word on Huston's public debate with his father-in-law, it's significant to note that Huston never stopped admiring Wieman for his commitment to improving the human condition; this aspect of naturalistic theology still drew his respect and always would. Later Wieman would strongly support the Civil Rights Movement and join protests against the Vietnam War, and Huston would admire him for walking his talk. Even in the first essay where Huston announced his split from naturalism, "Empiricism Revisited," he tells a story about how he kept some lines of Wieman's in his wallet for more than fifteen years, until that wallet had been "picked from my pocket at a High Pontifical Mass in St. Peter's." The central message of those lines, scribbled onto a piece of paper, was that we are morally bound to work for a better world and that we should react toward each other "as sensitively, intelligently, as appreciatively as we can." Huston would never argue with Wieman about that, taking his father-in-law to be exactly right.

## FINDING A NEW THEOLOGY

Vedanta allowed Huston to see each religion as a particular 'color of the spectrum' emanating from the same white light of mystical insight. Even when speaking about God specifically, Satprakashananda had taught Huston that there is no conflict between the traditions. Each god and goddess is only an emanation of the Divine Ground, the Godhead behind all the gods, and each religion's god is only a specific culture's interpretation of the personal-God principle. In Vedanta's universalism, where the world's gods are ultimately masks on the face of the one pre-cultural Sacred, Huston found a theology flexible enough for him to support the world's religions collectively while also moving easily back and forth between them as different paths up the same mountain.

One outcome of all this was that even religious holidays took on richer meaning for Huston; for example, there was one day each year in particular when the two poles of his religious life became sharply joined. On Christmas Eve he would attend the Christmas pageant at his church, along with Kendra and the girls, but afterwards he would slip out to the Vedanta Center to hear the swami's annual address, "Jesus Christ, the Light of the World." In that sermon the swami described Jesus as only one *avatar*, one "incarnation" of God among many, but this didn't bother Huston for reasons we've already discussed. Given Vedanta's theology, Satprakashananda's concomitant belief that Jesus was a true incarnation of the pre-cultural—and pan-cultural—Sacred was confirmation enough of his support of Christianity for Huston to feel comfortable.

## GETTING BACK ON THE CUSHION

Satprakashananda agreed with Huston that religious faith and philosophical conviction give us a useful perspective on suffering, but only enlightenment takes us fully beyond its grasp, and intellectual studies alone can't get us there. Satprakashananda made it abundantly clear that texts and teachings have value, but only if they become instigators to spiritual practice, given that they cannot directly cause or contain the Truth. "It is written in the almanac forecast," Satprakashananda wrote, "that there will be several inches of rainfall, but if we squeeze the almanac, we do not get even a drop of rain."[16] Whatever value Huston was getting out of his reading and tutorials, he still had to meditate if he really wanted to get anywhere.

Huston learned from the swami that experiencing enlightenment—the omega point of spiritual growth—is like no other experience and transcends all experience as commonly conceived. In the everyday world of time and space we experience discrete objects—flowers, bees, children, fish, emails, music, this book, etc.—but the Divine Ground, though a 'something' in the sense that it actually exists, is not a discrete physical object with discernible attributes, so we cannot experience it with the senses. We can't see it because there's nothing (i.e., no *thing*) to see. It is not blue, fuzzy, square, plaid or whatever else. Also, we cannot know it as a mental object—for example, as we know the sum of two plus two (we *can* understand it as a mental object but what we understand is not *It*. What we understand is only a conceptual analogue of It). We can really only know the Divine Ground *ontically*—that is, by *being* it. More accurately, we can only know It by experiencing the fact that we already *are* It, making conscious what was already and always true.

Huston understood all of this clearly, which is why he had been meditating daily for nearly six years, but meditation did not come easily to him. He had difficulty getting his mind to settle down and thoughts often crowded into his head, refusing to go away. However, every now and then, and usually when he had let go of trying, there were moments when he experienced a profound sense of well-being, far beyond simple relaxation, and other instances when he seemed to melt altogether into the Oneness. These experiences, though far too rare for his liking, encouraged him to keep going; like glimpses of a mountaintop that one gets while hiking up a trail, they betokened that the 'mountaintop' was really there and that time spent climbing 'through the woods' was worthwhile.

## THEOLOGY ASIDE, WAS HUSTON A VEDANTIST?

Huston's debt to Swami Satprakashananda was immense and he accepted Vedanta, including its view of religion, almost completely, but he never formally took initiation into the Vedanta Society. When I asked why not, he said simply that, "I didn't feel the need and Satprakashananda didn't press the point." The swami had made clear that conversion was not part of Vedanta, so why bother? "Vedanta does not make any converts in the ordinary sense," Satprakashananda wrote. "To Vedanta, real conversion is the transformation of the inner nature, lifting a person from a lower to a higher plane." [17] Huston was amenable to that type of conversion, in fact he was hoping to achieve it, but he saw no reason to bother with the other sort.

Huston thus became an insider/outsider with the Vedanta Society, and neither he nor they ever found a problem with that arrangement. Today, Huston sometimes still attends Vedanta Society functions and over the years he has been a featured speaker many times at their annual open house at Olema, a beautiful property north of San Francisco. Though in recent years he's been attending a Methodist Church, one would wager the congregation whose doctrine most closely fits Huston's own is that of the Vedanta Society.

Vedanta helped reinforce Huston's enthusiasm for the world's religions, giving him a way to see how each of them could have value, and now he was ready to defend those religions publicly. Some people would have predicted disaster, given that Wieman and Huston's other colleagues believed the religions to be mostly superstition, but what actually happened was that he became a celebrity.

# Chapter Nine:
# The Religions of Man

... the rediscovery of religion is the great intellectual, moral and spiritual adventure of our time.

Bede Griffiths

Surely it is a magic moment in the study of religion, when the experience or insight of someone who does not belong to your own tradition enhances your own understanding of it. Huston Smith has done it for me; and I am sure for many more. The best guide points out the way back to your home, and the best guest helps one discover the unsuspected wonders of one's own house. But then is he a guest anymore?

Arvind Sharma,
a Hindu and Professor of Religion at McGill University

... understanding, at least in realms as inherently noble as the great faiths of mankind, brings respect; and respect prepares the way for a higher power, love—the only power that can quench the flames of fear, suspicion, and prejudice, and provide the means by which the people of this small but precious Earth can become one to one another.

Huston Smith, from *The Religions of Man*

Millions of people have read Huston's classic work *The World's Religions*, but few today realize that that project began in the spring of 1955 as a television show.

When television came onto the scene, producers learned quickly it was a ravenous monster that continually needed to be fed new programs. What is today National Public Television started out as National Educational Television and the producers of NET in St. Louis had been looking for college courses they could put on the air to fill up some time. When they conducted an informal survey of courses at Washington University that were popular, Huston's "World Religions" course was at the top of the list. The next problem that the producers faced, after Huston agreed to work with them, was to figure out what to call the show. The solution came from serendipity. In those days there was a popular coffee table book of photographs entitled *The Family of Man*, so the producers decided to build off that success, dubbing their new program, "The Religions of Man."

## Becoming a Talking Head

Huston was delighted at the prospect of having a large audience for the ideas he was sharing in PHIL 221-222: 'Philosophies and Religions of the World,' but Channel KETC thought Huston had to jazz up his delivery. They assigned a young producer named Mayo Simon to coach him on the finer points of being a talking head. Mayo explained to Huston that he had to remember this wouldn't be like one of his classes, where he had a captive audience. If he lost his viewers even for thirty seconds, they would change the channel and never come back. The producer accepted that Huston had to make his academic points, but Simon urged him to "illustrate them immediately, with an example, an anecdote, a fragment of poetry, something that will connect your point to things the audience can relate to."[1] He also urged Huston to speak in short, clipped sentences, avoiding the jargon of college professors. Huston took all of Simon's lessons to heart, seeing them as the best instruction on teaching he had ever received, and ever would receive.

The television show, scheduled to run for seventeen evenings, already had twelve hundred people signed up in advance to watch it as tuition-paying students. The producers predicted the audience would grow much larger once it was on the air and a buzz was created, and they turned out to be right. Huston had a knack for television and thousands more soon tuned in. Within a matter of months the series was showing in twenty other cities, with a total viewing audience somewhere in the neighborhood of one hundred thousand.[2]

Each week Mayo met with Huston to discuss the upcoming episode, standing Huston before him for a dry run, "And I can still hear his withering remarks," Huston once related in a magazine interview, "along the lines of: 'Doesn't sound too red hot to me, Huston.' By which he meant, 'Back to the drawing board!'"[3] However, unlike other professors who had tried their hand at television, Huston got the hang of things quickly and the show was soon competing with commercial programming—an extraordinary accomplishment in those days, as Philip Goldberg has pointed out. In those days "'I Love Lucy' ruled the air waves and comparative religion for most Midwesterners meant Methodist vs. Baptist."[4] In response to this success, The *St. Louis Post-Dispatch* devoted a two-page spread to Huston, and, according to Kendra, "a few Reform rabbis even made Huston an 'honorary Jew.'"

Huston's ability to convey complex ideas in simple language had much to do with why he had become a successful teacher, but Mayo's coaching pushed him to a whole new level. His success was also helped by his personality, which was cheerful and non-threatening, radiating a kind of Midwestern wholesomeness and humility. "He has this 'everyman' thing about him," James Cutsinger, a colleague and friend of Huston's, once observed. "He comes across as the spokesman for just the average guy, and that's something that really touches people."

In every show, Huston was clear about what he was trying to convey. First and foremost he wanted to describe each religion accurately, in a way that adherents would recognize it. Second, he wanted to give his viewers a sense of how richly humans have conceived the universe, so that they could get a glimpse of how it would be to grow up with another view of things. He was handing out lessons in cultural relativity in order to make each religion seem, relative to its own culture's assumptions, not only viable but attractive—and he was doing a damned good job of it, as Mayo Simon acknowledged.

During the series, Huston described seven "wisdom traditions": Hinduism, Buddhism, Confucianism, Taoism, Islam, Judaism and Christianity. By showcasing them as a group, with equal time spent on each, he suggested, as Satprakashananda had taught him to believe, that none of them was more valuable than the others. Even Huston's own religion, Christianity, was presented as one of seven prospects, and this unbiased approach put him, as Philip Goldberg has observed, "ahead of the curve on pluralism and interfaith respect."[5] In 1956, when the world was threatened with nuclear war, Huston's lessons on cross-cultural respect were a breath of fresh air, urging the world away from conflict by trumpeting the dignity of difference.

Huston gave his audience an understanding of other societies by giving people a better grasp of other religions—and this was a viewpoint that resonated with the everyday person. With the war in Korea just ended, and with two catastrophic wars in the recent past, people recognized the value in taking other people's viewpoints seriously. As an early advocate for global understanding, at a time when the U.S. had not yet launched its first satellite or added its fiftieth state, Huston argued that even if we believe our own religion is best, "we must listen to the faiths of others," for, "daily the world grows smaller, leaving understanding the only bridge on which peace can find its home."[6] Many viewers agreed, so they kept watching, and they kept telling their friends about the show. Consequently, and despite the fact that he had little more in the way of 'special effects' than a map of the world, a blackboard and a statue of the Hindu god Shiva, Huston became a celebrity.

## An unexpected offer

After the series concluded, Huston became a sought-after speaker on the college tour, once teaching his entire series of programs at Stephens College, in Columbia, Missouri on closed-circuit television. The biggest opportunity that resulted from the TV show came when William Danforth, owner of the Ralston Purina Company, then one of the hundred largest companies in America, offered money for a trip around the world. Danforth had learned that the bright young guy on TV hadn't visited most of the countries he had described, so Danforth made him an offer: if the university would grant Huston a semester's leave, a check to fund a round-the-world trip would be in the mail for both him and Kendra. Huston jumped at the opportunity. It gave him a chance to travel and to research a book he was planning. Kendra also was eager, but what would they do with the girls? It didn't seem possible for her to leave. Friends interceded, telling her it was too great an opportunity to miss, and since they had small children with whom the Smiths' girls were friends, they offered to take Karen, Gael and Kim. It was a tough decision, especially for Kendra, since Kim was still only seven years old, but arrangements were made, and in 1957, just after New Year's, they finally set off on their seven-month trip around the world. Huston later wrote in *Tales of Wonder*, "So began my love affair with the world."[7]

## Globetrotting

While visiting different countries, Huston was able to witness the religions in context, and this had a powerful effect on him. He would later write in his third book, *The Search for America* (1959), that in foreign lands one's reality becomes "shuffled," and "the familiar is half strange, and the obvious no longer so." His journal entries from the Danforth trip make clear that he relished that experience. Driven by a desire not to waste time, Huston kept busy every day. At night, rather than checking into a hotel, he and Kendra boarded a bus or train so that when they awoke the next morning, they were at the next destination where they wanted to sightsee.[8] Kendra found this routine exhausting but she humored Huston, who just couldn't seem to slow down. Even on buses and trains he slept only sparingly, furiously writing in his journal about his experiences as they moved from place to place.

On February 6, while in England, he recorded the "pleasantness, cheerfulness and helpfulness of the British people," and soon afterwards, in France, he was intrigued by "the way people really look at you." On March 29, in Turkey, he wrote of "the strangeness of waking up before 2AM to the beautiful yet unearthly cry and drum of the man going through the street to awaken Ramadan observers to eat." In Egypt, he was amused by riding from the Cheops pyramid to the Sphinx on a camel named 'Fantastique,' and he wrote a long paragraph in Israel about the ferocity of guard dogs at a kibbutz they visited. In India, where they lingered from April 23 until May 27 (a long stay that reveals Huston's interest in Hinduism and Vedanta), he wrote fifteen full pages. He and Kendra didn't visit many of the tourist attractions there, besides the Ellora and Ajanta Caves, but they eagerly stopped at as many ashrams as possible, including those of the Vedanta Society, Sri Ramana Maharishi, and, on May 27, in Pondicherry, Sri Aurobindo. Huston was hoping to meet real adepts in India, but Ramana Maharishi and Aurobindo had both died, and he doesn't seem to have met anyone as impressive as Satprakashananda back in St. Louis.

This was something of a letdown for Huston, since meeting enlightened adepts had been a personal priority of the trip, and in Burma he had had a meeting with a person that boded well for what might come. At the behest of a Buddhist master named U Ba Khin, he and Kendra had visited Ba Khin's prize student, S.N. Goenka, who was said to be able to sit indefinitely in samadhi. When they were brought into his presence, the man was sitting in the lotus position as still as stone. "U Ba Khin invited us to stick a pin into Goenka to show that his concentration was so deep that there would be not a flicker of a reaction," Kendra noted. "We declined, but Huston clapped his hands loudly next to Goenka's ear. Not a flicker. I lifted his limp hand and took his pulse. His flesh was quite cold and his pulse was very low—around 30, as I recall." U Ba Khin then explained that his student would come out of samadhi only at a time he had set for himself or when U Ba Khin—and no one else—requested it. Then U Ba Khin spoke to Goenka quietly and the latter soon opened his eyes. "In answer to Huston's questions," Kendra reported, "he said he felt as though he had had a wonderful sleep." This occasion greatly impressed the Smiths, and later, in 1975, Kendra would attend a retreat with Goenka in India, following up on that first meeting. Sadly, and as was said, they weren't impressed with the quality of other holy men on their first trip around the world, and didn't believe they had met any saints.

## Paranormal Abilities

Beyond meeting people who were awakened to ultimate reality, Huston had no interest in witnessing any other wonders of the 'Mystical East.' What was his exclusive fascination with just one phenomenon of 'mysticism,' enlightenment? What about astrology, telepathy, faith healing, astral travel, precognition and spirit possession? "I could never see where they had any real value or offered any real meaning. Human nature being what it is, people would still manage to be unhappy and selfish even if they could read minds or fly under their own power or whatever else. I was looking for something deeper than a few magical powers or tricks." Huston acknowledged that having one's health restored by a faith healer would be a wonderful outcome for a sick person, and he didn't discredit that it was possible, but the focus of his search was elsewhere, on what he believed would have the greatest value for mankind.

Huston's journal from the Danforth trip reveals no interest in other so-called paranormal abilities, and this remained true for all his subsequent trips to Asia. In 1962, while leading an "Asian Seminar Abroad" for the International Honors Program (an independent organization affiliated with several universities), Huston had to be dragged by his students to an astrologer in Bangkok, Thailand. Later, back in his room, he filled two pages of his journal with logical deconstructions of how the astrologer's predictions had been made. "Regarding my past: items the man could have inferred from American mobility: that I was not living in the house where I or my father was born, [and] that I was not following my father's profession. Items vague enough to seem true if you were inclined to accept them [included] that I was a self-made man." Among the other predictions Huston dismissed (in this case because they were too future-oriented to be proven false) were that he would have two sons and would live to be seventy-eight years old. In fact, Huston would never have a son and would live far beyond the age of seventy-eight.

Like Evelyn Underhill, the primary authority on mysticism in 1950s, Huston approached his subject exclusively in terms of the enlightenment phenomenon, and here he was also following the lead of Vedanta. In the Upanishads—and later in Patanjali's *Yoga Sutras*—we are warned that unusual abilities like telepathy, precognition and levitation are dangerous for spiritual growth, even as they are also by-products of it. As the adept achieves higher and higher states of consciousness, these abilities come along naturally but they pose challenges if the adept's ego is not kept under proper control—and prior to full awakening, it is never completely under control. Consequently, the aspirant is better off to ignore these abilities rather than cultivate or improve them. This is the lesson that Huston had heard from Satprakashananda, who once told him, "Occult powers are real, but I have seen evil men become good and that's the only miracle that interests me." Huston has accepted this guiding principle of spiritual growth, and it resonated well with the bias against miracles he had learned earlier from Wieman and naturalistic theology.

## WRITING A BOOK TO TAKE RELIGION SERIOUSLY

Back in graduate school, Huston's education on the world's religions had been both biased and boring. "Looking back," he explained in his first article for *Parabola*, "I sometimes feel that those teachers must have been geniuses of a kind—geniuses in reverse, because they could make something so implicitly interesting into something boring—which takes a sort of talent too common among academics." [9]

The leading book on World Religions while Huston was on television for KETC (and the book he used in his classes) was *Man's Religions* (1949), written by John B. Noss, a professor of philosophy at Franklin and Marshall College. This book, which Huston later remarked was as "dull as dishwater," was rife with unfair judgments about the religions that were already out-of-fashion when Noss wrote them; for instance, Noss used the term "high religions" for the Western traditions and pretty much judged everyone else's viewpoint to be a waste of time. He referred to Tibetan Buddhism as a "corrupt form of Buddhism" that had "monstrously transformed original Buddhism," [10] and he insulted Muslims by calling their religion "Mohammedanism," [11] suggesting that they focused their faith on the Prophet rather than God. But the religion that Noss hit the hardest was exactly that which Huston found most compelling, Hinduism. Like Katherine Mayo, Albert Schweitzer and others who had written negatively about Hinduism, Noss judged it to be a form of escapism. In a section titled, "The Rise of Indian Pessimism or World Denial," he argued that, "the doctrine that complete reality can be experienced only by one's becoming absorbed in Brahman-Atman led inevitably to a devaluation of the more ordinary modes of consciousness," and Noss included in these "ordinary modes" any concern for the practical matters of everyday life.[12] Hinduism had such "serious drawbacks," he summarized, that the result was "either lethargy of mind, feeling and will, or a definite renunciation of the world." [13]

Huston found these verdicts outrageous. Hinduism was the religion of Chandragupta Maurya, the Indian king who fought against and defeated the armies of Alexander the Great; it was the religion of the Gupta Dynasty, which, during the 4th and 5th centuries A.D., enjoyed a grander civilization than was ever achieved by Rome; and it was the religion of Mahatma Gandhi, who, before his assassination in 1949 (the year Noss' book was published) had helped kick the British out of India without firing a single shot. "So much for a lack of initiative or worldly interest on the part of Hindus!" Huston commented when he discussed the matter. "Noss wasn't even remotely impartial in his judgments, nor were they remotely accurate."

Huston wanted to offer something entirely different in a book of his own, describing the religions as their followers understood them, while avoiding evaluations or judgments almost entirely. Today this is a familiar approach (Huston points to Karen Armstrong as a good practitioner of it) but in the spring of 1958, when Huston's book came out, religions were rarely presented without judging them and privileging Western values along the way. But Huston changed all that, making clear in his introduction that he wasn't filtering the religions through the lens of any particular ideology, including those of Durkheim, Malinowski or Freud, all of which were popular at the time. He didn't discredit their work, and, in fact, he found value in their descriptions of religion's sociological and psychological functions, but he wasn't comfortable with the belief that those functions exhausted the benefits of religion. Religion has its benefits for the physical and social aspects of what we are, but Huston wanted to emphasize that it may have spiritual value, too, and as its adherents claim.

Seyyed Hossein Nasr, a leading scholar of Islam, once summarized the significance of Huston's book by pointing out that Huston was the first professor of religion to demand the freedom to love what he studied. Where scholars of religion had generally been accepted by their colleagues only if they were not religious (a condition Nasr finds analogous to hiring music teachers only if they're deaf), Huston sought to study the religions "religiously," in ways that took their face-value claims—including their metaphysical claims—seriously as potential truths. William James had done this for mystical experience in his book *The Varieties of Religious Experience* (1901), but this had never been attempted for the religions until Huston came along, and Nasr applauded him for it.

## A FRESH APPROACH TO RESEARCH

To insure that his descriptions were accurate, Huston hit on a research method all his own, and this forms another reason why his early work was so important. "First I read their sacred scriptures—including the profound and trusted commentaries on those scriptures," he explained. "Second, I sought out the most authentic and profound living representatives of those views and asked them questions. And third, I would jump into the religions myself, doing the rituals and practices they prescribed to get an insider's view." Regarding this last aspect of his method, Huston apprenticed himself to adepts of the religions, including Satprakashananda, traveling around the world also to observe rites and rituals. This 'participant-observer model' is common in academia today, but before Huston's approach most, scholars worked mainly in their offices, basing their research on textual study.

As readers moved through Huston's *The Religions of Man*, each tradition was painted with such accuracy and respect that it was almost as if the author were converting to one position after another. When Jews read his description of Judaism they thought, 'Oh, I see, Huston's one of us,' and when Muslims finished the chapter on Islam they rejoiced, 'he's defending our religion!' Robert Thurman of Columbia University once said that the same had been true for Buddhists, and Arvind Sharma of McGill University related that when the book came out in India, his father exclaimed, "This man understands Hinduism better than I do!" Pico Iyer, whose Indian parents were both professors of religion, wrote that this quality of accurate and unbiased description is still the key to the book's staying power: "What distinguishes that work, even today, is how it sits inside every tradition that it describes, blending the rigorous eye of the scholarly outsider with the beating heart of the initiate. Like a kind of 'Method scholar,' the author seems to report on each tradition from the inside out . . . ."[14]

## BUT HOW DO THE RELIGIONS FIT TOGETHER, AND CAN THEY?

One of the most interesting sections of *The Religions of Man* comes at the very end, in the last five pages, when Huston asks the reader to consider the question, "How do these religions fit together?"[15] He tells us that he sees three possibilities. First, we can adopt what is likely the most common position about religion, that "mine comes first and is best and the others line up behind it."[16] The second possibility, often expressed by people who think they are being generous, is that "in all important respects they are the same." But this option, however appealing it might seem at first (since it gives a measure of respect to all faiths), neglects the fact that they have distinct differences in theology and practice that are difficult to reconcile with each other. And this is partly why Huston worries in his book that advocates of this choice of "all the same" merge the traditions inappropriately, trimming the corners to make them fit together. He warns that before believers in this option (broadly speaking, 'universalism') go "hiking off too quickly to Baha'i, the current syncretistic faith that is making the most serious attempts to institutionalize this conviction," they should ask themselves if the differences between religions are really as arbitrary as they assume.[17] "How does Buddha's '*anatta* doctrine' of no-soul square with Christianity's belief in man's individual destiny in eternity?" he asks. And, "How does Theravada Buddhism's rejection of every form of personal God find echo in Christ's sense of relationship to his Heavenly Father?" Huston concludes his assessment of this second 'solution' by observing that, "The religions of man may fit together, but they do not do so easily."

The third possibility of how the religions fit is that they may *not* fit together at all but that this may be all right. Why not? Huston argues that in this case one wouldn't assume all truths to be available in any single religion. Each tradition would be viewed as containing something uniquely valuable, adding its own distinct information to the human enterprise and the overall cultural heritage of mankind. Though this option didn't entirely reconcile the religions to each other, it had some real appeal for Huston, and he would work with it in the near future, for the reason that it didn't smooth over the religions' differences, which he thought important to consider.

## But what about the perennial philosophy?

Many scholars today see *The Religions of Man* as advocating Aldous Huxley's viewpoint, and indeed there are moments when it does. For example, the book can be read profitably by perennialists, those for whom the direct experience of the sacred underlies all great religions, to get glimpses of religions' core, whether or not we think the individual religions have any ultimate value or not. Furthermore, moving from Huxley's perennialism to Vedanta's, Huston agreed with the swami that 'what rises must converge,' with each pathway meeting at the same summit of Truth. However, Huston found a potential problem in the swami's perennialism that troubled him deeply. The Vedanta teachings seemed to suggest that Christians and Jews were trying to reach the same spiritual goal as Hindus, whether they realized it or not; for example, in their ignorance Christians might think they were shooting for heaven but *really* they were after the Buddha-like awakening that comes with enlightenment. To put it another way, Vedanta seemed to be another variety of Universalism, in this case privileging religions like Hinduism and Buddhism—or Sufi Islam—that hold mystical awakening to be the highest goal, but denigrating religions that see it otherwise, relegating them to a lower tier of spiritual clarity. To Huston this suggested that Vedantists believed they knew more about the true goals of Christianity and Judaism than the people practicing those religions—which, of course, might be the truth, but Huston hoped that it wasn't. Huston longed for a different answer that validated *all* the religions while still honoring their differences, including their different goals. At the time, when he wrote *The Religions of Man,* he saw no such solution, which bothered him greatly. Until such a resolution came along, he would have to console himself with having written a bestseller.

*The Religions of Man* received praising reviews from scholars as well as the popular press, and one result of this attention was that Huston's department promoted him to full professor. Offers for speaking engagements and book projects poured in, and his alma mater, Central Methodist College, awarded him his first honorary Ph.D., in tribute to his accomplishments. The highest and most unexpected praise came from the Massachusetts Institute of Technology, the high temple of scientific and materialist inquiry. The president of MIT, Carl Compton (the brother of Arthur Compton, Huston's chancellor at Washington University), was trying to strengthen MIT's humanities' program and felt that the time was ripe to add a philosophy department. Would Huston like to come and teach at MIT? "My St. Louis colleagues argued that the dream of humanizing scientists was romantic," Huston later wrote, while discussing how he felt about the offer, "but the task seemed worth attempting. Moreover, Cambridge was an intellectual magnet."[18] Of course Huston had some trepidation about how his metaphysical views would go over at MIT, but he couldn't think of a better place in the whole world to affect a reconciliation between science and religion, which was still his dream. He took the offer, eager to see what he could do.

*Changshu, the Chinese village where Huston grew up.*

*Huston's mother, Alice Longden*

*Huston (in front) with his older brother, Robert.*

*The Smith family, with Alice, Walter and Wesley in front, and Huston and Robert in back.*

*Huston, Robert and Walter, when Huston was in high school in Shanghai.*

*Huston during his college days in Fayette, Missouri.*

*Huston and Kendra at the time of their marriage.*

*Kendra's father, Henry Nelson Wieman, with Kendra, Karen (on far left) and Gael.*

*Gerald Heard (on right), standing with architect Felix Greene, on the construction site of Trabuco College in the Laguna Hills. (Permission of the Vedanta Society)*

*Swami Prabhavananda, Aldous Huxley and Christopher Isherwood in the Green Room at the Vedanta Temple in Hollywood. (Permission of the Vedanta Society)*

*Huston and Kendra, with Gael, Karen, and Kim, at their home in St. Louis (above).*

*Swami Satprakashananda.*
*(Courtesy: Vedanta Society of St. Louis).*

*Huston on television, in St. Louis, 1955.*

*Huston interviewing D.T. Suzuki on NBC television, for the series "Wisdom for Our Time," in 1958.*

*The marriage of Stanislav Grof and Joan Halifax, in Iceland, in 1972 (Huston in the foreground, back to the camera, acting as officiant). Permission: Stanislav Grof*

*Interviewing Jiddu Krishnamurti in 1968. (Copyright (c) Krishnamurti Foundation Trust, Ltd and the Blaisdell Institute.)*

*Huston with students in India, while leading the International Honor's Program in 1970 (and while he was still teaching at MIT).*

*Huston as an enthusiastic professor at Syracuse University in the 1970s.*

*A  supper on the banks of the Kentucky River with Gray Henry, Wendell Berry, Huston Smith, and Tanya Berry.*

*Joseph Cambell, Honolulu, Hawaii, 1985.  (Permission of Phil Cousineau).*

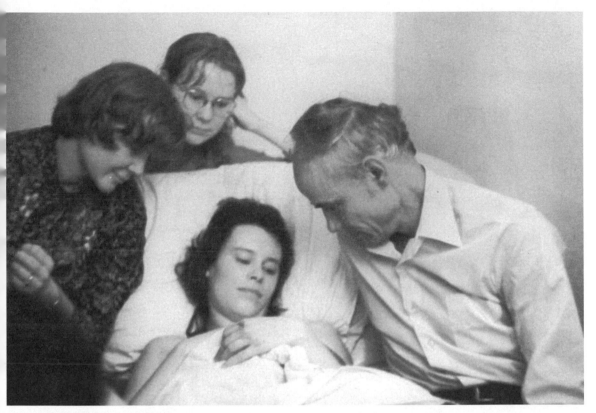

*The birth of Gael's daughter, Serena, with Kendra, Kim and Huston looking on.*

*Gael and her daughter Serena, about the time they moved in behind Huston and Kendra in Berkeley. (Permission Gael Rosewood)*

*Huston and Ram Dass, together at the Esalen Institute in Big Sur, California. (Permission of Cynthia Johnson Bianchetta).*

*Huston and Kendra, 1987.*

*Huston with his grandson, Isaiah.*

*Huston with Bill Moyers in 1996, at the time of their television show together.*

*Huston with Seyyed Hossein Nasr (in middle) and another Traditionalist, Jean-Louis Michon, at the Sacred Web conference in Edmonton, Alberta, in 2006.*

*Huston and Kendra with their granddaughter, Serena.*

*Huston in his home with Khen Rinpoche Lobzang Tsetan, abbot of the Panchen Lama's monastery.*

*Huston with Philip Novak (on the left), a close friend and colleague, and his favorite student at Syracuse, on the release of Tales of Wonder in 2009. Lance Trumbull, who studied at Berkeley with both Huston and Novak, is on the right.*

*Huston Smith interviewed by Phil Cousineau for mondayMEDIA DVD. (Permission: Jon Monday)*

*Huston being interviewed by the psychologist and gerontologist Ken Dychtwald (note that you can see Huston's cochlear implant on the back of his head in this photo). (Permission Jon Monday)*

*The Gyaltsens, the Tibetan family that takes care of Huston, with Dolma at the far right and her grandson, Ngawang Lekdup, in Huston's lap. (Permission Jon Monday).*

*Sufi master, Frithjof Schuon.*

*Pico Iyer, whom Huston has said he views as a "Dharma heir" of his perspective. (Permission Pico Iyer)*

*Huston with Douglas George, his first Native American student. (Permission Phil Cousineau)*

*Reuben Snake (at right) with a Huichol peyote man on our trip to Mexico to make The Peyote Road. (Permission Phil Cousineau)*

*Huston and the Dalai Lama at a conference organized by Gray Henry, in San Francisco, in April of 2006.*

*Huston in 2012.  (Permission Graeme Vanderstoel)*

# Chapter Ten:
# Temple of the Marvelous Mind

When this realization [of enlightenment] is completely achieved, never again can one feel that one's individual death brings an end to life. One has lived from an endless past and will live into an endless future. At this very moment one partakes of Eternal Life—blissful, luminous, pure.

Ruth Fuller Sasaki

If you want to see, see all at once. If you think about it, it's gone.

Zen master Lin Chi

*The Religions of Man* quickly established itself as the leading book in religious studies, and every publisher since that time has tried to knock it off its pedestal. "Failure," Huston commented with a laugh, giving a wink when asked why the book was still in print. He attributes its longevity to its readability and he credits that readability to the fact that the book began as a TV show. But what also appealed was that Huston placed the traditions on an equal footing, without sweeping their differences under the rug. "Today," Seyyed Hossein Nasr observed, "when there are 'inclusivists' who dilute all religious teachings into the claim that 'they're just saying the same thing,' and 'exclusivists,' such as fundamentalist Christians and extremist Muslims and Jews, who uphold their own religion but condemn all others, Smith's viewpoint provided a sense of dignity to all religions that was refreshing in its vision—and still is."

Deepak Chopra recalled that when he first read *The Religions of Man,* "as a fourteen-year-old coming of age in Delhi," what immediately struck him was, "the lucidity, the depth of understanding and the fact that it was totally non-opinioned." This respect for all cultures, combined with a genuine desire to build bridges between them, immediately made Huston the leading figure in comparative religion, though he had had no formal training in that field. His presentation of the religions helped invigorate interfaith dialogue, a project begun in 1893 at the World Parliament of Religions in Chicago that quickly fell by the wayside.

Even the military took an interest in Huston's work, flying him by bomber to the Air Command and Staff College at Maxwell Air Force Base near Montgomery, Alabama, to lecture one thousand officers on the topic of World Religion.[1] Huston spoke that day about the value of looking across the spectrum of faiths to learn something about religion in general. Each religion has its own domain of concern, but if a person wishes to understand *religion* as a global constant, he or she must explore its myriad manifestations, just as a linguist who wants to understand the phenomenon of human language must study more than one tongue. In addition, Huston told the officers that in some respects we can't actually understand our own religion if we don't contrast it with others, or as he put it in *The Religions of Man* (quoting an old British adage): "'What do they know of England who only England know?'"[2]

## EMPHASIZING THE VALUE OF DIFFERENCE

Huston was grappling with how the religions might fit together or interrelate. Based on conversations he had had with Gerald Heard, he was testing the theory that each religion has something unique to contribute to the human adventure and that the best human future would include insights from every religion and culture. Exactly what that would look like, beyond validating cultural differences, wasn't exactly clear to him. In "Accents of the World's Philosophies," published in *Philosophy East and West* in 1957, Huston offered his first, best guess. He began by giving a comment from Bertrand Russell, who once said that people are constantly engaged in three basic encounters: with Nature, with other people and with themselves. Huston then pointed out that in the mid-twentieth century, "The great surviving cultural traditions are also three— the Chinese, the Indian and the Western." Putting these two lists together, Huston theorized that each culture has had a better understanding of one of Russell's three encounters than the other two: "Generally speaking, the West has accented the natural problem, China the social and India the psychological."[3]

This solution to Huston's puzzle about religion suffered (and he wrote in his essay that he feared it might) from being overly simplistic, highlighting one aspect of each culture and religion over its other elements, including elements that members of those cultures might rather have had emphasized. But this failure, if one can call it that, simply highlights the magnitude of the problem Huston was wrestling with. It also reveals his determination to place himself, an American raised in China, in the role of global citizen, working for a solution that could help humanity avoid further conflict. He wanted to offer an answer that wasn't suggesting the 'West is Best' and everyone else is living out our evolutionary past. In 1961, when Huston was asked to give the Charles Strong Lectures in Australia, he was still arguing for this way of valuing the religions, based on Russell's three encounters, but he soon found himself going back to the drawing board. He had a strong inner sense, on which he often relied, that encouraged him to believe a more elegant solution was out there somewhere, even if he hadn't found it yet. The search for that solution became the grail quest of Huston's career, always present in the back of his mind as he continued to investigate the world's religions.

## EXPLORING YET ANOTHER TRADITION

When Huston moved his family to Massachusetts in 1958, he brought a regretful end to his ten-year apprenticeship with Satprakashananda, who had been his guru for a decade. But even before this separation, he had plunged into another religion, which was Zen. His reasons for exploring Zen in part came from its being the fastest growing Asian religion in America, which meant that it was quite easy to find Zen teachers. Huston had also become fascinated with Zen during his visit to Kyoto in 1957, on the Danforth trip. He had earlier visited the First Zen Institute of New York, a center founded in 1930 by Sokei-an Sasaki. Students there recommended that he visit Sasaki's widow, Ruth Fuller Everett Sasaki, when he reached Kyoto. Ruth Fuller Sasaki had already established a branch of the First Zen Institute there and was hosting Americans who wished to learn about Zen. Earlier in her life, she had been a wealthy Chicago socialite but after the untimely death of her first husband, Edward Warren Everett, began traveling with her young daughter as a way of sorting out her feelings and finding a new direction in life. In Kyoto, in the mid-1930s, she had taken part in a short workshop at a major Zen temple, Nanzenji, and after returning to the States met Sasaki. Eventually, in 1944, she and Sasaki were married, by which time Fuller was assisting him with his work.

When Huston and Kendra met Fuller, her husband had died. She was fluent in Japanese, living in Kyoto as a Zen priest of the Rinzai sect, becoming, in the words of *Time* magazine, "the first American in history to be admitted to the Japanese Buddhist priesthood and installed as head priest of a Japanese temple."[4] Ruth Fuller's daughter, Eleanor, no longer lived with her, having married another student of Zen, Alan Watts, who had studied with her mother in New York.[5]

Ruth Fuller Sasaki greeted Huston and Kendra with open arms, immediately assuming the task of introducing them around town, which proved very useful. "You have to have introductions to do anything in Japan," Kendra explained. "Ruth paved the way for us. She found a family that we could stay with, a Japanese family who was very nice, and she got Huston connected with Goto Roshi." Goto Zuigan Roshi was the abbot of the monastery connected to Myoshin-ji, Kyoto's ancient and revered "Temple of the Marvelous Mind," and as such was a deeply knowledgeable and respected Zen *roshi* or "master." He spoke excellent English, having lived in Los Angeles for two years. Among his students when the Smiths arrived were two young Americans, Gary Snyder, the Beat poet and close friend of Jack Kerouac (whom Kerouac depicted as "Japhy Ryder" in his novel *Dharma Bums*), and an ex-soldier named Walter Nowick, a virtuoso pianist who had trained at Julliard.

After meeting and making plans with Goto Roshi, Huston went off each day to train with him, riding to the monastery on the back of Nowick's motorcycle. Nowick, who was 88 years old when interviewed for this biography, was hosting a music camp each summer at his small "opera company" in Surry, Maine, in an old hay barn, and had become one of only three dharma heirs to Goto Zuigan Roshi when the latter died. In 1957, however, when he met Huston, Nowick was teaching English and music at a girls' school in Kyoto.

Huston was delighted that Nowick was willing to tote him around the city and that the roshi was willing to instruct him. Back in Cambridge, he had been experimenting with *zazen*, a type of meditation in which one watches the breath as a way of stilling the mind, but Goto Roshi recommended that Huston, if he really wanted to get anywhere, should take a *sesshin*, an eight-week training course, to refine his technique. Huston agreed, and so when the *sesshin* began, he joined in, again riding back and forth with Nowick. "Huston had a real passion for Zen," Nowick recalled as he walked to the place where he had buried some of Goto Roshi's cremation ashes, quite near the Opera barn. "There weren't many Westerners who were interested yet, so it was wonderful to meet someone else who was."

## WHAT ATTRACTED HUSTON TO ZEN?

Zen Buddhism began in China (where it was called "Ch'an") in the early sixth century A.D., started by an Indian monk named Bodhidharma who had been traveling across the countryside looking for adepts to study with but had no luck. This sparked the Indian monk to dedicate himself to rigorous meditation as a way of waking up on his own, and this emphasis on meditation inspired the tendency to label the school "Ch'an," a corrupted pronunciation of the Sanskrit word for meditation, *dyana*, as "Zen" is a corruption of "Ch'an."

Huston was interested in Zen philosophy because, like Vedanta, it emphasizes an experiential breakthrough into enlightenment rather than the collecting and processing of concepts and ideas, which is the usual task of philosophy in the West. In the Zen tradition, attention to concepts and ideas is actually said to get in the way of one's awakening, constituting an addiction to processing one's life through the thinking mind, the *chitta*, rather than opening oneself to the *prajna* mind, the "wisdom mind" that lies beyond it. In addition, Huston was attracted to Zen's riveted attention on reaching satori, "awakening," as quickly as possible, since this was also his goal.

Zen adepts stand out in Buddhist history for their aggressive attempts to awaken. Where other sects of Buddhism may approach spiritual growth as a slow project that requires patience, Zen—even in the school of "gradual awakening"—takes seriously the Buddha's claim that anyone can wake up quite quickly if they're willing to work at it. At the time of his death, the Buddha had said to his disciples, "Work out your own salvation with diligence," and in the idiom of Zen that meant, 'Don't wait for grace from above or for someone else to do it for you, just get to work!'

Huston was still exploring Huxley and Heard's experimental approach to mysticism, which William James had termed "radical empiricism" and which he believed paralleled the scientific method. Huston was testing in his own experience whether or not it's possible to reach higher states of consciousness, and whether Zen techniques could get him there faster than what he had been trying. Huston believed he was still aiming at the same target: enlightenment was enlightenment regardless of the religion or sect that promoted it. Thus, Huston felt no contradiction between Zen's view of awakening and Vedanta's.

Based on his acceptance of the perennial philosophy, Huston saw a basic agreement in the metaphysics of Hinduism and Buddhism. Buddhists describe the highest reality as *Shunyata*, 'Emptiness,' while Hindus describe it as Brahman, which is something of a 'Fullness'; furthermore, Buddhists describe the purest aspect of our psyche as *Buddhata*, our inherent 'buddha-*ness*,' while Hindus describe it as Atman, an absolute level of self. Huston believed Shunyata was basically equivalent to Brahman and Buddha-nature synonymous with Atman, so much so that, "I felt I was encountering the same truth in a different idiom."[6] Huston wasn't changing his goal when he shifted his attention from Vedanta to Zen, he was simply testing other methods of reaching it, in the hope of turning theory into experience even more quickly.

Many Buddhists today would cry foul, contending that Huston was wrongly equating terms that don't really fit together, but he was encouraged to do so by no less an authority on Zen than D.T. Suzuki, the best-known explicator of Zen to the West in the 1950s. Suzuki, whom Huston had hosted at Washington University the winter before going to Kyoto, has argued that the traditional controversy over terms was based mainly in semantic misunderstandings and philosophical nitpicking. Suzuki described Buddha-nature to Huston in a way that was perfectly symmetrical with the swami's description of Brahman, insisting that Reality is experienced in enlightenment as a mystical paradox in which Shunyata, "Absolute Emptiness," is *both* "an ultimate reality" and a "void of inexhaustible contents."[7] Suzuki believed Hindus and Buddhists *are* seeking the same goal. He even went so far as to claim, again in agreement with Vedanta (and, for that matter, the perennial philosophy), that Meister Eckhart's view of Godhead also was in "perfect accord" with the Buddhist doctrine of Emptiness.[8]

## ONCE AGAIN, AN APPRENTICE

Returning from the Danforth trip in time to teach for the fall semester, Huston was still engrossed with Zen, so he invited Suzuki to return to St. Louis for another visit to Washington University. Years before, Suzuki had been the disciple of Soyen Shaku, a Rinzai monk who had represented Zen at the Chicago World Parliament of Religions and had also served as his master's translator during a U.S. tour in 1905-06. Returning to Japan after that tour, Suzuki took a position as a university professor in Huston's discipline, the philosophy of religion. Soyen Shaku then charged him with the task of improving the West's understanding of Zen. To achieve that end, Suzuki published *Essays on Zen Buddhism* in 1927, and went on to become primary spokesperson of Zen in the West for the next four decades.

Like Huston, Suzuki was strongly motivated as a bridge-builder between cultures, and with that aim in mind he had attended the London 'World Congress of Faiths' in 1936. There he had met the young Alan Watts, who later wrote that Suzuki completely "stole the show."[9] By the end of World War II, Suzuki's efforts had gathered sufficient steam to exert influence on Western philosophy; for example, Martin Heidegger wrote, "If I understand [Dr. Suzuki] correctly, this is what I have been trying to say in all my writings."[10] Suzuki pitched his perspective in broad ecumenical terms that attracted the attention not only of philosophers but several psychologists, including such seminal figures as C.G. Jung, Erich Fromm and Abraham Maslow. Based on his success and growing reputation, Suzuki was eventually asked to teach at Columbia University, a position he held from 1951 to 1958. Huston felt he was in excellent hands with Suzuki as his new teacher.

During their meetings, Huston found that he was as attracted to Suzuki's personality as he was to his teachings. To Huston he was the perfect embodiment of what he taught and Watts agreed, once observing that Suzuki was "about the most gentle and enlightened person I have ever known."[11] And so Huston found himself traveling to New York City several times during Suzuki's Columbia years, hoping some of the old master's enlightenment would rub off on him.

## A STRANGE SORT OF WISDOM

In 1958, NBC television mounted a series of interviews with famous public intellectuals entitled the 'World Wisdom Series,' but when the show came together the producers realized they had positioned themselves to step on some toes. Every thinker enlisted for the program was a Westerner, which seemed to suggest there was no wisdom anywhere else in the world. Attempting to correct this mistake, they trotted out a token non-Westerner, D.T. Suzuki. To interview the Japanese author they picked the newly minted authority on the world's religions, Huston Smith, who, besides knowing what questions to ask Suzuki, also knew Suzuki himself. Of the twenty-two interviewees on the program, Suzuki was the only one who sat cross-legged on the floor, and Huston, to his credit, joined him in that pose. Together they made a somewhat comic image for 'Mom and Pop America,' given that both men were wearing business suits and Suzuki was sporting a bow tie (not quite the attire of the mystic and mysterious East).

Suzuki outlined the basics of Zen in his interview, explaining to Huston that it contains a belief in a truth that lies beyond all words and concepts; he continued, this highest knowledge can even be triggered without words. Suzuki related the story of Mahakasyapa, who was catapulted into *satori* when the Buddha answered a question by simply lifting up a flower. Hearing this, Huston observed: "The Zen perspective had passed from Buddha's mind to this disciple's mind. This is a very fragile thing." But Suzuki disagreed, arguing that communication is communication: "It's not fragile, in fact. You speak to me; I speak to you. Is that fragile?"[12] Huston acknowledged that it wasn't, gaining an insight of his own while also providing the context for a Zen insight for viewers. A year later the poet Muriel Rukeyser, a colleague of Joseph Campbell at Sarah Lawrence College, inspired by the exchange she had watched, put it into one of her best-known poems, "Fragile."

During that interview, later published with the others as *Wisdom for Our Time* (1961), Suzuki emphasized the value of enlightenment (describing it in broad terms that people outside his tradition could relate to): "Every one of us has God, or Godhead, in him. And to come in contact or to come into the presence of this Godhead, God, Dainichi [one of the so-called celestial Buddhas, also called Mahavairocana] . . . that is what Zen endeavors to lead us to. . . . When we come to that, we know what our existence means, what life is."[13] Huston appreciated how 'everyday' Suzuki made this possibility sound, as though enlightenment was something wonderful to experience but not superhuman in any sense. On another occasion when Suzuki was asked how it felt to be enlightened, he smiled and replied, "Just like ordinary everyday experience, except about two inches off the ground!"[14] He had brought his message to American television, and Huston had helped him do it.

## SORE KNEES AND 'PHILOSOPHER'S DISEASE'

Huston's first meeting with Suzuki the year before had already galvanized his desire to experience satori, "to learn what had produced such a gentle sage,"[15] and it was on Suzuki's recommendation that he had studied at Myoshin-ji.

Before Huston left on the Danforth trip, he had told his colleagues about his intention to spend a couple of months meditating in Kyoto and they had chided him for "whoring after the infinite." (Huston explained this one afternoon over Udon noodles at a Japanese restaurant near his home.) "But Suzuki had recommended Marvelous Mind and he was my teacher, so off I went. Besides," he added, "what better 'whoredom' is there?"

Huston's quest for a glimpse of awakening is what led him to undergo the eight-week retreat with Goto Roshi, as a sort of last hurrah for his trip around the world. But once at the monastery, he found the food (rice, pickles, twig tea, and little else) bland, and the monks' lifestyle austere, and it was only out of sheer determination that he stuck it out. He recalled that he and the monks meditated for ten or twelve hours a day in a long room with a raised platform on either side and when night came, they simply reached up and pulled down a sort of comforter. "One half of it was used as a mattress and the other half was a cover. So the private room that I might have wanted turned out to be a space about three feet wide!"

The monks meditated in the lotus position, with little chance for Huston to stretch his cramped legs except for a few brief sessions each day of *kinhin*, short periods of meditation performed while walking slowly in single file. And his difficulties weren't limited to his physical discomforts. He was a philosopher whose mind, like that of all Western philosophers, sometimes roiled and boiled with ideas. Even if those ideas seemed profound, Goto Roshi coached Huston to see them only as distractions. Early in the retreat Huston had sometimes written things down in a notepad he kept tucked away under the covers on the shelf over his head. When the presiding monk in the hall noticed he was doing this, Huston was called outside for a reprimand. In Huston's words: "He said, 'this is a holy place. We do not write in the zendo.' So I asked him, 'What if you have to write a note home or something?' And he answered: 'Well, try not to *have to*, but if you absolutely must, write it in the *banjo*,' which was the squat toilet we all used." Huston smiled. "So much for the prestige of being an author."

When Goto Roshi found out what Huston had been doing with his notepad, he immediately diagnosed him as having "philosopher's disease." Huston would later write that Goto Roshi then "retracted, acknowledging that there was nothing wrong with philosophy as such—he himself had a master's degree in philosophy from one of the better Japanese universities. 'However,' he continued, 'reason can only work with the experience that is available to it. You obviously know how to reason. What you lack is the experiential premise that makes reason wise when it is reasoned *from*. For these weeks put reason aside and work for experience.'"[16]

Huston remembered that another difficulty during the retreat was being away from Kendra, who was also training in Zen nearby at Sasaki's Institute, Ryosen-an Zendo. The fact was that she missed him, too. Her program gave her some time for sightseeing and other diversions, but she was so used to doing these things with Huston that she found herself continuously thinking of him. She wrote a note that she hoped would be delivered to him at the retreat, though, as it turned out, it was rejected. The note simply stated, in the pithy fashion associated with Japanese poetry: 'I long to cling to you like a wet shirt.'" This sentiment might suggest that Kendra wasn't as focused on her practice as Huston. In the years ahead she became the better and more dedicated meditator, spending four three-month silent retreats at the Insight Meditation Society in Barre, Massachusetts, and sometimes teaching meditation. In admiration of Kendra's spiritual progress, Huston recalled, with a little whimsey, "I began to wonder, you know—what if she gets beatified by these, and I, in my soiled self, have to live beside an angel?!"

## CLOUDS FOLLOWED BY SUN

Huston had learned from Goto Roshi that there are other meditation techniques besides putting one's attention on the breath. Goto had recommended *koan* practice as the rocket ride to awakening. But Huston soon learned that *koan* practice is no piece of cake, and especially for someone who has philosopher's disease. *Koans* are short sentences or stories that ostensibly make little or no sense but when contemplated from the right perspective are said to trigger a glimpse of satori. *Koans* are posed to students as if they were questions; however, they rarely accommodate a rational answer, and even when they do seem to have one, *that* is not the answer. As Suzuki had explained about *koans* during his television interview with Huston: "It is a problem which is to be experienced, not intellectually interpreted." And Huston has added to this, "*Koans* are Zen riddles that you do not solve so much as step through, as through Alice's looking glass, into Mad Hatterish conundrums designed to stun rational sense and in its place induce wordless insight. Perfect, simply perfect, for driving a professor of philosophy insane."[17]

The most famous *koan* is of course 'What is the sound of one hand clapping,' but Huston was given quite a different puzzle and the gist of his *koan* came to this: 'How could one of the greatest Zen masters have said that dogs do not have Buddha-nature when the Buddha has said that even grass possesses it?'[18] Armed with this *koan*, Huston's job was to focus on its true meaning and periodically report his findings to Goto Roshi during private interviews. For two months he banged his head against the *koan's* seeming contradictions for eight hours a day, an experience he later described as outrageously frustrating. His mind became like a "caged rat," he recalled, trying frantically to find a hidden way out.

Things went along for several weeks, with Huston's irritation intensifying as the retreat neared its completion. Every day he would come up with what he thought was another ingenious solution and every day, during *dokusan*, the private interview, Goto Roshi would frown and shake his head 'no.' Then, ringing a small bell, he would dismiss Huston from the room, telling him to try again. After two months of this, Huston hadn't gained even a brief glimpse of satori, only a sore back and tortured knees, and now, nearing the end of the retreat, he seemed to be facing total disappointment. "Lots of effort, no breakthrough," he recounted. He was worn down, worn out, exhausted and exactly where the roshi wanted him to be.

When the last week of the retreat arrived, the monks launched themselves into a seeming go-for-broke mode of operation, taking very little food and trying not to sleep at all. This, on top of what Huston had already been through, proved to be too much for him. "After the first night I was simply sleepy. By the third night I was a zombie. From then on, it got worse."[19] Even Huston's constitution was overwhelmed and he contracted a ferociously sore throat that convinced him he was going to die. Frustrated, bewildered, exhausted and, finally, exasperated, Huston stormed into the roshi's room for their last interview, his face flushed and contorted with anger. When asked how things were going, Huston shouted out, "Terrible!" To which the roshi remarked, "You think you're going to get sick, don't you?" When Huston said he already was sick and began to complain about it, the roshi, sitting peacefully, soberly remarked, "What is sickness? What is health? Put both aside and go forward."

Huston leaned forward to give the roshi a piece of his mind but found he had nothing to say. Goto's words had struck him like a bucket of cold water. With his intellect finally defeated, Huston broke through into a luminous moment of absolute stillness. "I despair of ever conveying the uncanny impact those twelve words had on me," he later wrote. "Sickness and health suddenly seemed beside the point of what it means to be human; compared to that more abiding reality [of the wisdom mind], health and sickness were two sides of the same coin."[20] Settling back into his cross-legged position, Huston's face softened and his eyes grew bright. Free of the philosopher's disease for the first time in years, he gained a great moment of clarity and insight, a brief glimpse of what Suzuki had so recommended. This moment profoundly affected him at the time and would stay with him in all the years ahead ("I have often been sick, but off it goes to the side, and I go forward").[21] Bowing deeply to Goto Roshi, who smiled in acknowledgement of what had happened, Huston got up without saying a word and left the audience hall in peace. He hadn't directly solved his *koan* about the dog (could it be solved directly?) but he had achieved its primary goal of gaining insight. This even more deeply confirmed for him that Truth is something experiential and higher states of consciousness are real.

## SAYING GOODBYE

After the retreat and just before Huston returned to the States, Goto Roshi invited him to come by for lunch and to say goodbye. During that lunch Huston gained another insight into the everydayness of Zen. When he arrived, Goto met him at the door of his tiny house dressed casually as though he were any old somebody—which, according to Zen, is exactly what he was. Then he introduced Huston to the old woman who cooked his food and showed Huston the small room where he slept, indicating a futon in the corner where, he explained, he liked to sit and watch Sumo wrestling on television. He then asked if Huston liked to watch sumo. "No." "Oh, too bad," Goto remarked. After that, to further make his point that a Zen master is just a ordinary human being who happens to have had an extraordinary breakthrough, the roshi showed Huston that in his backyard there were beer bottles, explaining that he liked to drink beer while watching the wrestlers go at each other. At first Huston wasn't sure what this tour of the mundane was all about but soon realized Goto Roshi was knocking himself off the pedestal Huston had placed him on. From a Zen perspective it's fine to respect a spiritual teacher but if we raise them up too high, we may simultaneously place ourselves too low, forgetting that we also have the Buddha-nature within us and that we too are a Buddha-in-the-making.

After lunch, as Huston made ready to leave, Goto Roshi gave him one last piece of advice. Bowing low, he said, "Turn your whole life into a life of gratitude." To explain what he meant, Goto Roshi pointed out that while Huston was traveling home, he would be relying on the actions and expertise of other people, including the airplane pilots and the ground crews—and even the efforts of those who were dead, like the Wright Brothers who had invented aviation in the first place. The master explained that people everywhere are the beneficiaries of people whom they've never met, and they should be thankful for what others have done for them. When asked if he had complied with Goto Roshi's request, Huston averted his eyes for a moment and reflected deeply, remarking, "Yes, I think I *can* claim that."

With the training at Myoshin-ji finished, Huston spent a few happy days sightseeing with Kendra and relishing a few good meals out, including several chances to fill up on Udon noodles, his favorite, which he had first enjoyed as a special treat during the eight-week *sesshin*. "That's when I came to love them," Huston remarked. "The head monk told me that if I wanted to give the monks a gift, I could pay for some noodles to be served. I still remember how grateful they were to get them—as was I!" When asked if he had brought back any other 'souvenirs' of the retreat, he mentioned that the head monk had given him a *keisaku*, a stick used to 'encourage' sleepy meditators. "I'm not sure whether he meant that as a reward or as a reminder that I tended to get sleepy, but either way—or both—I treasure it. It reminds me that the truth is always with us if we'll only wake up."

## WHAT HE TOOK FROM ZEN

Huston believed that even after his long efforts he was never a very good Zen meditator. Some authorities on the subject, including John Blofeld and Charles Luk, have disagreed with him in print about this opinion, both commenting that they were impressed with his knowledge and commitment. Luk, in his book *Secrets of Chinese Meditation*, observed that Huston was one of the very few Westerners with whom he bothered to talk about meditation. Joan Halifax Roshi, an old friend of Huston's and a very respected Zen master today, also compliments his practice. "He came to Santa Fe to a conference about six years ago," she remarked in an interview in 2008. "He had this amazing capacity to be very insightful and contemporary in his comments. There was this huge well of compassion and love between us. He was kind of a radiant being—and he was also a practitioner. He loved sitting in meditation and he knew what he was doing. I got the impression it was a very important part of his life."

In 1987, in a plenary address at a major international conference at Berkeley, entitled "Buddhism and Christianity: Toward the Human Future," Huston described three things he had drawn from Zen and Buddhism in general.[22] First, Buddhism reinforced his viewpoint that there are pathways for being religious besides the path of devotion he had learned from his parents. He was by nature a *jnana yogin*, as the swami had termed it, one whose primary approach to God was through understanding, and he believed Buddhism had helped him find validation for that approach. Second, Huston said in his lecture that he had had difficulty trying to cultivate the Christian virtues directly. "How, for example, does one go about trying to be more humble?" But when he read about Buddhism's postulate of 'The Three Poisons'—hatred, greed and delusion, which are considered the three main barriers to enlightenment, he found it easy to conceive of them as the "chief obstacles to the Christian virtues of humility, charity and veracity." He added that, "I started watching for the poisons, greed (to mention only the first one, including greed for self-aggrandizement) began to surface at every turn. Because poison is in the system now, one can deal more tangibly with it than with the health that lies somewhere in the distance." This worked for him, and so he recognized it as another debt to Buddhism.

Summarizing what he had taken away from these experiences, Huston explained, "A third transfusion of spiritual energy came from the Buddhist (as also Hindu and Taoist) unblinking recognition that there comes a time in our understanding of the Ultimate when not only personal categories but all categories must be set aside. At a certain point in my odyssey, the Christian emphasis on God's personal nature appeared excessive and confining: It made God seem cloyingly anthropomorphic." Huston realized once again that his own leaning was toward the "apophatic, transpersonal abysses of God's nature," the Godhead beyond God, rather than to the 'old man in the sky' conception of the Sacred he had grown up with—and Zen had reinforced the validity of that choice.

Huston never officially became a member of any Buddhist sect, Zen or otherwise, but the gifts it brought to him remained fresh and he looked upon those weeks at Myoshin-ji as among the most rewarding of his life.

# Chapter Eleven:
# The Search for America

And I myself—soft, weak, obscene, digesting, juggling with dismal thoughts—*I, too, was superfluous.* Fortunately, I didn't feel it, rather it was a matter of understanding it; but I was uncomfortable because I was afraid of feeling it (even now I'm afraid—afraid that it might catch me behind my head and lift me up like a wave from the depths). I dreamed vaguely of killing myself to wipe out at least one of these superfluous existences. But even my death would have been *superfluous.*

Jean-Paul Sartre, on life's meaninglessness

Oh how I wish for soothing rain,
All that I wish is to dream again,
My loving heart, lost in the dark,
For hope I'd give my everything.

Nightwish (a Finnish Goth band), from "Nemo"

Hope is an ability to work for something because it is good, not just because it stands a chance to succeed. It is not the same thing as optimism. It is not the conviction that something will turn out well, but the certainty that something makes sense regardless of how it turns out.

Valclav Havel

After returning from Japan, Huston continued to practice zazen daily and kept in close contact with his new mentor, Suzuki. This, along with the completion of his retreat at Marvelous Mind, gave him a definite cachet as an authority on Zen, and so throughout the 1960s he was often invited to speak on the subject or lend his name to the projects of others. For example, two pivotal books on Zen written for Westerners, *The Three Pillars of Zen* by Philip Kapleau and *Zen Mind, Beginner's Mind* by Shunryu Suzuki (no relation to D.T. Suzuki), feature forewords by Huston Smith, and it was Huston who had recommended Kapleau's book for publication. These books, soon to become 'must haves' on hippie coffee tables across America, provided excellent overviews of meditation for an increasingly eager audience, and in Kapleau's case there were also accounts of "eight contemporary enlightenment experiences," which helped bring the goal of Zen into focus, making it seem practical and attainable. Huston, based on his glimpse of satori, was eager to share this good news, his own experience justifying for him the value of yet another religion while also suggesting a possible cure for the frenetic and neurotic pace of modern life in industrial society. Maybe the Romantics of the nineteenth century had been right to believe that the East would become the cure for the West. "In the morning I bathe my intellect in the stupendous and cosmogonal philosophy of the Bhagavat Geeta," Thoreau had written in *Walden*, "and in comparison with which our modern world and its literature seem puny and trivial." And to this Thoreau added his recommendation that Westerners continue their cure by reading the *Tao te Ching*, the *Anelects* of Confucius, the *Vishnu Purana* and other Asian classics. Huston was reinforcing that viewpoint.

## ALAN WATTS

An irony of Huston's life in the late 1950s (and then in the 1960s) was that he, with expertise in both Zen and Vedanta, could have become a guru or spiritual guide himself; however, this was a role he neither wanted nor would accept. "I saw myself as a college professor," he remarked. "I would sometimes recommend spiritual teachers to people, but I never wanted to be one." However, something like the opposite was the case for Huston's friend Alan Watts, whom Huston first met when they were both out on the lecture circuit. Watts didn't like to stay planted inside any particular group or tradition; his autobiography is entitled, *In My Own Way*. For years he was a sort of 'roshi-at-large,' visiting college campuses to lecture on Zen and give workshops (while also writing books on the topic) even before he had visited Japan. Watts once described the specific character of his teaching like this: "I make it very clear to those who attend [my seminars] that my role is more that of physician than of minister, for the former works to get rid of his clients and the latter to keep them in a permanent following."[1]) However, it was difficult for him not to attract followers for the good reason that he acted the role of leader, moving out of academia (he was once the director of the California Institute of Asian Studies) into the position of loosely affiliated guru. Watts was on a different path than Huston, but their mutual expertise about Zen often brought them together, and, over time, they developed a friendship.

Huston never missed a chance to get together with Watts or host one of his lectures, bringing him to MIT several times during the 1960s. Huston has described Watts as not only brilliant but also an excellent dinner companion and storyteller with whom Huston liked to share tales and ideas.[2] The two of them were both close with D.T. Suzuki, and they would sometimes share information about how the old gentleman was getting along. Huston remembered Watts fondly: "The first thing is enjoyable, just delightful. He was so entertaining, but he was also one of the most articulate human beings I ever met. But," Huston chuckled as he reflected, "he was such an excellent performer that he couldn't resist a good line, leaving it to the scholars to cut the thin line between where truth and interpretation entered."

Kendra was more circumspect in her view of Watts than Huston. Watts had a reputation as a womanizer and rake, and because "some of my mother's Calvinism must have gotten into my genes," she found she couldn't fully approve of him. She did praise his writing and admitted that, as with Huxley, she found him to be "fascinating and charming company."

During one of Watts' visits to MIT, Huston had the chance to put him together with Aldous Huxley. As Kendra remembers the occasion, there was an unexpected meeting before they even sat down together. "Huston, Huxley and I were waiting for the elevator to take the three of us up to dinner at the Faculty Club. When the elevator doors opened, and before we could get in, Watts walked out." He and Huxley immediately recognized each other and Watts acted uncharacteristically deferential. "After a brief exchange we left Watts and got into the elevator and Aldous turned to Huston and me and said, 'What a curious fellow, half philosopher and half racetrack operator!'" Later, when Watts learned of this comment, he told Huston, "He got me just right!" Huston has said on several occasions that he believed this was the first time Watts ever met Huxley[3]—which would mean that he and Kendra had introduced the two British authors, but this seems highly unlikely. Huston first met Huxley in 1947, but Watts tells us in his autobiography that he first met Huxley "during the 1943 Easter vacation."[4] Whether or not Huston introduced the two men, he agreed with Huxley's assessment of Watts, once adding a wry bottom line of his own: "Watts was the guru of Zen who advised everyone to meditate but did not bother to do it himself."[5] But Huston offered Watts gratitude: "He introduced so many Westerners to Zen and wrote so beautifully about it that it's hard to fault him."

## A SECOND TV SHOW AND A THIRD BOOK

In 1958, Huston was 39 years old and had become *the* authority on world religions, the go-to guy on Zen, and also something of a television personality. He was offered another TV series, this one titled "The Search for America, a study in American values." His job was to interview renowned intellectuals on the program's theme while he played the role of attentive listener, posing questions to Erich Fromm, Reinholdt Niebuhr, Eleanor Roosevelt, John Kenneth Galbraith, Paul Tillich and a host of other cognoscenti. This series was as successful as "The Religions of Man" and it followed with an offer of a book adaptation. The book that appeared in 1959, with Kendra ("Eleanor Wieman Smith") as collaborator and co-editor, isn't known to readers today. While the interviewees have mostly faded from popular memory. *The Search for America* went through five printings in its first three years and flew off bookstore shelves.

Huston explained in this book's introduction that the objective was "to discover who we are by asking what we would like to become," which to his mind was an excellent way to proceed. Most of the essays, like F.C. Redlich's on "mental illness," or Harold Stassen's on "Our Relations with Russia," and even Margaret Mead's "The American Family" (in which she complains that American girls are too quickly rushed into marriage) are dated today and relevant mostly to history, though some of the contents still shine. In the essay "Love in America," the psychologist Erich Fromm argues that the "constant broadcasting and commodifying of love by Hollywood, songs and advertising" has caused us to swap real love for a cheap, "superficial, overly sentimental" substitute for it.[6] To remedy this, Fromm coaches that we must avoid deep immersion in media—whether electronic or otherwise—to protect the depth and authenticity of our emotions. While reading Fromm's essay, one can almost hear Huston cheering support from between the lines. In our age of internet addiction, virtual-reality sex, Tweeting and computer 'friending,' one is entirely inclined to cheer along with him. The essays that Huston wished even more for America to read, and *heed*, came at the end of the book (and TV program), and were offered by the two theologians whom he most respected at the time, Reinhold Niebuhr and Paul Tillich.

Both Niebuhr and Tillich had spoken strongly against the Nazis during the war and were now advancing positions they hoped would help a war-torn world heal. Niebuhr argued that the arrival of French Existentialism and the 'Beat Generation' (who said they had been 'beat' down by the modern world, even as they flowed with the beat of jazz) signaled that the West was losing confidence in its ideal of 'progress via technology,' falling by the wayside into meaninglessness. The World Wars had demonstrated that technology could as easily be used for destruction as creation, and the West, disillusioned by this realization, was slipping into despair and despondency, with the novels of Camus and Sartre illustrating the point. Human life is a tragic and meaningless affair, and though we might be god-like in certain ways, no creature is more ruthless and destructive. Niebuhr warned that this trend toward characterizing human existence as purposeless should not continue, since, to his mind, a consistent lesson of history is that despair and despondency are followed by decadence and destruction. Niebuhr argued that we could and should let go of our psychological and cultural dependence on the ideal of progress, but we must not give up hope. We should soften our grip on the psychological need to believe in an immanent technological utopia, but we should still strive to improve our lives.

Niebuhr argued that the best kind of hope isn't glued to *any* particular ideal, technological or otherwise; it is a predisposition of mind dedicated to the proposition that we are morally obliged to help each other survive and thrive. Niebuhr believed that in the final analysis the best form of hope is not only free of future-oriented or culture-specific goals or even the certainty that our efforts will succeed. We *must* help each other, Niebuhr maintained, simply because it's a moral imperative built into the nature of existence itself. Consequently, to remain *truly* hopeful we must accept that our efforts need not succeed. We have to do what we have to do and that's it. "Men do not have to believe they are permanently or progressively resolving their problems in order to take them seriously," Niebuhr commented in his interview with Huston, "Doctors do not depend for their sense of vocation on the illusion that if only they work hard enough, long enough, they will eliminate disease and death altogether."[7]

Huston, for his part, applauded Niebuhr's outlook for several reasons. First, because Niebuhr was agreeing with Wieman that we can and should act as God's agents on earth, while also agreeing with Huxley that whether or not our actions result in the perfection of a cultural ideal (whether it's that of a master race, a classless society, a technological Disneyland or Gerald Heard's utopia of super-conscious mystics), *we should still try to do something*. In addition, Huston found in Niebuhr's theory of a primordial morality an agreement with the ethical dimension of Huxley's perennialism, one in which hope is generated out of the nature of Reality itself rather than via attachment to the realization of a future-oriented ideal.

With Tillich's essay, Huston found a complement to Niebuhr's, and he agreed with Tillich's position entirely—perhaps because he actually wrote Tillich's essay, ghosting it with Tillich's permission.

Like Niebuhr, Tillich observed that meaninglessness and doubt were growing in Western society and he too believed that this was dangerous. "Doubt, as a questioning of one or a group of items in a belief structure, can be healthy," he said, "but total doubt, if it does not pass, is deadly. . . . With no visible way to proceed, we are left without hope." What particularly attracted Huston to Tillich's viewpoint was his cure for this meaninglessness. To survive, either as individuals or as a society, Tillich argued that we must have the "courage to be," and to gain that courage we must have something for it to depend upon—something that, as in Niebuhr's view, isn't future-oriented or overly conceptual. This 'something' for Tillich should be "faith," and while explaining what he meant, Tillich acknowledged that we can have faith in many things (including philosophies like communism that have no metaphysical elements), but then he asked the audience to consider what *should* inspire their courage. What is it that's most deserving of our faith? Here he hits upon what Huston had also come to believe:

> When we ask, to what should man give himself in the completeness of faith? We must begin with a negative. Not to any part of this spatio-temporal world. Nothing finite is related to man's total nature in a way inclusive enough to bring complete fulfillment. . . . Instead of one thing among others, the rightful object of faith must be the ground of all things. In the analogy of a room, it cannot be the lamp or rug or table; it must be the floor that supports them all. Religion calls this ground of all existence God, philosophy calls it Infinite Being or Being Itself.[8]

Huston saw in Tillich's philosophy a Christian viewpoint that broadly agreed with the perennial philosophy's postulate of a Divine Ground and the importance of experiencing it. "One whom faith leads to participate fully in the Ground of all Being," Tillich argued, "will find his life substantially changed." In this state of contact and awakening (into what Tillich called "the New Being"), one would have a platform for infinite hope and infinite faith based on the implicit and 'Infinite Good.' In summary, Huston reasoned that Tillich's theology complemented Niebuhr's view that hope didn't need to rely on any time-specific ideal while his view also jibed with Huxley's "minimum working hypothesis," and, in resonance with both Niebuhr and Huxley, Tillich was advocating spiritual growth as a platform for us to be of service to each other. This last position had been a non-negotiable part of Huston's philosophy since his boyhood in China, and as in Vedanta, Tillich was also postulating inner peace as the unit of world peace, enlightenment as a foundation for public service.

## A NEW HOME AND A NEW WAY OF SEEING THE WORLD

The Smith's new house in Massachusetts, located on Sandrick Road in Belmont, had a pond in the back yard where Huston would bathe quite regularly (and when the pond wasn't frozen) as if it were "his own private Ganges"—an allusion Thoreau had also made about his dips in Walden Pond. Kendra was entertaining the idea of going back to college, of starting graduate school at Boston University to study psychology and counseling (which she eventually did), but with three daughters at home and Huston's career sky-rocketing, she put the decision off for awhile. Fortunately for Huston, Kendra could be patient, and she was giving their daughters the sort of childhood she never had.

The new house, which was much more comfortable than their starter home in St. Louis, had a big front yard where the Smiths installed a stone statue of St. Anthony, picked up in the famous National Monte de Piedad pawnshop, established around 1775, during their trip to Mexico. "Seeing the statue made people think we were Catholics," Huston recalled. "This helped a few years later when I ran for the Democratic Council of Belmont. Saint Anthony helped me get elected!"

Huston was still in touch with members of the First Zen Institute of New York and one of them, Elsie Mitchell, happened to live nearby, in Cambridge. Elsie ran a small Zen group in her living room and sometimes, on Monday evenings, Huston went for meditation and group discussions, all of which he enjoyed. However, what most excited him about Cambridge was his new teaching post at MIT. MIT had added philosophy to its undergraduate programs for the first time in its history. Huston saw this development as a ripe opportunity to create an innovative philosophy program. This would be a curriculum that would fearlessly embrace new and promising ideas, a place where all the world's viewpoints could be explored without prejudice and a place where science and spirituality could finally meet and shake hands.

Hilary Putnam, later to become one of the most influential philosophers of his generation, was invited to join Huston at MIT in 1961, and soon afterwards took on the responsibilities of department chair. (Noam Chomsky, the linguist and political activist, was already at MIT and sat on the committee that hired Huston.) When Huston began forming the program into a department, there were only three members: Irving Singer, Jack Rawls, who had come from Cornell and Huston himself. But Rawls didn't last long. In those days, as Putnam explained in an interview, "Harvard used MIT as a stepping stone for philosophers. Rawls was the outstanding theorist on the issue of justice but Harvard didn't have a budget for him until another professor retired, so we had him at MIT until a place became open." Rawls moved over to Harvard in 1962, and Putnam soon followed him in 1965, while Huston and Singer stayed behind to anchor the department for many years to come.

In his classes, he concentrated mainly on the metaphysical theories found in the World's religions and especially Asian religions, which Western scholars tended to ignore. Huston, like Huxley and others, found in Eastern thought a possible corrective to the ills of the Western world. As noted, Huston agreed with Niebuhr that the West had become mesmerized by its dream of progress, causing not only a grisly 'morning-after'—since the dream hadn't come true—but also a continued tendency to focus too strongly on both materialism and the future. Regarding this last point, Huston told his students that there was a possible corrective in Zen because Zen emphasized the value of living in the present. "We understand the specific attraction of Zen Buddhism," he wrote in his introduction to Kapleau's *Three Pillars of Zen*, "when we realize the extent to which the contemporary West is animated by 'prophetic faith,' the sense of the holiness of the *ought*, the pull of the way things could be and should be but as yet are not. Such faith has obvious virtues, but unless it is balanced by a companion sense of the holiness of the *is*, it becomes top-heavy. If one's eyes are always on tomorrows, todays slip by unperceived."[9]

Huston also endorsed Zen's emphasis on the present because he believed in enlightenment, since if awakening were possible we should pay attention to the NOW, the only domain of time when the Divine Ground actually exists or can be experienced. Memories of the past and thoughts of the future are, according to Zen, abstract and conceptual distractions, affording no increase in one's fundamental state of consciousness. Memories and dreams are fine, Zen adepts believe, but the need is to ground them in the present. Huston recommended to his students that they explore the option of consciousness expansion as a real possibility, pointing out that he wasn't the only contemporary Western philosopher to make this recommendation. "Our final destiny," Tillich explained in his essay for *The Search*, "is to have our past, our present, and our future united, without being negated, in the eternal presence."[10]

*The Search for America*

Among the ideas that students at MIT, and Westerners in general, might learn from the East, besides understanding that Zen supplies our best orientation towards time, was a new view of *space* also. Huston gave his best guess about our proper relationship to the natural world in his essay, "Tao Now: An Ecological Testament," published in a collection of essays entitled *Earth Might Be Fair* (1962). This essay (coincidentally appearing at the same time as Rachel Carson's landmark warning against the dangers of DDT, *Silent Spring*) expresses the Taoist perspective that we must live symbiotically with the earth or face the dire consequences, or, to use a contemporary analogy drawn from baseball, we should remember that, 'Earth bats last.'

When today's environmentalists speak of a "cradle to cradle" approach to resource-management in which goods are continuously circulated through the 'industrial nutrient cycle,' and by-products of production never end up in landfills as 'waste,' Huston sounds far in advance of his time. He wrote this essay fifty years ago. "The guiding principle here is the closed system," he explains. "Instead of pouring industrial wastes and sewage into our waterways and puffing smoke into the atmosphere, convert the pollutants mechanically and chemically into useful substances and loop them back into the nutrient cycle. 'Pollutants are resources out of place.'"[11] Huston is also prescient when he argues that our environmental problems, including pollution, ecological-degradation and loss of species, are mostly symptoms of a much deeper problem, namely the way we view the natural world. Huston explains that "prudential measures" such as recycling and improved smokestacks are important, "but they need to be undergirded by an altered stance toward nature itself." Offering a corrective, he describes the Taoist view that all things in nature live in a "realm of interpenetration and interdependence," suggesting that we Westerners might do a bit of *meme* therapy with our ideology, adding Taoist elements and values before we cause entire ecosystems to collapse, and ourselves along with them. Environmentalists such as Bill McKibben, Lester Brown, Michael Pollan, Hunter Lovins, Paul Hawken and Jeremy Rifkin offer this same advice, and one must wonder if we wouldn't live with less worry today if Huston Smith and Rachel Carson had been listened to then.

## A VISIT FROM HUXLEY

Huston's primary axe to grind in the classroom was that the West needed to re-think its jettisoning of metaphysics. Science had proven itself competent in the world of matter but Huston was convinced that matter wasn't all that mattered. There must be a re-embracing of Reality's transcendental aspect as well, so that we would have a holistic view of the world. In class he illustrated this point with a lesson contained in Raphael's "The School of Athens." In the painting, one finds Plato walking arm-in-arm through a colonnade with his student Aristotle. Aristotle points at the ground to signify concern for material existence while Plato points to the sky, showing appreciation for what lies beyond it. Both heaven and earth should be honored, Raphael suggests, and Huston agreed—not to oppose science but to create a re-marriage of the worlds, the physical with the metaphysical. And this is why he invited Alan Watts to MIT several times. Watts had observed:

> For a long time we have been accustomed to the compartmentalization of religion and science as if they were two quite different and basically unrelated ways of

seeing the world. I do not believe that this state of doublethink can last. It must eventually be replaced by a view of the world which is neither religious nor scientific but simply our view of the world. More exactly, it must become a view of the world in which the reports of science and religion are as concordant as those of the eyes and the ears.[12]

He also called on his old friend Huxley.

In the fall of 1960, MIT was celebrating its hundredth anniversary, and to commemorate the occasion the Institute planned a wide range of events, including a series of lectures to help define MIT's direction for the future. Huston had already arrived at his own view of where MIT should go, and since the humanities department had an item in its budget for a distinguished humanist to participate in the reflection process, he suggested that it invite Aldous Huxley. Huxley had recently received, in May of 1959, the "Award for Merit for the Novel" from the American Academy of Arts and Letters, and in the two prior semesters he had been a visiting scholar at the University of California at Santa Barbara and at the Menninger Foundation. Huston easily convinced his colleagues to invite the author. (In fact, they suggested that Huxley might give a series of public lectures, which eventually became something of an event in Boston history, since those lectures caused numerous and epic traffic-jams that went on for hours.[13])

When Huxley, who was then 66 years old (and only three years from his death), arrived on campus, as a "Distinguished Visiting Professor of Humanities," Huston volunteered to be his social secretary, hoping to get as much time with his mentor as possible.[14] This chance to chum around with Huxley for a semester was improved further when Huxley received an office on the fourth floor of Building 14, just catty-corner from Huston's. Among the memories that stood out was a time when Huxley had laughed at a joke of Huston's while they dined at the nearby Faculty Club. Colleagues at Washington University had been pleased to learn that Huston's new office at MIT was listed as "Room 14-N" ( the N referring to the fact that his office was on the north side of the building), rejoiced in the letter N as testimony to the notion that Huston had brought the verbal humanities to an institute of numbers. And on another occasion, after returning to their offices from lunch, Huston had asked Huxley, "Aldous, what shall we do? Walk a long, long corridor and take the elevator or shall we climb four flights of steps?"[15] Huxley replied that he wouldn't mind taking the stairs, and as they climbed together, Huxley recited a bit of poetry from Christina Rossetti's "Uphill" to make the task more pleasant:

> Does the road wind uphill all the way?
> Yes, to the very end.
> Will the day's journey take the whole long day?
> From morn to night, my friend.

When the night of Huxley's first public lecture in Kresge Auditorium arrived, he and Huston were confronted and confounded by a completely packed hall. Latecomers were seated in the aisles and loudspeakers were placed outside in the corridor—as well as in two large rehearsal halls where 500 others waited to hear what he would say in his talk, "What a Piece of Work is Man." Visitors pouring in from neighboring Harvard, Radcliffe, Boston University, Wellesley, and other colleges across Boston were caught up in traffic jams set off by Huxley's appearance. As the crowd swelled, Huxley told

Huston that it wouldn't bother him to have people sit on stage behind him, and 200 or so came up out of the aisles and joined him there. Huston remembered, "It was amazing. The hall was entirely packed and Aldous took immediate control after I introduced him. He held the audience absolutely rapt for nearly two hours—and needless to say, my colleagues thought we had made a good decision by inviting him!"

Huxley's message that night (expanded upon posthumously in his book, *The Human Situation*) was an endorsement of both science and metaphysics. Huxley challenged the epistemic tool chest of the West, which he believed relied too heavily on the linear mind to nail down the truth of all things, and was acting like the carpenter who relies on his hammer for every job, when it would sometimes be better to use a screwdriver or chisel. Huxley considered Reality much too large to explore with anything less than all the tools at our disposal, and anything less than our full capacity—including our capacity for mystical insight. And even then we might have to accept that, on the level of ideas, there may be insurmountable mysteries.

Soon after his time at MIT, Aldous expressed this last message at the end of his final book, *Literature and Science*:

> Thought is crude, matter unimaginably subtle. Words are few and can only be arranged in certain conventionally fixed ways; the counterpoint of unique events is infinitely wide and their succession indefinitely long. That the purified language of science, or even the richer purified language of literature should ever be adequate to the givenness of the world and of our experience, is in the very nature of things, impossible. Cheerfully accepting this fact, let us advance together, men of letters and men of science, further and further into the ever-expanding regions of the unknown.

## Cleansing the Doors of Perception

During his visit to MIT, Huxley had some free time to go off and see the sights. What most interested him in Cambridge was happening over at Harvard where a young professor of psychology, who had gained acclaim for his book *The Interpersonal Diagnosis of Personality*, was researching the psychological effects and possible benefits of the psychedelic drug psilocybin. Timothy Leary, along with his research assistants, Ralph Metzner, Gunther Weil, George Litwin and one or two others, were as interested in Huxley as he was in them. Huxley, as it turned out, had written two books on psychedelic experience, *The Doors of Perception* and *Heaven and Hell*. Leary had read both of them. Consequently Huxley and Leary soon met and began to discussing their views.

Eight years earlier, in 1952, Huxley had read an article about "psychological medicines" written by two scientists working in Alberta, Canada, Dr. Abram Hoffer and Dr. Humphry Osmond, both of whom were doing research with mescaline, a synthesized form of the psychoactive ingredient of the peyote cactus. Huxley found their results fascinating, so he jotted off to Osmond—who, as it turned out, was already a fan of Huxley's. The next year, while attending a conference in Los Angeles, Osmond visited Huxley and the two men discussed the details of Osmond's research. Huxley explained that he was personally interested in mescaline for its possible value as a trigger for mystical insight, and Osmond related that several of his patients had reported what sounded like mystical experiences.

Huxley told Osmond that he had done some historical research on the topic that revealed some promise; for instance, Louis Lewin, a German toxicologist, had written as early as the 1880s that mescaline could hold the key to religious experience. Huxley also mentioned the work of William James, who wrote in *The Varieties of Religious Experience* that his episodes with peyote and nitrous oxide had converged into an "insight to which I cannot help ascribing some metaphysical significance." Osmond became so intrigued by what Huxley had to say that the two men decided it would be valuable if Huxley, who was well acquainted with mystical literature, tried the mescaline for himself.

Huxley believed there was no reason to dismiss chemically induced mysticism out of hand, for even the traditional technologies of consciousness expansion, including yoga and meditation, result in definite and measurable changes to physiology. Perhaps mescaline created the necessary physical circumstances in the body that could trigger mystical experience.[16] But there seemed only one way to be sure.

A description of Huxley's first psychedelic trip was published in 1954 in a short book called *The Doors of Perception*—named after a snippet of poetry from William Blake, who wrote: "If the doors of perception were cleansed, every thing would appear to man as it is, infinite." As the title of Huxley's book suggests, he had had a positive experience with the mescaline that Osmond gave him, believing he had actually experienced the Infinite, the "unitive knowledge" he had described in *The Perennial Philosophy*. Formulating a theory about what happened that day, Huxley argued that he agreed with C.D. Broad, a philosopher at Cambridge University who believed Henri Bergson had been right that the function of our brain and sense organs is mainly "eliminative" rather than revealing of things.[17] Huxley theorized that the nervous system works mainly to protect us from the huge amount of information in the world that is not necessary for our survival—but that can potentially pour through us from what Bergson had termed "Mind at Large." In order to get on with our lives, Mind at Large has to be funneled through the "reducing valves" of brain and senses, and yet "each one of us," Huxley believed, "is potentially Mind at Large" and we can experience ourselves as such.

Huxley interpreted Mind at Large as something analogous to Vedanta's Brahman or Eckhart's Divine Ground of Being and during his experience on mescaline he believed he had experienced THAT—or *been* THAT, which is more descriptively accurate. With Osmond's help, he went on to say that mescaline perhaps caused this experience by inhibiting the production of enzymes that regularly supply sugar to certain functions of the brain, including its more abstract and intellectual abilities. Freed from these functions, and with the reduction valve otherwise turned off, or greatly reduced, Huxley believed that Mind at Large had come flooding into his awareness. "The Beatific Vision, Sat Chit Ananda, Being-Awareness-Bliss—for the first time I understood, not on the verbal level, not by inchoate hints or at a distance, but precisely and completely what those prodigious syllables referred to."

After the drug had worn off, and in the years that followed, Huxley never changed his mind about what happened that May afternoon in 1953. He had been given a taste of Reality in its purest form, a glimpse of the fact that "All is in all—that All is actually each." *I am That, you are That, all this is That.* He didn't fool himself in thinking that he had reached complete enlightenment, since his experience had been temporary, but he concluded, as he wrote to Osmond afterwards, that, "What emerges as a general conclusion is the confirmation of the fact that mescaline does genuinely open the door...."[18]

## HUSTON MEETS LEARY

Tim Leary was interested in psychedelic drugs because of certain experiences he had had with psilocybin in Mexico, just that August before he met Huxley.[19] Reflecting on his first psychedelic trip, Leary wrote in his autobiography, *Flashbacks*: "In four hours by the swimming pool in Cuernavaca I learned more about the mind, the brain and its structures than I did in the preceding fifteen years as a diligent psychologist."[20] Getting specific, he then added: "I learned that normal consciousness is one drop in an ocean of intelligence. That consciousness and intelligence can be systematically expanded." This had also been William James' view and after arriving back at Harvard that fall, Leary shared these ideas with George Litwin, who then lent him Huxley's *Doors of Perception*.[21] There Leary found the theory of psychedelics he would carry with him for the rest of his life, and when he learned at a cocktail party that November that Huxley was actually in town, he immediately wrote Huxley a long letter describing his research plans and asking for help. "Two days later," according to Leary, Huxley "telephoned me at the office, even more excited than I was." The two of them decided to meet for lunch the very next day. During that meal Huxley agreed, over mushroom soup (!), to be an informal advisor for Leary's project. During the next few weeks, they would outline what Robert Forte has called a "non-clinical, supportive, yet objective and safe framework" for all of Leary's later experiments.[22]

Huston too had read *The Doors of Perception* and found Huxley's premise of Mind at Large deeply interesting. ("Far more than curious; I found his book riveting."[23]) In a very real sense, Huston was still "whoring after the absolute," so when he learned that Leary was looking for subjects to try out his supposed shortcut to bliss, he begged Huxley for information. Huxley then gave him Leary's contact information and Huston immediately wrote to him. That letter, dated November 3, 1960, said in total:

> In the course of conversations with Aldous Huxley, he spoke of some studies relating to mescaline which you are engaged in. At his suggestion I am writing to ask whether you are interested in further subjects for these experiments. I have known Mr. Huxley for a decade and shared throughout his keen interests in this line of research.[24]

Leary phoned Huston as soon as the letter arrived—and not just because Huston was a friend of Huxley's. After each guided session with psychedelics, Leary and his team had their subjects fill out questionnaires to give them feedback about what had happened, and in several cases there had been reports of what sounded like mystical experiences. Huxley, of course, believed that they *were* mystical experiences, and when he spoke to Leary about the matter he had already advised him to call upon Huston, who, as an expert on World Religions, could possibly evaluate the reports and lend insight.

Leary and Huston didn't manage to get together until after Thanksgiving, but when they did, Huston perused Leary's reports carefully, agreeing that they sounded like moments of spiritual breakthrough; however, it might be easier to discern the drug's mystical potential if he tried the stuff himself. The two men pulled out their date books and tried to schedule a session, about which Huston later wrote: "Several tries wouldn't work for one or the other of us, whereupon Leary flipped past Christmas and (with the faintest trace of a mischievous smile, as I remember the scene) asked, 'What about New Year's Day?'"[25]

# Chapter Twelve:
# Into the Fire

The orthodox Christian must accept by faith the miracle of Transubstantiation. By contrast, the mushroom of the Aztecs carries its own conviction . . . .

Gordon Wasson

The real voyage of discovery consists not in seeking new landscapes but in having new eyes.

Marcel Proust

When Huston arrived at Tim Leary's house around 12:30 on New Year's Day, 1961, he had Kendra with him, and she was as eager to have the experience as he was. Leary tells us in his memoir, *Flashbacks*, that in those days he was living in a house in Newton Center rented from a colleague who was off on sabbatical in the Soviet Union, and that the place was a rambling, three-storey mansion with wide lawns, a four-car garage and a gazebo, along with 185 steps leading up to the front door.[1] To help with the expensive rent, Leary, then single, had taken in a young couple who also acted as housekeepers. Once inside, Huston and Kendra were introduced to Frank Barron, a professor visiting from California, who had briefly been co-director with Leary of the Harvard Psychedelic Project, and Dr. George Alexander, a psychiatrist on hand in case something went wrong during Huston's session. Leary wasn't eager to be responsible for driving a famous scholar mad, so he had taken some precautions.

After coffee and a bit of pleasant chat, Leary laid out some psilocybin capsules on the coffee table and invited Huston and Kendra to help themselves, saying that one capsule would be a mild dose and three a strong one. Huston popped a capsule into his mouth and Kendra, whom Huston once described as "more adventuresome," took two. After about half an hour, when nothing seemed to be happening, Huston took another capsule and Kendra swallowed a third.[2] The young couple that was living with Leary (graduate students with a newborn baby) was ensconced upstairs, out of the way. Since Huston and Kendra seemed to be doing just fine, Leary and his colleagues left them alone, moving into another room to give them some quiet but checking in periodically to make sure things were going well.

Kendra sat back in a chair and Huston laid himself out on the couch. After only a few more minutes, the effects became vividly noticeable to him. Colors and light began to have depth, patterns in the wool rugs began to undulate, the draperies began to breathe, and, as Huston later wrote, the "world into which I was ushered was strange, weird, uncanny, significant and terrifying beyond belief."[3] Huston still knew who he was, and that he had taken psilocybin in Leary's home, but otherwise he had become completely transfigured and had to hold onto his seat. His inner space changed so intensely that he lost all sense of time—or rather time had become paradoxical. "A moment could be both just a moment and all time pressed into that moment."[4] He felt himself breaking through into higher states of consciousness, and, as had happened with Huxley, this confirmed for him that such states existed. He had had brief moments of this during meditation but now he was experiencing something like complete awakening. It was as if he had been struck by noetic lightening. "The emanation theory and elaborately delineated layers of Indian cosmology and psychology had hitherto been concepts and inferences," he would later write. "Now they were objects of direct, immediate perception, [and] I saw that theories such as these were required by the experience I was having. I found myself amused, thinking how duped historians of philosophy had been in crediting those who formulated such worldviews with being speculative geniuses. Had they had experiences such as mine, they need have been no more than hack reporters. . . ."[5]

Huston was immersed in what Huxley had termed "this timeless moment," a period in which all eternity felt compressed into each and every second, and he continued escalating into even higher states of bliss and transformation, so much so that the shifts became too fierce and incomprehensible to be characterized as blissful. He eventually felt exhausted and found that the experience was difficult to keep up with. He remembered that in many religions it was believed that no man could look into the face of God and survive. "The vision would be too much for the body to stand, like plugging an electric toaster into a major power source without a condenser, the body would simply shatter."[6] For obvious reasons this thought worried him and he wondered if he could keep his spirit connected to his body if the experience intensified any further—or if, given the fantastic insights he was having, he would even *want* to stay connected! The temptation might simply be to leave the body behind and melt into the all-consuming fire.

Huston called out to Leary sitting in the kitchen, "Do you know what you're playing around with? You could have a corpse on your couch."[7] Leary came into the room and sat down, speaking to Huston for a few moments, and assuring him that his usual sense of selfhood might die for a while but nothing else would. Huston's confidence increased—as did Kendra's, and this was important, given that she had taken more. "The effect was very difficult for me to cope with," she remembered. "I felt as though I were going through all of evolution, stage by stage, from one-celled creatures on up the ladder—and I was so tired from all of this. I am a very visual person, and I was absolutely fascinated by wood grains and lights and textures, but the experience was challenging and very, very long!"

After about eleven hours in Leary's living room, the effect had subsided to the point where Huston and Kendra felt comfortable enough to make their way home. Even after the intensity had died down there remained a definite residual effect—a transpersonal afterglow—that lingered with them in the days ahead. For Kendra it was so palpable that it catalyzed a transformation in her life; specifically, her dealings with other people became radically altered: where before she had been extremely shy, she now found herself more open and outgoing with strangers, and this shift stayed in place ever after. "It was a real breakthrough," she said.

Huston believed he had finally encountered the full sunshine of the world outside

Plato's Cave and now wore a bit of a spiritual tan. The experience hadn't changed his theories on the nature of Reality so much as confirmed them. Just weeks before the trip on psilocybin he had written an article speculating that since science had moved forward on the basis of breakthrough insights by extraordinary individuals, "Might not this be the case with religious truth as well?"[8] Maybe religions arose from the revelations of adepts with an unusually high level of talent for transpersonal experience. Having now touched the sacred fire, Huston believed he had completely confirmed both the fire's existence and the authenticity of reports about it. Moreover, if *he* could experience the fire, even without a congenital talent for doing so (as he believed his meager successes with meditation indicated), many people were likely to be able to do the same. The reality of mystical insight might soon become, with a bit of help from the Harvard Psychedelic Project, a matter-of-fact experience in Western culture, and for the first time in its history.

## THE PROJECT

One outcome of that New Year's Day with Leary was that Huston joined the Harvard Project as an advisor on religion and mystical states. Leary was very excited to have him on board because Leary, as Paul Lee, who was soon to become another member of the Project, once explained, was hoping to shift the interpretation of psychedelic experience from *psycho-mimetic* to *mystical-mimetic*, that is, from the view that the drug's effect mimicked mental illness to the view that it creates a healthy and valuable, albeit unusual, state of mind. Leary had accepted Huxley's perennialist framework for understanding the psychedelic experience, and as a psychologist he was particularly intrigued by Huxley's premise that there are positive aspects of the human unconscious that were overlooked by Freud. Freud believed the unconscious to be largely comprised of repressed desires and repressed traumas from childhood, and that, if not properly dealt with, these repressed contents of the mind result in neuroses and psychoses. Huxley offered no disagreement on that point, but he thought Freud's view of the unconscious was too narrow, arguing that we have beneath us not only darkness from our past but also light—light from the archetypal material of what C.G. Jung termed the "collective unconscious," and especially from Mind-at-Large, the Divine Ground of Being at the root of our existence. Huxley had commented on the limited views of psychologists exactly as Leary was beginning his project, explaining for instance that, "the only unconscious they ever pay attention to is the negative unconscious, the garbage that people have tried to get rid of by burying it in the basement. Not a single word about the positive unconscious. No attempt to help the patient to open himself up to the life force or the Buddha Nature."[9]

After reading Huxley's *Heaven and Hell* and *The Doors of Perception*, Leary began to pose new questions for his colleagues in psychology: What if neuroses and psychic frustrations were not only generated by repression but also from our *frustration* in not being able to access the deeper spiritual aspects of who we are? What if we intuit that there is something more to us than we commonly experience but have no way to access it? Furthermore, what if there is a more profound state of 'sanity' beyond that which commonly occurs, a state reachable only when we move toward enlightenment? Could spiritual enlightenment actually be a more complete state of sanity? Leary was intrigued by such ideas, and if Huston Smith could help him to establish and defend

Huxley's mystical-mimetic model of psychedelic experience, then the drugs could prove useful as aids for people who wish to access their positive unconscious. This was Leary's hope and Huston and Huxley shared it completely.

After each psychedelic session, participants in the Project filled out lengthy questionnaires to be analyzed and collated, and over the next twelve months these session reports gave Huston strong evidence that Huxley was right to say that psychedelics "genuinely open the door." They may be a "gratuitous grace," as Huxley had added, unnecessary for awakening (since people could reach enlightenment in a host of other ways) but useful tool nonetheless, triggering a blast of the positive unconscious for those who had no native talent for reaching it otherwise. "The experience is so fantastic in both its novelty and its power as to beggar all possibility of adequate depiction through words," Huston wrote in one of his own session reports, after an experience with LSD dated January 6, 1962. "The most that can be hoped for by way of description is an approximation, and only those who have had the drug can know how far removed from actuality the approximation must be."[10] Huston added that his dominant reaction was "astonishment at the absolutely incredible immensity, complexity, intensity and extravagance of being, existence, the cosmos, call it what you will. Ontological shock, I suppose. . . . Intellectually, the dominant impression was that of entering into the very marrow of existence."

With descriptions like this coming from Huston Smith, a definite buzz began to grow in the Cambridge intellectual community. "Huston was a renowned and authoritative expert on religion and religious experience," Ralph Metzner, one of Leary's colleagues, explained Huston's importance to the Harvard Project. "It meant a lot to Tim and all of us that he could and would validate the authenticity of these mystical experiences. It broadened our viewpoint beyond the standard psychological/therapeutic perspectives." With Huston lending credibility to Leary's reports,[11] other scholars of religion in Cambridge decided to join the party, including Paul Lee, a graduate student at Harvard Divinity School, and Walter Houston Clark (1902-1994), an expert on the Psychology of Religion who was teaching at nearby Andover-Newton Seminary. "I couldn't wait to try it," Paul Lee said, and Clark, as it turned out, was even more eager than Lee.

Walter Houston Clark was 60 years old when he joined the Harvard Psychedelic Project in early 1962, becoming the other major authority on religious experience to lend credibility to Huxley's and Leary's mystical-mimetic interpretation. In 1958, he had published *The Psychology of Religion*, considered the best book on that subject at the time, and just months prior to joining the Project he had received the American Psychological Association's "William James Memorial Award" for his life-long contributions to the field. Based on the earlier work of Rudolf Otto and William James, Clark had focused his research on the individual's experience of religion and spirituality, and so he was a perfect fit for the Project—and, as it turned out, for psychedelics also. Clark had been studying religious experiences his whole life but had never had such an experience until he tried psychedelics. The upshot was, as Leary later explained in *Flashbacks*, that, "After his session he became a committed project member."[12]

## THE GOOD FRIDAY EXPERIMENT

As work on the Project continued into 1962, the group looked around for ways to clinically test whether or not psychedelics could produce religious experiences. One of their newest members, Dr. Walter Pahnke, a physician then completing a second doctoral degree at Harvard Divinity School, proposed a double-blind experiment in which one half of a group of graduate students and guides would be given psilocybin while the other half took niacin as a placebo, but with neither half knowing who had received what. Huston and most members of the Project agreed that this test seemed promising. Because it eventually took place in Marsh Chapel at Boston University on Good Friday of that year, it became known as the "Good Friday Experiment" or the "Miracle at Marsh Chapel."[13]

When Huston showed up at the chapel that fateful Friday morning to act as one of the guides, he found that 20 graduate student who had volunteered from Andover-Newton were gathered in the basement, eager to participate. Leary himself wasn't around that day, instead visiting New York City where he had been conducting private "turn-on" sessions with artists and intellectuals. Leary later claimed in *Flashbacks* that he was a guide for the Marsh Chapel experiment, but Huston was absolutely certain that Leary wasn't there. Furthermore, Metzner and Lee, who were also guides that day, couldn't remember that Leary was present. The fact is that Leary hadn't supported Pahnke's proposal, saying that he "really had to laugh at this caricature of the experimental design applied to that most sacred experience. If [Pahnke] had proposed giving aphrodisiacs to twenty virgins to produce a mass orgasm, it wouldn't have sounded further out."[14]

Metzner has explained elsewhere that Leary "rejected the impersonal clinical atmosphere of the traditional psychiatric experiment,"[15] preferring an "existential-transactional" approach in which careful records of peoples' subjective experiences were kept and discussed (the approach that he had hit upon with Huxley). Jack Kerouac had suggested that Leary call this approach "Intuitional Research" or "Subjective Studies."[16] However one termed it, it was something very different from what Pahnke had in mind, which helps to explain why Leary wasn't present at Marsh Chapel that day. Huston, on the other hand, like Clark, saw a tremendous potential in Pahnke's approach, and believed that the experiment might turn out as they hoped.

The 20 students were gathered in the small basement so they could have their privacy while also being able to listen to the sermon and hymns piped in from above. After the thirty-milligram doses of psilocybin were distributed and had taken effect, it became crystal clear who had gotten the real drug and who hadn't, and Huston found himself among those who *had*. For the most part, the day passed pleasantly but there was one glitch when a young man who had received the psilocybin left the chapel and took to the street, convinced that he was chosen by God to announce the dawning of the Messianic Age that would usher in a thousand years of universal peace and prosperity. Huston and another guide were finally able to chase the man down and convince him to return to the sanctuary, where Pahnke administered a shot of Thorazine to get the fellow's feet back on the ground.

*****

A few days later, after filling out a detailed questionnaire compiled by Pahnke, Huston learned, to no surprise, that many of his experiences matched those reported by traditional mystics. Pahnke had arrived at this conclusion by comparing the experiences of the Andover-Newton students with those listed in a typology of mystical experience compiled from the work of W.T. Stace, a professor at Princeton whose book *Philosophy and Mysticism* was creating a stir at that exact moment. Stace himself had examined several attempts to glean from traditional accounts a "universal core of common characteristics of mystical experience," including those cited earlier by William James and D.T. Suzuki.[17] In the final analysis, Stace's typology included seven characteristics in all:

1. A sense of everything in the cosmos as interconnected.
2. An apprehension of the One—described variously as life, or consciousness or a living Presence.
3. A sense of objectivity or profound reality.
4. A feeling of blessedness, joy, happiness, satisfaction.
5. A feeling that what is apprehended is holy, or sacred, or divine.
6. Paradoxicality of experience.
7. Ineffability, or the sense that what is happening cannot be described with words.

In addition to these, Pahnke added two more criteria, as Walter Houston Clark—who had been in on the developmental stage of the Good Friday Experiment—later explained: "*transiency of the experience* and *persistent positive changes in attitude and behavior.*"[18]

Armed with this extended list, Pahnke then trained three judges, otherwise unconnected with the experiment, to recognize evidence of the nine criteria. These judges were later given the data collected from the students with no indication of which group had taken the psychedelic and then asked to identify, if they could, any evidence of students who were giving testimony of mystical experience. As it turned out, almost everyone who had taken the psilocybin that day—and *only* those who had taken psilocybin—had experienced something strongly resonant with Pahnke's typology, providing the first empirical evidence that psychedelic experience can actually *be* mystical experience. Today, this conclusion is far less controversial (the results of the Marsh Chapel experiment having been clinically replicated twice since that time, most recently at Johns Hopkins), but in 1962 the only people convinced of Pahnke's conclusions were those in the Harvard Psychedelic Project. Bolstered by this positive outcome, they immediately began working on how this new spiritual tool might be applied to the benefit of society. Perhaps, Huston couldn't help but wonder, this would prove to be the definitive tool for creating the inner peace Tillich had believed was necessary for freeing the Western mind of its addiction to the future.

## A DEFINITE DIFFERENCE OF OPINION

While deciding what to do next, the group split over the question of whether or not the drugs (which were not yet illegal) or the drug findings (which were not yet conclusive) should be shared with the general public. Everyone in the Project was in agreement that great strides had been made but they were in disagreement about next steps. By the late fall of 1962, Leary and Metzner were routinely giving psychedelics to as many people as possible, but Huston and Clark advocated going slowly and being careful. The tiebreaker in this dispute was Richard Alpert, Leary's new co-director at the Project, who had joined just after Huston—and who would later, after a life-changing pilgrimage to India, become the renowned spiritual teacher Ram Dass, the 'Servant of God.' Much to Huston's consternation, Alpert voted for turning on as many people as possible.

When Huxley had met Leary two years earlier, he had advised Leary to remember that "food and drug prohibitions go back to the Garden of Eden," and in *The Politics of Ecstasy* (1968), Leary would explain that Huxley had wanted him to avoid publicity specifically to keep society's gatekeepers from freaking out. But Alpert and Metzner disagreed with that policy; let people who were small-minded and unwilling to try the drugs freak out if they wanted to. Who cared? Well, for one, Huston cared.

In the summer of 1961, there had already been something of a parting of the ways between those who wanted to proceed slowly and those who wanted more immediate recognition of the drugs' value after Leary, Alpert and Huxley had attended a symposium in Copenhagen on psychiatric drugs at the "Fourteenth International Congress of Applied Psychology." Huxley believed they could advance their case at the conference by discussing the therapeutic use of psychedelics while also suggesting the mystical-mimetic interpretation of the experience. When Alpert took the podium he shocked everyone, including Leary, by claiming that the psychedelic experience is "an end in itself and that the drug-induced religious-mystical trip produced [unequivocally] love, Christian charity and the peace that surpasseth understanding."[19] Alpert argued that the drugs should be used for personal growth rather than as cures for specific illnesses. By so doing he crossed a definite line, pushing the Project into a much more controversial position, a position that months later he was still promoting even after the debate had heated up.

Truth be told, Huston agreed with Alpert's viewpoint, but this wasn't the time or place—in Cambridge in 1962—to admit to that or declare the theory as a fact, and Huston worried it would slow down their progress in the long run.

Huston agreed with his friend Huxley that it was better to go slowly, not just because he respected Huxley but because it made better sense to do so. By Thanksgiving of 1962, Huston had taken only six trips with psychedelics (two with each of the three substances the group was investigating: mescaline, psilocybin and LSD) and the Marsh Chapel experiment had yet to be replicated by scholars outside the Project. Until more conclusive evidence had been gathered, he thought it was wise to lie low and stay somewhat insulated in their conversations. But Leary, Alpert and Metzner weren't having any of it; they had grown tired of what they saw as the sclerotic attitudes of their Harvard colleagues, and longed for a quicker acceptance of what they noetically knew to be true. Before either side could convince the other, Leary and Alpert fell into considerable trouble at Harvard that had devastating repercussions for the Project.

## PROBLEMS AT HARVARD

Leary and Alpert first got into trouble in the fall of 1961, when their department head, David McClelland, aired reservations about the Project at a faculty meeting, writing that from Leary's and Alpert's behavior, one could "hardly fail to infer that one effect of the drug is to decrease responsibility or increase impulsivity."[20] But when everyone at that meeting had his or her say, things calmed down, and didn't flare up again until another department meeting the following spring.

At the second meeting, arguments about the Project quickly broke out and were subsequently reported in the student newspaper, *The Harvard Crimson*, under the head-line, "Psychologists Disagree on Psilocybin Research." From the *Crimson,* the story jumped to the daily newspapers and the wire service, and then all hell broke loose. Harvard's administration, embarrassed by the public attention, got involved in what had been a departmental controversy and forced the Project to turn over its supply of psychedelics. A faculty committee was given control of the drugs, and the committee gave the drugs to the head of the University Health Service for safekeeping, to be re-leased back to the Project only if and when the faculty committee gave its approval.[21]

This new protocol angered Leary and Alpert. One can almost hear Leary remark-ing, "Oh, yes? So how can we get them in case hell *does* freeze over?"

But there was little they could do about it. Their next move was to ignore the situ-ation and procure the drugs elsewhere. Leary had met a British ex-pat named Michael Hollingshead who was supplying him with LSD, and he had also found colleagues in the medical profession who were willing to give him access. He continued his excursions into Manhattan to turn on artists while also doing an end-run around the Harvard faculty committee.

Meanwhile, over at MIT (the place that Leary often joked to Huston was 'TIM' spelled backwards), Huston experienced none of the same problems. His credibility ac-tually helped protect that of Leary and Alpert, at least from the first waves of criticism. But it was clear that Leary and Alpert needed to behave themselves if they wanted to save their jobs, and, unfortunately, from Huston's perspective, they weren't very good at that. Given the intensity of their fervor for psychedelics, Huston believed disaster in one form or another was inevitable, and even after he enlisted Huxley to help rein them in, storm clouds continued to loom.

*****

In the summer of 1962, at the beginning of the most tumultuous decade of the twenti-eth century, a new chapter in world history opened when the United States launched Telstar, the world's first commercial communications satellite. In other news, "The Amazing Spiderman" first appeared in comic books and the Soviet Union was lagging behind in the race to the moon, since John Glenn had orbited the globe three times that February in his space capsule, Friendship 7. America was flaunting its confidence and ability, and still enjoying the post-war boost to its economy, though not all of the news was good. During that same year, the United States tripled its numbers of troops in Vietnam, and it began to seem that the conflict might not have a speedy solution, given that the Soviets were even more eager to prevent America's success in Southeast Asia than they had been to win the Space Race. They had formed an alliance with com-munist Cuba that led President Kennedy that October into a dangerous stand-off, the "Cuban Missile Crisis," when the Soviets tried to establish a nuclear missile base just fifty miles off the tip of Florida. The Soviets backed down after a very tense week of sabre rattling, but the Cold War had reached its hottest point ever. This was the setting when Timothy Leary was thinking of letting his psychedelic genie out of its bottle.

# Chapter Thirteen:
# IF Squared

And men go forth to wonder at the height of mountains, the huge waves of the sea, the broad flow of the rivers, the extent of the ocean, and the courses of the stars, and omit to wonder at themselves . . . .

St. Augustine

The very depth of the roots of the religious life in the unconscious frightens many, and it is at least one reason why the use of the psychedelic drugs causes hysterical fear. With intrepid courage man explores the ocean's depth, climbs dizzying and snow-covered peaks, penetrates the darkness of the Arctic or ventures into the vastnesses of space. For this he gains almost unanimous applause. When he peers into inner space he is likely to draw back in terror; and unless he does retreat, his companions brand him foolhardy or ridicule him for "contemplating his navel."

Walter Houston Clark

Huston, Huxley and Clark were having trouble getting Leary and Alpert to be discreet about whom they shared their drugs with—and for several reasons. To begin with, Allen Ginsberg, who had first tried peyote in the 1950s (in the same research program at Stanford University Hospital as the novelist Ken Kesey), was coaching them to be open and "democratic" in their policies about who should and shouldn't try the drugs, rather than acting as self-appointed gatekeepers. Second, Alan Watts had recently published his book *The Joyous Cosmology*, an endorsement of psychedelic experience that featured a foreword by Leary,[1] so the latter believed the cat was already out of the bag—and the bag had been opened even further by an unknown writer named Jane Dunlap (later identified as Adele Davis, the well-known nutritionist and author of a series of bestselling cookbooks) who had just published *Exploring Inner Space,* a favorable account of LSD experience.

As a compromise regarding how the Project should move forward, the group decided to start a non-profit organization to function independently of both the Project and their academic affiliations. "We decided to reduce the embarrassment to Harvard by separating the drug research completely from the university," Metzner later explained.[2] To which he added:

A nonprofit corporation was established under the name of The International Federation for Internal Freedom, or IFIF for short, and the Board of Directors included Leary, Alpert, Metzner, Walter Clark, Huston Smith, Alan Watts, Paul Lee, Rolf von Eckartsberg, Gunther Weil and George Litwin, Lisa Bieberman and Peter John. Elsewhere Huston has written of these last two that they "deserve to be mentioned for holding our 'church' together; without pay or public recognition, they gave virtually their full time to it.[3]

The goal of the new organization was to sponsor and support research into consciousness expansion with psychedelics (still not illegal), and, as their "Statement of Purpose" explained, to explore one puzzle in particular: "The issue is whether the world of normal sense is unqualifiedly real and, indeed, the only reality, or whether reality is far more than mind and sense disclose—not only quantitatively, but qualitatively as well."[4]

And so IFIF was officially launched on January 24, 1963, with offices in a little colonial building at 14 Story St. in Cambridge. Leary wrote later that the venture was immediately successful because it provided a nexus for public interest in psychedelics, and "within a few weeks over a thousand people sent in ten dollars each to join, and we were avalanched with inquiries."[5] Huston recalled that the organization grew rapidly but he was diffident about equating growth with success and as he has commented elsewhere, "IFIF was the iffiest organization Cambridge had ever seen."[6] Despite several noble enterprises, including the launching of *The Psychedelic Review,* a journal aimed at establishing the group's academic credibility, it was often difficult to get all members of the group pulling in the same direction. Lisa Bieberman gave them some semblance of order, opening the many letters that poured into the office and answering the telephone (everyone had a good laugh when someone realized their office phone number, 547-7244, could be remembered as "KISS BIG"), but she could only do so much with a collection of such intense personalities.

No longer under the thumb of Harvard in terms of when and to whom they could administer the drugs, Leary, Alpert and Metzner wanted to focus IFIF's attention on a project they were setting up in Mexico. They had been living (with nine other people, including Leary's two children) in a three-storey house in Newton Center, and over meals hatched a plan to open a psychedelic training center in Zihuatanejo, a sleepy, little tourist town. The goal was to initiate as many people as possible into the use of psychedelics, promoted as a tool for personal growth, while also using these same people as research subjects for IFIF studies. In preparation, Leary and Metzner had scouted out towns and hotels the summer before, and finally had settled on Zihuatanejo. "One couldn't imagine a more perfect environment for such explorations," Metzner once explained in an interview with Robert Forte:

> We rented the Hotel Catalina again and sent out brochures to our IFIF mailing list. The response was overwhelming, since the opportunity was unique. For $220, people could spend a month in one of the world's most idyllic tropical places, learning to expand their awareness with powerful new aids, in a protective and supportive environment.[7]

Huston didn't believe the Mexican venture was the best fit for IFIF but Leary and Alpert were going ahead anyway and by May had received more than five hundred applications for the program. No longer sure of where he fit in—or *if* he fit in—Huston was mostly working by himself to boost the credibility of psychedelic mysticism. One of his tactics while out on the lecture circuit was to juxtapose quotes from the traditional mystical literature with selected quotes from Leary's questionnaires. After reading the quotes, Huston would ask the audience to tell him which quotes were testimonies of psychedelic experience and which were from 'real' mystical experiences, and when the audience failed to do so—as they inevitably did, Huston had made his point. He wasn't saying that *indistinguishability* between the two sets of experiences proved they were non-different (some psychedelic experiences, after all, might also be indistinguishable from schizophrenic experiences), but that this similarity suggested the possibility that they *could be* non-different. If he could get academics to admit even that, he would have won some ground.

*****

Getting back to Leary, Tim had arranged his spring schedule so that he could be absent from his classes and focus attention on the project in Mexico. IFIF finally accepted three hundred of the applications sent to them, putting itself under the gun to pull off the program, so Leary and Metzner headed down to Zihuatanejo to get things ready, while Alpert, Clark and Huston held the fort at the IFIF offices in Cambridge. Everything went along smoothly for about a month, helped by the fact that the two factions of IFIF (slow track/fast track) were now living apart, but then another bomb fell on the group.

## CLOSING OF THE HARVARD PSYCHEDELIC PROJECT

Leary's department didn't realize until April that Tim wasn't actually teaching his spring classes. When the department head, David McClelland, asked what the hell was going on, Leary's secretary said he had gone to Los Angeles to solicit more interest in IFIF, having told her at the beginning of the semester to give his students a reading list and then dismiss them. McClelland blew his top, later explaining that he told Leary that if he didn't get back to Cambridge immediately he'd be fired for being AWOL, but "Tim thought it was more interesting to be fired so he didn't come back. And he was fired. But he was fired technically for being AWOL. Not for taking drugs."[8]

To make matters worse, Leary wasn't the only one in trouble. After Leary had left for L.A. (planning to go from there to Mexico), "John Monro, one of Harvard's deans, asked reporters at the *Harvard Crimson* to keep him informed about what Leary and Alpert were up to, and one of those reporters, Andrew Weil, later to become a doctor and popular author, agreed to his request. Among the things that Weil found out when he went snooping around was that Alpert had shared psychedelics with an undergraduate named Ronnie Winston, to whom Alpert, who was gay, was apparently attracted. To get Winston to snitch on Alpert, Weil approached Winston's father, explaining that Alpert had given his son drugs and that this was against the agreement the Project had made with the Dean's office. Weil explained that he wouldn't use Ronnie's name in his *Crimson* article if the dad would convince Ronnie to confess about Alpert, which he subsequently did.[9]

On May 28th, 1963, an unsigned editorial by Weil appeared on the front page of the *Crimson*, stating that "while the firing of Richard Alpert would be unfortunate were it to lead to the suppression of legitimate research into the effects of hallucinogenic compounds," Alpert should nonetheless be fired for violating "the one condition Harvard placed upon their work; that they not use undergraduates for subjects for science experiments."[10] Alpert defended himself by saying that he hadn't given Winston the drug in his role as a teacher but simply as a friend, and Winston supported Alpert, claiming that his trip had been "the most educational experience I've had at Harvard."[11] But Alpert was dismissed anyway and the Project was shut down.

Years later, in his book *The Natural Mind*, Weil did some soul searching about what happened, regretting his actions to a large extent,[12] but he would also report that he believed Leary and Alpert had acted unethically, whether he too had done so or not. Yet even if Weil had not become involved, most historians and biographers agree that it would only have been a matter of time before someone shut the Project down. "There were a lot of people gunning for us," Gunther Weil explained to one of Leary's biographers,[13] and in that lynch mob were most of the members of Harvard's psychology department. Weil broke the dam with his article, but once it was open, a flood of anger and venom poured through. Even the grad students attached to the Project became open targets for blame. In the end, most of those grad students had to scramble to realign themselves with other faculty in order to graduate.

When Huston learned about the fiasco at Harvard, he was deeply upset. Leary and Alpert had not been careful at a time when the Project was under the administration's close scrutiny, and he later would accuse Leary of being "frivolous in the sense of being reckless and not as responsible as he should have been."[14] But Huston was also offended that Harvard had taken the low road, engaging in what he saw as a definite act of censorship. "It really was a farce in many ways," Huston claimed. "Leary could be an ass, as Huxley had pointed that out, but most of what he and Dick got from the administration, they didn't deserve. There had been a general movement against research with the psychedelic drugs and Tim and Dick became the whipping boys of that movement." Walter Clark agreed with Huston that the Project had been censored, later explaining in his book *Chemical Ecstasy* (1969) that the crackdown had had several motivations, few of which were either noble or well reasoned. And in *Ecstasy*, Clark also offered a capstone judgment: "Behind the scenes burned a whole complex of charges and countercharges, passionate loyalties and vicious meanness, painfully arrived at administrative decisions, ambitions thwarted and fulfilled, passions, rumors, jealousies, gossip, wisdom and folly."[15]

## THE MANIFESTO OF ABSOLUTE FREEDOM

Following the scandal at Harvard and with the Project now over, Leary and Alpert were banking entirely on IFIF's seminars in Mexico to forward their agenda. Huxley, from his side, was disappointed in their choices, as he shared with Huston, because they had drawn so much negative publicity to the substances. If only they had been more prudent. In the future he would be more circumspect with Leary—and especially after Leary's Mexican project also ended in disaster, with the group first expelled from Zihuatanejo and then, after only one month, from two Caribbean islands, Dominica and Antigua. Bad press caught up with Leary and Alpert in all cases and local authorities weren't going to let a bunch of psychedelic crazies overrun their cash cow resorts. Returning to the United States that August, the group spent a few weeks licking its wounds at Alpert's house in Newton Center (meetings that included several "I told you so" moments with Huston and Clark) and then decided to move their base of operations to a rural mansion in Millbrook, New York. Huxley was dealing with health issues at that time, including a bout of cancer, so he was mostly out of the picture and unable to support Huston and Clark, though it is clear from his letters to Osmond that he worried Leary had run entirely amok.

Leary chose the town of Millbrook (population 1,700) as specific site for his new headquarters because Peggy Hitchcock, both Leary's and Alpert's close friend, had twin brothers, Tommy and Billy, who owned a house there. When Billy, a young stockbroker for Lehman Brothers learned that Leary, whose work he greatly admired, was looking for a new place to do research, he offered him the unused 2,000-acre estate. Leary of course accepted and quickly moved in with his entourage; so for the next three years, the white, four-storey, sixty-four-room mansion owned by the Hitchcocks would be Leary's center of operations.

With Leary, Alpert and Metzner out of Cambridge, Huston's involvement with IFIF was somewhat stymied. The pattern had been, as Huston once described it, "to meet about every other week, sometimes for an all-night session with one of the substances, sometimes simply to discuss the religious implications of the psychedelics";[16] but by the late summer of 1963, Huston and the other academics in IFIF were trying to figure out if they even still mattered. An article about psychedelics had appeared in *Look* magazine that summer of 1963, challenging the views of Leary and Alpert and again penned by Andrew Weil. After more such publicity Leary and Alpert had gone on the warpath, demanding absolute intellectual autonomy and posting a manifesto in *The Harvard Review* that stated they were now free from the "game of society."[17] Many years later, Robert Forte would ask Alpert what he and Leary had meant by the manifesto and would be told that they simply had wanted "freedom from being controlled by others." The manifesto only made things worse, with many authority figures, including the local police in Millbrook, taking it as a flagrant challenge to the established order.

From Huston's perspective, all this hoopla caused Leary to feel increasingly demonized, so, in a kind of childish retaliation, Leary moved closer and closer to being the demon conservatives claimed he already was. Leary's relative isolation at Millbrook—away from regular contact with his Cambridge colleagues—intensified his tendency to see himself as a heroic victim of a bankrupt society. In Huston's view, Leary increasingly moved away from being the brilliant scholar he first met and admired towards the self-indulgent renegade whose grandstanding wasn't helping anyone—including himself.

## MIND GAMES AT MILLBROOK

Free to follow his own thoughts, Leary conceived of Millbrook not only as a center for psychedelic research but also as an utopian commune where other experiments in lifestyle could be pursued, including group relationships and so-called "open" marriages. Earlier, while lounging on the beach at Zihuatanejo, he had thought to model a commune on the Polynesian society that Huxley described in his last novel, *Island*, but after moving to Millbrook he changed his mind, dubbing the new group the "Castalia Foundation" after a fictitious society of mystical scientists in Hermann Hesse's last novel, *Magister Ludi*. Leary's goal was to transcend the "mind games" of American society, encouraging his followers to drop their social masks and other hang-ups and coaching them to help each other wake up. Several of the methods for achieving this de-conditioned state of mind involved using shock tactics, for instance serving green eggs and black milk for breakfast to raise people's awareness of how conditioned was their way of seeing the world.[18] Another method required that whenever Metzner rang a certain bell, everyone on the estate's grounds had to stop what he or she was thinking or doing and tune into the NOW, a sort of Zen exercise in being present.

Walter Houston Clark, though somewhat stodgy and sixty-two years old, saw some method in Leary's madness and tried to swing with the exercises whenever he visited Millbrook. This was something of a surprise to the other members of IFIF, as Paul Lee has explained. "Now he was so square," Lee observed. "He looked like an old retired shoe salesman. I mean I never met a more square looking guy in my life but he and Leary just became the chummiest of pals and it was always to my total astonishment." But not everyone in the Cambridge cadre could go along with the changes Clark accepted—and not everyone, as it turned out, was allowed to. "I don't know what happened [the summer before] on those Caribbean islands," Lisa Bieberman later remarked in an interview, "but it was the beginning of the end of what had been our warm, dedicated little fellowship. Certain persons who had been in were out now. And, as it developed, I was one of them."[19] For his part, Huston was 'in,' but sometimes what was happening at Millbrook transcended both civility and common courtesy, and he found himself wondering how much longer he could participate. He was proud of the group's headway in suggesting the value of psychedelic experience, and he wanted to keep the two factions of IFIF together, but he was deeply questioning whether or not that was even possible.

"One time we went to Millbrook together in Huston's van," Paul related, referring to a visit they made over the Thanksgiving weekend of 1963. "His daughters were along— and this caused some problems for Huston and Kendra. I think they were somewhat worried about exposing the girls to more than they were ready for or could even comprehend." Millbrook, as Lee emphasized, "was a totally drug-infused atmosphere," and perhaps not a good fit for teenagers, as became clear when the weekend progressed. Kendra wrote that during the Thanksgiving meal she noticed the turkey was stuffed with Morning Glory seeds and that "someone's pet monkey had dragged his tail through the cranberry sauce." Huston related his views on what happened then in an interview with Robert Forte in 1998, and his comments are worth quoting *en toto*:

> ... differences began to appear with Tim and Dick on one side and Walter Houston Clark and me on the other. They were antiestablishment rebels, whereas Walter and I thought of ourselves as reformers. They were giving up on the university, where we were sticking with it. . . . So one night a formal parting of the ways took place. . . . Dinner was preceded by the traditional Thanksgiving touch football game, which Kendra remembers with delight because she was regularly assigned to block opponents and (as she put it) getting in people's way was something she was good at. Her moment of glory was when she was assigned to block Maynard Ferguson [a famous jazz trumpeter who also happened to be a stocky guy].
>
> Not surprisingly, the brownies were spiked with grass; but the pertinent part of my report came around midnight when Tim, Dick, Walter Clark and I decided, with our friendship at full tilt, to face up to our differences, and Walter and I officially withdrew from IFIF and the direction it was headed. As we were the 'squares' in the organization, I suggested that we might organize ourselves into IFIF Squared with the logo IFIF2, though we did not in fact institute a parallel organization.
>
> But after our 'parting-of-the-way' discussion was over and I was heading upstairs to join Kendra for the night, he [Alpert] sought me out for the first one-on-

one conversation we had ever had, as I recall. 'I am sure that we will remain friends and continue to see each other,' he said, 'but before we formally go our separate ways, I want to tell you that I have been impressed with the steadiness with which you have maneuvered these turbulent years.' It is self-serving for me to report that, but I do so because it was my first glimpse of the generosity of the man who was to become Ram Dass. Also, in a way that brief exchange was to prove prophetic, for in the years that followed I grew closer to Ram Dass than to Tim.[20]

Leary later claimed in his book *High Priest* that he hadn't so much changed the direction of IFIF when he moved to Millbrook as revealed its original intent: "In 1961 we estimated that 25,000 Americans had turned-on to the strong psychedelics . . . . At that rate of cellular growth we expected by 1967 a million Americans would be using LSD. We calculated that the critical figure for blowing the mind of the American society would be four million LSD users and this would happen by 1969. . . . That was IFIF's hidden agenda."[21] However, when quizzed about this comment, Huston strongly disagreed: "That might have been Tim's hidden agenda but it wasn't ours!" And after looking through various statements by Clark, Watts, Heard, Lee and others who had been involved with IFIF from its inception, it's clear that Huston has it right; in *High Priest*, Leary was giving a revisionist spin to the purpose of IFIF. If IFIF had sought to turn-on four million young Americans without a thought of what could happen next, Huston wouldn't have joined in the first place.

## STATES AND TRAITS

After the fateful breakup during Thanksgiving, everyone's cards were on the table and the parties began moving in their own directions; however, one thing stayed constant between them—and, for that matter, for all the pro-psychedelic factions of America—and that was Huxley's interpretation of the psychedelic experience. Leary, Alpert, Huston, Lee, Clark, Metzner—as well as Alan Watts, Allen Ginsberg, Ken Kesey, Oscar Janiger (the doctor who gave LSD to Cary Grant) and a host of others—still accepted that the drugs could trigger a glimpse of Huxley's "unitive knowledge." In gratitude for this landmark mystical-mimetic interpretation, Leary, Alpert and Metzner dedicated their manual for conducting drug sessions, *The Psychedelic Experience* (1964), to Huxley. But Huston believed that Leary and his team—as well as most others in the pro-psychedelic camp—weren't reading Huxley closely enough, missing one of his most salient observations about the psychedelic experience.

After Huxley's first trip on mescaline in 1953, he decided that the experience, though a definite breakthrough for him, was something less than an experience of enlightenment. A critical element of complete awakening had been missing; specifically, he had felt no impetus toward altruistic behavior, and he saw this as significant. Based on the traditional accounts, Huxley accepted that if one expanded one's consciousness to the point where it was synonymous with the Divine Ground, one's will would become synonymous with the Divine Will. Having freed oneself from suffering and delusion, one would then wish to end the suffering of others. Consequently, Huxley believed that if an 'enlightened' person did not have this desire, he or she hadn't yet reached the final breakthrough. Applying this principle to his trip on mescaline, Huxley believed that since he hadn't felt concerned for others or eager to do something for others, he had only experienced a facet of enlightenment. Huston took this to be a key point that Leary had overlooked and was still overlooking. Huston had believed since childhood that true spirituality involves and inspires service, and this had also been his legacy from Wieman, Satprakashananda, Niebuhr and Tillich, so he was sensitive to the wisdom of Huxley's final appraisal of his mescaline trip.

Most advocates of psychedelic experience in the 1960s believed such experience could be a subset of mystical experience, and though Huston agreed with this to a large extent, he, and Clark also, wondered if that were actually the case, given that the drugs' impact on the lives of those who took them didn't seem to match up with this theory. "Drugs appear to be able to induce religious experiences; it is less evident that they can produce religious lives," he wrote in an article at that exact time.[22] Clark was convinced that the drugs *could* have the same impact, as he reported later in his book *Chemical Ecstasy* (still considered by some to be the single best appraisal of the religious import of psychedelic drugs), but Huston wasn't sure—and Leary and Alpert's actions seemed to be providing evidence to the contrary. In October, less than a year after his breakup with Leary and Alpert, Huston published his particular views in an article, "Do Drugs Have Religious Import?" In that article, which went on to become the most reprinted essay in the history of *The Journal of Philosophy*,[23] Huston argues that the "object of the religious life is not altered states but altered traits of character,"[24] and yet most of the people who took the drugs didn't seem to have become either more compassionate or more socially aware, let alone more ego-less. This would be one of Huston's bottom lines about psychedelics in the years ahead; he would coach people to try the substances but to avoid the 'religion of religious experience.' He would argue for the importance of traits over states, of morality and charity over just blowing one's mind.

## THE BERKELEY LSD CONFERENCE

In the spring of 1966, two and a half years after IFIF's break up, Huston was invited to participate in a conference on psychedelic drugs at the University of California, Berkeley, put together by Richard Baker, later to be the head roshi at the San Francisco Zen Center. Baker wanted Huston to be on the conference's advisory committee with Frank Barron, Dr. Sidney Cohen, Paul Lee Alpert, and several other experts, and Huston accepted the offer, eager to air his own appraisals, including his point about 'traits over states.' The conference was supposed to take place in Wheeler Auditorium on the Berkeley campus, but when university officials learned that Leary and Ginsberg were scheduled to speak, they demanded that Baker "dis-invite" Ginsberg and the venue be shifted to a university facility in San Francisco.[25] Leary had become notorious by then, and, bolstered by the encouragement of Ginsberg, was endorsing his open-door policy on grand scale with loads of publicity. No moderating influence was available to him after the split with Clark and Huston, and after the death of Huxley, who had died of throat cancer nearly three years earlier, on November 22, 1963, the same day President John Kennedy was shot in Dallas.

The conference that eventually ran for five days (June 13-18) kicked off with a party the night before the first day of talks in a mansion in Marin County with The Grateful Dead supplying the music. Huston would, many years later, become a close friend of the Dead's drummer, Mickey Hart—even acting as the officiant at Hart's wedding—but in 1966 Huston found the music to be little more than noise; in fact, he felt completely out of place at the event, seeing it as inappropriate for people who were supposedly taking psychedelics seriously. After all, "he'd come to San Francisco not with flowers in his hair," as Don Lattin put it in *The Harvard Psychedelic Club*, "but to deliver a well-reasoned paper at a reputable academic conference." Paul Lee adds that the East Coast scholars were caught completely off-guard by the "full-blown, no-holds-barred, free-and easy San Francisco acid scene," and Lee himself, who wore a Brooks Brothers suit that night, felt nearly as square as Huston.[26]

When the conference finally got underway, and when it came time for Leary to take the stage, he began by saluting Ginsberg (standing in the back of the room) as his "beloved guru," and then launched into what Robert Greenfield has described as a "major policy address," announcing his "politics of ecstasy," and uttering for the first time his six-word mantra of psychedelic liberation. "My advice to people in America today is as follows: If you take the game of life seriously, if you take your nervous system seriously, if you take the energy process seriously, you must *turn on, tune in and drop out*." Many in the audience cheered Leary's advice, but Huston shook his head in disbelief, feeling Leary had finally gone over the edge. He later told Robert Forte that he had agreed with so many of Leary's criticisms of society but disagreed with Leary about how to effect responsible change. Leary was baiting society's controllers into full-on attack, basically taunting them to shut down all psychedelic research, while he also stirred up an audience that was too young to understand the consequences of their actions. In short, Leary's speech was too self-interested and self-righteous for Huston's taste.

"Smith looked at all the sexual immorality inspired by Timothy Leary, Richard Alpert and psychedelic religion," Lattin has written, "and was reminded of what Friedrich Nietzsche had said about Christ's disciples—how they 'should look more redeemed.' To Huston's mind, steeped in the history of religious movements, Leary and Alpert's actions smacked of antinomianism, the Christian heresy that asserts that true believers are exempt from moral and civil law because they're already saved."[27] Leary was playing a dangerous game, and given that Huston had been publicly identified as a supporter of Leary's views and of psychedelic experience in general, Huston thought it was time to speak up for his own perspective.

When Huston got to the podium, he first delivered his formal paper, "The Religious Significance of Artificially Induced Religious Experience," but then launched into a tirade against Leary's new policy. He criticized the advice that the youth of America should become revolutionaries—or that they would be revolutionaries simply by dropping acid, which struck him as absurd. Soon after the conference, in an article for a journal entitled *ETC.*, he offered the of summary of Leary's position he had given that day, and it is a view he still defends: "If the psychedelic movement were apocalyptic, revolutionary or utopian, it would present an alternative to the status quo. . . . Being none of these, its social message comes down to 'Quit school. Quit your job. Drop out.' The slogan is too negative to command respect."[28]

## WHEN THE DUST SETTLED

Over the years, Huston and Leary would—perhaps surprisingly—stay in touch, sometimes visiting each other when the opportunity arose. According to Ralph Metzner,

"Leary only ever expressed the highest regard, respect and admiration for Huston when he was around me." But never again would they work together as colleagues, Huston's message at the Berkeley conference having made public the permanent split between them that had occurred at Millbrook. Richard Alpert on the other hand, after his rebirth at the feet of his guru, Neem Karoli Baba, collaborated with Huston many times in the years following, teaching courses with him at the Esalen Institute, serving on panel discussions together, and, in 1995, co-launching the International Peace University in Berlin. To this day, Huston and Ram Dass remain friends and try to stay in contact. Huston would also collaborate with Metzner, contributing an article to Metzner's first major book and giving lectures at the California Institute of Integral Studies where Metzner was director for many years.

Huston ultimately believed that psychedelic experience is *potentially but not inevitably* meaningful. Paul Tillich once argued—to a Harvard audience that included Huston—that the primary religious question of the 20th Century was whether or not in our materialistic world it is still possible to regain "the lost dimension, the encounter with the Holy, the dimension that . . . goes down to that which is not world but is the mystery of the Ground of Being?" Huston agreed with Tillich that this is *the* critical question and he believed that psychedelics could be part of the answer, providing mystical insights for people who lacked an innate talent for having them. Operating like a Zen *koan*, the drugs might open a glimpse of the Sacred by freeing the mind from 'philosopher's disease' and other mental habits. In 1969, in an essay for the book *Transcendence*, Huston lauded the value of *koans* while suggesting, provocatively, that American society could use something of that sort. "Reason operates in contemporary life under such heavy unconscious conditioning from science that it might be good for us if at certain times, for certain purposes, we had a Western equivalent of the Zen *koan* to decommission reason, to simply knock it out, allay it, so it couldn't get in our way." [29] Was Huston recommending Huxley's psychedelic doorway into Transcendence?' He can no longer remember but admitted that it was likely, given his views.

Huston accepted that drugs were only one tool and ultimately unnecessary, but when they did trigger awakening, what was the gripe against that? One need not attain insight only through yoga, prayer, meditation or other traditional means, and on that point, he accepted what W.T. Stace had termed the "principle of causal indifference." Whatever worked, simply worked and that was that. Speaking directly to the possibility of psychedelics as a catalyst, Stace himself had pointed out that Jakob Boehme, a German mystic, once experienced the entire universe while looking at sunlight reflected in a pewter bowl, and yet, "Looking at a polished surface seems just as lowly and unspiritual a causal condition of mystical experience as the taking of a drug." [30] Huston agreed. It didn't matter how the experience was arrived at, it was the experience that counted, and he would never change his mind about this—as he makes clear in his own book on psychedelics, *Cleansing the Doors of Perception* (2000).

Huston's view in 1966 was that one could awaken one's sense of the reality of higher states of consciousness by taking LSD, but LSD didn't seem to be, in and of itself, enough of a spiritual practice to generate full enlightenment. As a result, he found himself agreeing with Alan Watts' conclusion about psychedelics, that "When you've received the message, hang up the phone." [31] The drugs had value but they were neither a panacea for the evils of the world (as Leary believed), nor a complete pathway to full awakening, as Huston, for a brief moment, had believed. He had been roasted in the sacred 'fire,' but now he looked for other tools to stabilize the significance of that experience—as would Alpert by going off to India. In the future, Huston would lend his endorsement to psychedelic spirituality many times, but never with the level of hope or commitment that he had demonstrated in the early 1960s.

# Chapter Fourteen:
# Trying to Count at MIT

For Westerners, the only real alternative to the boss-God religion has been the so-called 'scientific' view of the universe as a system of essentially stupid objects.

Alan Watts

The universe is vast. Nothing is more curious than the self-satisfied dogmatism with which mankind at each period of its history cherished the delusion of the finality of its existing modes of knowledge. Skeptics and believers are the leading dogmatists. . . . This dogmatic common sense is the death of philosophic adventure. The universe is vast.

Alfred North Whitehead

The winter of 1967-1968 was in many ways the winter of Huston's discontent. He had been struggling with feeling out of place at MIT for more than three years, and at 48, he was at the apex of a mid-life crisis. There were reasons for his worries beyond his confrontation with getting older. In 1963, Aldous Huxley died, creating not only the loss of this revered friend but an unexpected challenge. Huxley's death left Huston in the position of primary torchbearer of Huxley's ideas. Huston accepted gladly this role, seeing it as a privilege, but sometimes the position was difficult and unenviable, given the disdain for Huxley's ideas among Huston's colleagues. "They started to refer to Aldous as a lay preacher with little to say which he went on saying," Ram Dass remarked in 1994, on the occasion of the 100th anniversary of Huxley's birth. "Someone who had lost his genius into fuzzy, confused mysticism." Huston was now wearing Huxley's crown but it sometimes felt more like a dunce cap when he wore it in academic circles. It often seemed better to call the perspective he shared with Huxley the 'perennially ignored philosophy,' since few wanted to hear about it.

Huxley died of a painful throat cancer that had bothered him off and on for two years; however, he hadn't shared news of his illness with most of his friends, including Huston. Huston and Kendra only learned that he was sick after it was too late to visit his deathbed in California. In the last hours of Huxley's life, he asked his second wife, Laura, to inject him with LSD. He died while fully awake in a vivid psychedelic experience, determined, she said, "to wring as much meaning from his last moments as possible." Huston was devastated to lose this mentor of fifteen years, but he also found Huxley's last act heroic and inspirational, indicative of a great mind's enduring desire to explore, to grow and to awaken.

Huston was also still dealing with his disappointment over the failure of IFIF, which had put an end to his hope that psychedelics might become a socially accepted way for people to get a glimpse of enlightenment. Furthermore, he was worried about where the emerging hippie culture was taking 'research' with the substances. The summer before had witnessed San Francisco's rowdy "Summer of Love," along with its many LSD burnouts, which Leary's "politics of ecstasy" had certainly helped to incite. Huston, on the other hand, as the father of three daughters now ranging in age from eighteen to twenty-two, and as a professor who cared deeply about his students, worried that his own work might somehow contribute to the recklessness. Fire can illuminate but it can also burn, and there were definitely young people who had gotten burned by not having proper supervision during the trips on LSD (one is reminded of the story of the Sorcerer's Apprentice, when the apprentice learns the danger of going beyond what he is able to control). Huston hadn't helped the drugs to go public intentionally, but he worried that young people might read his essays as encouragement to trip out. It was the year of America's greatest escalation of forces in Vietnam and Huston believed young people had enough on their plates without compounding their worries with powerful, mind-altering substances.

Huston was also upset that his close circle of allies had dwindled to zilch following the IFIF split. Paul Lee had moved to California to teach at Santa Cruz; Walter Pahnke had been hired by the U.S. government to do research with psychedelics at the Spring Grove Hospital near Baltimore (and would drown two years later in a scuba-diving accident in Maine); and Walter Clark, soon also to transfer to Spring Grove, had left his teaching position under pressure to distance himself from psychedelic research. "The trustees at Andover Newton threatened me with dismissal," he confided in an interview.[1] Huston was still practicing Zen meditation but most of his Buddhist pals had also left Cambridge, and he was more alone with his thoughts than he had been for seven years. As if all this wasn't enough to put him in a funk, he was having problems in his marriage.

As a sought-after star on the lecture circuit, Huston was rarely home. "He had gotten his teaching schedule down to two days a week," Kendra recalled, "and he was away much of the rest of the time. He was abroad every summer for two to four months, usually leading trips with students. So I got used to making a life for myself." The family was no longer spending summers at Eagle's Nest, so Kendra found new ways of entertaining the girls. "As soon as the youngest was big enough, we started going camping." To Kendra's surprise, the girls liked it, and so did she. Each summer, she and the girls would pack up and take a trip, even driving as far away as Arizona. "It was great," Kim, their daughter reminisced. "We camped in the Grand Canyon and Canyon de Chelly, saw deserts and reservations, saw Native American beadwork, rugs and pottery, and ate piki bread, a sort of super-thin tortilla. It must have been a lot of work and responsibility for Mother, but for me it was carefree fun."

Kendra recounted that she came to enjoy the effort of putting these trips together, liking not only the trips themselves but the freedom they engendered. "Huston and I went skiing for a few years—as a way to create family time together—but beyond that and for the most part, the girls and I were on our own. We got very accustomed to camping in the wilderness on our own. I remember one time, on an island off the coast of Maine, Karen held an umbrella for me while I cooked our dinner in the rain. It was fun. We became self-sufficient in more ways than one."

During the summers when Huston was not abroad, he still often stayed on the lecture circuit or attended conferences. When the latter occurred, Kendra and the girls sometimes dropped him off before continuing on to one or another of the national parks. "Our entire family crossed the country a number of times when the girls were young because of Huston's projects or to see relatives," Kendra said, "and we drove to Mexico for two summers. These trips were great fun. We would all sleep in the car— Kim small enough to wind around the gearshift—and find country school houses that had a well, a privy and maybe swings." With a new measure of independence and a stronger sense of her self-worth, based on her success as a mother and bolstered, since 1962, by taking courses for a master's degree at Boston University, Kendra was less needy of Huston's attention—having grown accustomed to not having it.

Huston was becoming more and more unhappy at work and sometimes brought that frustration home with him, acting uncharacteristically cranky or critical. "He was displacing his anger at his colleagues onto me," Kendra remembered. Huston still found solace with the girls and still tried to make time for them, getting out his guitar to launch sing-alongs or thinking up games they could play together, but otherwise he was increasingly depressed and listless. While out on the road lecturing, he experienced the sort of respect for his views that he didn't get at MIT.

During the summer of 1967, Huston led a trip to India, an "Indo-American Seminar," with a group of 15 girls for the International YWCA. Gael, then almost 20 and a student at Wooster College, in Wooster, Ohio, was also along on that trip, so that she could see the world and spend time with her father, as Karen had done on an earlier trip in 1961. But that was not to be. One aspect of the trip involved a home-stay in which Indian families hosted the American students, in an attempt to bring together young women from two sides of the planet to make them real in each other's lives.

## DISGRUNTLED WITH MIT

Huston was out on the lecture circuit not only because he was a successful author but also as a way of spending less time at MIT. The major contributor to Huston's discontent at that time was that, after nearly ten years of teaching at MIT, he felt he hadn't made a dent in the Institute's philosophical allegiance to strict materialism, nor had he moved science and religion an inch closer to reconciliation. In fact, nobody even seemed interested in his ideas.

Positivism and modernism were in full swing and had almost completely taken over the academy, allowing little room for the significance of the humanities and none for religion and metaphysics. American colleges had first been created in the seventeenth and eighteenth centuries as seminaries to train Protestant clergy. Though Huston believed that goal had been "rightly retired,"[2] it had been replaced by a model just as dogmatically entrenched, based on the template of the German research university established in the nineteenth century by the German philosopher Wilhelm von Humboldt. This Humboldt model, focused on the sciences, had clear benefits for society, since technology was becoming more and more important and required experts to manage and develop it, but it denied the value of subjects that didn't deal directly with the physical world. At MIT, which had become the High Temple of the Humboldt model, and of all research universities, Huston was entirely a fish out of water (though this had been part of his initial attraction for going there). Once, after he complained

145

about this to a colleague in the sciences, the colleague, reflecting for a moment and then smiling, offered Huston an explanation for why he was so invisible: "The difference between us and you is that we count and you don't."[3] Huston found the double entendre both clever and painful, an apt summary of his situation.

Huston had been working for eight years to move MIT's pedagogy into a place where its administration and faculty could recognize, as Albert Einstein had once testified, that "Not everything that counts can be counted."[4] There are subjects of inquiry, like the natural human interest in art and aesthetics, that deserve attention, but that can't be put into a test tube or viewed through a microscope. To demand that only scientific tools are viable for investigating Reality was to commit the sin of "Scientism," a pejorative term for positivism, asking Reality to conform to science's tools, and confounding science's view of the world for the world itself (like a person who thinks the world is blue because he is looking through blue sunglasses). Scientism argues that only the categories and definitions of the natural sciences form the basis for enquiry, including philosophical enquiry, and all else is a waste of time. The physicist E. Rutherford once put it, "there is physics and there is stamp-collecting."[5] But Huston disagreed on what he saw as solid philosophical grounds so when he couldn't get himself listened to, he began launching diatribes against Scientism in his published work. During the mid and late 1960s, Huston spent as much time writing about the dangers of Scientism, positivism and the over-applications of technology as he did endorsing the perennial philosophy or the value of religion.

We find his philosophical disagreements with Scientism and its pernicious effects on society coming out strongly in an essay he wrote in 1967 for a book entitled *Human Values and Advancing Technology*, wherein he covers three problems he believed technology had created, though mostly as accidental byproducts of the nineteenth century's dream of a technological utopia. First, technology had generated engines for compounding wealth and power, which had compounded the control that some nations had over others. Where some people argued that this had increased America's safety by giving it the power to control its destiny, Huston argued the exact opposite, proposing that it was undermining America's security by creating an angry class of oppressed nations (he would return to this argument in 2001, when asked publicly to explain the causes of the 9/11 tragedy). Furthermore, Huston contended that increased technology and control had hampered America's safety from within, giving the State too much power over its people ever to be opposed by a popular revolution, even if such a revolution were necessary to overthrow despotism. Citing the ineffectuality of the protests taking place against the Vietnam War (a war that would claim the lives of nearly 60,000 American soldiers—most of them barely out of their teens), and the increasing violence perpetrated against war protesters (soon to reach a crescendo at the Democratic National Convention in Chicago in 1968), Huston pointed out that—good or bad, "the day when the Bastille could be stormed with pitchforks is over."[6]

Huston's second concern about the over-application of technology involved what he considered its pernicious effect on individuality. Like Huxley, he saw a dangerous trend toward a mass-mind growing in society, with individuality squashed under a robotic 'group-think' of canned rhetoric, rampant advertising and oppressive state mandates. "When man first built society, it was like a home that sheltered him from the wilds," Huston wrote in his essay. "But it has tightened to the point where it has become something of a trap." He blamed this effect on the fact that more and more

time in people's lives was being consumed by role behavior in which *what* was done
was more important than *who* was doing it. People were, he believed, becoming overly
identified with their jobs and social roles, and the more this happened, "the more our
individuality idles, or rather never comes into being." If the trend kept going, the individual—as Dostoyevsky, Kafka and others had also warned—would become little more
than a cog in a machine. To push this point home, Huston alluded to a play then popular on Broadway: "When Quentin in Arthur Miller's *After the Fall* announces: 'I can't find
myself,' it is no wonder. Like so many in our time, he has no self to find."[7]

Huston goes on in the essay to cite the current tensions in American society, explaining that part of Tim Leary's appeal with youth was due to mass society's squash-
ing of individuality. "Protesting the tyranny of technology with its over-emphasis on
control, the young today are striking up for opposite, countervailing values. Their
'Be-ins' celebrate being over doing. 'Turn on, tune in, *drop out*' celebrates the private
life over a public life that has become too controlling." Though Huston didn't agree
with Leary's tactics, he understood why young people were drawn to him. They wanted the freedom to think their own thoughts, as well as the freedom not to become
either cannon fodder or docile housewives. They were drawn to other heroes, Angela
Davis and Abbie Hoffman, voices of revolution and freedom, rather than Doris Day and
John Wayne, icons of the status quo.

Huston's last worry over technology relates not to the world that technology had
created but to the worldview it promoted, and here he gives some of his specific arguments against Scientism. "The vision turned the universe into a necessity emptied of
purpose, a chain of effects without final causes, wherein all that mattered was matter."
Disagreeing on the grounds that other ideologies, involving metaphysical elements,
could afford richer vistas, he added:

> I do not say that the human spirit cannot survive such an antiseptic vision. The
> point I want to make is that man need not continue it unless he wishes. For there
> is nothing privileged about this mechanomorphic view of reality. . . . [And] if we let
> our minds be guided by logical rather than psychological considerations [such as
> the comfort found in political correctness], we can see that this view is so incom-
> plete that to live in it would be like living in only the scaffolding of a house, and to
> love it like loving only the skeleton of a wife.[8]

Metaphysical views, Huston argued, had not been retired from the curricula of universities because they had somehow been proven false but because Humboldt's scientific
model had been over-applied to all human concerns, including those of philosophy and
the humanities. Looking through the lens of science, Humboldt could see no legitimacy or necessity for metaphysical theories; however, Huston believed this was confusing
"an absence of evidence for an evidence of absence." Again, it was like looking at the
world through blue sunglasses and denying the existence of the color yellow on the
grounds that it couldn't be seen through them. The methodologies of philosophical inquiry were determining which concepts could and couldn't be considered, and Huston
believed too much of reality was falling outside the purview of these methodologies.

Huston argued that metaphysics had become an excluded knowledge mostly because of cultural habit. Scientism had entrenched itself as the new Dogma and people
were accepting it out of the same sort of ideological momentum that had once made
Christianity so powerful—and sometimes still does. "The reason we resist science's

147

limitations is not factual but psychological," he would later write in his book *Beyond the Postmodern Mind*, "and we don't want to face up to them. For science is what the modern world believes in. Since it has authored our world, to lose faith in it, as to some extent we must if we admit that its competence is limited, is to lose faith in our kind of world."[9] Huston wasn't advising that we lose all faith in 'our kind of world' but that we also gain faith in Underhill's "other world to live in," the world outside Plato's Cave. The solution was not so much about subtraction as it was about addition, and when it came to the issue of technology, he advised the same principle: "The moral is not 'less technology,' but 'more other things.'"

## REASON TO LEAVE

Huston's isolation was compounded after IFIF because he had no allies to turn to in his department. In fact, he has written elsewhere that he had more problems with the philosophers at MIT than he did with the scientists (who, after all, were just doing their job) and this situation exacerbated his loneliness and restlessness. In the education of every rationalistic philosopher is the understanding that *contained within every theory is the possibility of its opposite* and Huston willingly conceded this point to his colleagues, but they seemed unwilling to do the same, dismissing his perspective before they had even considered it. Huston wasn't demanding like an adolescent child that he was right; he was arguing that he *could* be right—and not that the postulate of an Absolute Ground of Being contradicts no scientific laws whatsoever. However, his colleagues couldn't consider it even as a theory, and this became frustrating. "I knew I could run out the clock just trying to get them to grant that I, with my different point of view, was even doing philosophy," he once told John Horgan in an interview.[10] Elsewhere he has added, "As for my interest in religion, some colleagues reacted as though I were wearing a loincloth and nose ring. Eastern religions, especially, were considered on a par with black magic and witchcraft."[11]

Huston was advocating a re-exploration of metaphysics as one alternative to Humboldt's strict materialism, but for Huston's colleagues, in the heyday of Scientism, such a move could only constitute a return to the Dark Ages. To suggest that so-called 'enlightenment' or 'mystical experiences' were a viable means of knowing *anything* was to sink into touchy-feely nonsense, privileging subjectivism over objectivism. Huston argued back that if philosophy excluded metaphysical theories from its analyses, it became little more than "applied logic." Addressing the claim that mystical experiences are 'subjective nonsense,' Huston contended that such experiences need not and should not contradict scientific facts, but when mystics experience the Ground, the One, the Universal Self, Godhead, they have transcended the Cartesian duality of *subject* and *object* that takes place in the physical world. Their experiences are therefore neither subjective nor objective in the traditional sense—since the "Cartesian Split" has no relevance to that which lies beyond time and space, and so no relevance to the experience of That. Following Stace's lead in *Mysticism and Philosophy*, Huston theorized that Huxley's "unitive knowledge" is best described as "transsubjective." But it didn't matter what terms Huston used, his colleagues remained nonplused and uninterested. It was as if he were speaking in Swahili.

Huston eventually offered a humorous anecdote about his colleagues' disdain for metaphysical questions in his book *Why Religion Matters*. When the poet Robert Graves visited MIT for three weeks in the mid-1960s, the various departments were invited to host him for a dinner and the philosophers agreed to do so, mostly because the Institute had offered to pick up the tab. "When the table had been cleared for after-dinner drinks," Huston related, "Graves lit a cigar, leaned back in his chair, and addressing us squarely, asked, 'What do you gentlemen have against ghosts?' I thought that our chairman, Hilary Putnam, would choke on his brandy before he recovered himself and turned the conversation toward Graves' love poetry."[12]

In fairness to Putnam, who was interviewed at his Harvard office in 2008, he had locked himself into administrative duties "at too young an age" and was often too distracted by the needs of running a department to engage in conversations with Huston and other colleagues. Furthermore, soon after arriving at MIT in 1963, Putnam had organized one of the first faculty and student committees against the Vietnam War (a committee that Huston then joined), and this also took up his time. It wasn't so much that Putnam disliked what Huston was writing about or dismissed it out of hand but that it wasn't one of his interests and he didn't have time to look further into it. "We never argued," he commented. "Actually, I don't think we ever talked shop." Putnam agreed there was a general disdain in academia toward the sort of work Huston was doing but there was more disinterest than animosity on his part, and he liked Huston very much as a person. "The main thing is how very supportive Huston was. He was a very sweet guy, and gave me lots of help through all this crazy maneuvering we experienced with the humanities department. Even after I moved to Harvard two years later, in 1965, I always enjoyed running into him."

## ANALYTICAL PHILOSOPHY

Huston was frustrated with his colleagues not just because he felt ignored and left out, but because they often didn't notify him of department meetings and he wasn't allowed to teach graduate students. Apparently they didn't take him seriously. If they didn't like his approach to philosophy, he didn't like theirs either. His colleagues were mainly of the "analytical school" derived from the later work of Rudolf Carnap (1891-1970), with whom Putnam had studied, and Huston saw this orientation as problematic. In 1965, he published his only book of the late 1960s, *Condemned to Meaning*, wherein he argues against the notion that only analytical philosophy is authentic philosophy.

The book begins with a quote from the French philosopher Maurice Merleau-Ponty, who wrote: "Because we are present to a world, we are condemned to meaning." Merleau-Ponty argued that because we are born into a dialectical relationship with an external universe, we are naturally inclined to speculate about our relationship to it. Huston agreed with that, seeing this 'condemnation' as the root of all philosophy, generating from it such questions as '*What* is the nature of reality?' and '*Why* are we here?' During this period Huston was drawing inspiration from the work of Viktor Frankl, a respected psychologist and Holocaust survivor, who argued that the human drive for meaning lies deeper within us than even our drive for pleasure (Freud) or our drive for power (Adler). Huston agreed with Frankl (who was also in accord with Tillich and Niebuhr) that the need to find meaning is fundamental to our existence. Without it we fall into *ennui* and lose our will to go on. Conversely, human history has shown that, armed with a sense of meaning, people often become preternaturally resilient—as Frankl's own survival of the death camp at Auschwitz had demonstrated. "This illustrates," Huston wrote, "Nietzsche's contention that 'he who has a *why* to live for can bear almost any *how*.'"[13] Huston believed that humanity would always seek meaning because its situation required it to do so. Analytical philosophers had for the most part discarded the traditional questions of philosophy, focusing their attention instead on trying to form bulletproof categories of analysis. Here is where Huston thought they had gotten lost in the woods.

The premise of analytical philosophy was that philosophers must first get clear on what they are talking about and how they can talk about it before they launch into trying to solve specific problems. For instance, what do the terms *being, truth, mind, knowledge* and *communication* even mean? From the analytical perspective, many traditional questions of philosophy lacked clarity (and could perhaps even be proven irrelevant) because they arose from faults of language. For instance, when we say, 'Why do I exist?' or 'Why does the universe exist?' we may simply be misapplying the term *why* to a context where it doesn't belong. We *can* appropriately ask, '*Why* did you hit me on the head?' to someone holding a stick, looking for the rationale behind his action, but if we apply the term *why* to what science seems to have shown is an indifferent universe, what traction can we get? What insights does the question afford? Analytical philosophers were arguing, 'None.'

They believed they could correct this semantic mess by generating clearer terms for inquiry, weighing which terms had virtue and which were simply mistakes arising from the surface forms of everyday language. Putnam, while he was at MIT and after, was trying to clarify discourse on the nature of mind; from Huston's perspective, he and the other analytical philosophers were like fisherman who had become so caught up in cutting bait that they had forgotten to go fishing. So many long hours were wasted at conferences nitpicking over problems of logic and terminology that people never got around to dealing with the issues of life itself. "If I had to express in one word the defect of character that I find in analytic philosophy," Huston wrote in *Condemned*, "it would be *remoteness*—it simply is too withdrawn. . . ."[14] The masses were still "condemned to meaning," and they would continue searching for it with or without the help of professional philosophers, so why not lend a hand? Huston had dedicated *Condemned* to his three young daughters, and he certainly hoped his own work as a philosopher was not extraneous to their inevitable concern for meaning.

What also bothered Huston about his colleagues' approach was that when they did, from time to time, give judgments about man's quest for meaning, they mostly argued it is a wild goose chase not worth bothering with, an enterprise based in poor logic and bad terms. Peter Berger, a respected sociologist of the late 1960s, summed up this gripe of Huston's by observing:

> Modern society has not only sealed up the old metaphysical questions in practice, but . . . has generated philosophical positions that deny the meaningfulness of these questions. "What is the purpose of my life?" "Why must I die?" "Where do I come from and where will I go?" "Who am I?:—all such questions are not only suppressed in practice, but are theoretically liquidated by relegating them to meaninglessness.[15]

For Huston and Berger this position was absurd, and especially when it claimed to be the only meaningful possibility, relegating all others to the dustbin. Working separately, they were asking their colleagues to consider the same question: Is the claim that life *does* have meaning meaningless?

Later in his life Putnam would undergo the Bar Mitzvah he had avoided in youth, returning to Judaism as a source of truth and meaning. Huston would take this move as evidence of the impotence of Putnam's approach to philosophy, since even one of analytical philosophy's greatest protagonists had chosen to go beyond it for answers. When asked how he was able to reconcile his philosophical viewpoint (based in materialism) with his embrace of religion, Putnam offered a surprising answer, "I compartmentalize." And when this was related to Huston a few months later, he raised his eyebrows and exclaimed, "Not fair!" He saw it as the chicken's way out.

## A REASON TO STAY

If there was a bright spot for Huston at MIT, it was the students. Young, eager, and often brilliant, they flocked to his classes and many of them considered him their mentor. Tim Casady, a student from those days, recalled that after taking Huston's "Topics in Philosophy" he realized he had joined a cadre of students fascinated by Huston Smith. "That first semester Huston invited us out to his house, where his wife, Kendra, made a nice chicken dinner and we all got to know each other. There were about ten of us in that particular group. His ideas excited all of us so much that we decided to take as many 'Huston classes' as possible, but when it came time to register, we learned that we weren't alone. He stood out from the rest of the philosophy department, who all seemed very locked into rationalist thought and skeptical of anything 'Eastern' or 'mystical.' Anyway, Huston had a large following."

Casady's comments touch on an interesting irony of that time: exactly when Western philosophy was at the height of its disdain for metaphysics, popular interest in Asian religions reached its zenith. Young people from across America were reading the Upanishads and Buddhist sutras; studying with gurus to expand their consciousness; learning yoga and meditation; hungry for any intimations of enlightenment. This trend had a great deal to do with Huston's popularity. His talks on the lecture circuit were flooded with young people eager to hear his thoughts. But Huston's popularity with students was driven largely by the influence of the counterculture, which made it easier for some at MIT to dismiss him. "What was interesting about the situation," Huston related, "was that my popularity was taken as proof that I had nothing to say."

Huston's following would grow only stronger as the 1960s wore on. In 1967 the Beatles released their record-breaking album, "Sgt. Pepper's Lonely Heart's Club Band," including the song "Within You, Without You," a musical testimony to the value of mystical insight and a veritable Spark's Notes version of Vedanta. The next year, in 1968, the 'Fab Four' also visited Maharishi Mahesh Yogi at his ashram in Rishikesh, India, to study "Transcendental Meditation" and cultivate their inner peace. And the Beatles weren't the only rock group to take up the cause. The Doors (who took their name from Huxley's *The Doors of Perception),* The Grateful Dead, Donovan and a host of other acts also went on the bandwagon, helping to fuel the mystical leanings of the youth culture, which now had embraced not only the ideal of enlightenment but also Leary's theory that LSD could give a glimpse of it. The youth culture was creating and experiencing the largest outbreak of Romanticism in the history of Western civilization, and students in Huston's classes found that this suit-wearing, shorthaired professor actually supported many of their views. Even students from other colleges, including nearby Wellesley, where Hillary Rodham Clinton was then student body president, often came over to MIT to take classes or listen in, finding nothing like Dr. Smith on their own campuses. Huston, like the Beatles, Huxley and Leary, was a *bona fide* inspiration for seeing the world another way.

Much of what made Huston appealing came out in an interview in May of 1967 for the MIT student newspaper, *Innisfree*, and the exchanges give a sense of his rapport with students, along with a few of the particular ideas he was sharing with them. Here are the salient points of that conversation:

*Innisfree*: "You have been described as a man of diverse interests and talents. Is there any unifying theme that draws your interests together?"

Huston: "I think there is a theme that underlies and unites the variation. Can we, by taking thought add to our stature, to the quality, of our personal lives? Why am I on the boundary between philosophy and religion? Because both disciplines speak to my central question. Why do I straddle both eastern and western thought? Same answer: I want to know what both hemispheres concluded about man and his place in the scheme of things entire."

The reporter asks Huston next about the role of education in society.

Huston: "I shouldn't think that education's basic object should be pegged at anything less than maximization of man's potential [Huxley's original point]. Under this generous canopy we distinguish between professional education (which one needs to do his job), and liberal education (which, whether acquired formally or informally, one needs to live an adequate human life)."

*Innisfree*: "There is a lot of talk and publicity about the 'hippie' generation; for instance the groups in San Francisco's Haight-Ashbury district or the Village that preach a life-form based on love. Do they make any sense?"

Huston: "I wish I knew. I follow them with keen interest. Their stance is radical, but I'm disposed to be hopeful. At the very least, they must be credited with seeing aspects of our culture that are inhuman, unjust and deadening, and refusing to make an easy peace with them."

*Innisfree*: "Can you give an example?"

Huston: "Sure. Vietnam. . . . The question is: What is their alternative, and how viable is it? I like their endeavor to find values in simple things, the senses, nature, the here-and-now; likewise, their moves to establish enclaves of community to counter the impersonality of current society. And it's a nice touch for the Diggers to dispense free food and clothes to countermand our society's harsh and uncompromising commercialism. I'd like to believe that they are evolving some new and viable social patterns, but we must wait and see."

*Innisfree* [asking a question that was on the minds of so many spiritual seekers in the youth culture]: "Many of the religions, particularly in the East, have the concept of enlightenment. Do you yourself believe in the concept of enlightenment as expressed for instance in Zen Buddhism or Hinduism? If so, in what form?"

Huston: "I certainly subscribe to it as an ideal. If you are asking if I believe it is attainable, I would have to introduce the question of degree. I don't have a precise image of complete enlightenment, but I think it makes sense to regard some persons as more enlightened than others."

*Innispress:* "Do you feel that enlightenment should be the ultimate goal of every human being?"

Huston: "Not having defined it I feel safe in saying I can't think of a better one."

*Innisfree:* "Does our Western culture inhibit progress toward enlightenment or enhance it?"

Huston: "That's interesting—and difficult. I'm not sure how I feel about that. I think industrial society increases the range of man's freedom, but to move in any direction [positive or negative], contemporary Western man gets less help from his tradition than did his predecessor, but concomitantly he's less encumbered by it—more free to move out in new and more creative directions. I guess what I really believe is what Shaw once said; that there's no such thing as this world becoming an easy place to save one's soul in. So in aggregate it's neither harder nor easier to become wise in our time than in others."

Regarding Huston's conundrum at MIT, it is of note that this issue of *Innisfree* became one of the most popular of the year, even as he was thinking of leaving the institute out of frustration.

## A MIXED BLESSING

Huston was enjoying his success with America's youth, who, like Zooey in J.D. Salinger's novel *Franny and Zooey* (1961), which was popular with young people at that time, longed for wisdom to accompany knowledge in their educations.[16] When Huston related that the Western philosophical tradition may have been wrong to assume that Ultimate Truth can be captured with concepts, and that the East might have it right that Truth is an existential state of mind and spirit instead, his students were right there with him. His popularity, which made him attractive as a commencement speaker, is partially what resulted in his receiving the prestigious Harbison Award for Teaching in 1964, along with four more honorary doctorates, from Concord College (1961), Franklin College (1964), Lake Forest (1965) and MacMurray College (1967). But Huston was tired of being kept away from the 'adult table.' Yet every time he made up his mind to leave, or he received a job offer from someplace else, the administration, realizing his appeal for students, raised his salary and decreased his teaching load. "Thus," he wrote in his memoir, "each year I became better off and more depressed."

# Chapter Fifteen:
# Teaching Science to the Dalai Lama

Silence is only as worthy as what we can bring back from it, and what we can weave of it into the clamor of the world.

Pico Iyer

When the Dalai Lama was asked what most surprised him about humanity, he answered: "*Man*. Because he sacrifices his health in order to make money. Then he sacrifices money to recuperate his health. And then he is so anxious about the future that he does not enjoy the present; the result being that he does not live in the present or the future; he lives as if he is never going to die, and then dies having never really lived."

Throughout the 1960s Huston continued practicing Zen meditation and studying Zen teachings. There were far fewer resources available in English in the late 1950s than there are today but he had come across two books that really struck him as brilliant, *The Zen Teachings of Huang Po* and *The Zen Teachings of Hui Neng*, both written by John Blofeld.[1] Huston admired Blofeld's writing so much that, as had happened when he read Gerald Heard, he became determined to meet the man himself. Blofeld lived in Bangkok, Thailand, but Huston was undeterred. He wrote to Blofeld, who, as it turned out, was familiar with Huston's work, and asked if they could meet sometime. Blofeld was amenable to the idea, so it only remained for Huston to get away from his teaching duties long enough to get to Thailand. In 1961, that opportunity presented itself when he was asked to deliver a series of lectures in Australia.[2] The idea was to drop in on Blofeld after Australia, while returning home.

"Blofeld went to China as a young man," Huston said, "then he fell in love with China and even married a Chinese wife, but he had to leave when the Japanese invaded in 1936. However, when the Communist Revolution came along after the War, China kicked out foreigners, suspecting them of being imperialists, so Blofeld would have had to go sooner or later. He ended up in Thailand."

Blofeld, Huston reminisced, turned out to be as gracious in person as he had been in his letters, but upon arrival there was still a surprise. The books by Blofeld that Huston had admired were on Zen, and so he had expected Blofeld to be a student of Zen. "Not so, I found out that he was mainly studying Tibetan Buddhism and his guru was a Tibetan!" Huston said he didn't flinch. He had hoped to scrutinize Zen but the Tibetan tradition would present just as interesting a topic of discussion, given that Huston knew very little about it and hadn't included any mention of it in his book on

World Religions. Huston had fallen in love with teaching people about religions other than their own, so here was another chance to learn a new tradition he could pass along, and Blofeld was one of the few Westerners who understood the intricacies of Tibetan Buddhism.

Information about Tibet and its religions was scarce in those days. Prior to the 1950s, the so-called 'Forbidden Kingdom' had lived for centuries in isolation, protecting its beliefs and customs from outside contamination. Two centuries ago, the Tibetans had consciously rejected the Industrial Revolution as counterproductive to their ultimate goal of cultivating an enlightened society, believing that faster communication and transportation, joined with 'improved' production, would turn their attention in the wrong direction, distracting them from their spiritual pursuits. When the French opera singer, feminist, journalist and adventurer Alexandra David-Neel visited Lhasa, Tibet's capital, in 1923, she estimated that 40 percent of the adult population was made up of monks and nuns, with Tibetans in general more focused on attaining enlightenment than any society had ever been. The situation changed after the invasion by the Chinese in 1950, when the communists began their systematic takeover of Tibet and the eradication of its religions, including not only Buddhism but also the ancient shamanistic religion of Bon. The Chinese contended that Tibet, which had existed for centuries as an independent kingdom, should be liberated from the despotic rule of its powerful lamas. "Religion is poison," Chairman Mao told the young Dalai Lama when the latter visited him to discuss his peoples' religious freedom. And in 1959, fearing an assassination attempt by the Chinese, the Dalai Lama, along with his family and advisors, was forced to flee to India, where they joined tens of thousands of Tibetan refugees, becoming a nation in exile.

For the Chinese, the Dalai Lama's departure at first seemed like a victory. They had swept the religious leadership of Tibet out of the country. They predicted an end to Tibetan Buddhism, which they saw, in Marx's view, as an "opiate of the masses," a hypnotic and toxic ideology that kept the peasantry from overthrowing their oppressors. Today, of course, the situation looks much different—even to the communists. By shattering the "Forbidden Kingdom" and chasing out its religious leadership, the Chinese have made the entire world aware of the Dalai Lama and his teachings. In hindsight, it is as if they decided to put out a campfire by throwing its burning embers out into the forest. "Look, the fire is gone!" they might have said, looking at where the 'fire' had been, but inadvertently they had created a blaze all around them. By creating a diaspora of refugees, they have actually globalized a religion that had long kept to itself.

Today we are accustomed to seeing "His Holiness the Dalai Lama" on the cover of *TIME* magazine or the daily newspaper, smiling back at us from the newsstand, but in 1962, when Huston visited Blofeld in India, and just three years after the Dalai Lama had fled from Tibet, that was not the case. The world would not realize the plight of the Tibetan people for several years. Huston Smith had a great deal to do with that increase in awareness.

*****

Blofeld spoke with Huston about the influence of the Tantric tradition—a set of Fourth century Indian descriptions of the universe in terms of primal male and female energies—on Tibetan Buddhism. In some ways analogous to the Chinese' own traditional cosmology that the world is woven together from the forces of *yin* and *yang*, Tantra speaks of energies that can be cultivated and channeled in the service of health and spiritual awakening. Lamas and other adepts harness these energies using *mantras* (sacred syllables), *mandalas* (sacred geometry), *mudras* (special hand gestures), *asanas* (yoga positions), *pranayama* (breathing techniques) and the manipulation of sacred objects, moving one scholar of religion to term their practices a "ritual assault on enlightenment." Huston was intrigued by Blofeld's descriptions, and true to his habit of seeking apprenticeships, he asked Blofeld where he might study the religion firsthand. Blofeld, eager to help, came up with a list of five locations where Huston could find the religion intact, but he didn't prioritize that list, telling Huston to pick whichever place interested him most. Huston settled on Dalhousie, India, but he wouldn't be able to travel there for two more years when he would have a sabbatical from MIT. Completing his tutorial and thanking Blofeld and his wife for their hospitality, he returned home to Kendra, Gael and Kim. Karen, the oldest daughter, had gone off at college.

## INDIA, 1964

By the time Huston got away from his duties to visit Dalhousie for a couple of months in 1964, he had read what little he could find on Tibetan Buddhism and added two or three stops to his list of destinations in India. However, his first encounter upon arrival was with a Christian mystic. Huston later commented on how that had happened:

> I was conversing with one of a number of gurus whose reputations had taken me to the foothills of the Himalayas, when suddenly there appeared in the doorway of the bungalow I was in a figure so striking that for a moment I thought I might be seeing an apparition. Tall, dressed in a white gown, and with a full beard, it was a man I came to know as Father Lazarus, a missionary of the Eastern Orthodox Church who had spent the last twenty years in India. Ten minutes after I was introduced to him I had forgotten my gurus completely—he was much more interesting than they were—and for a solid week we tramped the Himalayan foothills talking nonstop.[3]

During one of their hikes together, Huston confessed to Lazarus that he was strongly attracted to the Hindu doctrine of universal salvation—that everyone, without an exception, makes it in the end—and that the lack of this in Christianity had been a problem he had wrestled with. "Its alternative, eternal damnation, struck me as a monstrous doctrine that I could not accept." Hearing this, Lazarus responded that his personal view of the matter was drawn from St Paul, who, in Second Corinthians, describes a man's entry into the highest heaven, where he "heard things that were not to be told, that no mortal is permitted to repeat." Lazarus was convinced that the secret the man had been told was that ultimately everyone is saved and nobody stays in Hell forever, but this truth should not be repeated lest the uncomprehending take it as a license to act irresponsibly. Lazarus told him that "God is all in all," the import of which is that the perfection of God prevails in all matters—a variation on Huxley's perspective that "everything is ultimately All Right, capital A, capital R." Huston heard the ring of truth in Lazarus' interpretation and he held to it ever after, believing it resolves what seemed to him like a cruel aspect of Christian doctrine.

The encounter in India that left the deepest impression on Huston was with Lama Anagarika Govinda, whose book, *The Foundations of Tibetan Buddhism*, had given Huston many insights. Blofeld had told Huston about Govinda, while writing elsewhere that Govinda was a "golden eagle amongst adepts,"[4] but it was Timothy Leary who had first mentioned Govinda to Huston. Allen Ginsberg had visited Govinda the year before, in Almora high in the Himalayas, and raved to Leary about the encounter, causing Leary to read Govinda's books (he then included some of their contents in *The Psychedelic Experience)* and telling Huston of his desire to meet the man. When Leary went to India as part of his honeymoon with his second wife, Nena von Schlebrugge, a former model born in Mexico and raised in Beijing, the couple had stopped in Almora. (Schlebrugge's marriage to Leary lasted barely longer than the honeymoon. She would later wed to-day's most important American scholar of Tibetan Buddhism, Robert Thurman, later having a daughter with him named Uma, and two sons, Ganden and Dechen. But they had a memorable stay at Govinda's hermitage, learning upon arrival that Huston had already been there.)

Lama Anagarika Govinda (1898-1985), though a recognized authority on Tantric Buddhism, was not actually a Tibetan, having been born Ernst Hoffman in 1898, the son of a German father and a Bolivian mother. He first traveled to Asia in 1928, visiting Sri Lanka to study Buddhist burial mounds; however, during a conference in Darjeeling in 1931, he met Tomo Geshe Rinpoche, who so greatly impressed him that he trans-ferred his spiritual allegiance to the Tibetan tradition, taking the Rinpoche as his guru.[5] When Huston, Leary and Ginsberg eventually visited him, he was happily settled in the Himalayas with an Indian wife, the artist Li Gotami.

Govinda's hermitage was situated in a remote area that had attracted several West-erners before the crew from Cambridge, all of them interested in the spiritual life. A famous American scholar of Buddhism, educated at Oxford, W.Y. Evans-Wentz, had built the very cottage where Govinda now resided.[6] When Huston had come to the area, he hiked into the foothills, up trails scattered with pilgrims and beggars, before finally arriving at "Holy Man Ridge." There he spent two weeks undergoing tutorials with Govinda, each lasting "until the sun set behind the Himalayas,"[7] and during these sessions he prepped for his upcoming visit to the Tibetan refugee camp in Dalhousie that Blofeld had told him about. Huston had an ascetic streak in those days, enjoying the challenges of getting by with very little, so he was undeterred by the discipline at the hermitage. He had been raised in rough conditions in China, and his father had been both frugal and austere. Some of that had rubbed off on Huston, becoming part of his own view of what constitutes the spiritual life. Reflecting on this trait in Huston, Kendra recalled that soon after their marriage, she was spreading jam on her toast one morning when Huston warned her not to be so indulgent, telling her to have her first piece without jam. When Kendra pointed out that she wanted only one piece, Huston acquiesced, but she took this remark as part of the parsimony he had inherited from his father. However, whatever its origin, the tendency to 'use it up, wear it out, make it do, do without' served Huston well during his travels in Asia, and he actually relished the austerity Govinda was recommending, making a substantial donation to the ash-ram at the end of his stay for the privilege of having roughed it.

After saying goodbye, Huston returned to New Delhi for a brief rest before head-ing off to Dalhousie, about twenty hours away by train. Dalhousie had been one of the British "hill stations" during the Raj, a place where both the frail and high-level bureaucrats could beat the heat of the plains each summer. Situated in the north-ern Punjab, it became the major town in a valley surrounded by snow-capped peaks.

The environment was particularly suited to Tibetans, who, after their flight from their homeland, had established several monasteries-in-exile there, including the Gyuto monastery. Talking with several people in Delhi, Huston learned that when he reached the valley, he would be within walking distance of Gyuto. Once rested and rejuvenated, he boarded a train and headed west along the Grand Trunk route. Once in Dalhousie, in October of 1964, he was awestruck by the scenery, the mountaintops stretching up into the thin air, the valleys green with crops and giant deodar trees, so big that shepherds camped beneath their roots.

## A UNIQUE DISCOVERY

As an American citizen, Huston was barred by the Chinese from entering Tibet, which is why it hadn't been on Blofeld's list. In Dalhousie he could witness traditional Tibetan practices with no constraints. "When I got off the bus that had brought me from the train and asked where this monastery was, they pointed to a path and I was climbing up and up. And when I got near the summit, I heard chanting and I knew I was where I wanted to be." Gyuto monks are known for a particular style of chanting, and as luck would have it, Huston had reached Dalhousie on the full moon of October, a Tibetan holiday when much chanting would take place. The holiday commemorated the arrival in Tibet of two renowned statues of the Buddha, one each from Nepal and China, and would be observed with a four-day *puja*, including chanting. "The ceremonies began at three o'clock the next morning in the 'ceremonial hall,' which—we were in refugee quarters—was in fact no more than a large tent."[8] Dusty and tired from his long journey, Huston was welcomed with traditional Tibetan hospitality; however, after being given a room, he was also told: "We have no special toilet," which he recognized to mean that they had no toilet at all, "at least other than 'god's great out-of-doors.'"

Over the next few days, while witnessing the circumstances around him, Huston found himself increasingly concerned about the suffering of the Tibetan people. Now without a homeland and forced to take menial jobs in India—a country where most jobs are menial, they had to accept the worst of the worst. Huston lamented what seemed to be the imminent demise of the Tibetans' religion, since it was illegal for them to practice in their native country and of little interest to the Hindus and Muslims in India. And so Huston made a pledge to help the Tibetans if he could. First he wanted to learn more about their customs.

The morning after reaching the monastery, having shared a simple breakfast of *momo* (vegetable dumplings) and butter tea, Huston went off to observe the special holiday puja. "Some 80 lamas, richly robed, seated themselves on cushions on the dirt floor in six rows running the length of the tent, three on each side of the center, all facing the center. I was end man on one of the back rows, near the altar."[9] Then the lamas began to chant, which caught Huston's interest at first simply because it was so exotic, but, given the fact that he didn't speak Tibetan, the chanting quickly became monotonous. After an hour or more, Huston was on the verge of dozing off when the chanting abruptly changed pace and he was brought back to his senses by "what sounded like an angelic choir." The monotonous monotone had now given way to a rich, full-chorded harmony. "If the accompanying bells and cymbals had begun to simulate the tones of the King's Chapel organ," Huston later wrote, "I would hardly have been more astonished."[10]

Having inherited a love of music from his mother, Huston found himself wondering what the monks were doing. At first he thought they were singing in parts but quickly realized that the "angelic choir" was really just one monk. "And he, seated perhaps ten feet to my right and two rows in front, was singing by himself what sounded like a three-tone major chord composed of a musical first, third and fifth." Realizing that he was hearing something extraordinary, Huston resolved to figure out how the sounds were being made and what their significance was.

The next day he located a tape recorder in a nearby schoolhouse and borrowed it to record the unusual chanting. Over time he learned that the lamas were actually using their sinus cavities and the space at the back of their throats as resonating chambers to make audible the natural harmonics contained in the sounds they were singing with their vocal chords. These harmonics are acoustical overtones, higher in frequency than the fundamental tones that were being sung, but Huston hadn't realized it was possible to make them clearly audible, so he was shocked and delighted by the effect. Enquiring about its significance, he learned, and would later explain, that, "Overtones awaken deep feelings because, sensed without being explicitly heard, they parallel in man's hearing the relation in which the Sacred stands to his life. The object of the lama's quest is to amplify life's 'overtones' that hint of a 'more' that can be sensed but not seen; sensed but not said; heard, but not explicitly. . . ."[11]

Later, after returning to MIT, Huston would take the recording of the chant to a colleague, Professor Kenneth N. Stevens, who specialized in the physics of the human voice. Stevens had never heard anyone sing like this and after a spectroscopic analysis of the tape, he and his colleague, Raymond S. Tomlinson, produced an acoustical description of the phenomenon. But it was Huston who was credited by the journal *Ethnomusicology* (January, 1972) with discovering an "important landmark in the study of music," and even earlier—in his essay for *American Anthropologist* (April 1967)—he had termed this new discovery *multiphonic chanting*, defined as a "tonic chord issuing from a single throat." Today, Huston maintains this was the only unique contribution he has made to human knowledge.

Decades later, Huston would have the delightful opportunity to hear the Gyuto monks again in his own country because Mickey Hart, the drummer for the rock band The Grateful Dead and an avid musicologist, decided to stage a concert tour for them. In 1995, Hart hired a series of concert halls from coast to coast and began arranging publicity, approaching Huston as the person to best explain to America what the lamas were all about. When Huston first learned of Hart's project, he thought, "Tibetan monks? Who is going to put out any money to go out for an evening to see them?"[12] But Hart had done his homework, and, as a member of a famous rock band, was able to get onto any radio program he chose. "So he really did the circuit before this first tour, and he dragged me along to give it a little historical credibility."[13]

Huston has said that he especially remembers one particular radio program with Hart, when, toward the close of the show, the interviewer remarked that he had one more question for Mickey, and he was going to give it to him right between the eyes. "Professor Smith is no problem, he teaches this stuff. But what is a member of The Grateful Dead doing with Tibetan monks?" According to Huston, Hart "Didn't blink an eye," responding immediately: "We're both in the transportation business." Huston considered this brilliant, explaining that it "comes close to saying everything about the relationship between great art and religion, because both transport us to another world." The tour became a huge success—followed by other tours—and one consequence of this was that Huston formed a close friendship with Hart, eventually performing the ceremony for his wedding. "Mickey's a fantastic guy," Huston said to me one morning, "and I'll never forget what he did for the Tibetan people by bringing their music to the West. He really helped them out—and in a way that I couldn't."

## TEA WITH THE DALAI LAMA

After three weeks in Dalhousie, the Tibetans became very comfortable with Huston's presence and one day a monk asked him if he had ever met the Dalai Lama. Learning that he had not, the man remarked, "Oh, you have come halfway round the world to study our culture and you're not going to visit His Holiness? That is a mistake." Huston, realizing the monk was probably right, asked if he could somehow get an invitation. The Dalai Lama lived fairly close in another hill station at Dharamsala to the east of Dalhousie so Huston packed up his rucksack, grabbed his procured letter of introduction, and hiked to the bus stop.

The Dalai Lama has become to the West an icon of happiness, serenity and non-violent opposition, winning the Nobel Peace Prize in 1989, but for the Tibetan people he is so much more. In Tibetan Buddhism, the Buddha manifests in three bodies: as the *nirmanakaya*, the historical person who became the Buddha, but also in two other forms. The second form is the essence of the Buddha, specifically the eternal Truth to which the historical man became awakened, and this essential truth is the *dharmakaya*, the "body" of the Eternal Law. The third form is called the *sambhogakaya*, or the "enjoyment body."

Tibetans believe that when a human being reaches Buddhahood, he has the ability to choose his next reincarnation. No longer having to work out his karma from past lives in this world of impermanence, he avoids the dissolution into nothingness that otherwise would comes with death (his having reached enlightenment), and he does this to share his insights about reality with those of us still in ignorance—which, from a Tibetan perspective, is most of us. Preferring to take form into stronger bodies that will last longer, these Buddhas take celestial bodies of tremendous beauty and power, like those of angels in other religions, and though this is a common belief in all sects of Mahayana Buddhism, these celestial Buddhas are particularly venerated by Tibetans. Among them Avalokiteshvara, the "all-seeing lord," is especially important. He has made a vow to guide them in their quest for awakening, gifting to them his special mantra *Om mani padme hum*, while also taking human form in every generation as the Dalai Lama. In their world, Tenzin Gyatso, the "14th Dalai Lama," represents the fourteenth time Avalokiteshvara has reincarnated as a human being to lead the Tibetan people to enlightenment. When Huston met him in 1964, the young lama was just twenty-eight years old.

Huston had scheduled an appointment with the Dalai Lama, but also resolved not to spend any longer than ten minutes with him, hoping not to take up too much of his time. During their conversation, Huston suggested that the lama visit America to make the plight of his people known to the world, and His Holiness agreed that it was a good idea. After a bit more give and take, and while preparing to leave, Huston overheard the Dalai Lama saying softly to himself—unexpectedly, in English—"I must think what is important."[14] Then he asked Huston if he would mind reseating himself for a few minutes, and Huston gladly obliged—soon realizing that his calling card, which read "Massachusetts Institute of Technology," had suggested to His Holiness that Huston was a scientist. Having a deep interest in a range of scientific theories, the high lama wanted to enquire about some of them, taking Huston's visit as a ripe opportunity to do so. Huston later explained what followed:

> There were two things in which he was particularly interested. He wanted me to fill him in on the 'Steady State' and the 'Big Bang' cosmogonies. Coincidentally, I had just heard a lecture on the 'Bang, bang, bang theory,' which holds that the world expands like an accordion, collapses and expands again, ad infinitum. When he heard about that, the Dalai Lama said, 'Well, that's the right one.'
>
> The other subject was DNA. He was sorting out in his own mind the interface between reincarnation and DNA. It was interesting listening to the interpreter trying to get the equivalents of sperm, semen and genes. He finally concluded that it had no bearing on reincarnation; in other words, it didn't undermine reincarnation.[15]

After nearly an hour and a half of animated discussion, the Dalai Lama was finally willing to let Huston go, but neither of them would ever forget that first exchange. Huston has described it as "the most wonderful morning of my life," and in 2005, the Dalai Lama, in his book *The Universe in a Single Atom*, remarked that, "When I count my teachers of science, I include Huston Smith among them, although I am not sure whether he would himself approve of this."[16] Huston, of course, did approve (though he was happy and relieved that the lama found other, more knowledgeable teachers after his visit) but what struck him most that day was how strongly they had agreed on the value of religion in an increasingly materialistic world. The Tibetans had rejected industrialization out of fear that it would generate too much concern for material objects, and reflecting on American consumer culture in the mid-1960s, with its ethos of 'keeping up with the Joneses,' Huston thought they had been right to do so.

*****

For decades, Huston has had a reputation for having achieving a definite level of spiritual maturity, so his own reference points for spiritual attainment are of some interest. When asked who he looks up to, Huston responded, "The Dalai Lama," adding, "This man is a marvel!"

Of course, this begged the question of 'why is he a marvel?' "He is so completely himself and without any pretentiousness," Huston replied, illustrating his point by remarking that for nearly twenty years he had never witnessed anyone in the 'Mystic East' who performed a miracle until he met the Dalai Lama. And what miracle was that? "How anyone could have been raised as that man was, like a queen bee, really, surrounded from the age of four by no one except people who assumed as a matter of course that he was God-incarnate for Tibet—how, to repeat, a mortal could have survived this kind of upbringing and yet escape the slightest trace of a big head is, I am inclined to think, as close to a miracle as I need come."[17]

In the Fall 2001 issue of *Tricycle* magazine, Huston called the Dalai Lama "my guru," but knowledge definitely flowed in both directions. The Dalai Lama was fond of saying, "My religion is compassion," and his teachings acquired an ecumenical tone over the years. Reaching out to the world, the Dalai Lama made clear that he'd rather find the seeds of peace in all religions than suggest that people convert to his own. Pico Iyer, who knew the Dalai Lama for thirty years and wrote a biography of him, *The Open Road* (2008), indicated he suspects some of this "anti-proselytizing stance" came from Huston Smith. "I'm sure," Iyer wrote about the Dalai Lama, "that he must have found great sustenance from knowing and talking to Huston, the most open-minded and sympathetic of religious explorers. And the fact that he met Huston so soon after he came into exile must have opened the door to his understanding that there were Westerners, born into other traditions, as eager to explore the major religions as he was, while never wishing to deny or minimize the useful differences between them." Moreover, Iyer also saw something similar in their characters and appeal:

> Only a very few people alive today can make me smile just to think of them: the Dalai Lama is one and Huston Smith is another. And when I reflect on it, I realize that this is partly because both celebrated teachers are voracious in their pursuit of wisdom and able to push back their own assumptions in order to learn from everyone they meet; both radiate a calm and openness that can come only from an inner shrine that is unwavering. More deeply, with both of them the sense of wisdom is infectious because they are light in every way: alive with mischief and sparkle, unimpressed with themselves and ready to see, and bear out in their every action, that delight is as much a part of life's adventure as is sober rumination.

## SETTING A NEW STANDARD FOR 'ENLIGHTENMENT'

After meeting the Dalai Lama, Huston felt he had a whole new conception of what it was to be enlightened. What had really impressed him was the vigilance, yet ease, with which the Dalai Lama embodied his religion. He was a living example of how altered states, cultivated through rigorous practice, could result in altered traits of behavior. Though treated like a god, his concern was always for his people, and he always pressed the point that all people should work for interests of others. In Tibetan Buddhism, it is believed that we can recognize those who have found true awakening by the degree to which they exhibit compassion for other beings, human or otherwise. And, with regards to practice, the cultivation of compassion is said to result in wisdom, for as we think more about others, we focus less on our own concerns and do less to inflate our egos. To achieve "Buddhahood," which is the definition of enlightenment for Tibetans, a practitioner must cultivate the six *paramitas*, the six "perfections," one of which is the perfection of *karuna,* "compassion." This sets the bar for enlightenment very high indeed, and it could have discouraged Huston, since this new standard pushed enlightenment even further out of reach, but for the effect it had created on the Dalai Lama and his people.

Even toward the Chinese, who had invaded his country and conquered his people, His Holiness seemed to hold no animosity, coaching the Tibetans to let go of their own. In fact, he lectured them about how to use their circumstances as an opportunity to *help* the Chinese. Buddhists believe that it is the *kleshas,* the "afflictive emotions" of greed, anger, fear, hatred, jealousy and pride, which cloud our minds and keep us from achieving the awakening that would otherwise bring true happiness. From the Tibetan perspective, the Chinese were doing many reprehensible things that were causing them to accumulate horrible karma, but they were doing so only because they had become the puppets of their own negative emotions. If the Tibetan people could set a strong enough example of compassionate behavior, perhaps the Chinese would come to their senses, serving their own higher selves by stopping their oppressive behavior. And so the Dalai Lama reminded his people to stay true to their ideals, cultivating the clarity of mind that generates awakening, and Huston saluted his success in this regard and still does. "On the political side he has turned the issue into a kind of laboratory of how oppressed, dominated people can relate to their oppressors," Huston once told Michael Toms in a radio interview. "The judiciousness with which he walks that terribly delicate line with—and I absolutely believe him—no hatred of the Chinese as a people at all, while at the same time not shelving his critical judgment [of their behavior] and being outspoken."[18]

In Dalhousie and Dharamsala, Huston witnessed the hardships of the Tibetan people, but like their leader they seemed to embody a stoical embrace of their problems, trying to mine their suffering for spiritual insights. Their desire to attain enlightenment "for the sake of all sentient beings" became a testimony for Huston of the value of their faith—and of all religious faith, for he saw first hand how religion gave them meaning and purpose, and how religion provided a practical platform for the cultivation of social harmony. Religion not only opened doors to the transcendent for them, it provided moral direction as well. In short, he saw that religion worked—or at least that it could—and this gave him further reason to disagree with Huxley, Heard and Watts that religion is only old baggage to be gotten rid of.

## "REQUIEM FOR A FAITH"

Turning his attention from the oppressed to the oppressor, Huston found in the behavior of the Chinese a living example of how exclusive allegiance to scientism and secular materialism—as with dogmatic allegiance to *any* ideology—could become dangerous. In our own society, he had observed how secularism raised to the level of a complete ideology was weakening traditional religions, including mainline Protestantism, but with the Tibetans he felt he was witnessing materialism's first complete victim. Chinese Communism, under Mao and based on Marx, was systematically eradicating Tibetan Buddhism, and since the West tended to see such religions as quaint, primitive and outdated, nobody seemed to mind or even notice. Huston hoped to change that. Once back in the States, he eventually hit on the idea of making a film. His view was that even if the film didn't reach a wide enough audience to wake people up, he would have documented the practices and values of this ancient religion before it evaporated, so there would be some record of this noble culture for future generations to study.

Huston learned from Alan Watts about a filmmaker named Ella Hartley who might help him with the Tibetan project. Ella had been impressed with Watts' books, so when she found out from friends, a few years earlier, that he was about to leave for a three-week tour of Japan, she offered to tag along and film him, which is what she did. Watts told Huston that Hartley was living in New York City with her husband, and gave Huston their phone number. "So when I got this grant to go back to Dalhousie in 1967, with this recording engineer to make a high quality recording of the Gyuto monks, using equipment from the Voice of America, on impulse I contacted Ella."

Huston was ecstatic when, over lunch in New York, Ella agreed to make a film, but the only convenient time for either of them to be in Dalhousie was exactly when the monsoon would be in full swing. "Well, we went up there for ten days to do this film and for seven days it rained," Huston reminisced. "Not an inch of film was shot! Just when we were on the verge of giving up and going home, and as if in answer to a prayer, the skies suddenly cleared." The two began running frantically from one site to the next, trying to film as many Tibetan customs as possible before the rain resumed, and Ella was able to shoot footage of the Gyuto monks, along with other rituals, and almost all of the film was usable.

Huston scripted the film, linking the episodes into a coherent storyline, while also acting as narrator (he would eventually do so for two other films produced with the Hartleys, "The Sufi Way" and "India and the Infinite"), making sure that he conveyed just the right tone. Elaborate rituals and whirling dances had been caught by Ella's camera, preserving what Huston assumed would soon be gone forever. "We needed a title, and since I thought this tradition was going down the drain, I called it, 'Requiem for a Faith.'" To Huston and Hartley's surprise, the film became something of a hit, not only as a favorite on college campuses but also as a documentary aimed at the general public, winning a bronze medal at the New York International Film Festival in 1968.

The award pleased Huston tremendously, not for himself but for what it insinuated for the Tibetan people, who finally had an interested public. Huston hoped that "Requiem" could —if nothing else—embarrass the Chinese into allowing some measure of religious freedom in Tibet. And he believed the film made clear that it was on the conscience of the rest of the world to save this unique and ecologically sustainable culture from extinction. Could the world just stand by and watch as an ancient religion dedicated to wisdom and compassion disappeared forever? Huston was calling upon the people of the world and he was getting results, setting off a wave of Western concern for Tibet and a ray of hope for the Tibetans themselves. Consequently, Tibetans have often given glowing reports of Huston when asked about his role in putting them on a world stage. Khen Rinpoche Lobzang Tsetan, a high-ranking lama and abbot of the Panchen Lama's monastery near Bangalore, related that even before he met Huston, he had heard about a Westerner who was a "great champion of the Tibetan people." Huston had gained from the Dalai Lama a new benchmark of what enlightenment might entail, and a new respect for the power of religion in people's lives. He wanted to give back in return.

# Chapter Sixteen:
# Leaving MIT

A certain irony brings smiles to the lips of boomers who lived through [the guru cults of the 1960s]: many members of the most antiauthoritarian generation in the history of the most antiauthoritarian nation in the world relinquished their spiritual autonomy to authority figures.

Philip Goldberg

Others see traditional religions as works of beauty whose holy texts have been polished over the centuries by many minds; to take an idea from here and there, they argue, is like stealing bricks from ancient temples to build a rickety shrine of one's own.

Jeremiah Creedon

As an advocate for the perennial philosophy, Huston was willing to find heroes in any religious tradition—including his own. During the 1960s, one of the luminaries among spiritual seekers in America was Thomas Merton, a Christian monk of the Trappist order who was also a gifted poet and writer. Born in France in 1915, and raised in England, Merton came to the United States (his mother's country) for college and then stayed on, eventually joining the Gethsemani Abbey in Kentucky. His mother had died when he was six and his father when he was fifteen, so Merton was accustomed to making his own decisions at a young age. In his autobiography, *The Seven Storey Mountain* (1948), he describes the journey that led him to Catholicism from an amorphous Protestantism inherited from his mother's family. Merton's viewpoint, as illustrated in his many books, always remained open to the teachings of other faiths. As a professing Christian, and the best-known Christian monk of the twentieth century, he gained popularity for insights he had actually gleaned from Zen, and this is what brought Merton close to Huston's heart.

Huston had wanted to meet Merton for some time, and the chance finally came along in October of 1968 when Huston was invited to an interfaith conference in Calcutta, called the "First Spiritual Summit." Huston intended to decline the offer due to a full teaching schedule that fall, but when he learned that Merton would also be there, he changed his mind, deciding to "move heaven and earth" to attend.

Huston's interest in Merton stemmed from several commonalities. First, both men were Christians influenced by Zen and both were respected for their Zen insights—even among Asians (the Vietnamese monk Thich Nhat Hanh even wrote a poem entitled, "Thomas Merton is My Brother"). Theirs was a fundamental attraction; second, Huston continued to believe in the value of meeting wise adepts, quizzing them for insights; and third, Huston hoped to speak with Merton about the challenges of remaining loyal to one's own religion when someone else's had more appeal. Quickly putting together a presentation for the conference, Huston packed up his bags and headed off to his beloved India, now for the fifth time.

"I arrived at the hotel," Huston would remember later, "and in the evening went down for hors d'oeuvres before dinner. As I entered the dining room there was Merton all by himself. He was alone at a table with his fruit punch, and so I went over and right off I had about half an hour with him before anyone else arrived."[1]

Huston introduced himself to Merton and after the preliminaries were out of the way, he, in his usual deferential manner, began pumping Merton for information. While discussing Zen and their mutual friend, D.T. Suzuki, Merton explained that he had now become interested in Tibetan Buddhism, and Huston, amazed by the coincidence, explained that he too was interested, telling him that he had met the Dalai Lama four years earlier. Merton expressed another coincidence. He would be going to Dharamsala to meet the Dalai Lama right after the conference ended. Huston, excited by the news, offered Merton some pointers on what to see and what to avoid in the Himalayas. Then he posed the questions he most wanted to ask: what was it like to be a monk? "I confessed I had monkish leanings," Huston wrote later, "but the man-woman thing was too strong for me."[2] Merton thought for a moment and answered, "You know, it's very nice," explaining that being a monk gave him a set schedule and presented few distractions from his spiritual pursuits; however, there was one aspect of monastic life that he truly struggled with. Huston leaned forward for the answer, and it was quick to come.

Merton made clear that he had no problem with two of his three monastic vows. "*Poverty* was a snap—a cinch," Huston recalled Merton saying. "*Chastity* was more difficult but manageable. But *Obedience* was a bugger! And we know from his life how it weighed upon him." Merton had been drawing heat from the Catholic Church for his endorsement of Buddhist thought, which teetered, from the Church's perspective, on the brink of heresy. He had been denied a coveted trip to Asia for several years out of fear that he might never come back, but now, with the guarded permission of his abbot, he was finally in the midst of the journey. Instead of leaving the Church, Merton's approach to dealing with its conservatism had been to stay true to his religion while also pushing for changes in its doctrine, hoping for a more ecumenical and tolerant Catholicism to result. Huston saw wisdom in Merton's approach and explained that he was trying to do much the same thing. Though, as a college professor, he didn't make his Christianity as public as Merton did, Huston had never left the Methodist Church and relished the liberalizing influence his work had on many Christians. He had witnessed the value of organized religion with the Tibetan refugees in Dharamsala, and he had witnessed the downside of spiritually 'going it alone' in Leary's behavior, which had become self-serving rather than selfless. Huston found himself working from a similar stance to Merton's: keep religion but work to make it more generous, open-minded and relevant.

When it came time for Huston to deliver his own paper at the conference, he titled it "The Relevance of the Great Religions for the Modern World." Huston began by explaining that, "Religion can, of course, be irrelevant and often is. No human endeavor is immaculate and one that traffics with millions is bound to emerge a mixed bag."[3] He went on to say that religion could also be valuable, as it once had been, if it was willing to work at being more relevant. The traditional faiths needed to gain traction with the problems of the modern world, finding ways to help solve the population explosion (then a talking point because of Paul Erhlich's recent book, *The Population Bomb*) and the environmental crisis, and when Merton heard this message, he applauded it. Religion couldn't remain satisfied with its past glories; it had to do something to improve the world and the daily lives of its people—or else it had no point to exist. As the conference progressed, the two men found opportunities to chat about their common views, forming a friendship.

One week later, when the conference ended, Huston and Merton flew together from Calcutta to Delhi, reluctantly parting company at the airport. "We were in high spirits and fantasized about becoming pilgrims together in Nepal. 'I'll write Kendra,' I said, 'and if she doesn't agree I'll divorce her.' 'I'll write my Father Superior,' Merton laughed, 'and if he doesn't agree, he can defrock me.'"[4] That pilgrimage would never happen.

Leaving Delhi that day, Merton headed north to meet the Dalai Lama, while Huston headed west for home.[5] They had promised to reconnect in the States. After visiting Dharamsala, Darjeeling, and Sri Lanka, Merton arrived in Bangkok to attend a Conference of Benedictine and Cistercian Abbots. On December 10, 1968, after delivering his paper on "Marxism and Monastic Perspectives," he went back to his hotel room, took a hot shower, and while getting out of the bathtub touched a faulty floor fan and was electrocuted.

Huston was devastated to hear the news. It had been less than a month since he had said goodbye to Merton, and he marveled at the strange karma that had brought them together so soon before Merton's death. Pico Iyer, in his foreword to Huston's *Tales of Wonder*, remarked on this fortuitous meeting, saying, "Some would call this [Huston's] characteristic luck; to me it sounded like a kind of grace," and Huston agreed. "I've always felt blessed to have met him, and I always lament the loss of so generous a spirit."

## UTOPIA

Huston's excursions to Asia were often solo, but there were also times when he took Kendra (on three trips) or one of their daughters along, and in 1969-70, Huston and Kendra helped lead a nine-month trip around the world with 32 college students for the International Honors Program (IHP). Kim, their youngest daughter, was now twenty and spending a college year in Mexico, which meant the trip posed no feelings of guilt for the Smiths, as had happened with earlier excursions (when they worried that the girls would feel abandoned). They were free to fully enjoy themselves. Kendra described that IHP trip as "a wonderful year, the happiest of my life." The program was titled "Quest for Utopia," and along with the Smiths were several other specialists and their spouses, including the director, David Plath, an anthropologist who studied Japanese culture, and Robert Kragalott, an expert on Yugoslavia. Huston, who had just turned fifty, was the point person while they were in India.

That trip was a true walkabout, with stops in many countries, including Israel (for its kibbutzim), Morocco, Iran, India (where they met Indira Gandhi and her husband, sharing a photo together), Japan, Russia (for its alleged 'classless society') and Sweden (for its free health care and concern for the common good). Huston kept only a few pages of notes in his journal, and most of them have to do with what struck him as funny as they traveled: "In Katmandu [right after the Vice President of the United States had visited] a sweet young Tibetan monk had said to Kendra in reverential tones: 'I saw your King Agnew.'" And Huston also wrote, "Hippies are taken [here] to be some tribe of American Indians who have migrated to Nepal!" In Japan: "Dozo on the double," and, "Well, my family killed the fatted carp again." After multiple disasters in India, one of the students, Carl Weese, commented, "this just isn't my incarnation," and Bill McFarland, another student, exclaimed, "how can I weigh 198 pounds? I'm starving to death!" Huston loved these comments from students and took particular delight when Jim Cort, another student, yelled, after a bout of group squabbling: "what this program needs is a couple of good executions!"

Ray Gawronski became a close family friend of the Smiths during that trip and continued to keep in close touch with them. Gawronski related: "I was very much influenced by Huston, who really was the only person I knew who had a real living sense for mysticism. My Jesuit mentors at Holy Cross had that as well, but traditionally mysticism was something for recluses, not students! However, Huston 'understood.'" During the trip, Gawronski also became close with Kendra. She has said that she and Huston came to see him as the son they never had, and a few years later, in 1974, he would move into their house for a year while attending graduate school in Syracuse. He would later become a Jesuit priest.

Japan was the highlight of the tour for both Huston and Kendra, who reveled in the chance to revisit old places they had seen twelve years earlier on the Danforth trip. In Tokyo, the group staged a protest against the Vietnam War outside the American Embassy and, in their search for possible utopias, also visited several communes. "Plath, who had visited Japan many times, took us to a very successful commune where we stayed for three or four days," Huston said. "To support themselves, they made very thick *tatami* mats for sleeping. And here's a bit of whimsy. At dinner, just like you'd have a purified water dispenser, they had a sake dispenser. I got a bit tipsy and it ended up they also had grapes and the students were lobbing grapes over the table to see if I could catch them in my mouth! Not the most dignified behavior, but we were having fun."

The one touchy moment in Japan occured after they visited the Communist Party headquarters in Tokyo. While in the Shinjuku subway station, the largest such station in the world, Huston went to look for someone who could give them directions to find their way home. The polite man that he approached turned out to be a plainclothes cop who said, "Step right this way" and delivered Huston to the police! Once they were all at the station, the police, interested in why Huston had been visiting the communists, grilled him for hours "on the assumption that I must be a spy for the Soviets."[6] But after learning who he really was, they not only let him go but gave him an expensive book on Japanese Art, assuring him that they had meant no disrespect.

As the IHP program moved toward its conclusion, members of the group realized how deeply they had bonded during their travels. So much so that when Huston asked if they felt they had ever glimpsed utopia, to his surprise they said they had—though not in Israel, Japan or Sweden. They had glimpsed it in themselves. "While we had discussed utopia, utopia had become the discussion itself, when thirty people had imperceptibly become one," Huston later wrote.[7] And Kendra agreed: "Everyone—students and faculty—decided that our group was the paradise we had all been looking for."

## Leaving MIT

By 1970, Huston was spending as little time at MIT as possible while also thinking about what he might do next. Several job offers had come his way but none had felt like a good fit, until, in 1972, he hit the jackpot when Syracuse University offered him an endowed chair as the Thomas J. Watson Professor of Religion. It was a prestigious post, and if Huston accepted it, he would join a Religion Department, affording him more elbowroom to share his ideas than he had in the philosophy department at MIT. Syracuse had a Methodist background and more openness toward religious studies in general, so after talking things over with Kendra, they left Cambridge in the summer of 1973, soon to settle into a new home in Syracuse at 887 Salt Springs Rd.

The attractions of Syracuse for Huston came out in an interview for the MIT student newspaper, *Free Parking*, conducted by Steve Reuys on March 8, 1973.[8] The article reads like Huston's exit interview from MIT, with Reuys asking him pointedly why he was leaving. "Here my interests are peripheral to the main thrust of the philosophy department," Huston answered, "and I am, as it were, token representation for other kinds of philosophy. There I expect to be part of a continuing dialogue, an ongoing colloquium. Second, I'll be actively involved there in graduate teaching, whereas here my work is almost entirely with undergraduates." When Reuys asked how his views differed from those of his MIT colleagues, Huston spoke openly against scientism, quoting Ludwig Wittgenstein: "Philosophers constantly see the method of science before their eyes, and are irresistibly tempted to ask and answer in the way that science does."[9] For Huston, this addiction to one way of approaching the search for truth had become confining and oppressive.

Huston went on to clarify that he wasn't upset with what his fellow philosophers were working on ("A lot of what my colleagues do interests me very much."); the problem had to do with what they left out. Huston explained that, for instance, the desire to awaken to the Absolute—a deep concern of Indian philosophy—was off their radar and appeared to them as nothing more than subjectivism or touchie-feelie nonsense. Huston had worked to secure "a respected beachhead" at MIT for viewpoints outside of analytic philosophy, including not only Asian philosophy but also existentialism and phenomenology, since proponents of those perspectives also argued that, "truth does indeed have subjective, contradictory (or better, paradoxical) and ambiguous aspects." But he felt his work hadn't paid off. No such beachhead was allowed.

Reuys wondered if this void in MIT's curriculum presented problems for students. Huston responded: "I do see students, as in certain respects, the losers, not in what they get but in what they don't get. . . . Analytic philosophy appears to serve logical sensibilities admirably, but onto transcendence, the sacred, the meaning of life and humanity's potentials it opens no vistas. Who, here at MIT, will be working with students whose sensibilities and concerns lie in these directions? Are we to say that these concerns are unimportant? Spawned by neuroses? Intangible to the life of the mind?"[10]

Huston explained to Reuys that in Syracuse he would work to restore components of the humanities that had been eroded over the past century, allowing students to explore truth and meaning with the binocular vision created by giving equal attention to qualitative as well as quantitative appraisals of the world. Science had done so much for humanity—and the global community was still riding the high created by the

Apollo moon landings—but inner space should also be explored. Huston's excitement is palpable in the article, and when he reached Syracuse he would prove as good as his word, opening new vistas for the students in his classes.

## THE DEATH OF HENRY NELSON WIEMAN

Huston immediately settled into his new job, working alongside James B. Wiggins and scholars who, for the first time in his career, respected his metaphysical theories. He and Kendra loved their new city, which was large enough to afford cultural opportunities, but small enough to escape when they needed time in the country. In short, Syracuse was just the right size, and this was the beginning of a happy period for both of the Smiths. It was also a period of sad farewells, with the death of several of Huston's major influences, including his father-in-law. This spate of goodbyes began in 1971 with the death of Gerald Heard, whose career had taken some quirky turns over the years, including one in 1941, when he published *A Taste of Honey*, a bestseller about an attack of killer bees. But the transition that had made Heard most notorious came when he authored several books on UFOs, starting in 1950 with *Is Another World Watching?* Huston was mostly nonplussed by these flying saucer books, believing Heard's intelligence was better applied to other topics, but before Gerald himself could say whether or not another world *was* watching, he suffered a debilitating stroke in 1966, leaving him mostly bed-ridden until his death five years later at the age of eighty-one.

Heard's several books about space aliens, which were definitely 'money makers' for him, received mixed reviews, and not just from Huston. Most scholars continue to see them as kooky and something of a sell-out, though sophisticated scrutiny of the UFO craze (for instance, by Jeff J. Kripal of Rice University, who has mined the phenomenon for its relevance to the study of religion in *Authors of the Impossible*) has created a more nuanced reassessment. Heard's mind had wandered over myriad topics that were rarely explored in academia during his lifetime, including the psychological import of 'little green men,' and the world of ideas is better off for it. Like his friend Huxley, Heard was willing to explore even those areas of enquiry that Aldous once termed the "odd and sometimes malodorous wells, at the bottom of which poor Truth is so often condemned to sit."

In 1973, the year Huston and Kendra moved to Syracuse, Alan Watts, another colleague and erstwhile mentor, also died. Watts, whom Huston had admired for being so entirely himself, warts and all, and whom Jack Kerouac had admired for the same reason (depicting Watts as Arthur Whane in his novel *Dharma Bums*), died of lung cancer at 58, probably from his long habit of cigarette smoking. With Watts gone, Huston became the best-known Western advocate of Zen in America.

The death that most affected both Huston and Kendra during this period was the loss of Kendra's father on June 19, 1975. After leaving Carbondale, where Wieman had spent what he called the "ten best years of his career,"[11] and settling in Grinnell, Iowa, in 1966, he had gone through bumpy shifts into old age. Continuing to write while teaching part-time, he had turned into something of a curmudgeon. "In his early eighties, still teaching, he became irritable, and in debates sharply combative," Kendra remembered. "Some comments indicated his fear of being a has-been and his apprehension that rivals in his field would have a greater legacy."

Wieman worried that his work had been lost in the shuffle and this disturbed him greatly. As evidence of this, in 1970, and with his memory and vitality declining, Wieman gave one of his last professional presentations in Grinnell, and though it was titled, "My Failures," it insinuated that the failures were really those of others. Tired of the mysticism and romanticism that had become part of student culture (a culture that embraced the work of his son-in-law but not his own), Wieman had begun to sulk, urging his students to change direction. "The culmination of man's quest through the ages, if ever there is a culmination," he exclaimed, "will not be to build the house of his dreams. It will be to climb above the fog of his dreams and see that the greatest values are shining summits very different from his dreams."[12]

Then Wieman managed to snap out of it, and especially after he let go of his career ambitions; admitting to himself that his best work was behind him, he began to soften. Kendra, who visited him whenever she could during his last years, was glad to be on close terms with her father again; she described what he was like towards the end of his life:

> Apparently contented and peaceful, he did a little gardening, walked in the woods, and limbered his stiff limbs with yoga. . . . Often his face was suffused with pleasure as he gazed at younger people. For me the change in him is encapsulated by one event. Happening to look out a window at my father as he was doing some yard work, I noticed that he was stock still, transfixed by something in a rough patch of grass, his face radiant. After he had moved on I went out to inspect the spot that had enthralled him. In some grass that the mower had missed I found a wild pink trillium—Blake's "heaven in a wildflower!" I believe my father was identifying with life itself. Rather than believing life to be one's possession, life itself is embraced with its ongoing creativity, becoming and dying, and becoming anew.

Kendra admired her father for finally facing his old age, and she gained new respect for his work as well. In 1957, during the Danforth trip around the world, she had met the scholar who had translated Wieman's work into Japanese, and he had told her, "He really is a Buddhist, you know." She, who was well acquainted with both Buddhism and her father's work, saw this as a stretch, but could also see the connection. "My father defined God as creative process, inherent in nature, a mystical concept. No created thing, belief, theology or theory should have our final allegiance because so doing would shut us off to the ever new—that is, to 'creative process.' And human beings, by meeting certain conditions, can align themselves with creative process, thus creating value in the world. My father knew zero about Buddhism, but these 'conditions' could be described as *metta*, one of the Brahma Viharas or 'Divine Abodes' of Buddhism. My father would say, like the Buddha, do not trust any authority, book, expert or tradition—test truth for yourself." Huston agreed.

When the end came, it came with a shock for Kendra. She had visited her father just a few months before. He hadn't seemed weak to her, and there had been no news from Laura that he was weakening. When the call finally came, Laura explained to her stepdaughter that Wieman had died in the night, apparently in his sleep, and that his passing had been peaceful. Huston consoled Kendra, even as he dealt with his own grief, since he had enjoyed his last visits with his old mentor, especially after Wieman had turned his attention to gardening. Reflecting back on their relationship, Huston said that he had always appreciated what Wieman had done for his career, and for the field of theology, "even when I disagreed with him."

## TROUBLE WITH GURUS

By the early 1970s, Huston had met only a handful of people whom he believed were experiencing anything resembling a total spiritual awakening. Satprakashananda, D.T. Suzuki and the Dalai Lama topped his list, and not all of those on the list, beyond those three, seemed to be free of their egos. Once, while in India, he had witnessed a yogi who cultivated such control of his body that he decided to enter death while situated in a prolonged headstand. Though the yogi was reputed to be enlightened, when Huston reported this extraordinary headstand to one of the yogi's neighbors, the neighbor had dismissed the yogi's remarkable death by saying, "Well, he always was a show-off!" Huston wondered: Was it possible to experience the Ground of Being continuously (which was the definition of enlightenment he had first learned from Huxley and Satprakashananda) and not have let go of one's selfish ego? And if it was possible, couldn't pride attach itself to one's spiritual attainments, rendering them in some sense null and void? Could one be both enlightened and self-absorbed? This didn't ring true for Huston, for if it were the case, would enlightenment even be worth bothering with? Wouldn't spiritual maturity also include emotional maturity?

Huston generally adhered to the Vedantic view that experiencing the Divine Ground of Being had profound value, giving the individual a new perspective on his or her life and death, but what about the social aspects of religion and spirituality? What about the aim of being of service? Was it possible that enlightened traits weren't awakened spontaneously upon experiencing the Ground? Maybe a continuous experience of Huxley's "unitive knowledge" was only a first stage of enlightenment, or a facet of it, and the Tibetans, with their emphasis on cultivating the Six Perfections, had established a better criterion for full awakening. From a utilitarian perspective, the Tibetan standard would bear sweet fruit even if no form of enlightenment were possible, since the worst that could happen was that people would learn to be kinder to each other. But were the social benefits enough? Not for Huston—at least not ultimately. He was still "whoring after the infinite" and longing to experience it as a continuous awakening, though the creation of a compassionate society was certainly a better outcome than having a bunch of wise egotists running around.

Huston's first encounter with a guru who seemed stuck on his own viewpoint had come in 1968, when he interviewed the Indian holy man, J. Krishnamurti.[13] The film of that interview, which took place at Claremont School of Theology, hosted by the Blaisdell Institute, is easily obtained from the Krishnamurti Foundation in Ojai, California, but one wonders why they bother to sell it. Any viewer who is not a true believer in Krishnamurti's outlook is continuously put off by the guru's haughty manner. Only once did Huston, a respected authority on spiritual matters in his own right, openly disagree with his interviewee—who had been cringing at almost everything Huston had said, and that came when they discussed the topic of love. Huston stepped into Krishnamurti's trap when he remarked that when we love someone, "we are both separate and united."

Krishnamurti winced and asked a leading question in his high-pitched British accent: "Sir, when you love somebody with your heart, not with your mind, do you feel separate?"

After considering the question (to which he was supposed to have said, "no"), Huston answered: "I do in some . . . both, I feel both separate and united."

"Then it's not love," Krishnamurti stated flatly, dismissing Huston's right to have an opinion, presumably because Krishnamurti himself knew better.

"I wonder," Huston remarked, daring to contradict a reputedly enlightened person (who had been a close friend of Huxley's). "Because part of the joy of love is the relationship that involves some sense [of separation]. Like Ramakrishna said, 'I don't want to be sugar. I want to *taste* sugar.'" Krishnamurti barely gave Huston's comment the time of day. But why should he? And when I asked Huston how he felt about the interview in retrospect, he responded, "I was surprised. It was the opposite of my experience with Satprakashananda and the Dalai Lama. It seemed to me that enlightenment should be more civil and patient."

*****

During the 1960s, a flood of yogis, gurus, and swamis flowed into the United States. Huston generally assessed them as having the same problem as Krishnamurti, an over-attachment to their own views. Hinduism includes within its scope the goal of transcending ego and being compassionate, and even of using direct action to achieve enlightenment—termed the path of Karma yoga—but the gurus coming to America seemed generally to ignore those teachings. Sticking to the position that a continuous experience of the Absolute, the Ground, constitutes "enlightenment"—whether ego-attachment is still there or not—they trained their devotees in techniques to cultivate that experience as quickly as possible. But the result, either of their practice (usually some form of meditation) or their interaction with their gurus, was not always very edifying.

An interesting blank spot in Huston's written reflections on the spiritual scene of the 1960s and 1970s is his general disregard for the guru phenomenon that rocked America. When asked why he hadn't said much about the various guru movements, he remarked that he hadn't been interested. "The gurus all seemed to be about creating their own domains of followers. It was too much about them for me."

Huston had a point, given that so many of the guru groups ended in scandal when one after another of their teachers was caught with his pants down—or his robes up, as the case may be. In 1968 (the same year that Huston interviewed Krishnamurti), John Lennon accused Maharishi Mahesh Yogi of making a pass at Mia Farrow when they were studying together in India, resulting in John's song, "Sexy Sadie" ("Sexy Sadie, what have you done? You fooled everyone!"). Though this accusation seems to have been false,[14] in the decades that followed there were many other scandals with gurus, including those of Swami Satchidananda, Swami Muktananda, Swami Rama, Amrit Desai and Baba Free John (a Western guru who changed his spiritual name as often as the others changed their clothes). "We've just been through forty years of gurus with feet of clay," Huston offered as a summary point, "and I think we're better off without them. The true guru-disciple relationship has value, but these fellows were mostly interested in creating empires."

In Vedanta, as in Huxley's perennial philosophy, the essence of the individual and the essence of the universe are one and the same; the Divine Ground of All Being is the essence of all beings. And so from that perspective, one's essence is no different from God's, and this viewpoint is common to the views of many mystics from the past, including Shankara, Meister Eckhart, al-Hallaj and Jacob Boehme. In the 1960s and 1970s, it also found a deep resonance with the counterculture; for example, Jimi Hendrix illustrated the "I AM THAT" principle on the cover of his album *Axis Bold As Love* in an image of Jimi's head superimposed over that of the Hindu god Vishnu, causing the image to suggest, "I am God!" However, the mystics, and one hopes Hendrix too, knew that to say, 'I am an expression of Godhead, the Oversoul, the Divine Ground,' is something quite different from insinuating that one has an exclusive right to the Divine Ground or that one is somehow 'God.' Some Westerners, like Huston, understood the true import of Vedanta's message, while others mistook their guru—or themselves—for God.

The saddest example of this misappropriation of Vedanta by the hippie culture, as the Oxford scholar R.C. Zaehner pointed out in his book *Our Savage God* (1972), came when Charles Manson decided he was not only Godhead but God. Believing that the Beatles were sending him secret messages in their songs (though he clearly missed the point of "Sexy Sadie"), Manson instigated a killing spree that shocked the nation. Nearly half a century later he remained in prison—still convinced he was God.

What did Huston take away from the guru scandals? "The value of staying inside the traditional religions, which put safeguards on behavior and help correct misinterpretations of teachings. The gurus opened many peoples' eyes to the Asian traditions but they also wreaked havoc." However, Huston didn't put all the blame on the gurus, recognizing that their followers had also duped themselves, colluding in their own enslavement. Furthermore, he saw culpability in our culture's turn toward strict materialism, which had eroded religious sensibilities and given young people who have a spiritual bent no place to turn, a recipe for disaster. Regarding this last point, he has explained elsewhere that this is part of what made the gurus so attractive: "We seem to be so hungry for spirituality as a people that we tend to latch on—uncritically—to something that has any aura of authenticity."[15] If the traditional religions could regain relevance—as he and Merton hoped they could—maybe young people wouldn't jump at the first teacher to offer them some truth.

Huston wasn't sure whether the rogue gurus had been dysfunctional because they were charlatans or because they had themselves confused a facet of enlightenment for the 'full monty'—a condition that Lama Surya Das has termed today "premature immaculation." However, he had arrived at the same conclusion as the Buddhists: spiritual growth is never complete until the ego is left behind and one's behavior has become supremely compassionate. He liked the Tibetan model of enlightenment, where only the most audacious would dare to claim absolute authority or insight. Perhaps this kind of ideal would help relieve the over-zealous guru-adulation happening in America, moving respect for spiritual teachers in a healthier direction.

## AFFIRMING THE VALUE OF RELIGION

Though Huston was popular with hippie culture—mostly for his embrace of Asian mysticism and LSD—there were aspects of hippie spirituality that made him shake his head. Foremost among these was the tendency of young people to pick and choose the pieces of religion they liked best, while leaving the rest. Huston has referred to this as "cut flower" religion, or "cafeteria-style" religion, an approach in which we, like a child at a buffet, "take too much of what we want and not enough of what we need." Huston understood why young people were longing to throw off authority, and why women wanted to get rid of the patriarchy endemic to most religions, but he believed they would be better off sticking to the established trails up the mountain of truth than bushwhacking their own way up. In his opinion, taking components from the religions and trying to fit them into a homemade matrix of one's own ideas only made for a crazy quilt. "Cultures resemble organisms more than mechanisms," he explained in 1972, "which means few if any items can be picked from one and stuck down into another to good effect."[16] An example of this, with reference to the guru groups of the 1970s, is that Americans had embraced Indian gurus but then plunked those gurus down into a society where there are no traditional checks and balances on their power, allowing them more leeway to become despotic.

While discussing what has also been termed "pastiche spirituality" or "religion *à la carte*"—or more popularly, the "New Age"—Huston brought up the name of Chogyam Trungpa. One might have assumed he was going to criticize the Tibetan teacher, who had been a drinking buddy of Allen Ginsberg's and had an unorthodox style of teaching, but no.

> Trungpa was a goofy and erratic guru but he had a lot to say when it comes to cafeteria-style religion. Trungpa said that if we knew the difference between what we like and what's good for us, we'd be at the end of our journey, not the beginning. And here come the traditions, the religions, because they have served out of centuries of experience and they are the better guides to what's good for us than our taste buds.

Robert Bellah, a friend and colleague of Huston's, who was for many years the dean of American sociologists of religion, held the same opinion on spiritual dilettantism, reinforcing Huston's perspective. Bellah knew that many young people were trying to find themselves by flinging their nets wide, but he couldn't understand or condone their approach—and he disliked that it seemed to be spreading. "For Americans, the traditional relationship between the individual and the religious community is to some degree reversed," Bellah wrote later in his book *Habits of the Heart*, citing a "Gallup poll found that 80 percent of Americans agreed that 'an individual should arrive at his or her own religious beliefs independent of any churches or synagogues.' From the traditional point of view, this is a strange statement—it is precisely within church or synagogue that one comes to one's religious beliefs."[17]

Huston agreed with Bellah that the trend was becoming dangerous. "Bellah really understood the social dynamics of the religious life. Not only does religion have value in one's search for identity—since very few people ever get to the bottom of themselves by themselves—but it also provides a strong foundation for shared values and social interactions." Finding oneself was great—and so was personal freedom—but not if it led to self-involved isolation that distanced young people from their communities. Better to stay inside a traditional religion and push for reform than to spend one's days in loneliness or a cult. "[Religious] institutions give traction, give spirituality traction in history," Huston commented in an interview. "So we have to take on the burden of those institutions if we're serious. Just like if you're serious about politics, you'd better join a party. I mean, is there a perfect political party on our planet? The whole idea! But if you don't get in there and get your hands dirty, then you're just talking to yourself and your friends."[18]

Predictably, the most condemning evidence against countercultural spirituality in Huston's estimation pivoted around the issue of service to others; in *Mother Jones,* in 1997, he praised New Agers for their optimism, but noted their failure to produce any true heroes of compassion and justice, for instance, like Mother Teresa or the Dalai

Lama. Their approach might make them feel good about themselves, but it was too self-centered for Huston to see as beneficial.

## CONTACT WITH A SECRET BROTHERHOOD

With reference to Huston's growing certainty that spiritual growth comes easiest if one follows tried and true pathways, he soon learned about a spiritual brotherhood of scholars who agreed with him on that point. The discovery of this spiritual order would become the most significant event in Huston's professional life during the 1970s. It was also the most significant event in his life beyond his meeting Heard and Huxley, for it resulted in the discovery of what he believed was the missing puzzle piece of how the religions might relate to each other with equal respect. It all began during the IHP trip in 1970, when the group stopped in Tehran and Huston had a chance to reconnect with Seyyed Hossein Nasr, a Muslim scholar who was scheduled that year to lead the annual hajj to Mecca from Iran.[19] Nasr was Huston's key to the brotherhood and opened the door to his third great epiphany, following his embrace of philosophy as a career path and his acceptance of the perennial philosophy.

Huston had first met Nasr a few years before at a dinner party in Nasr's honor at the Harvard Center for the Study of World Religions. Huston was scheduled to be out of town for the event, and so he had asked Kendra to take his place, and when he returned, Kendra raved about meeting one of the most impressive men—and women (Nasr's wife)—she could ever recall. "On the strength of her hyperbole I took pains the next time he visited Cambridge to invite him to my class. His lecture was a landmark." Huston has said many times that in the early days of his career, he had had trouble wrapping his brain around Islam and had no feeling for it at all,[20] but Nasr, during his lecture, unfolded the religion from its mystical core and that had made all the difference. In fact, Huston was so impressed with Nasr that when they met again in Tehran, he had the "Utopia" students join one of Nasr's classes for a week, and the two men began a long-lasting friendship.

Seyyed Hossein Nasr is professor of Islamic Studies at George Washington University and a leading apologist for Islam, presenting it in a well-received series of books, including *The Heart of Islam*, published after 9/11. Known for his erudition (he speaks English, French, Persian and Arabic fluently), Nasr was born in 1933, in Tehran, where his father was physician to the Persian royal family. He traveled to the United States at the age of twelve to begin his education in New Jersey, later moving on to study physics at MIT. In 1958, at the age of 25, he completed his Ph.D. in the history of science from Harvard, and then took a job at the American University in Beirut as the first Aga Khan Chair of Islamic Studies, teaching there for three years. When Huston caught up with him in Iran, Nasr had become the academic Vice-Chancellor of Tehran University and a respected public figure. When the revolution led by the Ayatollah Khomeini erupted in 1979, Nasr's liberal views, along with his connections to the aristocracy, forced him into exile. Eventually (in 1985) he accepted the position at George Washington. Nasr is the author of more than 50 books and widely known in academic circles as the only Muslim ever to give the prestigious Gifford Lectures in Philosophy. This is the highest distinction paid to a philosopher, and one that he shares with several other scholars mentioned in this book, including William James, Paul Tillich and Hillary Putnam. But in 1970 Nasr was at the beginning of his career, which would not really take off until two years later at the time when Huston wrote the preface for Nasr's breakthrough book, *The Ideals and Realities of Islam.*

In Tehran on the IHP tour, Huston was grateful to his new friend for helping with his difficulties over Islam, but he soon became grateful for something more. Nasr told him of a circle of Sufi mystics existing off the radar of academia while also functioning as a group of well-known scholars.

# Chapter Seventeen:
# Becoming a Sufi

The sacred is the presence of the center in the periphery, of the motionless in the moving; dignity is essentially an expression of it, for in dignity too the center manifests at the exterior; the heart revealed in gestures.

Frithjof Schuon, *Understanding Islam*

If God were on the side of one religious form only, the persuasive power of this form would be such that no man of good faith would be able to resist it.

Frithjof Schuon

My soul is a Mosque for Muslims,
a Temple for Hindus,
an Altar for Zoroastrians,
a Church for Christians,
a Synagogue for Jews,
and a Pasture for gazelles.

Ibn Arabi

During his stop in Iran, Huston had informed Nasr that the IHP group would also visit Sweden in its quest for Utopia. Nasr's ears pricked up and he told Huston that while in Sweden he should meet a friend of his, Joseph Epes Brown, an anthropologist who studied Native American religions. In 1953, while teaching at Indiana University, Brown had published a definitive book on the Lakota religion, *The Sacred Pipe*, based on interviews he had conducted in 1947 with the shaman Black Elk, already famous because of John Niehardt's book, *Black Elk Speaks*. However, Nasr wasn't recommending that Huston meet Brown for his expertise on Native Americans; Nasr assured him that Brown could provide insights on how the religions relate to one another.

Arriving in Sweden, Huston set up a meeting with Brown and the two men were able to sit down together and talk. Huston quickly bypassed the chitchat and laid his cards on the table: he knew what the religions had in common (the perennial philosophy in one form or another), but he was stumped over the "problem of relativism," not understanding how they could each be true and yet have so many differences among them. Brown was well aware of why Nasr had sent this fellow to him, and listened attentively to Huston's comments, assuring him that his conundrum was not insuperable though the solution would take longer to explain than he currently had time for. Brown suggested, since the IHP tour was about to stop in England, why not drop in on another friend of Nasr's? Brown recommended Martin Lings, the Keeper of Oriental Printed Books and Manuscripts at the British Museum, who surely could help him solve his problem. It was becoming something of an Easter egg hunt for Huston; he worried it might also be a wild goose chase.

Arriving in London, Huston immediately phoned Lings, but Lings was uninterested in meeting with him, saying that he was too busy and would have to beg off. Lings had finished his Ph.D. in Arabic studies at the University of London, writing his thesis on an Algerian Sufi mystic named Ahmad al-'Alawi. Since 1955, he had been working at the British Museum where Huston phoned him, and just before Lings could hang up, Huston explained that Brown had recommended they meet. Hearing this, Lings' tone changed abruptly and he told Huston to come right over.

Putting two and two together, Huston realized a cadre of scholars were passing him along and sizing him up, doling out their views on religion one spoonful at a time to see how he reacted. "When I traced the remarkable sequence of events that had brought me to Ling's door," Huston recalled, "subtly, ever so subtly, he suggested that there might be a kind of brotherhood linking the people I had met on my journey around the world, and he dropped the hint that I might learn about it from Nasr."[1] Huston was becoming both curious and frustrated. Lings, whom Huston later came to view literally as a saint, hadn't explained his theory of how religions fit together and Huston couldn't imagine what the skullduggery was all about.

Once back in America and able to resume correspondence, Huston wrote to Nasr and Nasr informed him that there was a group of scholars following a certain Western mystic named Frithjof Schuon, and he suggested that Huston think of joining them. If Huston wanted more information first, he should begin by reading some of Schuon's published work. This last comment startled Huston. "Exactly when the brotherhood was passing me around on the IHP tour, I had been reading books by Frithjof Schuon!"[2]

When he had packed for the IHP trip, Huston had taken Schuon's *In the Tracks of Buddhism* along with him, because he was scheduled to give a talk on Shintoism when he reached Japan and had noted that Schuon's book contained a promising chapter about the religion. "I badly needed an entrée, and more in desperation than in hope, I wedged the book into my bulging flight bag."[3] The material, much to his relief, gave him some wonderful clues, and two months later, while he was in India, lightning struck again. He was due to give a lecture on Vedanta and while "perusing a bookstore in Madras, my eye fell on a study of the Vedanta entitled *Language of the Self*, again by Frithjof Schuon."[4] Twice he had found a book by Schuon just when he needed it. "But would you believe a third episode?" he asked. After the group arrived in Iran, he picked up Schuon's *Understanding Islam* and was for a third time impressed. So even as he had been passed around for inspection by Schuon's followers, he had become a fan of Schuon's work.

Learning all this, Nasr recommended that Huston read Schuon's "most important" book, *The Transcendent Unity of Religions*, which, he assured him, held the missing puzzle piece Huston had sought for 25 years. Determined to decide for himself, Huston dug up an English edition of the book (first published in French in 1953) and read it. He had finally found what he was looking for.

## HOW THE RELIGIONS FIT TOGETHER

Fourteen years later, in 1984, Huston would write an introduction to the revised edition of Schuon's *The Transcendent Unity of Religions,* noting that when the book first came out, T.S. Eliot had applauded it, commenting, "I have met with no more impressive work in the comparative study of Oriental and Occidental religions." But the book generally went unnoticed, partially, one could guess, because of Schuon's intricate metaphysical writing style, but also, as Huston surmised, because it didn't connect with the discourse on religion then going on in academia. Schuon never mentioned the respected theologians of the past, including Schleiermacher or Barth, or his own contemporaries, like Tillich and Wieman; instead, he approached his subject in a way that carried him entirely outside the range of academic interest. Schuon didn't seem to care if he reached an academic audience or not, preferring to describe what he understood to be true on the highest level of inquiry. If the academic world—or the Western mind in general—were too set in its ways to consider metaphysical theories, he would write for those who weren't.

Huston quickly saw that Schuon's views were in many ways consummate with Huxley's and Heard's—including their belief that the unitive knowledge of the Divine Ground links mystics of all cultures—but Schuon was much kinder toward religion than Huston's earlier mentors, and this was the key for Huston.

Schuon's solution to how religions interrelated depended upon a particular analysis that held that every tradition has two primary aspects, the physical and the metaphysical, and religion has these aspects because reality does also. On the physical level, which he termed the *exoteric* level, the various traditions are as unique as the times and places in which they arise, each exhibiting its own personality and values; however, on the metaphysical or *esoteric* level they merge, becoming identical for the simple reason that mystics share an experience of what transcends all differences, the Oneness of the Divine Ground. Where other scholars had differentiated the religions based on their physical characteristics—such as the discrepancies between their beliefs, rituals or social values—Schuon made only one primary distinction: between their exoteric contents, which differ one from the other, and their collective, "transcendental unity" on the esoteric level. Schuon argued that cross-referencing the "forms" or characteristics of the various traditions reveals no consistent essence between them (any more than cross-referencing the colors of the rainbow suggests white light) but that mystics of all cultures, in their direct apprehension of what Rudolf Otto, an earlier, German theorist, had termed the *mysterium tremendum,* know the same Truth, to which the various paths lead and from which, like the colors of the rainbow, they all spring.

This raised an obvious question for Huston: why would the exoteric forms of religion be different if their core experience is the same? He was happy to see that Schuon stated the same question in his book: "Seeing that there is but one Truth must we not conclude that there is but one Revelation, one sole Tradition possible?" To this Schuon answered resoundingly 'No,' Truth is ultimately situated in the Transcendent, and therefore knowledge of it is beyond all forms, but "Revelation, or the Tradition which derives from it, belongs to the formal order."[5] God reveals each religion to a specific people in a specific place at a specific time, providing a container for the Truth that makes sense in their cultural context. The religions arise from the same Divine Ground but they take form in a particular society that has pre-existing mores, languages and histories, so it is only on the esoteric level that unity between them is fully recognizable.

## Becoming a Sufi

Schuon argued that there are no consistent threads of belief and practice between the religions in terms of their relative characteristics. Some religions have a messiah concept (e.g., Lord Maitreya in Buddhism) and others do not. Some describe a Creator God but others leave it out. Some believe there is a heaven beyond this world, while others don't. Furthermore, with reference to this last example, even when two religions posit a transmordial paradise, that does not mean they give it equal value. Hindus and Buddhists believe in various *svargas, lokas* and heavens beyond this world, but unlike Christians and Muslims, they don't place so great a premium on getting there, seeing enlightenment as the higher goal. Consequently, if in our attempt to find some common ground among the religions we surmise that, "the majority of religions have a heaven concept, so 'heaven' must be fundamental," we have arrived at a wrong conclusion. We have favored religions that consider heaven as primary while skewing those that don't. From Schuon's perspective, the differences between the traditions must therefore be preserved to protect them from being subsumed into a false universalism, and believers in each tradition should weigh the specifics of their faith according to their own values. However, Schuon also believed that 'what rises, must converge,' and so on the esoteric level, the religions find both their individual perfection and their ultimate unification. When the mystics of the world experience the Divine Ground, they transcend the relative differences between their religions, grasping the Truth at their core, and this is when the testimonies of mystics begin to sound alike—suggesting to both Huxley and Schuon the existence of a perennial philosophy.

Huxley would have agreed with Schuon that there is a division of classes within all religions (the esoterics forming the elite class), but Schuon offered an addendum with which Huxley would not have agreed: that, given the relative perspective of both *exoterics* and *esoterics*, they were each justified in holding their respective claims. Every tradition contains those who have been burned by the 'fire' and those who have not. For the esoterics, the physical characteristics of a religion have only a provisional importance (since they constitute a means of gaining the ultimate insight and are not the insight itself), but for the exoterics the characteristics are 'The Truth' and therefore absolute and non-negotiable. Huston sided with Schuon's view that those of exoteric persuasion are justified in believing this. The goals of exoteric religion are to provide meaning and purpose in people's daily lives, and even when a pathway to esoteric insight is included (purposefully or not), the tradition's value lies in its impact on the world. Saying this, to suggest that the forms of religion are epiphenomena or less than ultimate, could mislead the common ranks of believers.

Huston and Schuon believed that mystics who experience the "transcendent unity of religions" shouldn't confuse their exoteric brethren by giving them descriptions of what is literally beyond their comprehension, nor should they preach what might be construed as a universalism that threatens the beliefs that have guided their societies for centuries. Mystics may discuss their insights with those who can comprehend and within their own inner circles, but they should not misinterpret the esoteric unity of religion as either a clarion call against exoteric religion or an impetus for merging the traditions. People need the forms of religion they have relied on, that shape their daily lives. In addition, esoterics should recognize that even for those seeking esoteric insight there is a benefit to preserving the exoteric structures. Each religion is a unique gift of God with specific resources "sufficient unto salvation" for a particular society, so if its traditions are preserved, its unique pathway to the Ultimate will also be protected.

Huston agreed with Schuon that exoterics were right to fear those mystics who preached the arbitrariness of religious forms, but he also agreed with him that exoterics would be wise to respect mystics who didn't. Mystical adepts, when properly integrated into their congregations, become spiritual beacons and even extensions of God's own will. Priests memorize the words of God but mystics apprehend 'His' Truth directly. Priests speak, mystics listen. And based on their unitive experience, they are not only conduits for revelation and inspiration, but also what Schuon called the "life-giving sap" of those traditions that already exist. When deprived of its esoteric adepts, Schuon argued, "the religious edifice is shaken, or even suffers a partial collapse, and finally becomes reduced to its most external elements, namely, literalism and sentimentality."[6]

After reading Schuon, Huston was convinced that the problem he had outlined in *The Religions of Man* was finally solved. Considering how the religions interrelated, Huston had rejected both the committed position that "only my religion is right and everyone else's is wrong" as well as the universalist position that "all the religions are really saying the same thing." Schuon had opened the door to a third position, and Huston could now argue for something he had intuited all along—that the religions are 'the same but different,' leading to and encountering the same truth on the esoteric level, but different on the exoteric level. Huston said he had "learned more from Nasr than any other person alive." Nasr, in turn, offered an explanation of the reason why: "The viewpoint of Schuon dazzled Huston when he discovered it, and it was through me, which is why he says he learned so much from me, because Schuon's position gave him a closet in which to hang all his clothes, one could say. He had found a space within which everything he had learned could be placed in all honesty without distorting things. This was very, very precious for him." After twenty-five years, the missing puzzle piece was in his pocket. "To use the 'Tailor's Analogy,'" Huston said with a smile, offering a redacted version of the position, "Religion is ultimately like pants: plural at the bottom and singular at the top."

## THE TRADITIONALISTS

Huston had accepted a new position from Schuon but Schuon hadn't actually thought it up. Today this version of perennialism, reifying the value of the historical religions, is commonly termed "Traditionalism," and its earlier proponent was René Guénon (1886-1951), a French writer of metaphysical theories. Guénon had a few intellectual colleagues, most significantly Ananda Coomaraswamy (1877-1947), who was a friend of William Butler Yeats and the curator of Indian Art at the Boston Museum of Fine Arts. Princeton's Bollingen Series published a three-volume work of his essays on metaphysics, art and symbolism. Coomaraswamy has been lauded by Thomas Merton, Joseph Campbell, Wendell Berry and others. But Guénon had laid the foundations of the perspective by himself. In the 1920s, he had made his living in Paris writing for a Catholic periodical. He was also beginning to articulate his own views, soon to be shared in such books as *Man and His Becoming According to the Vedanta* (1925) and *The Symbolism of the Cross* (1931). Following the death of his first wife, in 1930, Guénon moved to Cairo, where he hoped to join a Sufi brotherhood. There he converted to Islam, marrying a Egyptian woman and starting a family.

Like Huston—and Huxley, Tillich and Niebuhr—Guénon believed the West had become too enamored of its industrial toys and the science that had generated them, eventually advancing his position in *The Reign of Quantity* (1945). The pretensions of science to authority in all realms of inquiry had incubated a recalcitrant view toward metaphysics that he thought was misleading, instituting both an individuated and collective myopia toward reality. To modern man, esoteric insights were nothing but delusions or ruses based on sentimentality and emotionalism, but Guénon contended that, "If one were to ask the 'positivists', as well as the partisans of Herbert Spencer's famous theory of the 'unknowable', by what authority they affirm that there are things [such as the Divine Ground] which cannot be known, the question would run a good risk of remaining unanswered, the more so because some of them seem quite simply to confuse the 'unknown'—that is, what is unknown to themselves, with the 'unknowable.'"[7] Without the guidance of religion and its visionaries, the West had devolved into a state of decadence, cynicism and immorality that upset Guénon—which is another reason why he had abandoned Paris and the West.[8]

For Guénon, the necessary growth into a healthier and more holistic way of living would not happen in this epoch. Individually, and for select groups who had found their way into the Infinite, the situation was not so completely abysmal, but the situation was terrifying nonetheless, given that the masses were so clearly floundering. Guénon wrote his books for those few readers who were awake enough to cut through the delusions of the modern world and free themselves, and Schuon, from the moment he first discovered Guénon, agreed with him overall in both outlook and approach.

Schuon read Guénon for the first time while living in Paris in the 1930s, and after visiting the man in Cairo in 1938 became the St. Paul of his perspective; however, the two men disagreed over how modernism should be dealt with, as Jacob Needleman has astutely pointed out.[9] Guénon called for an abandonment of the industrial world and its technological upgrades, while Schuon hoped to reform this world by reinvigorating its religious traditions. Schuon wasn't as nostalgic about the ancient world as Guénon was, or as pessimistic about the future. Schuon believed that with the right approach, metaphysics could be returned to its rightful place in Western ideology, thus, as Needleman explains, he wished to do what Guénon didn't think possible.[10]

Huston again sided with Schuon, finding Guénon's critique of the West "so uncompromisingly negative"[11] that it had little ability to inspire, despite his brilliant metaphysical theories. Modern man may have gotten lost in the woods, but his way out couldn't be found by overly criticizing him or by destroying his institutions outright. If the traditional religions were revitalized, perhaps Scientism's death grip on the humanities would be loosened and the West could correct its course toward a different sort of Brave New World. Mark Sedgwick, a professor at the American University in Cairo, titled his personal view of the Traditionalists *Against the Modern World* (2004). The title isn't an entirely accurate characterization. Not all of the Traditionalists pined for the past, and Huston, more accurately, pined only for the Timeless and Eternal—a different orientation toward time altogether and one that to his mind could never be out of vogue.

## Joining the Maryamiyya sufi order

Schuon contended that if the initiatory circles inside the various faiths were revitalized, and if members of those circles could meet with each other to discuss their esoteric insights, foundations of mutual understanding and respect could be fostered among the religions, even as adepts bolstered their respective traditions. This was the ground that Huston had in common with Schuon and Nasr, and this is why he decided to join their spiritual order. It wasn't a requirement among Traditionalists that he should do so—and many of them were firmly rooted in other traditions—but becoming a Sufi (albeit a "Methodist Sufi," as Huston characterized it) would give Huston yet another chance to understand a religion from the inside out.

Frithjof Schuon (1907-1998) was born of German parents in Basel, Switzerland. He moved to France as an adolescent to attend school and later wrote all of his books in French. After serving in the French army for nearly two years, he moved to Paris and started working as an artist and fabric designer, though his deeper interest in religion and spirituality kept pulling him away from that career. During the 1930s, and after discovering the works of Guénon, he made several trips to Algeria and Morocco to meet with Sufis—and to Cairo to meet with Guénon. While in Africa, Schuon sought out reputed adepts and then, when back in Paris, worked on his Arabic. After World War II, he settled in Lausanne, Switzerland, becoming a Swiss citizen, and in 1949 married a German Swiss woman. His trips to Africa would become the pivot around which his life turned for many years to come.

Schuon shared with Guénon the view that there is no spiritual path outside the revealed religions, and no entry into esoteric insight except through an initiatic circle. In addition, he also accepted Guénon's view that among the most vibrant and intact circles of mystics were those of the Sufi brotherhoods of North Africa, and hence he made his fastidious trips. The result was that in 1932, he met and became the disciple of Shaykh Ahmad al-'Alawi, the Sufi about whom Lings later wrote his doctoral dissertation, published as *A Sufi Saint of the Twentieth Century* (1961).

From his studies, Schuon learned that Sufism arose from the teachings of itinerant, Muslim holy men and women living in the Middle East in the Eighth and Nineth centuries C.E. These mystics, who were poor and wore only rough wool—in Arabic, *suf*, from which it is possible that their name derives—believed that the techniques of esoteric awakening should only be practiced under the direction of a master, called a *shaykh*. Furthermore, to protect the purity of their methods, these *shaykhs* demanded secrecy and would offer initiation only to disciples (*murid*) whom they deemed worthy. When the proper requirements had been met, novices were then trained in the methods that lead to *haqiqa*, the 'Truth,' having as its essential element *dhikr*, the 'remembrance' or 'recollection' of God.

As Sufism established itself and became formalized, various techniques for 'remembering' rose up in its brotherhoods. In Turkey, the Mevlevis twirl in place, earning the name 'whirling dervishes'; but the most prevalent practice in North Africa and in the rest of the Islamic world is the repetition of God's name. By repeating the holy name of Allah like a mantra, the novice remembers God—or more accurately, 're-members' himself or herself to God—and when this reconnection becomes complete, the adept experiences *fana* or 'extinction,' a state in which the Sufi has no part of his or her soul separate from God. This is the Sufi definition of enlightenment. Schuon learned from al-'Alawi that this was the goal of all Sufism, and he became intent upon achieving it.

Shaykh al-'Alawi, must have been quite remarkable, given the many testimonies that we have of him, and Schuon seems fortunate to have been accepted by him as a disciple so quickly. Sadly then, in 1934, only one year after Schuon became his disciple, the Shaykh died unexpectedly of heart failure, catalyzing a strange set of events in Schuon's life.

Schuon was in Paris when the master died. Schuon calculated that at the precise instant of al-'Alawi's death, he had been given a vision. Finding his mind suddenly and unexpectedly filled with the name of God, Schuon had left work and wandered along the quays of the Seine for hours in a sort of trance. Later taking this trance to be more than coincidental, he dropped everything and went to Africa to visit the grave of al-'Alawi, and to meet with al-'Alawi's successor. According to Schuon, the new shaykh, Adda Bentounes, also believed the trance had been providential and conferred on Schuon the position of *muqaddam* or 'deputy,' allowing him to initiate new members into the order. Eventually he renamed his branch of the *tariqah* the Maryamiyya, those "of Mary," to distinguish them from their Algerian brethren, the 'Alawiyya.[12]

Before Huston joined the initiatic circle, Schuon was living near Lausanne, which became the center of his growing group of followers. Nasr had put Huston in touch with Whithall Perry, Schuon's secretary, who told him he would be welcome to visit the Shaykh any time he wished. Huston got his chance in February of 1972. After arriving in Switzerland, Huston quickly realized that Perry acted as a sort of gatekeeper for the Shaykh:

> I had to first pass an interview with an attendant—the keeper of the gates, as it were—who had to approve of my position on matters important to Schuon. Did I, the attendant asked, believe in evolution? I sensed that if you accepted evolution, and Majestic Divinity, as the key to explaining life, you would be bidden a polite *adieu*. In fact I do believe in evolution.... But on the technicality that evolutionary theory has not yet adequately explained consciousness, I answered a resounding, 'Me? Evolution? Absolutely not!' I was then ushered into my audience with Frithjof Schuon.[13]

Huston recounted what Schuon was like that day. "He was very austere and I was somewhat intimidated. He looked something like an Old Testament prophet. He always wore robes." James Cutsinger, a professor of theology and friend of Huston's who also knew Schuon, offered further details that suggest what it must have been like to meet him: "Schuon was off the scale [and] certainly a spiritual genius of some kind. He seemed to have a quality where his ontology was the same as his epistemology, if I could put it that way. He knew with his being and not just his brain." Cutsinger elaborated: "Whenever I asked him a question it was as though he'd been waiting fifty years to be asked exactly that question, because the answer always came like a thunderbolt, just like lightning. There was never 'well, hmmm, I guess this is what I'd say about that.' There was never any pause or deliberation, and the answers always had a curious ring of truth to them."

Part of the reason for Schuon's formal bearing, Huston later learned, was his belief that a "truly spiritual man must always be a personification of nobility." This caused him to require specific rules of decorum in both dress and behavior, not only for himself but also for his disciples. Certain artworks were preferred in the *tariqah's* facilities. Sometimes Huston saw wisdom in these rules and sometimes they just seemed quirky. For example, one of Schuon's idiosyncrasies was that he would not allow the "hideous dialect" of German-Swiss to be spoken at his center in Basel or Lausanne. He expected followers to address each other in pure German if they were not speaking French or Arabic.[14]

During Huston's first visit with him, Schuon explained that he wanted Huston to be initiated in the United States since he was an American. Huston was amenable to this, so when he returned home, he contacted Schuon's group in Bloomington, Indiana, where the American center was—and still is—situated. Huston visited a few months later and an initiation ceremony followed. "It involved various people who were at different stages, holding hands and swaying and so on," Huston reminisced. "And then we sat down and the signal was given and the person leading the ceremony turned to me, shook my hand and said, 'I give you your Islamic—your initiatic—name.' And that was it. And when I was given that name, meaning the 'Glory of the Religion,' I think I audibly sighed. I mean I felt unworthy. It was the highest name he could have given me!" [15]

Huston was now 53 years old and a Sufi with a new set of practices, including praying five times a day and observing the fast of Ramadan. He stopped his Zen meditations ("I realized that meditation isn't the only way, and I wasn't doing well at that at all."), and focused entirely on Islam, writing at the time: "No other faith now interests me more, and in none are explorations more rewarding. Over the Arab world too the heavens have opened." [16] For the next ten years he would remain deeply involved with the Maryamiyya order, reporting to Nasr regularly as the group's stateside representative. "That's when Schuon just moved into my life," he remarked.

## A BRIEF MEETING WITH TIMOTHY LEARY

While visiting Schuon in Switzerland, in February of 1972, Huston didn't realize that his old pal Timothy Leary was also living there. During the five years that had passed since Huston had last seen him, Leary had gone on a wild adventure—in fact, several wild adventures, including getting arrested for marijuana (twice); getting sentenced to several years in the California State Penitentiary at San Luis Obispo; undertaking a daring escape from that prison; taking a trip to Africa under an alias; spending a few months hiding out in Algeria with Eldridge Cleaver (a Black Panther and, like Leary, on the lam from the FBI); escaping from Cleaver (who hoped to use money from Leary's books to fund his militant projects); initiating a plea for asylum in Switzerland; and then, in 1971, being put into a Swiss prison. Just a few months prior to Huston's visit, Leary had been released from jail and was living peacefully in Basel, Schuon's hometown and the place where LSD was invented in 1938.

Michael Horowitz, who was Leary's archivist, recalled the man's state of mind. "I visited Tim in Switzerland in the winter of 1972. Tim said that even with angry cops and Black Panthers out to get him, his life was still easier than it had been when he had had to cross the Bay Bridge in rush hour traffic." Leary was putting a good face on things, but Horowitz admitted that Tim was under terrific pressure both personally and politically. "Richard Nixon had declared him the 'most dangerous man alive,'" Horowitz observed, "so Tim was worried that the Swiss government might extradite him to the United States."

Some of the IFIFers had helped Leary make bail (e.g., Walter Houston Clark mortgaged his home to send Tim $20,000) but Leary—by then without a passport—could, as Horowitz surmised, "only wait to see what the Swiss would do with him."

Richard Alpert, calling himself Ram Dass, had just published *Be Here Now*, a bestselling manifesto on the need for spiritual awakening, but Leary's own book projects were on hold. "He was trying to work out several book deals," Horowitz commented, "but he didn't have access to his manuscripts and papers, which I was keeping safe for him but didn't dare travel with. There was real danger of them being confiscated by the FBI. So

I had gone to Switzerland to see what Tim wanted me to do. It was a crazy time. Many forces were arranged against Tim, hoping, as they were, to keep him out of print."

When Leary finally tracked Huston down in the resort town of Lugano, he was still worried about extradition, whereas Huston was sailing along smoothly, having just received two more honorary Ph.D.s, one from Hobart College and one from William Smith College. Leary was a political refugee, while Huston was a featured speaker for the Jung and Kazantzakis Seminar. By coincidence, the six-week program in Switzerland was titled "Castalia," focusing on the connections between the work of Jung and the novelist Herman Hesse, whose last book, *Magister Ludi*, described an order of scholarly monks living in a fictitious institute named Castalia—the very name that Leary had used for his 'utopia' at Millbrook. As representatives of two very different Castalias, the two old friends were experiencing quite different fates.

Leary came roaring up on the back of a motorcycle driven by one of his Swiss supporters. "I was happy to see him," Huston recalled, "but he looked rough and I knew he was having lots of trouble." What Huston didn't know was that in the past year, Leary had, according to Greenfield, one of Leary's biographers, started experimenting with heroin, one consequence of which was that he was even more manic than before.[17] Leary, who was still wearing his trademark white tennis shoes, white slacks and a white sweater, spoke with Huston on the street for a bit and then suggested that Huston and Kendra visit him when they had a chance. A few days later, Huston, Kendra and a young professor named Katz from Harvard piled into a cab and went to Leary's hotel.

Leary mopped his brow incessantly and chain-smoked as they discussed old times and new directions. Tim told Huston about Horowitz' visit, and that Horowitz was hiding his papers (which included letters from Huston) from the FBI; the hope was that Horowitz could somehow put together a publishable manuscript for Leary that would get him out of debt. Huston listened attentively and wished him well with the project, but worried to himself about how fidgety Leary had become. Leary grinned continuously but somehow looked sad. He seemed to be confirming he had taken the wrong path that night long ago at Millbrook when they had dissolved IFIF. "Judging from his appearance," Huston related, "he seemed near the end of his rope."

The two friends said goodbye, and as Huston walked back to the conference, what stuck in his mind was the question Leary had greeted him with that day. Smiling, Tim had said: "Nobody ever changes, do they?" Huston found himself reflecting that for Tim at least, no truer words had ever been spoken. Greenfield described Tim as a "self-proclaimed cheerleader for change who himself had never been able to change," and Huston fully agreed. "Tim was an Irish Rebel and nobody—including Huxley, Dick Alpert, or me—was ever going to get him to be something else. You had to accept Tim for what he was, and he could be quite brilliant at times, though he also tended to be self-destructive." Horowitz agreed and disagreed when we discussed the matter. "Tim was certainly his own person, and Huston is right about that. But I don't believe Tim was 'strung out' in those days on anything but the terrific pressure he was under—not that Huston says he was doing drugs. Tim *did* experiment with heroin, like at least half the Beat artists and rock celebrities that he knew, but he never got hooked. John Higgs, in his book *I Have America Surrounded*, gives a more accurate view of Tim's years in exile than Greenfield does."

Whatever the case, it would be several years before Huston and Tim met again, in California for one of Leary's book signings, with which he had asked Huston to help.

Huston was convinced Tim had unintentionally proven that operating inside of the system was a healthier way to create change than advocating social anarchy, all-out revolution, or asserting oneself to the point of personal breakdown.

# Chapter Eighteen:
# Forgotten Truth

What the power of the Slowing taught me is what the Source of All is constantly yearning for: that each of us will know without doubt that we are loved, and that we are intimately, irrevocably part of the endless creation of love, and that we will join, with full freedom and consciousness, the joyous creativity that is Nature.

Gerald G. May

All that exists, in whatever mode this may be, necessarily participates in universal principles, and nothing exists except by participation in these principles, which are the eternal and immutable essences contained in the permanent actuality of the Divine Intellect. Consequently, it can be said that all things, however contingent they may be in themselves, express or represent these principles in their own way and according to their order of existence, for otherwise they would be purely and simply nothingness. Thus, from one order to another, all things are linked together and correspond, to come together in total and universal harmony, for harmony is nothing other than the reflection of principial unity in the manifested world; and it is this correspondence which is the veritable basis of symbolism.

René Guénon, *Autorité spirituelle et pouvoir temporel*

There were no visible signs that Huston had become a Sufi (he did wear a beard, though for the reason that Kendra liked it) and he never went to a mosque to perform his daily prayers. However, he was formally involved in the sense that he spoke with Nasr by phone quite regularly and sometimes worked on projects with other members of the spiritual order, forwarding the viewpoints of his branch of the *tariqah* (a Sufi order). Huston was travelling a lot in those days, and whenever his journeys took him anywhere near Washington, D.C., he would stop over for a day or two and visit with Seyyed Hossein, who then mounted a lunch for members of the group who lived nearby. "It was always a Persian lunch," Huston remembered. In a later age of terrorist attacks, along with the backlash of Islamophobia that followed, this peaceful circle of Sufis would probably be on a CIA watch list as a potential terrorist cell.

## SCHUON'S PANENTHEISM AND THE 'INTELLECTUS'

Schuon and Nasr were pleased to have such a distinguished scholar as Huston in their midst, especially since no other member of the group, including Nasr himself, was as well known to the public as Huston. And Huston was delighted also, in that Schuon not only provided the answer to his riddle about how the religions fit together, but introduced him to a competent set of allies in his fight against Scientism, the killing jar of spirituality. Many of the Traditionalists, including Brown, Lings, Titus Burckhardt, Marco Pallis and Nasr, were respected scholars in their own right who could be characterized as 'focused' or even 'pious' but never as irrational, cultish or absurd. This was important to Huston, who had carefully groomed his credibility in academic circles. The Traditionalists had gleaned many useful ideas from their scrutiny of the metaphysical theories of the past, and Huston believed those ideas had potential for addressing the shortcomings of the modern world. Why not work with scholars who were on the same page?

Huston was also in the Schuon camp for other reasons, including Schuon's breakdown of religion into its exoteric and esoteric aspects. He had also taken over Schuon's views of why the universe exists at all, and how mystics are able to know their place in it.

Schuon's latter views are similar to what Arthur Lovejoy had termed the "Great Chain of Being." In traditional cultures, Lovejoy pointed out, people believed that life is arranged according to a hierarchy of existences, starting from the most crude, humble and basic, and moving up through myriad layers of sophistication to an ulitmate *ens perfectissimum*, which usually takes the form of a supreme Being or Divinity. Adapting this viewpoint, Schuon argued that everything in the cosmos, and even the cosmos itself (as a context for all the other things), manifests out of the one Divine Ground. As it arises, it becomes distinct and differentiated. This creates a falsehood of sorts (Hindus and Buddhists term it *maya*, or "illusion") since nothing can ever completely break away from the Oneness, as waves on the ocean can never achieve complete separation from the ocean itself. In this world of seemingly autonomous existences, there is a hierarchy of physical structures and nervous systems, ranked from least sophisticated to most, as well as a range of conscious states, ranging from that of a bacterium to that of a Buddha.

Huston had already heard much about this viewpoint from Swami Satprakashananda, since in the Hindu iteration of the Great Chain of Being the various levels of the hierarchy form the steppingstones by which a reincarnating soul (*jiva*) moves closer and closer to experiencing its true identity as the Divine Ground. Each step up the Chain affords a more complete view of the landscape because each step brings a more complex physiology and consciousness capable of having such an experience. These steps are taken by the soul because the illusion of ultimate separateness from the Divine Ground creates a sense of limits that feels somehow false and claustrophobic—particularly since each soul is ultimately THE Soul. On the human level, this claustrophobia generates a desire to know one's true condition, which is what generates the 'seeker' mentality that some people find themselves experiencing in life. It is this desire to throw off false boundaries and touch the truth of one's own being that drives us toward Buddhahood, but, for Schuon, that is not all it does. Schuon believed this desire to know oneself comes originally from the Divine Ground itself. It is this desire to know Itself which caused the Ground to create the cosmos in the first place. For Schuon, as well as for Swami Satprakashananda, the Sacred Oneness has created this universe as a context in which to become aware of its own nature.

Offering an analogy, Schuon explained that as the eye cannot see itself, the Divine

Ground, in its unmanifest state, cannot know its own being. To gain self-knowledge, the eye must look into a mirror, creating a second, 'illusory' eye that it is capable of perceiving as an external object. Similarly, the Oneness creates a false duality (a sense that there is something outside of itself) by rising up into waves of multiplicity that provide a context for reflecting on its true nature. Using another analogy, sugar is sweet but doesn't know it's sweet for the simple reason that it doesn't have a tongue; so by creating a physical universe as a context, the Oneness is trying to grow a 'tongue' with which to 'taste' its own nature. As this context arises in the universe, with all its illusions of separateness and duality, the Oneness becomes restlessness in its desire to transcend the boundaries it has imposed on itself, and this friction causes its drive to create physical structures (ants, aardvarks, and apes) of varying capabilities of grasping the reality of its situation. The Oneness becomes aware of itself, or comes to know itself, ultimately through the human being, which is the center and apex of creation precisely because of its ability to know the Divine Ground. For Schuon, the import of the human state lies in this ability to know. When a person (for example, the Buddha) experiences the Divine Ground at his or her core, the Divine Ground simultaneously realizes its own true nature, since the essence of the person experiencing the Divine Ground *is* synonymous with the Divine Ground itself. Again, at that point it is the Divine Ground within the person that is waking up. Schuon saw this as the eternal, spiritual dynamic of all existence and believed that the generic religiosity of man is born out of it. "The *religio perennis* is fundamentally this," Schuon once summarized, "the Real entered into the illusory, so that the illusory might be able to return unto the Real."[1]

Huston wondered why the Oneness, in its original undifferentiated state, would want to know itself in the first place. (If there was originally no duality, why would it pine for something else? How would it even be aware that it was missing out on something?) But he learned that for Schuon and the Traditionalists this was a moot point. From the level of the Transcendent there can be neither hunger for knowledge nor a context for asking questions like 'why.' But what we do know is that it *does* happen, since the world in fact exists. For the Traditionalists, the closest we come to a reason why is that manifesting is an aspect of the Divine Ground's inherent nature—and otherwise a great mystery.

For some reason, perhaps related to its quality as consciousness, the Oneness simply wants to know Itself. It is only after the world of forms comes into existence that its sentient beings come into existence and experience the desire to know and awaken and to live fully. According to Schuon, Revelation helps us to know that this desire, the desire to know and awaken and live fully, originates in, stems from and echoes the Divine Nature. Schuon believed that because each discrete moment of creation is an iteration of the Divine Ground, we can infer that the general 'longing for more' that we find in all creatures—including the plant world's desire to follow the sun—is a subset of the Transcendent's cosmic desire for awakening. Every desire of every living thing has its ultimate purpose in fulfilling the cosmic desire, which can only be quenched when the Transcendent knows that it is the Transcendent, and this occurs whenever a person wakes up to his or her full nature.

In theology, this viewpoint that the cosmos is the Divine Ground in some process of becoming more conscious is termed *panentheism*, and Huston, like Schuon, was fascinated by the idea of it. Is the Oneness trying to *know* itself as some sort of an improvement on simply *being* itself? ('I don't just want to *be* sugar, I want to taste sugar!'). And when the Oneness is awakened in a person, does that person then become a conduit for the living presence of the Divine Ground in the world? Does that person become the eyes, ears, tongue and fingertips of God? Schuon believed that the answers to all these questions was 'Yes.'

*****

Besides the Great Chain of Being, another view of Schuon's that Huston appreciated concerned the aspect of mind that is capable of knowing the nature of the Cosmic Plan. When mystics are revealing the secrets of life (from the inside out as it were), what function of mind allows them to do so? Plato termed this faculty the *nous*, translated as *intellectus* by medieval Western European theologians and mystics. This is the faculty to which Schuon refers with the term "Intellect," which he distinguishes from what we have come to mean by that word in the modern period, namely the cerebral mind. Cutsinger, a contemporary Traditionalist, explains the difference between the two functions of mind:

> While reason operates one step at a time, proceeding by stages from premise to conclusions, the Intellect goes straight to the conclusion, although in this case to speak of a conclusion could be a little misleading, for there is no summing up or synthesis of prior particularities. 'Reason obtains knowledge like a man walking about and exploring a countryside by successive discoveries, whereas the Intellect contemplates the same countryside from a mountain height.' . . . Reason conceives—that is, it holds things together. But the Intellect *perceives*. It cuts right through those things, directly apprehending their esoteric meaning or essence. It is to the spiritual or suprasensible order what vision and the other physical senses are to the material or empirical order.[2]

The Intellect or Intellectus is, for Schuon, a faculty for knowing the Infinite, and in this way is analogous to a sense organ such as the eye. Yet Schuon was always very careful to point out that even if someone had a good facility with the Intellectus, that did not mean he or she was necessarily enlightened. Enlightenment could come only when the person grasped the Transcendent with all aspects of his or her being, while the Intellect is only that part of the human mind that 'senses' the Absolute and its plan. Cutsinger summarizes Schuon's perspective like this: "The Intellect is only 'a mirror.' . . . Realization means that 'our being, and not merely our thought, participates in the objects which the mirror reflects.' This is why intellection must be joined with Virtue and Prayer if we are to grasp, and then become, what we see."[3]

The Intellect then is a clear noetic intuition that functions somewhat like a spiritual Geiger counter, sounding off when a hunch or theory has the ring of truth about it, and this entirely resonated with Huston's experience. At significant moments in his life, he had 'just been sure' of what he had read or heard from others; this had been the case during his 'Night of Fire' and when he first read Heard. Something inside had yelled out, 'That's it!' He found he couldn't deny that inner voice. And as his life progessed, his many insights and awakenings taught him to trust that aspect of his mind, the Intellectus. His powers of reason had been applied to the project of articulating and defending its choices, but reason was secondary to intellection.

*****

Schuon was Huston's spiritual master, but did he consider Schuon enlightened? "No, he was a *savant*. He had a direct window onto the Absolute, but it's only a window and there's a lot that doesn't fall within that. As long as he was looking out that window, he was almost infallible. He had a gift but he wasn't enlightened, at least not in the Buddhist sense."

Schuon believed that even accurate descriptions of the Oneness are provisional, given that by their very nature they are less than the Oneness. "Descriptions proceed through forms," Huston once observed, "and the Absolute is formless."[4] Huston's personal goal as a philosopher—like Huxley's before him—was not to uncover a systematic philosophy but to challenge Scientism's death-grip on philosophy. He wanted to present alternatives, and so he didn't see himself as hitching his wagon to Schuon's to the exclusion of all other possibilities. He was exploring a particular approach to Truth, as he had also explored Vedanta and Zen, and he still had no intention of become dogmatic in his views.

Sedgwick has called Huston's Traditionalism "soft," maintaining that Huston is more open-minded than the hardliners of the camp—who, for instance, believe that esoteric insight is only gained if one joins an initiatic circle.[5] Gray Henry, a close friend of Huston's for many years and the director of Fons Vitae, a publisher of books on religion, pointed out that Huston had never believed there was only one way to do anything, and told a story to illustrate her point. Once, when Huston had visited her in Louisville, Kentucky, he had spoken to a group of students about the value of the Intellectus. "The path of *jnana yoga*," he said, "is that in which the Intellect discriminates between the Absolute and the relative." One of the young people then asked if it were ever possible to follow two levels of the same faith—for instance, the path of devotion to God AND the path of the Intellect. "Huston whirled around on his cane," Gray continued, "remarking, 'My Dear, we have both a heart and a mind!'" Gray laughed. "It was so typical of him," she said, "to want to embrace all possibilities and settle for no one approach to things. Reality is much too mysterious for that." That day, Huston and Gray had finished filming his views on death and the different faith traditions, *Death and Transformation: Personal Reflections of Huston Smith*. And that evening, they would head out to Wendell and Tanya Berry's farm for supper, where the two men discussed their youth on farms and their early experience as church goers.

## SETTLED IN SYRACUSE

By the mid-1970s, Huston and Kendra had put down roots and were enjoying themselves immensely. Huston was finally settled into an institution where he felt fulfilled. Huston's department at Syrcuse was supportive and he was delighted by the opportunity to mentor graduate students in their program. Phil Novak, whom Huston had met at the conference in Switzerland the summer he met Leary there, had come to Syracuse to work on his Ph.D. directly under Huston. Ray Gawronski, whom Huston had met on the 1970 IHP trip, arrived for the same reason—actually moving in with his mentor's family. "When I went to Syracuse," Gawronski said, "I was to have had some sort of Teaching Assistantship, but when I showed up, it had somehow disappeared. . . . I was left high and dry, but the Smiths instantly came up with the plan that I would live with them and help out with things in their house. So I had the great blessing of living with them for the year 1974-1975, and I was treated like one of the family."

Kendra enjoyed Gawronski's company. He was useful around the house, sometimes cooking wonderful Polish dishes, playing Chopin on the piano and attending to other duties, such as driving Huston to work. "Huston was so much the absent-minded professor," Gawronski recalled, "that he tended to forget he was stopped at a traffic light until the cars behind him reminded him. It was better if someone else drove him." In exchange for such services, Huston gave Gawronski advice on his professional direction. Though Huston was practicing Sufism, he counseled Gawronski to reclaim his family's traditional heritage. "I had gone to Syracuse to study comparative religions, but with Huston's help I became intellectually re-wedded to my earlier Catholic faith, and after my master's degree, I entered the Jesuits."

The Smiths accepted Gawronski as a friend, and Kendra grew close to him, enjoying his company and the pleasure of having someone else in the house, now that the girls were gone. Karen, their eldest daughter, had finished her B.A. in psychology and her M.A. in anthropology at Berkeley in the 1960s and now had a daughter, Sierra. Gael had moved to California in the late 1960s, where she worked at the Esalen Institute and met Ida Rolf, an innovator of techniques in deep-tissue massage. In August of 1971, Gael married Stuart Karlan in what Kendra described as a "Big Sur hippie wedding," and in 1972, she gave birth to Serena, who would become the apple of Huston's eye. (Serena was born in New York City, in an apartment where several of her parents' friends chanted to keep the room calm, and later became, according to one relative, "the quintessential flower child.") Kim, the youngest, had also moved to California. She left the family home outside Boston in1967 to attend Antioch College in Ohio, and after finishing a B.A. in both Ceramics and Chemistry, headed west to be near her family. Once settled, she started work as a self-employed potter, switched to acupuncture, and then settled into a job for a corporation handling international money transactions. Later, and for many years, she was a first grade teacher.

Kendra completed her Master's degree in 1964 and later received a Ph.D. in psychology from the experimental program at Union Graduate School. She wrote her dissertation on Buddhist psychology under the direction of Don Klein, with Daniel Goleman also serving on her committee. Since finishing her Masters, she had worked in mental health clinics, "doing counseling and therapy with children and adults, mostly parents," and at Syracuse worked in the university's counseling center while also a state-run clinic in the city. She sometimes worked long hours but enjoyed helping young people sort out life's challenges.

Huston and Kendra were experiencing a whole new life. Even America felt different to them now, with the war in Vietnam finally over and, in 1974, with Richard Nixon stepping down as President to avoid impeachment over the Watergate fiasco. The draft was ended; relations with the Chinese had resumed (thanks to Nixon); Daniel Ellsberg[6] had released the Pentagon Papers; and in terms of economic stability, America was enjoying the largest middle class and the greatest economic equality in its history. Both Smiths remembered their ten-year period in Syracuse as the best years of their lives, and part of the reason for this was that during that period Huston published his first bestseller (and arguably his most important book) since *The Religions of Man*.

## Forgotten Truth

In 1975, Huston wrote *Forgotten Truth*, dedicated to Kendra and published with the subtitle, "the Common Vision of the World's Religions." Here for the first time he laid out in print the details of his mature viewpoint, and in less than 200 pages introduced a new generation of readers to the perennial philosophy, delivering a book that was more readable than Huxley's earlier description and much kinder to religion. Regarding this last point, Huston presented Schuon's Traditionalist perspective but again outdid one of his mentors, writing with greater clarity and a much warmer tone than Huxley. Ken Wilber (whose career Huston had recently helped take off by recommending Wilber's manuscript for *The Spectrum of Consciousness* to his publisher) would write in his own book that *Forgotten Truth* was the "best introduction" to the perennial philosophy ever written. When Wilber updated *Spectrum* in 2001, he saw no reason to revise that comment.[7] Huxley had teased out many more nuances of the perennial philosophy than Huston, and given many more references to the spiritual adepts of the past, but his book was an "anthology of mysticism," while Huston's was intended only as a brief outline and overview. Together these two books are complementary and many readers move from one to the other and back again.

Whether or not one believes there is a perennial philosophy (and, if so, whether or not one believes there is a transcendent unity of religions that goes with it), Huston's humanitarian desire is admirable, then and now. He provided a philosophical position that makes sense of reality and also gives people a common roof under which their religions can live peacefully. In seeking a way to create social harmony within nations and between them, Huston believed it could be found in Traditionalism. Here was a view allowing for the 'dignity of difference' to shine while positing a unification of all religions on the esoteric level.

Months after the book was released, Huston republished an article he had written in 1968 for *The Eastern Buddhist* while returning home from Japan on an ocean liner.[8] In "Four Theological Negotiables," he argued that we must be careful to avoid conceptual straitjackets that suggest we are either saved by grace or self-effort; that God is either inside us or outside us; and other such diametrical opposites. These 'either/or' theories can only lead to conflict. In the article, he also offered ways to reconcile these polarities, reminding us that we should play fair with each other and listen to each other's views, for we live in too small a world to do otherwise. "The moral for my thesis is obvious," he wrote. "However different the theological alternatives I listed above may seem—and in ways are—those who are divided by them are [still] on the same ship; in the same boat, we might say."[9] The sooner we wake up to this fact, Huston believed, the better off we'll be. He hoped that *Forgotten Truth* would help pave the way.

*****

Not everyone in academia was happy with *Forgotten Truth* or with having Huxley's views brought back to life. Some scholars applauded it as a brave and well-argued thesis against Scientism and in favor of metaphysics, but others attacked it as a set of mystical meanderings. One of the more interesting sets of criticism, which quickly led to a series of exchanges in print, came out in the *Journal of the American Academy of Religion*. Soon after *Forgotten Truth* was released, Schuon's *Transcendent Unity of Religions* was also reissued. This timing led to an unfavorable review in *JAAR* by Dr. Richard Bush. Huston responded in the December issue,[10] coming immediately to Schuon's defense. This exchange is worth taking a look at, for it summarizes the four main criticisms of Schuon that were popular at the time.

First, Bush argued that Schuon's tiered view of reality placed the Transcendent "too far beyond the world in which we live," to which Huston replied that the tiered view is more metaphorical than scientific.[11] "Logically," he explained, "the Infinite could not *be* such if anything—our world included—lay outside it," but, when speaking of the Infinite with terms gleaned from the world of everyday experience, "it is useful to use the tiered model."[12] However, Huston added, "Its higher levels are not literally elsewhere; they are removed only in the sense of being inaccessible to ordinary consciousness. . . ." We may speak of the Oneness as having parts but Huston believed there is ultimately only the Oneness; from the highest level of reality we realize that *every* aspect of reality is the highest and only aspect. Each part rests and nests within the One—which is why Huston would later sometimes follow Ken Wilber's habit of speaking of a "Great Nest of Being" rather than a "Great Chain."

Bush's second point was that it's difficult to argue against a thesis that claims only to be comprehensible to an elite few, to which Huston responded that the truth of the thesis may be experienced only by an elite few but the thesis itself is a rational position that can easily be understood and discussed. Huston then went on to refute Bush's third argument, that Schuon underplays the ethical dimension of religion, which, of course, was a key point for Huston. Bush had contended that Schuon—by emphasizing the esoteric aspect of religion—had left ethics out of the mix, but Huston contended that, "It is certainly not the case that esoterics consider the ethical unimportant. They will be the first to join exoterics in insisting that if one thinks that he is growing in his love of God but is not in fact growing in his love of man, he is deceiving himself. . . ."[13] Having said this, Huston was, however, willing to acknowledge that for the mystic there IS a level of insight from which nothing is or can be perceived as wrong or out of place. In the relative world there are consequences, but from the perspective of the Infinite, all flux is only the play of the universe (here Huston uses the Hindu term, *lila*) and has no final consequence.

Bush's fourth concern was that Schuon showed "little sympathy for other points of view," and Huston acquiesced to some extent on this charge; however, he then raised a charge of his own. "This opens onto the general question: Assuming that truth matters and one is not a total relativist, what *should* be one's stance toward what one sees to be error?"[14] Huston agreed that Schuon was adamant in his views, but disagreed that Schuon was unwilling to hear arguments against them, or inclined to use Revelation rather than reason to defend them. If Schuon was wrong, *why* was he wrong? To say that he was convinced of his position was not an argument against its validity. The fact was that most scholars, including Bush, were also convinced of their positions. Was Bush criticizing Schuon for being certain, or just for being certain of an unpopular theory? Huston thought the latter was the case, and in the months that followed other scholars were roused against Schuon's views by their incongruity with received knowledge and because of the popularity of *Forgotten Truth*.

It's important to note that in 1976, with Huston then nearly 60 years old, he had finally found and expressed the complete position on religion that he would hold for the rest of his life.

## PLUNGING INTO SUFISM

In 1976, Huston and Kendra took a victory lap of the world, helping to lead another IHP trip abroad, this time entitled "Reality as Truth and Construct: Three Great Perspectives." Huston related to me that, "The first perspective to be covered was Islam, so we went first to Morocco, and then, for another view of Islam, we went to a Muslim *zawiyya* in India. And the second perspective was Hinduism, so we had three weeks in the south, in Pondicherry, and then in the north, in Brindavan. Then for the last perspective, which was East Asia, we visited Hong Kong and, since we couldn't get into Mainland China, Japan."

Huston was the faculty leader this time, and with him went Victor Danner, an Islamicist from Indiana University, and Robert L. Gross, an expert on South Asia at the University of Minnesota. In terms of students, Huston's journal tells us that "eighteen women and fifteen men" signed up for the trip, and four children of the various faculty members were also along. The Danners brought their two young sons and the Grosses brought Almora, their five-year-old daughter. "So there were about forty people in all," Huston remembered.

While getting ready to leave, a handbook was put together and circulated that held short biographical notes about each member of the group, and even Almora got her own bio blurb, saying that she liked to draw, "especially on her legs," and that on the trip she hoped to "ride a camel, an elephant and a lion." Huston couldn't remember if all of her dreams had come true, but then added, "Perhaps not the lion."

Huston's journal tells us that daughter Kim, age 26, was also with them, finally getting her chance to travel around the world with her father as Karen and Gael had done earlier. Huston also outlined the proposed itinerary in his journal: "Sept.15-19, Turner, Maine, for orientation [and a week of group-building exercises]; 20-22 in Bath, England; 23 to Oct.27, Fez, Morocco; Oct.28-Nov.1, vacation in Israel; Nov.2 5, Tehran; Nov.6-Dec.7, Isfahan, Iran; Dec.8-11, Delhi, 12-13, Agra, 14-Jan.9, Varanasi; Jan.10-16, Kumbha Mela; 17-Feb.1, Kathmandu or Bodhgaya [Bodhgaya won out]; Feb.2-21, Madras, 22-Mar.17, Kandy, Sri Lanka; 18-24, vacation in Hong Kong; 25-May 14, Kyoto." Schedules were difficult to keep and there were always contingencies, so the itinerary changed a few times as they moved along, including visiting Israel before Morocco. "We went lurching around the world on those excursions. Kendra and I have both said they were the most demanding years of our lives. No pain, no gain. On one of the trips, we had a student who had an abortion. We had another female student, Gertrude Toll, who contracted head lice and couldn't be welcomed by her host family when we arrived in Japan. Another time we left a student, Bill Becker, behind in a remote part of Morocco and he had to hitchhike back to Fez—you take it from there. We really lurched!"

Huston recalled several highpoints from that trip, including a visit to the Kumbha Mela, a Hindu festival listed in the *Guinness Book of World Records* as the largest annual gathering of human beings on the planet. The Kumbha occurs every three years, but only once in every twelve years is it held in Allahabad, which is considered the most auspicious gathering of all, attracting more than ten million people at the high point of the celebration. Pilgrims arrive on a plain situated between the Ganges and Yamana Rivers where they live in tents, attend devotional celebrations, listen to sermons by swamis, watch yogis tie themselves in knots and, on the propitious day appointed by astrologers, take a ritual bath to insure freedom from rebirth in the confluence of the two sacred rivers. Huston was stunned by this outpouring of spiritual exuberance and happy to have a front row seat for it. He and the group camped right in the thick of the festivities and the intensity of the pilgrims' devotion was infectious, with the IHP group often joining in the dances and chants. It was a weeklong experience that Huston described in glowing prose. But he was even more impressed by something the group witnessed at its next stop, a Sufi enclave in Iran where they had the chance to participate in a Sufi gathering, called a *majlis.*

Huston had learned with joy that Nasr had set the whole thing up before the group arrived. Danner, the Islamicist for the IHP trip, was also a member of Schuon's Sufi order[15] and also eager to participate, since he had never witnessed a *majlis* in Iran before.

Only the men of the IHP group were allowed inside the *zawiyah*, the Sufi residence. The women felt a bit left out on the appointed day when the men were led down the narrow lanes of the old section of Tehran into a compound where fifty or sixty Sufis were seated in a circle on the floor of a large hall. After entering and removing their shoes, Danner pointed out an inscription in Arabic over the door that he then read and translated: "This is not a mosque for the ignorant to clamor in, nor a Ka'ba for idiots to circle. This is a temple of total ruin. Inside are the drunk, gone from themselves."[16]

Phil Novak, Huston's student at Syracuse (later a professor at Dominican University), was acting as a teaching assistant for the trip, and shared details of the *majlis*:

> It was extraordinary. I had heard about the practice of the repetition of the name of God in Sufism. Well, I had heard about that and read about that but here we find ourselves invited in, not to sit on the sidelines but to gather in the circle. And the evening starts. First some words by the Sufi master, then some preliminary chants—it seemed to go on for hours. The lights go down and it gets pitch black . . . they get taken over by the pulse of things.
>
> Maybe some of our guys thought, "I'm going to be an observant anthropologist about this," but I always wanted to be a participant anthropologist, so I threw myself into it completely. And I had one of those little openings, those little *satoris*, altered states of consciousness that at least gave me very concrete evidence of the power of this technique. And as the chant repeated and they rhythmically swayed—of course Sufi practice is very emotional—it's like a calling out—to cry out and yet the chant goes on and who knows when it stops.

Huston offered his description of what happened, including his eyewitness account of Sufi 'drunkenness':

> The hour had grown late. For the climax of the ritual, the few candles that had dimly lit the hall were extinguished, and a hypnotic, pounding chant took over. Gradually I became aware of a man who was sitting opposite me in the swaying circle, his form dimly silhouetted against the faint light from a transom behind him. His movements grew erratic and then agitated as they broke with the swaying rhythm of the circle; then, after a minute or two, convulsions set in, punctuated with a loud outburst of "Allah, Allah, Allah." Quickly two 'bouncers' (as I found myself thinking of them later, because of their hefty size) appeared behind him, smothered him in their embrace, and held him pinioned until his seizures subsided. In ecstatic moments such as that, it could be literally the case that there

was only God in what that *dervish* experienced. Allah could very well have filled his entire mental horizon.[17]

As the *majlis* moved towards its conclusion, there was a murmuring down of voices and the lights slowly came up. "There were people with tears in their eyes," Novak remembered. "People had just been bathed in something deep, and I looked around at everyone and you could really see it. You felt like everybody was your brother. It was a transforming experience. Everyone was so relaxed. Fear was gone and there was a kind of total presence among us." Then food was brought into the room, and as a feast began, the IHP students felt a tremendous camaraderie with the Sufis, though the two groups spoke no common language. Smiles were exchanged and food was eaten from large plates, around which they sat on the floor. Near the close of the evening, Huston stood and approached a Sufi elder who had sat next to him during the repetition of the name. The man rose quickly, smiled back at Huston, took his hands and looked into his eyes. "For several moments they just stood there," Novak reminisced, clearly moved by what had taken place. "I thought it was a case of wisdom staring into wisdom, or self-surrender staring into self-surrender. I'll never forget that moment."

When the meeting concluded, Huston said goodbye to everyone and made his way out onto the street with Nasr. He seemed to be somewhat 'drunk' himself, given what happened next. Talking to Nasr about the *majlis*, Huston suddenly became animated, expressing his excitement and gratitude to Nasr for setting things up. The street was crowded and the traffic, though congested, was moving quickly, presenting a challenge for Nasr, since Huston wasn't adept at crossing the busy streets of Tehran. "So I took his hand and said, 'look, come with me.'" Nasr chuckled as he told this story. "So I navigated through one side of the street and then we were stuck in the middle, with the traffic coming from both ways. There were these two streams of cars whizzing behind us and in front." Nasr had no problem moving forward but worried that his friend was scared; however, when he looked over at Huston, the man seemed to be in a trance. Huston was oblivious to the cars and kept badgering Nasr with questions about the *majlis*. "We're in the middle of the street and in danger of getting run over," Nasr remarked, "and he can't wait until we get to the other side to start asking me questions about Sufism! That's how caught up in it he was!"

## A LONG-OVERDUE APOLOGY

The meeting with the Sufis was the most inspiring event of the trip for Huston but the most *meaningful* moment had come earlier, while they were visiting India. Kim had fallen in love with the beauty of India's art and architecture, along with the deep devotion of its rural people; she had heard her father lecture about India's ancient and profound philosophies many times, but it was actually the lives of the people, so close-knit in their clans and castes—and so devout in their religious practices—that had the greatest impact on her. One day, while sitting in Huston's hotel room, Kim told her father about all this, and their conversation lead to an emotional breakthrough. "Her reaction startled me," Huston later wrote in *Tales of Wonder*. "A memory, long forgotten and walled off, came back into consciousness. 'Kim, if there is one thing in my life I regret,' I said to her, 'it was leaving you and Karen and Gael when I went on Mr. Danforth's trip in 1957.'"[18] Kim stared at him in astonishment and it took a moment for her to realize what her father was saying. In her bio blurb for the trip's handbook, she had written that when she was seven years old her parents had taken a seven-month "business trip" around the world, and that in their absence she had "formed stronger bonds with her sisters, looking to them for love and guidance." There had been some benefit in this, but there had also been feelings of loneliness and abandonment.

According to Huston, Kim had, as a child, bragged to her friends that her parents were "explorers" but "what she really felt but could not express was: her parents had died."[19] Twenty years later, sitting in an Indian hotel, Huston knew that though he had made the right choice for his career in 1957, those choices had caused emotional distress for his children—and especially for Kim, the youngest. "And that understanding allowed me, in that hotel room, to apologize. When I asked her forgiveness, Kim broke down and cried. And cried. And cried. And I cried with her."

## ANOTHER SAD GOODBYE

While the IHP group was in Japan that May, Huston got word that his mother had passed away. He quickly put together a small bag and flew home for a few days to attend the funeral.

Huston's parents had been living for many years in Marionville, Missouri, in The Ozark Methodist Manor, a retirement home whose services were available free to missionaries. Wesley and Alice had enjoyed it there, where the townspeople were friendly and the location, in the southwest of the state, was scenic and pleasant, and where they could also be amused by the colony of white squirrels that had lived on the property since the founding of the town in 1845.

During their years in Marionville, the Smiths had lived in several facilities on the Manor's property. "It was a gradual thing," Huston recalled. "First they had their own little cottage, and when that became too much, they had an apartment in the big building. Then they were moved to the nursing center. My father was the first to become frail, so mother moved mostly so she could stay with him."

Huston's father had died in the spring of 1968, at the age of 89. "The chief nurse in the nursing center told us later that she had admired my father and had written out an account of his death—and she gave us a copy of that. It was titled 'Give Us a Holy Rest,' and was based on something my father had wished for a dying parishioner: 'And if it pleases Thy will, give us a holy rest.' That's where the nurse got the title. She considered that my father had managed his decline in an exemplary fashion, and from her account—and my visits to him—I would have to agree."

When asked what a "holy rest" meant to his father or to himself, Huston answered, "As the body declines, the thing we can give to the next generation is how to age gracefully. I think that is a wise thought. What does it mean to age gracefully? Well, to act your age, to realize that you're shutting down and not to bemoan it but to accept it with good grace. My father did that, and I'm trying to do that, too."

Huston lamented that he hadn't been present when either of his parents died. "But we visited them quite often over the years, and brought our daughters to see them, which was very nice for everyone." Kim, the youngest, recalled that when they made the long drive to Missouri, the whole family used to amuse themselves in their usual fashion, by singing songs. "During the last trips, we sang Beatles songs, reveling in the harmonies." And a similar memory came back to Huston as he flew from Japan to say goodbye to his mother. "I remembered that she was the one who taught me music, and I've loved music all my life. I owed her that great gift, so I was heartbroken to lose her without having the chance to say goodbye."

Alice was 91 when she quietly passed away in her sleep, and Huston, when he arrived, was consoled that she, like his father, had been given a Holy Rest.

# Chapter Nineteen:
# Stan and Joe

It had always seemed to me that, by and large, psychotherapists lacked the metaphysical dimension; in other words, that they affected the mentality of insurance clerks and lived in a world scrubbed and disinfected of all mystery, magic, color, music and awe, with no place in the heart for the sound of a distant gong in a high and hidden valley.

Alan Watts

Hardly had I finished the manuscript when it struck me what it means to live with a myth, and what it means to live without one. . . . [The] man who thinks he can live without myth, or outside it, like one uprooted, has no true link either with the past, or with the ancestral life which continues within him, or yet with the contemporary human society. This plaything of his reason never grips his vitals.

C.G. Jung

The 1970s was one of the most productive decades of Huston's career, setting a precedent that wouldn't be rivaled until the 1990s. Though *Forgotten Truth* was his only published book of that period, it was his boldest book to date, and, in addition, he also produced sixteen professional articles and chapters for other books on a wide range of topics. He wrote about the moment of death, the value of prayer, the need for heightened ecological awareness, the validity of the Traditionalist position, the weakening of the humanities in our universities, the theory that the Western philosophical tradition constitutes another "Great Religion" (since, like all other 'religions,' it offers answers to life's pressing questions), and he continued to write favorably about psychedelics. What is remarkable is that he found time to write at all in those days, since he was still crisscrossing the country almost weekly, which forced him to do most of his writing on notepads in airports. In 1971 alone, Huston delivered the Mendenhall Lectures at DePauw University, the Gates Lectures at Grinnell College, the Merrick Lectures at Ohio Wesleyan University, and the Distinguished Lecture Series at the University of Oregon,[1] while also presenting talks at dozens of other colleges and attending eight professional conferences in Europe and Asia.

This was a period when he lost several close colleagues (along with his older brother, Bob, who died in 1977 at the age 60 due to a brain embolism), but it was also a period of gaining new allies, not all of whom were from among the Traditionalist camp. For instance, he met and befriended Saul Bellow when the distinguished novelist visited Syracuse—and what an ally Bellow proved to be. Bellow was regularly attending a discussion group in Chicago on the philosophy of Rudolf Steiner, founder of the Waldorf School, and Bellow believed very strongly that a wrong appropriation of science had pushed the humanities back onto their heels, compromising education at every level. Huston of course agreed, and so the two often found themselves discussing the dangers of dogmatic materialism over lunch, with Huston impressed over Bellow's insight. Even before they had met, when Bellow had received the Nobel Prize for Literature, he had given testimony at the awards ceremony to what became their shared perspective on materialism's effect:

> The images that come to us in this contractual daylight, so boring to us all, originate in the contemporary worldview. We put into our books the consumer, civil servant, football fan, lover, television viewer. [But] there is another life, coming from an insistent sense of what we are, that denies these daylight formulations and the false life—the death in life—they make for us. For it is false, and we know it, and our secret and incoherent resistance to it cannot stop, for that resistance arises from persistent intuitions. Perhaps humankind cannot bear too much reality, but neither can it bear too much unreality, too much abuse of truth.[2]

Bellow and Huston had little to no contact in the years that followed and did not work on projects together, despite their mutual opposition to materialism. That role of collaboration in Huston's life was filled by two other people in particular, Stanislav Grof and Joseph Campbell, both of whom influenced him deeply and were his close colleagues during the 1970s and 1980s.

Grof, a psychiatrist, and native of what is today the Czech Republic, had embraced Huxley's perennial philosophy as a logical outcome of his research with psychedelic drugs, while Campbell, a professor at Sarah Lawrence, had arrived at that same position by studying the world's mythologies. Together, Huston, Grof and Campbell came to form an extraordinary three-way allegiance, arguing similar positions from different angles of expertise, and to synergistic effect. Often meeting at conferences in America or Europe, while also teaching workshops at the Esalen Institute in Big Sur, California, they reinforced each other's work for more than two decades. Together they rate among the most significant theorists and proponents of the perennial philosophy ever to have lived, Huxley notwithstanding. Grof's book *The Cosmic Game*, Campbell's *Myths to Live By*, and Huston's *Forgotten Truth* give a breadth to Huxley's "minimum working hypothesis" that extends into the fields of psychology, mythology and religion. That said, what was it exactly that these three men admired about each other's viewpoints?

## STANISLAV GROF

Stanislav Grof was born in Prague on July 1, 1931, receiving his doctor's degree in medicine from Charles University in 1956, but only a few months after graduation he participated in a formal experiment with LSD that profoundly influenced his career ever after. The Sandoz Laboratory in Switzerland had pitched the idea that LSD could have profound benefits for mental health workers by giving them a brief glimpse of the mental disturbances that their patients experienced constantly. However, Grof's first 'trip' had been entirely beautiful and life-affirming, seeming to contradict this *psy-*

*chotomimetic* model from Sandoz. In fact, the experience didn't seem 'sick' in any way, and Grof was actually so inspired by what it seemed to reveal about the psyche that the study of non-ordinary states of consciousness became his lifelong profession, vocation and passion. In 1965 he added to his medical degree a degree from the Czechoslovakian Academy of Sciences (Doctor of Philosophy of Medicine).[3]

Prior to the LSD session, Grof had been an orthodox Freudian, but, as had happened with Walter Houston Clark (Huston's colleague from IFIF), his experience shattered his strictly materialist assumptions about the psyche. Grof came to believe there are transpersonal and metaphysical dimensions of the psyche too evident to be ignored; furthermore, he theorized that the limited Freudian model had promoted a gloomy view of human motivations and potentialities. Freud's letters make clear that part of the reason he had framed his theories in such confined terms was so that they would appeal to his materialist colleagues in the academy, who would have accepted his theories in no other way. If he wanted psychology to be viewed as a legitimate 'science of the mind,' Freud had to let go of any metaphysical mumbo-jumbo. And so, for instance, in *Civilization and Its Discontents*, he dismisses the mystical experience of Oneness with Reality as a misinterpreted "infantile longing" of the subject for the unity he or she once felt in the womb and while at the mother's breast, and there was nothing more to it than that. Grof understood Freud's concern that Psychology should be taken seriously, but as had happened with Freud's student C.G. Jung, he no longer was willing to ignore evidence that contradicted Freud's materialist view of the psyche. In fact, he didn't believe he could do so and still call himself an empirical scientist.

In the years ahead, Grof accumulated considerable evidence that the mind has metaphysical aspects that lie beyond the surface of our everyday awareness, and based on this evidence—drawn mainly from his research with LSD—he framed new models of the psyche. However, in the early years of his work, before those models were formed, he drew the attention of his colleagues by insisting that LSD had proven itself a useful tool for accessing and treating his patients' unconscious influences. Specifically, he argued that psychedelic experience catalyzes and magnifies the subject's ability to access repressed memories while also facilitating the emergence of unconscious motivators in the subject's behavior. In short, Grof thought psychedelic drugs were to psychiatry what the telescope had been to astronomy, a tool for observation via magnification, and over time, he stated his case with such conviction in so many journal articles, and backed by so much empirical evidence, that his work formed the gold standard for LSD's potentialities as a research tool—once causing Albert Hofmann, the Swiss inventor of LSD, to remark: "If I am the father of LSD then Stan is the godfather."[4]

Grof's work in Prague gained so much attention and respect that in 1967, he was invited to join a research team at the Maryland Psychiatric Center in Baltimore, housed within the Spring Grove Hospital. Walter Pahnke and Walter Houston Clark were already on staff there when he arrived, and Grof was pleased to make their acquaintance, given that they too were working outside the psychotomimetic model.

The Spring Grove project, financed by the United States Government, was the last sanctioned research endeavor with psychedelics in the country, following a nationwide crackdown on the substances that resulted from San Francisco's infamous "Summer of Love." One goal of the project was to train mental health professionals to deal with the burn-outs of the youth culture. "This made it possible," Grof explained, "for psychiatrists, psychologists, social workers and priests doing pastoral counseling to have up to three high-dose LSD sessions—so they could understand what the experience is like."

Grof described how the drugs were administered. "After several hours of preparation, experimental subjects were given a single overwhelming dose of 400 to 600 micrograms, after which their eyes and ears were covered, as a way of helping them to focus inward, and then the session began in earnest." Since this procedure resulted in intense experiences—and given that LSD was already highly controversial with the public—subjects were constantly monitored by what Grof termed "a male-female dyad of therapist and nurse."

In 1968, Huston was one of the professional subjects who arrived on the doorstep of Spring Grove, and Grof was scheduled to work with him. Grof had read Huston's articles on the relationship between psychedelics and mystical experience and was eager to meet the man himself. In terms of first impressions, Huston struck him as "friendly, gentle and intelligent," but when the drug took effect, other aspects of his personality loomed forward; for instance, Huston's smile faded and he became agitated and impatient. "It was very powerful," Grof remembered. "In earlier sessions, Huston saw the light side of the cosmic design, but in this session he had the opportunity also to look into some of the shadows." Huston had been under considerable stress at MIT, where he was still teaching at that time, and this pushed his experience in a challenging direction. Feeling tremendous trepidation, he relied on Grof to keep his feet on the ground and his mind away from the need for administering a strong sedative.

Recalling that first day with Grof, Huston had a pained expression on his face, observing: "It turned out to be a bummer. You don't forget any psychedelic experience, but one like that really stands out! It was a strong dose and I was so thankful that Stan was there."

But why was Huston there? Hadn't he 'received the message and hung up the phone' as Watts had advised? He was convinced that psychedelics could trigger mystical insight but his conclusion had been that traits mattered more than states, so why bother with the drugs? The first answer is that though traits mattered most, Huston still believed the experience had value, since, for him, it had helped to affirm the reality of the Divine Ground. Furthermore, he was aware of recent studies, including Grof's, that suggested psychedelics could have therapeutic value even for 'sane' people (given that everyone has repressed unconscious content that needs to be dealt with), so why not see what a session might reveal? At this time, Huston was also experiencing a midlife crisis and he was looking for help from all quarters. The experience was terrifically unpleasant and revealed little of interest, so that when the drug subsided, he abandoned psychedelic therapy once and for all. The one benefit that came out of the session was that Huston became acquainted with Grof.

## Ancient Wisdom and Modern Science

Grof maintained that his research had revealed extraordinary aspects of the human mind; for instance, during LSD sessions, he repeatedly observed two levels of the psyche that were unrelated to his subjects' personal biographies: a "perinatal level" derived from the trauma of biological birth, and a "transpersonal level" suggesting that the psyche, in its farthest reaches, might be "commensurate with all of existence and ultimately identical with the cosmic creative principle itself."[5] This transpersonal aspect was, Grof theorized, metaphysical in nature, and Huston, for obvious reasons, celebrated Grof's willingness to explore such a theory.

Grof's description of the psyche's transpersonal aspects resonated deeply with Huston's own convictions, but this was only part of what soon made them allies. Grof was looking into traditional descriptions of the psyche drawn from the very religions that Huston studied, hoping to find valuable clues about the psyche's essential make-up, and so Huston helped steer him toward valuable resources, including contact information with swamis, shamans and other adepts of the traditional paths. "As this work continued," Grof wrote later, "I realized that I was rediscovering ancient knowledge of human consciousness that had been around for centuries or even millennia."[6] He also began noting important parallels and consistent content between the shamanic traditions and the spiritual philosophies of Asia—and this lead Grof to reify not only the ancient religions but also Huxley's and Huston's view that there is a perennial philosophy underlying all of them.

Grof first described his perennialist re-mapping of the psyche in 1975, in his book *Realms of the Human Unconscious: Observations from LSD Research*, and Huston became so impressed by it that he shared Grof's findings in a long appendix in *Forgotten Truth*. Huston was convinced Grof's research offered clinical evidence that the mind is something more than the brain, and this was the specific reason that Huston was still interested in LSD research. "In contradistinction to writings on the psychedelics which are occupied with experiences the mind can *have*," Huston observed, praising Grof's work, "the concern here is with evidence they afford as to what the mind *is*."[7] Grof had argued that consciousness is "not a product of the brain, but a primary principle of existence, and that it plays a critical role in the creation of the phenomenal world,"[8] and this converged perfectly with what Huston had first learned from Huxley, Heard and Swami Satprakashananda.

## THE ZAEHNER CONTROVERSY

Many scholars disagreed with both Huston and Grof over their view that the psyche has metaphysical aspects, or that psychedelic drugs could trigger true insights into them. In fact, regarding the latter claim, the leading academic authority on mysticism at that time, an Oxford don named R.C. Zaehner, disagreed with them completely, having argued in 1961 (in *Mysticism, Sacred and Profane*) that the highest form of mystical insight depends upon a sense of profound intimacy with the living God, while Thoreau's reverie in the forests of New England, or the buzz of the shaman on peyote, and even Huxley's rapture in the "unitive knowledge" were all something inferior to that experience. Aiming a barb at Huxley in particular, Zaehner contended that since Huxley's description of his experiences on mescaline had closely corresponded with what he had described in *The Perennial Philosophy*, his conclusions were only a bit of wish fulfillment, based on preconceived assumptions he had inherited from studying Vedanta.

After Zaehner published his critique, Huxley offered a careful rebuttal, but many scholars (due to their own biases?) followed Zaehner's lead and the controversy died down for a while; that is, until Huston revived it again, starting a back-and-forth with Zaehner that lasted for more than eight years.

Zaehner had originally given three reasons for why Huxley was wrong about psychedelic experience, and Huston addressed each of them in his article, already mentioned, "Do Drugs Have Religious Import?" Zaehner had said that no drug could guarantee a mystical experience and Huston agreed with him on this first point, but then argued that Huxley did too. Huxley had claimed that under the right circumstances psychedelics *could* induce a mystical experience, but didn't claim they necessarily *would*.[9] Zaehner's second argument was based on the fact that he himself had tried mescaline and nothing of significance had happened. To this Huston responded that, "This of course proves that not all drug experiences are religious, but not that none is."[10] And lastly, Zaehner contended that a close scrutiny of the historical records showed that there are three sorts of mysticism: nature mysticism, monistic mysticism (of the Vedanta, Huxley and Emerson sort); and theistic mysticism, but that the last has generally been recognized as the highest form. Zaehner was willing to grant that drugs might inspire something like the first or second sorts of experience, but the third, involving a connection with the personal God, was beyond their reach. However, Huston argued back that Zaehner was not only going against the evidence, he was proceeding in the face of it. "James Slotkin reports that the Peyote Indians 'see visions, which may be of Christ Himself,'" Huston reported. "[And] Sometimes they hear the voice of the Great Spirit.'"[11] In short, Huston gave evidence that psychedelics *can* trigger theistic experiences.

In the months ahead, Zaehner proved unwilling to back off from any of his three initial arguments, and in 1972, in *Zen, Drugs & Mysticism,* he added that it was "deplorable that a reputed authority on comparative religion and the history of religions, Professor Huston Smith of M.I.T.," should write "with evident satisfaction" about how psychedelic experience had even the possibility of being truly mystical.[12] Zaehner accused Huston of focusing so intently on the "monistic experience" that he couldn't see the other, "higher" form, adding, somewhat unprofessionally, that "The worst fool of all . . . is the learned fool who is also ignorant."

Zaehner contended that if Huston would take off his blinkers, he would see that "for the 'orthodox' mystical traditions, in all the major religions that have mystical traditions at all, knowledge or 'wisdom' is balanced by an intense love for a God personally experienced and adored."[13] However, Huston didn't see any such thing. That same year, he had published an article in the *Journal of the American Academy of Religion* concerning R. Gordon Wasson's discovery that Soma, the sacrament of India's ancient Vedic religion, had most likely been *Amanita muscaria,* a variety of psychedelic mushroom,[14] and Wasson's findings suggested that even Hinduism, which, even in Zaehner's own view, was an "orthodox" and "major" religion, most likely had its roots in psychedelic experience. Furthermore, Huston bristled at the cultural chauvinism and snobbery—not to mention abject provincialism—of Zaehner's view that shamanic religions are neither orthodox nor major. Perhaps Zaehner's conclusions were themselves a bit of wish fulfillment, given that Zaehner, as a practicing Catholic, had a strong bias against both Huxley's "unitive knowledge" and the 'primitive' religions.

Before this debate was ended or resolved to anyone's satisfaction, it became irrelevant, not only because Zaehner died in 1974 but for the reason that the U.S. Government outlawed the use of psychedelic drugs even by research professionals. In 1973, the Spring Grove program was closed down, and Grof, now out of work, left Baltimore. This marked the end of formal research with psychedelics in America for the next two decades, but it was the beginning of his collaboration with Grof; for instance, Huston would write the preface to Grof's next book, *The Human Encounter with Death* (1977).

## JOE CAMPBELL

Huston's other major ally during the 1970s and 1980s was the mythologist Joseph Campbell, himself the main bridge between the work of Carl Jung and Aldous Huxley. The *Christian Science Monitor* once lauded Huston as "Religion's Rock Star,"[15] but if there was another —and there *was*—it was Joseph Campbell.

Campbell had a similar talent for explaining complex ideas in simple language, and in many ways he and Huston formed a 'one-two punch' while out on the lecture circuit. "Joe and I met while I was at MIT," Huston remembered, speaking fondly about his friend, "and after that we often met in airports to coordinate our efforts while we each toured the country. In those days, Joe and I realized that we were working different sides of the same street. We were both talking about religion and spirituality, but he was emphasizing the power of myth, while I was dealing with the transcendent Truth that myth points to. We had a good division of labor!"

Campbell, fifteen years older than Huston, was born in New York City, in 1904, and had earned both his B.A. and M.A. in the study of mythology at Columbia University. In the 1920s, Campbell had read the works of Freud and Jung and became profoundly influenced by the latter. Jung offered a theory of symbols and metaphors in mythology and literature that totally captivated Campbell's attention, forming the foundation for all his later work. In 1934, he had accepted a position in Comparative Mythology at Sarah Lawrence and taught there for the next thirty-eight years, retiring in 1972.

In 1938, Campbell had married Jean Erdman, a member of Martha Graham's Dance Company (Alan Watts once observed that, "Erdman is to dancing what Vivaldi is to music."[16]), to whom he would remain happily married all his life. The other significant event of that time was that he met and befriended Swami Nikhilananda, another swami of the Ramakrishna Order, like Huston's friend, Swami Satprakashananda. From Nikhilananda, who lived in New York City while Campbell attended Columbia, Campbell got the same strong dose of Vedanta that Prabhavananda had given to Huxley and that Satprakashananda had given to Huston—including the view that there is an eternal religion implicit in reality itself. Over the next three decades, Campbell would give lectures at the Ramakrishna-Vivekananda Center whenever he was in New York City, though in 1954 he became somewhat disillusioned with Vedanta (in form, if not content) after a visit to India with his teacher. During that trip (described in Campbell's fascinating book, *Baksheesh and Brahman)*, Campbell rebelled against the Hindu tendency to fawn over gurus, along with Swami Nikhilananda's indulgence of it, and after that visit, was a Vedantist only in the broadest of terms.

The same year that Campbell met Nikhilananda, he also befriended Heinrich Zimmer, a German scholar of Sanskrit and Indian Culture who was teaching at Columbia. When Zimmer, a close friend and colleague of Jung's, died unexpectedly of pneumonia two years later in 1942, his widow asked Campbell if he would edit Zimmer's unpublished works. The project took Campbell more than twelve years. In Zimmer's writings, Campbell found many of the ideas that would define his mature viewpoint, and the majority of those ideas were borrowed from either Vedanta or Jung, with the latter being most important.

Scanning world literature (including religious texts, mythology and folk tales), Jung had observed that if one looks closely enough, and beyond superficial differences such as names and places, it is possible to see recurring cross-cultural patterns of character, plot and outcome that he termed *archetypes*. For example, Merlin, Lao Tzu, Gandalf and Moses are ultimately iterations of the archetype of the 'wise man.' Similarly, there are also archetypes of the demon who must be overcome, of the maiden who must be rescued, of the trickster who deceives but also can help, of the Mother Goddess whose favor should be sought, and so on and so forth, throughout world literature. What most interested Jung about this phenomenon was that these prototypical patterns could not be attributed to the historical migrations of people from one place to another; they occurred in all cultures independently and with equal force, regardless of whether any two of those cultures had overlapped. Furthermore, Jung recognized that these archetypes surfaced also in the dreams and fantasies of his patients, and he concluded, based on this, that these patterns bubble up in all people, everywhere, because they are endemic to the human psyche itself.

Freud postulated a "personal unconscious," an aspect of the psyche that is filled with the repressed or ignored content of our past, but Jung added to this a "collective unconscious," a level of our psyche that doesn't depend upon personal history and is not characterized by neurosis. As a psychiatrist, Jung was engrossed by the import of this theory of a positive unconscious on the dynamics of personality, mental illness and self-actualization, but, in addition, speculated that the archetypes of what he termed the "collective unconscious" might be the wellsprings of all art and culture. He believed there could be consequences of his views that stretched far beyond psychology *per se*, and this is where both Zimmer and Campbell staked their claim.

Campbell saw Jung's theories as not only plausible but likely, applying them to his own research with mythology. In 1949, in his breakthrough book *The Hero with a Thousand Faces*, Campbell pointed out that the myth of the hero who leaves his homeland in search of some power object (a Holy Grail, golden fleece, golden goose, sacred fruit, curative waters, magical ring or whatever else) and goes through hell to bring it back for the sake of his people, is endemic to all cultures, whether they call this hero Hercules, Jason, Arjuna, Arthur, Siegfried, Beowulf or the Whale Rider. To Campbell's mind, analysis of world mythology gives concrete evidence to the view that there is a *hero archetype* in the *collective unconscious* of humanity, and that we are all hardwired to express and respond to it. Consequently, the family of man, below the surface of its historical and social differences, is connected inextricably on a transpersonal level of its being. Jung was interested in this possibility for its psychological import, but Campbell, based on his deep interest in spirituality, focused on what the theory implied for religion and the quest for individual awakening.

It has been said that every person is the hero of his or her own life's story, but Campbell didn't agree. Each person *should* be the hero of that story but many people are not. Campbell hoped to rectify this lack by encouraging people to embrace mythology as something more powerful than a collection of false histories or archaic follies. For Campbell, the Holy Grail and the Golden Fleece are psychic euphemisms for the self-actualization that we all seek (whether we realize it or not). The hero's quest actually points to "a constant requirement in the human psyche for a centering in terms of deep principles."[17] Campbell believed that people everywhere, and always, seek the wholeness that comes with self-realization, and that stories of the hero's journey give them psychic pointers in symbolic language about how that can be accomplished. Reading myths or sharing folk tales around a campfire, people are really using archetypal patterns of the collective unconscious to trigger healthy configurations within their own psyches.  All these propositions were right up Huston's alley.

Huston found Campbell's and Jung's description of the collective unconscious to be a good fit with his own viewpoint, since it included the idea of a transpersonal and trans-cultural knowledge to which all people have access.  Huston speculated that this particular level of the psyche might exist somewhere between our everyday consciousness as individuals and the Divine Ground at the root of all Being.  Campbell, in fact, had spoken in exactly these terms, believing that the power of myth was in helping us to activate the archetypes in the service of realizing Huxley's unitive knowledge.  Like Huston, Campbell believed that self-realization could never be selfish, pointing out that the true hero always brings the 'lost treasure' or 'power object' back to help his or her people.  "The ultimate aim of the quest," Campbell wrote, "must be neither release nor ecstasy for oneself, but the wisdom and power to serve others."[18]  Bingo!  Huston reveled in this belief as an advocacy of his ideal of 'traits over states,' and grew even more excited by Campbell's view of why this is so.

Campbell had accepted Schopenhauer's theory that compassion arises in the hero because his quest has taught him that his own inner being "actually exists in every living creature . . . [and this] is the ground of that compassion (*Mitleid*) upon which all true, that is to say, unselfish, virtue rests and whose expression is every good deed."[19]  For Campbell, the collective unconscious includes motivations for individual behavior that transcend our individuality, deriving from its close intimacy with the Divine Ground itself; in other words, the hero cares for others because he has awakened to the fact that he is ultimately—and on the deepest level of his being—inseparable from them.  In this way, Campbell set Jung's view of the psyche into the context of both Vedanta and the perennial philosophy, winning over Huston in the process.  Here was a viewpoint akin to Schuon's 'transcendent unity of religions' but drawn from the study of myth, legend and literature, rather than from formal religion, and revealing new aspects of perennialism.

## METAPHOR AND ALLEGORY AS THE LANGUAGE OF THE SOUL

Based on careful consideration, Campbell concluded that there's no set formula for interpreting myths or configuring the import of the various archetypes.  Myths are too metaphorical and slippery for their meanings to be exhausted by any one interpretation; moreover, each culture creates its own constellation of how the archetypes fit together, which also must be considered in any analysis.

These views rang true for Huston, who liked how they implicitly showed respect for the differences between cultures.  Huston appreciated Campbell's view that myth-making is more a species of poetry than an attempt at didactic description, having the same power as poetry to inspire us aesthetically, based on symbolic and allegorical use of language.  For Campbell, myths are rendered impotent if they are interpreted literally, since their archetypal power is ignored in favor of something far less substantial—and far more arguable.  For example, as a thought-poem the tale of lost innocence in the Garden of Eden, with its lessons on the dangers of temptation and owning a power beyond one's control, makes perfect 'sense'; whereas, forcing the myth into the straightjacket of literal interpretation not only reduces its power but pushes it beyond the limits of credibility.  Can we accept that Adam and Eve were the first human couple, created in the current form of our species (though presumably without belly buttons), and taking poor advice from a talking snake? Huston thought Campbell was on the right track: the power of myth lies in its non-rational (but not *irrational*) nature, and the slippery character of metaphor is what prevents any interpretation of a myth from being exhaustive.

Huston enjoyed Campbell's ability to see the world through a mytho-symbolic lens. "He was brilliant in many ways, including his powers of analysis, but what stood out for me was his embrace of symbols and metaphors. Once, when we bumped into each other at Chicago's O'Hare Airport, he told me that on his way to a lecture, just a few days prior, he had moved his car from a parking spot when a little boy in a red shirt had told him, 'You can't park here.' Joe asked, 'Why not?' The boy answered, 'Because I'm a fire hydrant!' 'All right,' Joe said. 'Thank you for telling me.' Joe was the only person I ever met who would move his car for such a reason, accepting that a small boy could somehow be a fire hydrant just because they wore the same color!"[20]

## A WEDDING IN ICELAND

After Campbell retired from teaching in 1972 and Grof had moved to Big Sur in 1973, Huston sometimes teamed up with one or other of them to lead workshops at Esalen; however, the first time all three were together was in 1972, during a conference in Iceland, which unexpectedly turned into a wedding ceremony.

Grof, jointly with Michael Murphy and Richard Price, had created an organization called the International Transpersonal Association (ITA), dedicated to exploring the transpersonal aspects of the psyche, and in 1972, Grof helped organize the First International Transpersonal Conference in Bifrost, near Reykjavík, Iceland. Among the seventy-two participants were Lawrence LeShan, Walter Houston Clark, Einar Palsson (an expert on Icelandic mythology) and Joan Halifax, an anthropologist who studied shamanism and had been working closely with Grof for about a year. "There was a tremendous charge in the air at that conference," Halifax recalled, "a real feeling of synchronicity. I think Carl Jung was probably smiling from the heavens at this extraordinary gathering of people who were engaged in therapy, and also at scholars like Huston who were looking at religion cross-culturally, and mythology, of course, in terms of Joseph Campbell's work."

Halifax is the presiding Roshi at the Upaya Zen Center in Santa Fe, New Mexico. Though she had met Huston twice before, it was at the conference in Iceland that she really got to know him:

> My first impression of Huston, which has stayed very much the same since that time, was of a person of great wisdom and compassion. He had such a delightful sensibility. He wasn't an egotistical person. He had tremendous humility—and he had a very refined sense of humor. He also had a tremendous meta-cognitive base. He could step aside from things and see them from a vast perspective. I think he was able, throughout his lifetime, to hold things in very much the same way as the great religious teachers of our time—like the Dalai Lama or Thich Nhat Hanh, which is to say that he was in touch with the truth of the suffering in the world, but he also, somehow, had a deep, inner stability, and was psychologically so fundamentally integrated that he was able to put that suffering into a perspective that was basically transformational.

Halifax had met Grof at a conference in Dallas, in 1971, just four years after Grof came to the United States, and while she was teaching at the University of Miami, learning that they shared a strong interest in shamanism—which quickly segued into a strong interest in each other. After a few more meetings, their relationship moved quickly, and so when Grof told her he was going to attend a ten-day conference in Iceland, she took a leave of absence and went along. There they toyed with the idea of getting married, and, as Grof tells the story in his book *When the Impossible Happens*, everyone at the conference quickly became involved.[21]

Campbell and Palsson decided that the wedding should have a solid mythological foundation, so they reconstructed an ancient Viking marriage ritual. "The joining of the bridegroom and the bride reflected *hierosgamos*, the sacred union of Father Sky and Mother Earth," Grof wrote, "and the symbol of this union was the rainbow."[22] In free time between academic sessions, some of the conference-goers began making costumes and masks to wear at the ceremony, while others worked on the menu for the banquet that would follow. Huston was charged with the role of priest or hierophant to join the couple, and Campbell was asked to stand in as the father of the bride. Campbell's wife, Jean, choreographed the ceremony and oversaw the rehearsals.

The wedding became a two-day affair, starting with a purification ceremony in a sauna that was performed separately for the bride and groom, as was the Icelandic tradition. Grof remembered that the men "drank mead, sang appropriate songs and told many jokes," and that afterwards the two groups met for dinner. Huston recalled that it was to be a sunrise marriage, but, given that they were in Iceland, the sun rose at 2 A.M., "so nobody went to bed that night." When the time was deemed auspicious, everyone was brought to an old volcanic crater as the sun appeared above the horizon and the ceremony commenced.

"I was dressed in the national costume of Iceland," Halifax recounted, "which is a long sort of black woolen dress with gold embroidery at the hem and cuffs. The dress itself symbolized the Central Mountain of the World and the Great Mother. I wore a gold crown and a big white veil, like a kind of glacier cascading off the crown on my head." Grof wore an Icelandic wool sweater, while Erdman danced in front of the couple, leading the way to where Huston stood waiting to perform the ceremony.

"I don't really remember what Huston said that day," Halifax added. "You know, it was one of those events that when you're in it, it's so overwhelming. There you are in this volcanic crater with Joseph Campbell standing by your side and Huston Smith standing before you. And there's your beloved. And there is this bower under which you're standing. It was all very dramatic and extraordinary!"

After wedding rings were exchanged, Walter Houston Clark offered a benediction that was taken from Ruth's pledge in the Old Testament: "I will go where you go and your people will be my people," and the ceremony was deemed complete.

"It was one of the most beautiful things I've ever witnessed," Huston remembered with a broad smile, "a myth had come to life. So appropriate for that group of people. I'll never forget that day! It was like something outside of the everyday world, and it cemented my relationship with both Stan and Joan, two lovely friends."

## A BONE OF CONTENTION

As Huston began to work more closely with Grof and Cambell, it became clear that he disagreed with them on one subject in particular, namely that neither Grof nor Campbell had any respect for organized religion. Grof, like Huxley and Heard, believed that organized religion is too chauvinistic, dysfunctional and authoritarian to be relevant in modern, democratic societies. "Once religion becomes organized," Grof wrote later, "it often completely loses the connection with its spiritual source and becomes a secular institution exploiting the human spiritual needs without satisfying them. Instead, it creates a hierarchical system focusing on the pursuit of power, control, politics, money, possessions and other secular concerns."[23] Grof borrowed insights from the traditional faiths but believed that the goal of every seeker should be to push beyond the 'isms' of any particular tradition, and—as the Sufis had put it—to catch fire directly from THE fire at the core of all reality.

Campbell, like Grof, Heard and Huxley, believed that organized religion is mostly a barrier to spiritual growth, though looking across the mythologies of these traditions is useful for understanding the collective unconscious. When Campbell spoke of God, he talked in broad terms about the god archetype and its significance in history or for the psyche, rather than as a means of advocating worship. Between 1959 and 1968, Campbell published four volumes on the various gods of the world, analyzing them in his *Masks of God* series, and he explained in these texts that each god—of whichever culture—is really just a mask on the face of the 'God' concept, exhibiting a particular aspect of Its personality, and describing Its multitudinous nature that recedes into the ineffable. For Campbell, the organized religions too often confuse their particular concept of the inexpressible for the only possibility. Furthermore, with regards to religion in general, the tendency to use one's own religion as a platform for denigrating the religions of others, measuring someone else's faith by the yardsticks of one's own, skewed religion into a force for unity only within one's tribe, creating division in all other regards.

Huston agreed with Campbell on each of these points but drew the different conclusion that religion was redeemable. Certainly it was wrong to be a fanatic, mistaking one's religion for the only possibility, but why couldn't the religions be recognized as separate yet valuable pathways to the same sacred goal? No one religion, or even religion is general, held an exclusive approach to God, but did that mean they had no unique value? Huston didn't think so. He believed Campbell had been too turned off to religion in his youth by a "joyless, judgmental Calvinism,"[24] but Campbell has argued that his reasons were of a philosophical nature, closely related to those of Huxley.

Huston enjoyed working with 'Joe,' elucidating the common ground between various traditions and their mythologies, but continued to defend organized religion. Certainly there were people like Campbell and Grof who could rely on their own efforts to reach self-realization, and who derived all the community they needed from their colleagues and friends, but they were among the exceptions that prove the rule. The majority of people need guidance and support, and they rely on the shared sense of purpose that religion affords. Without a hand to hold, or the certainty provided by a specific religious ideology, most people would lose their sense of direction in terms of both meaning and morality, drifting into isolation and cynicism, Huston believed. Campbell didn't seem interested in the needs of the common man who has neither the time nor skill sets to find his own way in life.

"Campbell, whom I loved dearly, missed something that Huston got," Phil Cousineau, an author, filmmaker and friend of both Huston's and Campbell's, observed. "Religion gives a context that keeps you from drifting away into self-indulgent rhapsodizing and navel-gazing. What Huston's onto is that unless we have some kind of structure or discipline, we can get caught up in our own illusions. And people also need a sense of community. Janis Joplin used to say, 'Every night I make love to ten thousand people and then go home alone.' She grew sad and tired from her isolation. Joe didn't understand her need to belong, but Huston did. Huston knew that for hundreds of millions of people, religion gives not only a sense of purpose but a sense of belonging, and that's no small gift. Religion can definitely be useful and Huston has that right."

# Chapter Twenty:
# Esalen

My brain is only a receiver; in the Universe there is a core from which we obtain knowledge, strength and inspiration. I have not penetrated into the secrets of this core, but I know that it exists.

Nikola Tesla

... but if the psychologists readily recognize the existence of a 'subconscious'—which they sometimes abuse in making of it an all too convenient explanation, indiscriminately attributing to it everything that they are unable to classify among the phenomena they study—they always forget to envisage correlatively a 'superconscious,' as if consciousness could not as easily be prolonged above as below ...

René Guénon

In the 1970s and 1980s, Grof, Campbell and Huston participated in a mutually beneficial, three-way admiration for each other's work, and though none of them was interested in formalizing a systematic philosophy, each believed in an iteration of the perennial philosophy that they worked closely to compare and develop. At conferences on such topics at "Psychology and Religion," when a question arose that dealt with one or other of the world's religions, all eyes turned to Huston; when it was about mythology, they swiveled to Joe; and when it had to do with psychology, Grof offered an answer. Grof had performed more clinical research on the psychological effects of psychedelic drugs than anyone in history. Campbell knew more about the world's mythologies than anyone else (with the possible exception of Claude Levi-Strauss); and Huston was one of the top three scholars of World Religions (along with Mircea Eliade and Wilfred Cantwell Smith). Together they were a compelling and charismatic team, forming a strong presence at the Esalen Institute for more than two decades. Esalen became Huston's truest home, offering him his most open-minded audience.

While traveling around the world on the Danforth trip in 1957, Huston and Kendra made a stop in Pondicherry, at the ashram of Sri Aurobindo, where Huston met a bright young man from California named Michael Murphy, recently graduated from Stanford. Murphy, soon to establish the Esalen Institute with the help of his friend Dick Price, was at the ashram out of a deep fascination for Aurobindo's theory that human beings are still evolving biologically, and that we can speed up that evolution by focusing on our spiritual lives. Aurobindo had received a good understanding of Darwin's viewpoint while studying at Cambridge University, and many years later had merged those views with theories drawn from Indian philosophy, especially Vedanta. The result was that Aurobindo believed we are currently in the process of actualizing extraordinary physical and psychic abilities as natural by-products of our spiritual growth toward enlightenment, and that our ever-increasing physical abilities are driving our spiritual evolution. Each works as an engine of change for the other. In the same way that biological evolution has generated astonishing enhancements of the brain's structure (and in a relatively short period), Aurobindo believed other physical advancements were also coming along (especially as we work to channel more and more of the divine energy at the root of our being into the process).

Aurobindo believed this was happening because the Divine Ground, or what he termed "Supermind," is actually using us as a context for it own awakening, even as we are using it for ours. Aurobindo argued for a form of what philosopher's have termed *evolutionary panentheism*, in which the Supermind is playing out a series of awakenings about its nature by biologically enhancing human beings as the instruments of those awakenings. Thus we are both expressions of the Supermind as well as its contexts of insight. This theory (very much in tune that of Gerald Heard) is what had brought Murphy to Pondicherry, where Aurobindo had his "laboratory of evolution" to develop and apply techniques of spiritual (and therefore biological) awakening, much as Heard had done at Trabuco. Murphy wished to assess the project, hoping to set up something of the sort back home in California.

"He told me that he had inherited some coastal property in Big Sur," Huston reminisced about his long-term friendship with Murphy, "and along with meditating every day he was using his stay at the Aurobindo ashram to figure out what a Western ashram could look like." Murphy, who many years later would write *The Future of the Body*, a book in which he would share his Aurobindo-based theories of human development, was particularly intrigued by the idea that we can develop athletically by developing spiritually, and vice versa. He didn't go along with everything that Aurobindo had written however, and he disliked certain aspects of the ashram's formal arrangement. Murphy found the place too hierarchical and authoritarian, based, as it was, on a cross-pollination of the Indian guru system and the Western corporate model. Murphy, as a firm believer in American individualism, democratic equality and freedom of expression, hoped to develop safeguards for his own institute that would mediate the tendencies toward spiritual monarchy so prevalent in Hindu culture. He wanted a place where all ideas would be explored freely and where no particular viewpoint—or any one personality—would ever, as Murphy put it, "capture the flag."

Murphy saw a definite wisdom in the template of the Western university model, with its ideal that disparate viewpoints can co-exist on the same campus if each is backed by rigor and defended by rational argument; however, like Huxley, Huston and Grof, he also believed that the dogma of strict materialism was holding the universities hostage, preventing them from reaching their full potential.

Murphy wished to explore all theories of human development, so he advocated at Esalen a "radical empiricism" like that once championed at Harvard by William James, an approach that could be faithful to the full spectrum of human experience and not ignore anomalies simply because they didn't fit into the reigning paradigm.[1] For Murphy, a comprehensive scientific study of consciousness would have to take into account the phenomenological reality of subjective experience, embracing methods that are first person as well as third person. Scientific rigor could be equally observed if it was demanded that subjective experiences be verifiable through repetition; that is, if the same practitioner, or others after her, could attain the same experience using the same methods. In short, Murphy was picking up where James had left off, and Huston was excited that such a research institute was being developed.

When Murphy came back from India, he enlisted Richard "Dick" Price to help him realize his dream, and as they laid their plans, they solicited the support of intellectuals who were investigating human physical, psychological and spiritual potentialities. Chief among these were Aldous Huxley and Gerald Heard. Murphy and Price invited them to give their input, and the two Brits were delighted to do so, even taking the time to visit Big Sur. As Jeffrey Kripal has pointed out, in his excellent history of Esalen, what followed was that Murphy and Price soon began to cross-reference Huxley's theories of "Human Potentialities" with Heard's and Aurobindo's views on evolution.[2] Once they had set this hybrid vision into place, they opened their doors for business in 1962, naming their institute after the Esalen people, an extinct tribe of Native Americans who had once lived in the area.

The next step, a step that would never be finished, was to find people besides Huxley and Heard whose ideas were worth exploring and sharing. Joseph Campbell was asked to give some talks in 1966, at the recommendation of Alan Watts (who was one of the first presenters when the institute began, and supplied their first mailing list), and Huston also arrived in 1966, having bumped into Murphy at a conference in Cambridge, Massachusetts. Asked why he invited Huston, Murphy said, "the obvious reasons: his perennial philosophy, his general charisma and light, his personality, and his great sympathy for mysticism." Asked why he had accepted, Huston said he had been delighted to learn there was a new venue for unusual viewpoints, a place where neither the "scientististic controls of academia" nor the "group-think" of most ashrams held sway.

## Psychology, religion and Esalen

Arriving in Big Sur in 1966, Huston soon sensed a definite negative attitude toward organized religion, with the general viewpoint on campus being that religious organizations are too set in their ways and too authoritarian to be relevant to the modern world. The emphasis was on personal development and the individual's need to take charge of his own growth—physical, psychological and spiritual. This predisposition against religion, which Grof and Campbell shared, was, Murphy admitted, an inheritance from his religion professor at Stanford, Frederic Spiegelberg. Spiegelberg (1897-1994), a German aristocrat who had fled the Nazis in 1937, believed in mystical experiences (claiming he had had one himself), but argued in his classes against all forms of organized religion. If Huston's viewpoint can be characterized as the "religion of all religions" (and it can), Spiegelberg's was the opposite: the "religion of no religion," which, in fact, was the title of one of his books. Murphy, and Price too, had taken on Spiegelberg's viewpoint, and that vantage was shaped further by Murphy's study of psychology.

Psychology, as an academic discipline, is similar to religion in that it seeks to help individuals achieve wholeness and fulfillment, but its focus is far more personalized and its successes have done much to undermine the value of religion. The traditional religions provided people with sets of ideals to live by, but they—arguably—encouraged little insight into themselves as individuals, regarding them as members of various congregations or discreet examples of a generic type (e.g., Christians, sinners, Muslims), rather than as unique personalities with inner dynamics and needs. Psychology, on the other hand, not only favors a person's right to see himself as a unique personality, but also the right to direct one's own path toward wellness. This approach made the most sense to Murphy and Price, and this raises an important question: if religion was mostly cast aside at Esalen, why was Huston there?

At Esalen, people were encouraged to glean from the established religions whatever they found useful to their own journeys. In brief, Murphy and Price were advocating something like the cafeteria-style religion that Huston disdained, which seems to suggest that he was 'odd man out' by being there. Huston agreed with them that there should be a place in the world where the full range of human potentialities could be explored without bias—even religious bias. Strict Traditionalists like Schuon were claiming that only the established faiths could lead to awakening, and Huston saw the wisdom in keeping those pathways open and intact. But the Traditionalists also believed that people should beware of what Huston has called the "sin of particularity," the evil of believing that only one tradition can lead to the ultimate insight. From Huston's perspective (again, a more "soft" and nuanced Traditionalism), he was extending the warning against the sin of particularity in such a way that it applied even beyond the organized religions. Where the strict Traditionalists recognized only the established pathways up the mountain of spirit, Huston saw also a value in blazing new trails, including even those derived from modern psychology. He had looked successfully between and beyond the religions, so why shouldn't others? Huston didn't see Esalen as a replacement for the church or temple, as Murphy and Price (and Grof and Campbell) most definitely did, but rather as a valuable addition.

By participating in workshops at Esalen, Huston also hoped to monitor the accuracy with which the traditional religions were represented, improving those descriptions when necessary, while pointing out the positive side of religion along the way. As someone who professed the value of faith, Huston hoped to be an example of what healthy religiosity looked like—which might be especially valuable for the droves of young people pouring into Esalen at the time. Many of these hippie kids were not grounded enough in their own spirituality to cast aside the religions they had grown up with (whether they thought they were or not), and Huston might be able to point this out to them before they got lost along the way, or worse, fell under the sway of a bogus guru of the Charles Manson sort.

With the influx of the counterculture and its Eastern-inspired viewpoints, pumped up by LSD and the electric music of The Beatles, The Doors and The Grateful Dead, things often teetered on the edge of chaos, but Huston was adept at pulling things back. During the late 1960s and throughout the 1970s, Huston was one of the stabilizing influences on Esalen exactly at the time when it needed this most. "It's good to be open-minded," Huston remarked, "but not to the point where the hinges come off! I had seen young people at Millbrook who had gotten in over their heads with drugs, and so I worried about some of these kids at Esalen."

Huston described how the natural hot springs on the campus would, on occasion, become the site of spontaneous orgies, and how the 'do your own thing' and 'if it feels good, do it' ethos of the 1960s often tipped the scales toward bedlam. "On Friday evenings there would be this drumming, with these big bongo drums. And there would be a multitude of people twirling and doing whatever else. It was sometimes fun and exciting, but other times it was quite dangerous and out-of-control. Mike and Dick realized they were flying by the seat of their pants, and some participants in the workshops clearly took on more than they could psychologically handle." When asked about those early days of Esalen, Murphy agreed with Huston: not everyone was ready to handle absolute freedom. "I wouldn't take anything back, but you only want to go over Niagara Falls in a barrel once!"

In summary, Huston didn't believe psychology had rendered religion obsolete but he agreed that it contained insights worth investigating. He had even come to hope that psychology might help fulfill his long-time dream of splicing science and spirituality.

## Enter Abraham Maslow

In 1962, just when Esalen had first opened its doors, Abraham Maslow published his landmark book, *Toward a Psychology of Being*, outlining his theories about the pinnacle of wellness, informed by a close scrutiny of Asian philosophies. Murphy read Maslow and was so impressed by the book that he gave copies of it to all his staff, holding discussions on its implications in the evenings after Esalen's workshops closed. For Murphy, the book had come along almost by providence and just when he needed it most, and what felt like kismet, karma and destiny intensified when Maslow himself showed up at Esalen's door, by accident just one month later.

While driving down the California coast on a stormy night, Maslow and his wife had wearied of taking the dangerous curves and decided to check into a motel. Having no luck finding one, they remembered a sign earlier for some sort of institute, so they backtracked. When they pulled up to the front gate, Maslow asked the desk clerk if a room was available. The clerk, instantly recognizing Maslow's name (he was reading Maslow's book at that very moment), began jumping around excitedly, telling Maslow that he could definitely stay and then running off to fetch Murphy, who later interpreted the coincidence as a bit of Jungian synchronicity. Even Maslow found the coincidence uncanny, and in the years that followed he would recognize Esalen as the perfect crucible for his ideas, giving numerous workshops there until his early death in 1970 at the age of 62.

What had drawn Murphy to Maslow was the latter's emphasis on human potentialities and the possibility that psychology could not only help neurotic people become sane but help sane people become more sane, reaching higher stages of clarity and insight. Like William James, Frederic Myers, Jung and only a few other psychologists before him, Maslow was more interested in the higher end of the psyche's functioning than its dysfunctional pathologies, and in this regard he considered that human beings might even have metaphysical aspects. Investigating beyond the limits of Depth Psychology, with its emphasis on neurosis and psychosis, and Behavioral Psychology, with its emphasis on behavior modification, Maslow was working to establish a "Third Force" in Psychology that went beyond the need for improved social behavior and the limits of strict materialism.

Maslow had earlier laid out what he termed the psyche's "hierarchy of needs" in his book *Motivation and Personality* (1954), and there he also outlined his vision of a new Psychology. Where Freud had explained that we have a primal set of drives, Maslow argued that Freud's list was far too limited—and much too primal. Yes, we have drives for food, shelter, sleep and sex, but that is not the whole story of our needs. Maslow believed our natural drives can be arranged into a hierarchy, depicted as a pyramid, with Freud's primal drives at its foundation and our higher motivations stacked on top of these, in stages that reach toward the summit of psychological fulfillment. After our most basic needs are met, new and more sophisticated drives awaken in us and other aspects of our psyches beg to be heard. Moving up the pyramid, we find that we also have a drive for safety and security that leads us to join communities; a desire to love and be loved that causes us to make friends and start a family; a drive for self-esteem and meaningful work; and finally, at the pinnacle of our development, a drive to know who we are in the fullest sense. This last, in Maslow's terms, is the desire for "self-actualization," and he argued that this highest drive could be fulfilled only when and if we open ourselves to our metaphysical dimensions. Like Frederic Myers, C.G. Jung, Aldous Huxley and William James, Maslow believed in a positive unconscious, free of pathology and based in the transpersonal dimensions of our nature, and he believed that by opening to these dimensions we come to full awareness of what we are, achieving the highest level of both sanity and spiritual fulfillment.

To describe and illustrate this high level of development, Maslow compiled a list of self-actualized people that included both Huxley and James (along with Ralph Waldo Emerson, Thomas Jefferson, Eleanor Roosevelt, Walt Whitman, John Muir and others),[3] and in almost all cases, these people reported having gained their highest insights as the result of what Maslow termed "peak experiences." These breakthrough moments in their lives were characterized by a sense of timelessness, transcendence, ecstasy and strong feelings of love and connectedness with all reality, and Maslow saw in these experiences, and in descriptions of their relevance to self-actualization, neglected realms of psychological inquiry. What if our psyches *do* have transpersonal and metaphysical aspects? What if connecting with these aspects *does* lead to self-actualization? What if staying cut off from them is at least one cause of mental illness and emotional instability? What if Eckhart's "Divine Ground of Being" actually does exist and the freedom it brings to the psyche when experienced is the fullest definition of sanity and wellness? Maslow had reached the conclusion that such possibilities should at least be investigated.

Maslow speculated that we often suffer and mope about at the bottom of the hierarchy of needs because of our culture's entrenched materialism, which has wrongly convinced us that if we're not yet happy, we only need acquire more of what we already have. We need more food, bigger houses and sexier spouses, rather than chasing after delusional religious experiences or mumbo-jumbo like the so-called "Divine Ground." Fulfillment is possible, but only if we seek it within the framework of our everyday desires in the material world. Maslow of course disagreed, believing that what drives us is more than primal urges and worldly concern. For him, fulfillment would come only if we grasped the transcendental roots of our being, and each time we did so, we would trigger the highest sort of "peak experience," and as these experiences accumulate, we move toward self-actualization. Maslow termed this process of evolving the existential condition of our being "Being-cognition therapy" because it depends on contacting *The Being* underlying our psyches; however, the task, from a therapeutic perspective, was to figure out how to generate such an experience on demand. By the time Huston arrived at Esalen, four years after Maslow's first visit, many there thought the answer had come along in the form of LSD.

# Esalen

A wide range of approaches were eventually tried, and many of them, including Feldenkrais energy work, the Rolfing form of deep tissue massage and the so-called "West Coast" form of Gestalt Therapy (forwarded by Gestalt's founder, Fritz Perls), were first developed at Esalen, but LSD had its turn in the spotlight, and that made Huston even more valuable, since he was well-acquainted with the experience of it. And, even after the drugs became illegal, what stayed in place, for both Huston and Esalen, was Maslow's framework of believing we have transpersonal aspects that elicit awakening when they are brought to bear on our conscious awareness. In brief, Huston believed that Psychology, via Maslow (and also Grof), was proving more open-minded as a discipline than either Philosophy or the academic study of religion, and that a splice seemed to be coming together, quickly gaining support from Stan Grof, Richard Tarnas, Anthony Sutich, Frances Vaughn and other transpersonal psychologists working at Esalen.

## Tightening the Braid

When Grof became a scholar in residence at Esalen in 1973, the Aquarian Age of Love and Peace seemed to have found a focal point. So much positive growth was taking place at Esalen so quickly that many people believed a new world order was on the way. Grof had left his job at the Spring Grove Hospital and LSD was now illegal, but attendees at Big Sur were already floating in sensory-deprivation tanks, using biofeedback machines, taking sensitivity training, exploring past-life regression and trying out other techniques to trigger peak experiences.

Of course, Grof was aware that not all the techniques for self-actualization were new, and sometimes he and his colleagues were actually reinventing the wheel. Ancient cultures had already found methods of consciousness expansion, including shamanic drumming, T'ai Chi, hatha yoga, *pranayama* (yogic breathing) and Zen meditation, and perhaps the ancient techniques had lasted so long for the simple reason that they worked. Grof believed that some cultures, including those of Tibet and India, might actually be centuries ahead of Western civilization, and if that was the case, he was eager to explore them. Grof had done his research and in Huston Smith, an expert on world religions, as well as a long-time practitioner of several spiritual techniques, he found a perfect resource.

Over the next fifteen years, Grof and his wife, Christina (herself an expert in nonordinary states of consciousness), conducted more than 30 month-long workshops and scores of shorter ones, and they often called on Huston to attend as guest faculty and expert adviser. Jeffrey Kripal has given us a detailed account of Grof's work there, and what comes across is that Grof actually knew he was trying to braid science with the traditional spiritualities. Looking at the names of several of these month-long courses, "Buddhism and Western Psychology," "Ancient Wisdom and Modern Science" and "Aboriginal Healing and Modern Medicine,"[4] we see this was one of his conscious goals, and Huston was trying to help him reach it.

Another resource for Grof, as he sought metrics from the traditional cultures to gauge and cultivate psychological growth, was Joe Campbell. Indeed, Grof's clinical research with LSD suggested that during sessions, patients sometimes tapped into the collective unconsciousness, and Campbell helped convince Grof that this was not only so but that this transpersonal content has healing power. Campbell believed that these experiences, however achieved, resonate with the mythic content of ancient cultures for the simple reason that they spring from the same transpersonal roots. Campbell saw tremendous therapeutic value in studying the world's mythologies, which for him is why they have stood the test of time despite science's attempts to kill them off. They have survived because they have psychological benefits. And so, like Huston, Campbell—despite his disdain for organized religion—helped to weave ancient strands of knowing into the braid that Grof was creating.[5]

In summary, the three guiding visions at Esalen, which continue, were Huxley's postulate that we have latent potentialities, Aurobindo's vision of our evolutionary purpose and Maslow's theory that our highest need is to self-actualize, all of which were compatible with Huston's, Grof's and Campbell's philosophies as well as with each other. The overall goal was to awaken into a secular enlightenment of hyper-sanity, and Huston was happy to help explore that possibility. And thereby he accomplished a significant hat trick in his career, finding a way to appeal to both New Agers at Esalen and religious conservatives elsewhere. Note that as the 1970s wore on, and just after he had become a member of Schuon's Sufi brotherhood, he was also soaking in the hot tubs at Big Sur and discussing the virtues of LSD—not easy to pull off without being a hypocrite, which he was not.

Huston believed that most people are *exoterics* who require religion, but there are also *esoterics* whose proclivities allow them to be more experimental, engaging in what he and Huxley termed "empirical mysticism."[6] Few of his friends at Esalen would have agreed with his first premise and even fewer of his Traditionalist friends would have agreed with the second—since the latter argued that even esoterics must follow established channels of growth—but Huston had reached a rationale all his own. The choice of which path one followed simply depended upon one's abilities and personality type.

## A RE-EVALUATION OF 'ENLIGHTENMENT'

The piece that had stayed in place for Huston since he first accepted the perennial philosophy was the goal of spiritual awakening; however, during the late 1970s, his views on enlightenment—whether secular or religious—changed significantly, and he lost faith in the notion of a complete or final breakthrough. He had no doubt that it was possible to mature spiritually (since he had done it himself) but he had become suspicious of traditional claims of a final or highest possible awakening. Consequently, in some ways, he was a good fit at Esalen, where numerous theories of self-actualization were being investigated without any of them being cast into dogma.

In 1996, during a television interview with Bill Moyers, Huston observed: "I'm a heretic among the Hindus in questioning the reality of what they call *jivanmukta*, a completely enlightened soul within this body. I do not think this happens. I think our mortal coils are too firm and too binding to allow that complete attainment within this life...."[7] Huston hadn't stopped believing that there is a Divine Ground or that there is a unitive knowledge that comes with experiencing it, but after 25 years of intense spiritual practice, as well as innumerable visits with holy men all over the world, he had become convinced the unitive knowledge can't be held onto all the time, nor is there anything like human perfection. "We strive for spiritual perfection," Huston remarked when we discussed this matter, "and it is good that we do so, but we cannot get all the way there, for we are fallible instruments."

When asked what he meant by "fallible," Huston made clear he wasn't saying we are tainted by sin, or suggesting that we are somehow inherently evil, but rather he meant something more like 'limited creatures with limited abilities.' The unitive knowledge is indeed valuable but it can't be held onto continuously (which is the common definition of enlightenment), and even if it were, we would still be, on the level of our relative selves, temporal creatures with limited memories, imaginations and knowledge. In short, not perfect.

Even the enlightened person would still have to interpret his or her experience of the Divine Ground with a relative mind that had been trained in a specific language and given a specific set of cultural beliefs and values. As in the case of what might be termed the 'relative absolutes' of sun, moon and sexuality (which are *relative* in that they are bound by time and space, but *absolute* in that all human minds must take them into account), the significance of the Divine Ground would still be weighed by a particular mind and applied to a worldly context. In short, even if a person was continuously experiencing the Divine Ground, he or she would still also be a person, and this brings with it a set of endemic limitations.

So Huston adjusted his criteria for spiritual maturity, believing now that it required coming to terms with both our timeless nature and our temporal natures as well. We may certainly grow in wisdom, and that should be our goal, but to imagine we will ever arrive at a place where growth is complete, or where we are omniscient or infallible, is the stuff of legend.[8] Huston still believed, as he wrote in *Forgotten Truth*, that the goal of spiritual practice is to turn our "flashes of insight" into "abiding light," but, he had added that this stabilization of wisdom "need not require that the terrain the light discloses remain in direct view."[9] He now argued that if our memory was "operative rather than idle, the mystic's experience of the inner light stabilizes to become his defining sense of reality." The mystic need not continuously experience the Ground for wisdom to exist; she need only let the experience of THAT inform all her actions. This was the new model of spiritual maturity that Huston adopted.

Another point to add here is that Huston saw an unexpected value in this reassessment of enlightenment, for if perfection or a final breakthrough were not possible, there was no ground for a division in the human race between the "enlightened" and some or other spiritual peasantry. Everyone is simply on the road to becoming clearer and more compassionate, co-learners on a vast journey that leads ever upward but to no final arrival. Furthermore, this open-ended model of self-actualization gave the spiritually mature person permission to keep on growing, finding new chances to apply the unitive knowledge—along with other insights of life, philosophical and emotional—to the circumstances of their everyday lives.

'Enlightenment' could still function like any other ideal, including those of beauty and goodness, and so, for example, the artist might never capture the perfection of Beauty, but reaching for it would still inspire him or her. The perfection of all ideals is embodied in the various archetypal forms of mythology, with Hercules or Bhima giving us examples of the ideal of physical strength, or Venus or Lakshmi as examples of ideal beauty, and these ideals resonate in our collective unconscious, providing reference points for our psyches to feed upon. It is not possible to be perfectly beautiful or perfectly good or perfectly strong, but that doesn't mean we couldn't strive for such ideals. The Buddha, Jesus, the Mahdi of the Sufis are all *hierophanies* of the 'Perfect Person' whose attainments we should celebrate and cultivate, even if we can't fully become them.

"My old student at Syracuse, Phil Novak, shares my general view of enlightenment," Huston mentioned one afternoon. "He talks about enlightenment as an 'asymptote.'" When asked what he meant by that term, Huston remarked, "Go ask Phil!" Novak shortly thereafter explained that *asymptote* is a term from mathematics, referring to a situation in which a straight line is approached by a point that is moving toward it perpendicularly, but (and this is what makes the point an asymptote) it never quite reaches the line, since as it moves closer, it increasingly curves away from the line toward the parallel. "An asymptote is something that keeps getting closer to its goal but never reaches it," Novak explained, "and that is how Huston sees enlightenment. A person might get closer and closer, but there is no end to the journey. We are infinitely *betterable*, but never *perfectable*."[10]

Later that same day in Berkeley, Huston agreed with Novak's description, but then quickly offered an addenda, "Well, maybe accepting that we will never be perfect—at least, in any way other than accepting all aspects of what we are—*is* a kind of perfection." What he implied was that without a final breakthrough, the wise person is free to own his or her limitations as well as his or her limitlessness. "Even Jesus prayed," Huston wrote in an essay for *The Eastern Buddhist*, "and the Buddha continued to sit after his enlightenment."[11]

An interesting addendum to this is that when Huston's views were discussed with Mike Murphy, Murphy began to laugh, challenging his old friend's position. Murphy agreed that spiritual growth never stops (whether continuous awareness of the Divine Ground is possible or not), but he seemed more willing to talk in terms of stages of enlightenment than to throw out the term altogether. He pointed out that Huston himself was often accused of being enlightened, and when I asked Murphy if he thought that was true, he answered that it might be, citing the unusual quality of Huston's personality and presence. "Huston told me once that he wasn't enlightened," Murphy remarked, "but I told him something I had once heard said about Emerson. When Emerson claimed he wasn't enlightened, the person who had accused him of it replied: 'Sir, what you ARE is shouting at me so loudly I can't hear what you're saying.'" Murphy laughed again. "Over the past fifty years, we've only had a handful of presenters at Esalen who really 'glowed in the dark' and Huston is one of them."

As a kind of last word on Huston's reappraisal of enlightenment, and reflecting his old viewpoint that mystical experiences are useful only when they lead to compassionate action, he once wrote: "It is easy to make too much of direct mystical disclosures. Desert stretches provide opportunities for growth that are as important as mountaintop experiences, and theologians assure us that souls can be established in an abiding relationship with God without being sensibly aware of God's presence. The goal is not altered states but altered traits. Aldous Huxley's observation that the task of life is to overcome the fundamental human disability of egoism comes in here, for every step we take in overcoming that is in God's direction."[12]

# Chapter Twenty-One:
# Wisdomkeepers

A long time ago the Creator came to Turtle Island and said to the Red People: 'You will be keepers of Mother Earth. Among you I will give the wisdom about Nature, about the interconnectedness of all things, about balance and about living in harmony. You Red People will see the secrets of Nature. . . . The day will come when you will need to share the secrets with other people of the Earth because they will stray from their Spiritual ways. The time to start sharing is today.

A Mohican prophecy

Nature has spread for us a rich and delightful banquet. Shall we turn from it? We are still in Eden; the wall that shuts us out of the garden is our own ignorance and folly. . . .

Thomas Cole,
Nineteenth Century American landscape painter

In the summer of 1983, after ten years of teaching in Syracuse, Huston and Kendra moved to Berkeley, California, to be closer to their daughters. Their first home was on Avenida Avenue, but eventually they moved to Colusa Avenue. This was the beginning of the most productive period in Huston's career, and although he had technically retired, he was still running at full tilt. During the 1980s, he picked up several more honorary Ph.D.s, including ones from Alaska Pacific University and Hamline University, and he would be a visiting professor at Villanova; furthermore, as the best-known scholar of religion in the world, he was still a favorite on the lecture circuit—delivering talks at venues as far away as Kyoto and Bombay.[1] However, the bulk of his work took place near home and on campus at Berkeley, where he was now an adjunct professor, offering regular courses in World Religion while also anchoring an annual program for visiting scholars. Berkeley, along with the University of Chicago and Harvard, had been given a grant by the National Endowment for the Humanities to explore 'A Global Approach to the Study of Religion,' and Huston was picked to lead the program at Berkeley. In that capacity, he offered workshops over three summers and participated in a wide range of discussions with scholars from all over the country. His lecture for the program in 1987, "'Another World to Live in,' or 'How I Teach the Introductory Course,'" summarized the approach he had used for nearly forty years, which had now become the approach used by many religion professors, the author of this volume included.[2]

Huston was now free from his regular faculty responsibilities for the first time in his career, which gave him more opportunity to work on personal projects, including regular visits to Esalen, just two hours down the Coast Highway. At Esalen, he offered workshops (sometimes with the help of Kendra or Gael) or participated in the programs of others, including, in 1986, a conference organized by Stanislav Grof and Robert Forte on "Entheogens and the Future of Religions."

Huston was suspicious of the term *entheogen* ("god-revealing") because it suggested that psychedelics somehow contain God or guarantee a glimpse of the Divine—which, as we've seen, he didn't believe was possible. (An experience might come if the right person was in the right frame of mind, but wasn't guaranteed by putting a pill in one's mouth.) However, he agreed that many shamanic cultures—at least those employing a psychedelic sacrament—might see it that way. But whatever the case, he was entirely delighted to be getting back together with old friends, including Walter Houston Clark from the IFIF days, who was now studying with a Mexican shaman named Salvador Roquet.[3]

Huston also appreciated that the conference on entheogens was academically sound and ambitious, covering a wide range of opinions on the subject. LSD's inventor, Albert Hofmann, was there, along with other experts, including: R. Gordon Wasson, the ethno-botanist who first argued that Vedic Hinduism's *soma* was probably a magic mushroom; experts on the subject of religion, including Huston, Jack Kornfield (an American Buddhist who had trained as a monk in Thailand and Burma) and Brother David Steindl-Rast (a Benedictine monk with a Ph.D. in psychology); respected experts on psychedelics, such as the biochemists Alexander and Ann Shulgin; visionary theorists such as Terence McKenna; and, informed psychologists such as Clark and Grof. Many years later, in 1996, Forte would compile these presentations into a book of the same title as the conference, which remains today the single best text on the subject of entheogens and religion.[4]

## THE WORLD UNDER OUR FEET

In the 1980s, and ever after, California offered so much opportunity to Huston that he rarely missed his life back in Syracuse, but there *was* one exception. In New York, he had enjoyed a ten-year relationship with several Native American elders of the Onondaga tribe, which had a definite influence on his life and work.

In 1973, soon after he had arrived at Syracuse, Huston learned that a tribe of Native Americans was living only five miles from the campus. "Up until then I had dismissed the whole family of indigenous religions—namely, the tribal and the oral—as unimportant," Huston later wrote in his book, *A Seat at the Table*. "I blame my teachers for this, for *they* dismissed them. 'After all,' they said, 'they can't (or until recently couldn't) even write, so what did they know?'"[5] But Huston was curious to find out, deciding that this was a great chance to learn. He drove out to the reservation early one morning and met with Chief Leon Shenandoah and another "wisdomkeeper" of the Onondaga, Oren Lyons, to share a discussion that lasted late into the afternoon. Jumping into his car for the trip back home, Huston felt an excitement growing inside him that finally detonated into a realization: "'My God, Huston,' I heard myself saying in the car. 'For three decades you have been circling the globe trying to understand the metaphysics and religions of worlds different from your own, and here's one that has been right under your feet the entire time—and you haven't even noticed it!'"[6]

What started out as a one-time visit to the Onondaga soon became another of Huston's close apprenticeships with experts of a traditional religion. Over the next ten years, he spent most of his free weekends on the reservation, and came to feel guilty for not having mentioned Native American religions in his book *The Religions of Man*, suggesting by omission that they didn't deserve what Huston later termed "a seat at the table" with the other great traditions.

The first step in Huston's reassessment of what he termed the "primal religions" was to get over his prejudice against cultures that store their wisdom orally. Huston quickly realized that he, like most Westerners, held a bias against societies that don't use written language, seeing them as primitive, backward and childish. 'True' or 'sophisticated' societies build cities, create monuments and record their religious views in written scripture, right? "Wrong," Huston said. "These people have a very sophisticated culture; it's simply built on different values and viewpoints than ours." Most Native American societies, including that of the Onondaga, were nomadic and eschewed written language for the simple reason that it was impractical to carry written texts around as they traveled from camp to camp. Given their belief that they should live softly on the earth, they avoided building cities and fixed roads that would scar the face of their "Great Mother." Their own ultimate 'monument' for proving their sophistication was to live in such a way that nobody could tell that they had existed. Preferring the 'Seventh Generation' ideal, that seven generations hence their descendents would have the same bountiful resources that they had enjoyed, they were careful to live in harmony with the natural world, building no statues of steel and cement. What had made them seem barbaric to the Europeans, all of whom had put a premium on written texts and urban landscapes, was actually what made them civilized in their own eyes. And when Huston caught on to this, he felt both humbled and embarrassed.

While studying the dynamics and functions of the Onondaga's oral tradition, Huston gained new respect for their ways. "We think of writing as simply an addition to oral communication," he later told Michael Toms in a radio interview, "but it came as a shock—and yet as a moment of truth—when it dawned on me that from their perspective . . . writing is not simply an addition but an invasion of the oral tradition, meaning that it excises or . . . overshadows certain virtues which an exclusively oral society possesses."[7] Huston saw how an oral tradition functions with an inherent prioritization of information that literary cultures lack. "It is clear to me," he explained to Toms, "that one of the prices of literacy is that we become inundated and swamped with information. We live in the 'Information Age,' and we think of that as a total good, and yet what about finding one's way around in it?" Huston then gave Toms the example of visiting the Widner Library at Harvard with the intent of discovering which books had the most useful things to say about the meaning of life: "Which isle [aisle] should I walk down? There's nothing in that system which gives us the slightest clue to priorities." He didn't want to overly romanticize tribal peoples, but he understood how the great informing myths of the Onondaga, which keep in place such persistent questions as *what is the purpose of life?*, gave them a sense of orientation, "of where they were in the world and the direction they should move in their life."

Huston's respect for the Onondaga intensified further when he looked into the content of their philosophy. Specifically, he celebrated their view of nature as benevolent rather than evil, angry or inferior; nature demands respect, but if respect is forthcoming, the Onondaga believed the Great Mother would give them all that is necessary for life—if not all that greed and avarice would want. The Western world had "positioned itself in opposition to nature with a stance that was reserved and critical," Huston explained in an article for the journal *Philosophy East & West*,[8] but "Native America has sided with the world itself." The Onondaga posited no separation between themselves and the physical world, and no separation between the physical world and the spiritual world. All things have spirit and the land itself is sacred. Where Medieval Christians had cowered from the evil they projected onto Creation, hoping for deliverance from the "Vale of Tears" and the "Pageant of Suffering," the Onondaga celebrated this earth as paradise, with no concept that they had been exiled from Eden.

Huston learned that the Onondaga saw themselves in a situation of "mutual relatedness" to all other beings, whether two-legged, four-legged, equipped with fins or otherwise.[9] The Onondaga considered all creatures—and even all *things*—part of the divine plan, giving humans no special place of importance. All species in the "web of life" exist because the Great Spirit wishes them to exist, and humans have no right to claim dominance or preferential treatment. Nor should humans demonize nature, as the popular Hollywood movie "Jaws," about a giant shark, was doing at that very moment. And with this in mind, Chief Lyons, in 1977, and with Huston's help, visited a conference at the United Nations in Geneva, Switzerland, reprimanding the attendees for acting as though only people mattered: "I do not see a delegation here for the Four Footed. I see no seat for the Eagles," he remarked. "We forget and we consider ourselves superior. But we are after all a mere part of Creation . . ."[10]

During the ten years that Huston regularly visited the Onondaga, he had ample opportunity to observe how they specifically participated in the Great Order, and he used this as a reference point for his own spirituality in the years ahead. Did he recall an experience of seeing through the Onondaga lens? "Oh yes," he said, "I think the first time was when my granddaughter, Sierra, came to visit us during a school vacation." Though only six-years-old, Karen's daughter wasn't content to watch television all day or play in the yard. "She wanted projects!" Huston reminisced with a chuckle.[11] Realizing that the compost heap in Kendra's garden needed tending, Huston asked if she'd like to help him turn the whole thing over to make it active. "I told her we would be like Native Americans, returning some energy to the Earth. And so one brisk morning, we went to work."

Sierra was inquisitive, questioning her grandfather: What would their shoveling accomplish? Why was it important to turn the pile over? Huston struck up a short lecture on composting, explaining that getting more air into the pile would accelerate the process of breaking down the grass, leaves and plants into useable soil. "She was fascinated by all of it. Part of the heap was ripe, but it contained stones and various kinds of bric-a-brac, so we seized on a wooden crate that was lying around, covered it with chicken wire, and sifted out the intruders." Over the next few days, they created a magnificent heap of friable soil that Sierra kept sifting through her fingers as though it was treasure. Huston felt that their creation deserved a title, so after discussing the possibilities, he and Sierra settled on "Perfect Dirt." The last step was to put the perfect dirt intp plastic bags to be delivered by hand to various neighbors, office secretaries and friends on the last day of Sierra's visit.

"Sierra went on later to study marine biology," Huston remarked, "but she never forgot our project together—and neither did I! I kept monitoring the compost pile after she left, and in the years ahead it would be one of my daily spiritual practices—until osteoporosis made that sort of work impossible for me." Huston thought at first he had kept up the composting duties for his granddaughter, but soon realized it was also for himself, and about what he had learned from the Onondaga. It started to feel as if the project was drawing him into something larger, assuming its own proportions. "The first word that came to mind was *participation*—in composting I was participating in nature's rounds. Then, though, an adverb moved in to underscore that word. I was *consciously* participating in nature's rounds. Willy-nilly, everything participates in nature's gyrations—'ashes to ashes, dust to dust.'"[12]

Huston's apprenticeship with the Onondaga had expanded his view of spiritual maturity in a significantly new direction. The Onondaga, like most Native American tribes, had no equivalent concept to *jivanmukta* or enlightenment, but their embrace of the natural world, and their desire to live in harmony with all species, had become a true measure of wisdom for him. He had accepted from his parents, his father-in-law and the Tibetans also that spiritual maturity must include concern for others, but now he extended that principle to include the planet itself—right down to the dirt. Maybe the Onondaga were right that it is more than enough enlightenment to live in peace with the natural design of all things.

## AMERICA'S SHADOW STRUGGLE

Given his newfound respect for Native American religions, Huston took on "two projects of correction and inclusion." The first was to add a new chapter on "The Primal Religions" to *The Religions of Man* (updated in 1991 as *The World's Religions*), about which he commented elsewhere that, "To omit them from the first edition of my book was inexcusable, and I am glad I will not go to my grave with that mistake uncorrected."[13] In addition, and as had happened when he had studied Tibetan Buddhism, Huston took up the Native Americans' cause, leading a delegation of tribal elders to the World Parliament of Religions in Cape Town, South Africa, in December of 1999.

During the 1893 World's Fair in Chicago, a featured piece of artwork had been the sculpture "The End of the Trail," displaying a Native American warrior on horseback, slumped in his saddle with the tip of his spear pointing to the ground in defeat. As Phil Cousineau has written, many Americans and Europeans viewed this statue as a literal rather than symbolic description, "proof that the Indians had been conquered and removed from the land—and from sight."[14] The catch phrase of the World's Fair had been "A Century of Progress," and the taming of the plains tribes was considered one facet of that progress. Though the Fair also featured the First World Parliament of Religions, Cousineau has pointed out that "not one group of indigenous people was invited." So Huston hoped that after more than a century of being suppressed and ignored, Native Americans would finally be granted a "seat at the table," a chance to share their spiritual views with the world.

The delegation consisted of eight Native American leaders, including Oren Lyons, Vine Deloria Jr., Winona LaDuke (chosen by *Time* magazine in 1994 as one of America's fifty most promising leaders under the age of forty), Leon Shenandoah, Charlotte Black Elk (granddaughter of the famous Lakota holy man, Black Elk) and others with whom Huston would act as interlocutor. Inspired by the trickster advice of his friend Reuben Snake, "Listen, or your tongue will keep you deaf," Huston urged the audience to pay close attention to what native people—silenced for so long—had to say.

Rather than dwelling on old wounds from the past, the elders emphasized the need for all people in the world to wake up to our shared influence on the environment—and, given the pressures of over-population and climate change, the world seemed ready to listen. After a century of silence and four centuries of "shadow struggle," the delegates were able to share their concerns on a world stage for the first time in front of an audience of seven thousand attendees. "These are our times and responsibilities," Chief Shenandoah proclaimed during his time on stage. "Every human being has a sacred duty to protect the welfare of our Mother Earth, from whom all life comes. In order to do this we must recognize the enemy—the one within us. We must begin with ourselves. We must live in harmony with the Natural World and recognize that excessive exploitation can only lead to our own destruction. We cannot trade the welfare of our future generations for profit now. We must abide by the Natural Law or be victims of its ultimate reality."[15] Huston, sitting on stage with Shenandoah, led the cheers when the chief was finished, and later, when asked about his own viewpoint, added, "I stand with the native peoples on this: The people of the world will either hang together on solving environmental issues or we'll hang separately."

After arriving home from South Africa, Huston worked with his friend Cousineau, as well as the filmmaker Gary Rhine, to produce not only a book about the visit to Cape Town but also a film with the same name, *A Seat at the Table: Struggling for American Indian Religious Freedom*, and in 2004 this film was a big hit at the Amnesty International Film Festival. "Phil and I felt really grateful to have been able to do something for the Native American 'shadow struggle,' and I felt it was partial compensation for having left them out of my first book on world religions. They still don't get the attention they deserve, but we were trying to correct that."

## THE INTERNATIONAL YOUTH SEMINARS

Returning to Huston's semi-retirement in the late 1980s, his extra time allowed him to focus on new projects, and new projects came along. He and Kendra were asked in 1985 to help facilitate "The International Youth Seminar: Building Bridges Between the World's Religions," a program in which one hundred college students from all over the world would go on pilgrimage together for the summer, visiting the world's great religious shrines in Jerusalem, Turkey, Italy, India, Thailand, Korea, Hong Kong and China. Seeing this as a noble cause, they agreed.

The idea for the seminar came from the Reverend Sun Myung Moon, leader of the Korean Christian movement often termed the "Moonies." Reverend Moon had been repeatedly accused in the press of fanaticism and dictatorial control of his followers, and in 1982, the United States Government also convicted him of tax evasion; consequently, he spent a year in the Danbury Federal Prison. His public image had been tarnished to say the least. "I think the Youth Seminar was partially for public relations purposes," Huston speculated as he discussed the program, "to show that he was actually a nice guy, and more broad-minded than he seemed." But whatever was Moon's intent, Huston's goal was to support inter-religious understanding on a global scale, and he was happy to let Sun Myung Moon foot the bill.

Huston and Kendra were brought in at the beginning of the trip at the Unification Church's facility near Tarrytown, New York, to help prepare the participants for what they would encounter on their travels. Then, at the end and once the trip was winding down, Huston was flown to Seoul, South Korea, to help celebrate what they had learned. The first Youth Seminar was such a success that Moon decided to fund another one, and then another one. Huston and Kendra would participate in three seminars in all, being flown to Anzio, Italy, for the beginning of one and with Kendra a leader for the trip round the world on another.

When asked what he remembered most from the Youth Seminars, Huston offered that he had reconnected with his friend John Blofeld, who was a leader on one of the trips. "He was along as the expert on Buddhism," Huston commented, "and we had many opportunities to be together and discuss common interests." When asked what had made an impression on her, Kendra recalled a forty-six-year old Tibetan lama, Lobzang Tsetan, with whom she often sat during long bus rides. "Two memories about him really stand out for me. In India, it was very hot and the bus had no air conditioning. For some reason, it always felt ten degrees cooler when I sat beside him! My second memory of him is that one morning our luggage had been removed from the hotel and placed by the curb for the bus driver to load. The driver was an old man, so it was going to be difficult for him, but without saying a word, Lobzang hitched up his maroon robes and began helping the man. How many monks or priests would do something like that? Lobzang really was marvelous."

Huston and Kendra reconnected with this monk three or four more times after Kendra's Youth Seminar with him and after he rose in the ranks of his monastic order. Lobzang Tsetan bacame Khen Rinpoche Lobzang Tsetan, abbot of the Panchen Lama's monastery in exile, located near Bangalore, India.[16] He currently works closely with the Dalai Lama and lectures in Europe and America to raise funds for his monastery. During the Youth Seminar he was one of the ten leaders who each oversaw ten students as they traveled together. When contacted about what he termed the "Moonie trip," Rinpoche was happy to share memories of his time with Kendra and Huston. "Huston is a generous person, with great love for the Tibetan people," Rinpoche observed. "Actually, he loves everyone. He doesn't discriminate. Maybe that's why he is a good friend of His Holiness, the Dalai Lama. They both love everyone! And that's what the Youth Seminar had really been all about, learning to live together peacefully in this world."

In 1989, the 10th Panchen Lama died suddenly at the age of 51, soon after giving a speech that was critical of the Chinese leadership's treatment of Tibetans. Whether he was murdered or not is still a topic of controversy, though few Tibetans doubt what happened. Sadly, from Huston's perspective, the shadow struggle of the Tibetan people continues in the same vein as that of Native Americans. He continues in his disappointment over their persecution at the hands of the Chinese, whom he has never stopped thinking of as countrymen.

## An unexpected homecoming

Huston and Kendra have an in-laws cottage behind their home in Berkeley, and for many years it was reserved for Tibetan refugees sent to them by the Dalai Lama. As one set of guests learned English, along with the necessary skills for living in a new land, they moved out and a new group replaced them. Today Kendra lives in the cottage and the Tibetans have actually moved into the house with Huston, where Dolma Gyaltsen and her husband Ngodup cook and clean and act as his caregivers. But this is not the first time that the Smiths shared their living space.

In the mid-1980s there came a chance for Huston to get closer to his daughter Gael and with her daughter, Serena. Soon after Huston and Kendra first arrived in Berkeley, and while they were still living on Avenida Drive, Gael got a divorce and moved into the apartment on the first floor of their house. Gael, as a trained expert in massage, movement and somatics, and a recognized heir to the work of Ida Rolf, had no trouble supporting herself financially. But her work caused her to travel often and her 12-year-old daughter was relocating to a new school, so part of Gael's rationale for living near her parents was to give Serena's life more stability. "I did not want her to be a latch-key kid," Gael recalled, "but Serena didn't really need a baby sitter either. Living near my parents seemed like a good solution."

Serena had been born in New York City. When the birth occured, Gael had felt such peace and serenity that she and her husband, Stuart, decided to name the baby "Serena." Since her head popped out at exactly 11:59 PM, followed by her body two minutes later, they gave her the middle name of "Midnight."[17]

Trying to be a steadying influence, Huston spent as much time with her as was possible, given his busy career. "Serena was beautiful inside and out," Huston said with pride, "and greater love hath no man than for his granddaughter." And so he began to reminisce:

> When she was going to Berkeley High, during her Junior year, she was trying-out for the crew team and I shuttled her back and forth to practice. Every morning that Fall, I would get up at 5 o'clock and drive her to where the team rowed during home meets. They would have an hour of vigorous exercise, then put the shell on their shoulders and carry it back to the clubhouse. Serena was finding herself through sports at that time, and I encouraged her as much as I could. In college, I had played tennis and it was good for us both—on many levels. Unfortunately, Serena didn't make the starting team, and that was very hard on her.
>
> I tried to cheer her up—since she had been picked as an alternate and that wasn't really so bad—but there was only so much I could say. But she and I became very close because of that. She knew how much I cared about her, and how badly I felt that things hadn't gone her way. I started giving her even more attention, and we enjoyed our time together.

When asked for a happy memory of Serena in those days, Huston replied that there were too many to count, and he felt a deepening of family connections. Serena graduated from Berkeley High in 1992 with a beaming Huston Smith watching her from the audience. And later that year he took her to a rock concert. "Mickey Hart and I were good friends in those days, and he invited me to come to a Grateful Dead concert in San Francisco. But the only reason I accepted the offer was so that Serena could see them. When we got to the auditorium, she came with Mickey and me and we went into the greenroom and met everyone in the band, and then we had these front row seats. It was a special night, and wonderful for Serena. She was just beaming!" When asked how he had reacted to the concert, Huston smiled and replied, "Well, when the music started, people began to sway and Serena and I just swayed along with them. For me, it was about being with her."

# Chapter Twenty-Two:
# Car Trouble in Tanzania

Seriously, what are the principles of their theories, on what evidence are they based, what do they explain that wasn't already obvious, etc? These are fair requests for anyone to make. If they can't be met, then I'd suggest recourse to Hume's advice in similar circumstances: to the flames.

Naom Chomsky on Postmodernism

David Bohm, physicist and close colleague of both Oppenheimer and Einstein, was a theorist whose work greatly interested Huston in the 1980s. Shortly before leaving Syracuse, Huston was asked to chair a committee to bring important speakers into the religion department, and he suggested that they invite Bohm. "My colleagues were a bit upset with me at first," Huston remembered. "They said, 'Bohm should be brought here by the physics department, not us. Why waste our sop of a budget on him?" How had Huston responded? "Well, Bohm was making such interesting claims about the nature of reality, I couldn't think of anyone whose theories had deeper ramifications for religion and philosophy. Anyway, after a bit more discussion, I was able to convince them to bring him to Syracuse."[1]

When asked how that had worked out, Huston replied, "Brilliantly, even my colleagues had to agree that his work was exciting, and for me, personally, it was a chance to get to know him better and talk shop. We had some very stimulating conversations that week."

Huston had met David Bohm in June of 1980, at a conference on "Knowledge, Education and Human Values." sponsored by Columbia University and held in Woodstock, Vermont. He had learned quickly that Bohm was an unexpected ally in the fight against dogmatic materialism in the academy. Bohm, who was teaching at the University of London at the time, made it clear at the conference that he stood with Huston. James Hillman (a student of Carl Jung's), Rollo May (another psychologist) and other intellectuals were arguing, according to one news reporter, that "The scientific method . . . has created an economic, political and educational system that values facts over curiosity, financial gains over social contributions, precision over insights."[2] And to Huston's further delight, Bohm's lecture also included comments supporting the theory that the universe has a metaphysical aspect; in fact, Bohm described a transcendent level of reality that sounded almost identical—*if not identical*—to Eckhart's and Huxley's Divine Ground of Being, as well as Hinduism's *Brahman*.

Just before the conference began, Bohm had published his landmark book, *Wholeness and the Implicate Order*, in which he presented a distillation of a theory he had been working on for more than thirty years. He had been nudged toward his revolutionary views by the unusual behavior of quantum entities called photons. In brief, the aspect that intrigued Bohm was this: if two related photons of light (related because they result from the splitting of the same *positron,* which is a larger quantum entity) are traveling in opposite directions, they somehow maintain the same angles of polarization (basically, the same orientation in space relative to their point of origin) no matter how far apart they travel in space, *or even if one of them is affected by an outside force along the way.* For example, if a scientist changes the orientation of one of the photons, the other one will instantaneously be found to have the same new angle of polarization. This phenomenon was proven conclusively by experiment two years later, in 1982, at the Institute of Optics at the University of Paris. It had already been accepted as most likely even at the beginning of Bohm's career, and what drew Bohm's attention—and everyone else's—was that it seemed to present a contradiction to Einstein's theory that nothing could travel faster than the speed of light. This business about one photon changing its orientation in summary with another seemed to suggest a sort of instantaneous communication between two distant objects. *Instantaneous* occurs outside the realm of speed altogether, let alone faster than the speed of light. For Bohm, who agreed with Einstein that nothing was likely to break light speed, this phenomenon of the 'communicating' photons suggested that quantum theory must somehow be incomplete, that perhaps a better theory could resolve or explain away what appeared to be a contradiction from inside the current view. Maybe nothing could travel faster than light but instantaneous communication is somehow also possible.

Bohm began to draft a new and broader perspective, and after more than two decades finally arrived at his theory, arguing that quantum reality is actually based on what he termed an "implicate order." His view was that there is a fundamental but *unobservable* level of order in the universe that gives rise to all observable phenomena, including not only light photons but, at higher magnitudes of reality, children, trees and Buicks. The underlying level, which he termed the "enfolded order" (synonymous with what others have termed the "quantum potential"), sometimes "unfolds" into discrete quantum moments of physical being. However, Bohm believed that on the "enfolded" level, where nothing is manifest as an observable entity, all things are really part of *one* thing—though this thing is not a *thing* at all, at least not in the Newtonian sense. Bohm described it as an "implicate order" that underlies the "explicate order" of the physical universe. He theorized that as various quanta emerge from it, they retain some characteristics of their implicate—and infinitely interconnected—original state. The beauty of this theory for the problem of those pesky photons that seem to instantaneously communicate with each other was that it allowed for the photons to exist as discrete particles on one level of their being (as they moved away from each other in the explicit order) but explained how they could also change their orientation simultaneously. On the explicit level, the photons were in cahoots simply because *they still retained characteristics of the implicate level from which they had emerged;* they were not communicating across a vast distance at a speed greater than light; they were simply behaving as the one thing they fundamentally were on the implicate level of existence.

This summary is a redacted explanation of Bohm's theory in *Wholeness and the Implicate Order* and intended to illustrate the components of Bohm's work that so appealed to Huston. First and foremost, it contained the premise that there is a level of things that transcends physical reality and this level of quantum potentiality not only exists but is the foundation for all existence, a view which sounded to Huston very much like Vedanta's Brahman and Eckhart's Divine Ground. Though its presence of the implicate order is strongly suggested by the behavior of quantum entities like split photons, it cannot, because of its implicit and unmanifest nature, be quantified directly by scientific methods, since there is nothing to 'see' with the tools of science. This concept also jibed with the claims of mystics, who had written that the purest level of Being exists beyond both time and space.

As Huston dug more deeply into Bohm's view of Reality, the points of resonance with his own views kept mounting. For example, Bohm's theory supported and expressed the notion that the universe, at least at its quantum level, is *non-local*, meaning, in the jargon of physics and argued earlier by John Stewart Bell, that the events and entities we encounter in the explicate order are not ultimately autonomous or disconnected. Bohm argued that at the implicate level, all knowledge of the universe is stored as pure potentiality in a state of "dynamic vacuum," and at that level, where there are no observable phenomena, reality is entirely non-local and non-temporal. On that enfolded level, it is Oneness—or 'Noneness' (since it's difficult to speak of a singularity from which nothing can be separate, including a place from which to observe its oneness)—that then unfolds into physical patterns and events. The closer we get to the subtlest and most implicate level of Reality, events express themselves with increasing degrees of profoundly interconnected, self-referential and therefore "non-local" behavior.

One of the characteristics that really grabbed Huston about this aspect of Bohm's theory was that he had heard something very much like it before. In Hinduism, there is the premise that the physical world, the realm of change and impermanence, rises out of an unmanifest reality, and that Reality itself is also non-local. For Hindus, information about the totality of the universe is contained in each discrete moment of creation, which they then describe with the visual analogy of the "Jewel Net of Indra." Reality is depicted in the analogy as an expansive net created by the god Indra, and at each junction in the threads of the net there is a highly reflective jewel. Each of these jewels can be seen reflected in all the other jewels, and the reflections of all of the jewels are contained in each jewel. So in the Vedantic conception, each discrete moment of creation contains the blueprint of the entire universe—or, to mix metaphors, the entire creation is contained in the 'DNA' of each moment of creation. For Vedantists, the entire universe can be—as it were—cloned from any aspect of the universe, though it is also, and somewhat enigmatically, a discrete moment in the jewel net of Indra.

Bohm was arguing, in accord with Advaita ('nondual,' or even 'non-local') Vedanta, that all of reality is interconnected, and to Huston's delight, Bohm didn't leave the phenomenon of consciousness out of his theory regarding this interconnectedness. In fact, Bohm had devoted two full chapters of his book to a discussion of the nature of consciousness, arguing that as matter and energy were once treated as separate entities, along with space and time, perhaps nothing, including consciousness and matter, is ultimately separate from anything else. Reality merely comprises varying densities of one infinitely self-referential and all-inclusive phenomenon. Where Newtonians and strict materialists had argued that consciousness is an epiphenomenon of matter (consciousness having developed slowly as a by-product of increasingly sophisticated stages of biological evolution), Bohm wondered if it might not be the other way around. Perhaps material creation is actually an epiphenomenon of consciousness. And this started Huston thinking, what if, in terms of another context altogether, it could be that people are all connected on the level of Jung's and Campbell's *collective unconscious* because that level of physical existence retains more of the absolute interconnectivity endemic to the deepest level of Being? Could the collective unconscious exist closer to the Pure Consciousness from which all superficial levels of our psyches (and all other things in the world) arise?

It was ironic that at this time when metaphysics had been barred from philosophy and couldn't be taken seriously in the academic study of religion, it was being legitimately considered in the discipline of Physics, the hardest of the hard sciences. Einstein had replaced Newton's view of a three-dimensional universe floating in linear time with a four-dimensional space-time continuum where matter and energy are transposable. Quantum mechanics had suggested that the universe isn't built out of atoms or any other absolute or indivisible particles, but rather is a complex interaction of energetic processes arising from pure potentiality. The universe, composed of interrelated vibratory events, is more like a cosmic interference pattern than a structure comprising discrete material objects. In fact, with reference to objects, quantum physics was—and is—entirely undermining the materialists' viewpoint, and so Bohm was simply adding support to this position. Even he came to see that his views had a definite resonance with certain ancient viewpoints, and later in his life he would discuss these similarities with mystics of several traditions, most notably with Jiddu Krishnamurti, the Indian holy man Huston had interviewed many years before.

The similarity between Bohm's views and certain tenents of Hinduism suggested to Huston that science was bringing metaphysics out of mothballs, and this couldn't happen soon enough for him. Now that metaphysics had been returned to physics perhaps it could also be returned to philosophy and the academic study of religion. Strict materialism had had its day, and the next step in the development of the hard sciences suggested that the ancient traditions hadn't been as wrong as the modernists had supposed. A few years later, Huston would tell Michael Toms in an interview: "The developments in science have undercut a kind of crass Newtonian view of reality as consisting of ultimate little atoms that are unrelated to other things—our century has undercut that. The interrelation between the parts of being—which David Bohm emphasizes with his concept of implicate wholeness—clearly is a move back toward the unity which traditional philosophies, those of Asia included, emphasized."[3]

It's important to note that Bohm wasn't the first quantum physicist to allow metaphysics back into the discussion or to suggest that mystics of the ancient world had had accurate intuitions about the nature of reality. Huston was well aware of that fact. Thirty-four years earlier, in 1946, Erwin Schrodinger, the winner of the 1933 Nobel Prize for Physics,[4] had commented in his book *What is Life?*, "The point of view taken here levels with what Aldous Huxley has recently—and very appropriately—called *The Perennial Philosophy*."[5] Schrodinger agreed with Huxley, though he knew Huxley's views contradicted the scientific dogma of their time, because Shrodinger believed metaphysics might actually be important even to physics, and so he later commented in *Mind and Matter* (1958):

It is relatively easy to sweep away the whole of metaphysics, as Kant did. [. . .] But you must not think that what has been achieved is the actual elimination of metaphysics from the empirical content of human knowledge. In fact, if we cut out all metaphysics it will be found to be vastly more difficult, indeed probably quite impossible, to give any intelligible account of even the most circumscribed area of specialization within any specialized science.[6]

*****

Today this viewpoint, of which the painter Salvador Dali once gleefully termed "quantum mysticism," is fairly commonplace in the discussion of quantum theory (see especially the recent work of Nick Herbert and Amit Goswami), but it's important to note that Bohm was the first to give a complex explanation of how it actually worked. This formalizing is what excited Huston most and is the reason he had brought Bohm to Syracuse.

Modernism, with its view that humankind can only know what science can prove, held sway in academic circles for nearly a century, so to suggest, as Bohm had done, that this was an antiquated view constituted an attack on modernism's root assumption. Bohm, like Schrodinger, was saying that the best understanding of the universe necessitated the acceptance of the view that reality has a metaphysical aspect, an aspect that by definition could never be directly quantified or measured, though its effects in the realm of time and space could be. In short, Bohm, who later entered into discussions with Krishnamurti on the overlaps in their perspectives, was arguing that there is a facet of reality that science cannot see.

## What else science cannot see

In the 1980s, Huston went about trying to revitalize the discipline of philosophy in two particular ways: First, he suggested that philosophers consider the possibility of metaphysical entities such as Bohm's *implicate order*, Hinduism's *Brahman*, Emerson's Oversoul and Tillich's "God beyond God," along with the human capacity for experiencing them. Second, he questioned the limits of science and pure reason even for telling the story of life as we experience it on a daily basis. In an essay titled "Excluded Knowledge," for the *Teachers College Record*,[7] Huston argued in 1979 there are areas of human concern with which science finds no traction and provides no insights. Broadly speaking, he subsumed these phenomena of artistic taste and moral values under the term *qualia*, and unlike Bohm's implicate order, here was a blind spot in science's ability to offer quantification that hid in plain sight, situated in our everyday experience.

Life's central issues, Huston argued, are issues of *quality*, dealing with judgments regarding the value of our thoughts and actions—political, moral and aesthetic. They deal with evaluative choices regarding the nature of existence and our place in it, rather than simply with descriptions of life's quantitative aspects, like those of distance, size and weight. When we ask, 'How many paintings are in this room?' we are asking a question that can be answered quantitatively by counting, but when we ask, 'Which of them is the most beautiful or interesting?' our enquiry turns qualitative. Similarly, if we ask, 'How many people died in the Iraq War?' we are asking about something we can measure, but it is a qualitative process to wonder, 'Did they die for a good reason?' Referencing Plato's categories of the True, the Beautiful and the Good (mostly for their descriptive usefulness), Huston pointed out in his article that we deal with qualitative mysteries every day; for example: what constitutes right action and moral *goodness*? What, if any, value does *beauty* have and how can we define it? In terms of ontology, what is the *true* nature of our existence? And also, by what methods of gaining knowledge may we know the answers to these questions or the truth of our judgments concerning them? Science cannot quantify that a thing is either good or beautiful, so questions such as those regarding art, music and morality are left to the subjective and inter-subjective worlds of human discourse.

In his lectures, Huston described to his audiences the frustration modernists feel when they try to deal with *qualia* such as moral values. He quoted Wittgenstein, who once remarked, "Values. A terrible business. You can at best stammer when you talk about them."[8] Huston explained that this stammering derived from science's inability to locate any indisputable norms of behavior to guide our actions. "It can tell us that nonsmoking is conducive to health, but whether health is intrinsically better than so-matic gratification it cannot adjudicate. Again, it can determine what people like to do (descriptive values) but not what they should do (normative values)."[9]

On its own, science cannot tell us whether or not to choose long life over short-term gratification, and pure reason can only give us options about why we should or should not gamble with cigarettes. The decision about what is *best* lies with us, and what we want out of life. To give another example, science is well equipped to take us to the moon, but has no power to tell us whether or not we should bother to go. We must find our own reasons to do things, and those reasons will depend upon views and values that can't be quantified; they are prior to science, or as Huston told an audience at the American Philosophical Association, in March of 1987:

> The deepest reason for the current crisis in philosophy is its realization that autono-mous reason—reason without infusions [from our value systems] that both power and vector it—is helpless. By itself, reason can deliver nothing apodictic. Working (as it necessarily must) with variables, variables are all it can come up with. The En-lightenment's 'natural light of reason' turns out to have been a myth. Reason is not itself a light. It is more like a transformer that does useful things but on the condition that it is hitched to a generator [of pre-existing moral and aesthetic assumptions]."[10]

The problem for both science and philosophy was that modernists, as Huston argued for the *Teachers College Record,* like the positivists before them, had a recurrent tendency to pass off their qualitative judgments as quantifiable facts, maintaining that science had proven our existence to be purposeless, when what they were really saying was that science could neither find nor prove one. They argued that only physical param-eters should be considered when formulating a civil code, school curriculum or foreign policy because they couldn't prove the relevance of any other consideration. The in-herent flaw in their position, according to Huston, was that it included the assumption that their inability to quantify other people's qualitative judgments (including those found in the world religions) somehow proved the validity of their own. Huston be-lieved that accepting such an illogical premise had distracted the general population from the fact that even if we rely only upon quantifiable facts when formulating our qualitative judgments, *those judgments still remain qualitative.* For even when we use scientific facts as a foundation for our decisions, we still must decide what is "right and wrong," "good and bad," and "true and false," and even when we say it is "good" to rely only on quantifiable information, we are still making a qualitative choice. This being the case, Huston argued, quoting Karl Jaspers, that science "fails in the face of all ulti-mate questions," and consequently (now quoting Wittgenstein), "leaves the problems of life . . . completely untouched."[11]

Huston, of course, saw this gap as an enormous problem and with regards to the circumstances of human existence, no improvement on religion. In fact, modernism's meaninglessness discouraged Tillich's "courage to be," given that it offered no sustenance for why we should bother living (other than that we could—if we wanted to—make the most of our meaningless existence). Modernism's position also made a mockery of Frankl's conclusion that the search for meaning is our most basic psychological drive—since, modernists argued, we are looking for what does not and can not exist. What was needed, Huston believed, was a philosophical understanding of the limits of science and the mistakes of Scientism, and Bohm agreed with him. And just when Huston was working his hardest to make these points, along came a movement in philosophy that also seemed to agree with him.

## THE FRENCH CONNECTION

Huston's friends at MIT were still grinding their axes within the analytical philosophy, but during the 1970s a philosophical movement arose in France that soon sent shock waves across the Atlantic. Beginning with the work of Jacques Derrida, Jean-Francois Lyotard, Michel Foucault and Jean Baudrillard and championed in the United States by Richard Rorty, this viewpoint, termed *postmodernism*, raised compelling questions about modernism's assumptions and conclusions. Huston, at least in the beginning, saw it as aligned with his thinking. Like Huston, the postmodernists believed that modernism had been wrong to raise scientific materialism to the level of an absolute ideology, masking its qualitative judgments as logical conclusions. Postmodernism had called 'foul,' rejecting "the scientific, one-dimensional worldview into which modernity slipped," Huston later wrote, "because it recognizes it to be not scientific but scientistic."[12]

Huston sided with postmodernism's reaction against modernism's earnest confidence in 'progress,' often summarized in the slogan "The West is Best," assuming that utopia is guaranteed by an endless application of European culture and scientific know-how. Too often this ideology had been used to justify colonialism abroad and rampant industrialization at home, with all but the rich being ground away in the wheels of progress. Based on an ideological commitment to defend oppressed sexes and social minorities, Foucault and others had become cultural watchdogs on the lookout for dogmatic ideologies that set up bases for oppression against people who disagree with those ideologies. Consequently, postmodernists occupied themselves with "unmasking" and "deconstructing" the structures of power, hierarchy and control that make oppression possible. Through these deconstructions, de-mystifications, and "decenterings," they pointed out how "centers" and "presences" and "absolute truths" have been used to create hierarchies based on the "binary opposites" (Derrida) that spin out of them. For example: right and wrong, true and false, just and unjust, beautiful and ugly, etc. In short, the postmodernists were deconstructing the philosophical assumptions and concomitant power structures of modernism, and for that Huston was very grateful. However, there was another side to postmodernism with which he did not agree, and over time he came to see postmodernism as even more dangerous than modernism.

The movement sometimes went too far, claiming that no truths or "centers" should ever be allowed (or even explored), since they implicitly create a divide between believers and non-believers, with the latter subsequently being marginalized and oppressed. Huston felt that this position swung the pendulum too far to the other extreme. "What if we become so phobic of wholes and truths that we only endlessly avoid them?" he wondered. "And who, once *pre-modernists* [defined as those who believe in the traditional religions] and modernists have completely died out, would generate the truths that postmodernists feel compelled to deconstruct? *'What then?'*"

Postmodernism began to seem parasitic to Huston, dependent on identifying other viewpoints to rail against. Ideologies could certainly be or become dangerous, oppressive and totalitarian—but must we suspect all attempts at truth-building? Or should we mainly be wary of those that are dogmatic and oppressive? Huston believed the latter was closer to the right course. If no truth or meaning was *ever* sought (and regarding truths or meanings which might be useful, postmodernism offered no guidelines), how could we establish a moral basis for our behavior? Postmodernists often seemed detached from such considerations, viewing them as quaint or naïve, and maintaining an ironic stance on issues of 'right and wrong.' While avoiding all claims of right and wrong certainly prevents anyone from being marginalized, it also suggests that there are no 'wrong' positions in the world. For this reason postmodernism arguably supports the *status quo*, since it can come up with no proof that the *status quo* is wrong. And so Simon Blackburn has observed in the *Oxford Dictionary of Philosophy* that,

> While the dismantling of objectivity seems to some to be the way towards a liberating political radicalism, to others it allows such unliberating views as the denial that there was (objectively) such an event as the Second World War or the Holocaust, and to others such as Rorty (*Contingency, Irony and Solidarity*, 1989), it licenses the retreat to an aesthetic, ironic, detached and playful attitude to one's own beliefs and to the march of events. This retreat has been criticized as socially irresponsible (and in its upshot, highly conservative).[13]

Back here in the world where we live day to day, outside the realm of rarified concepts, life calls for choices and guidelines for making them. These choices may be made with reference to values that are held provisionally and with an open mind, but values must be held—for they will be expressed in our daily actions whether we hold them or not. This imperitive is where postmodern theorists often fell mum—raising the ire not only of Huston but of social activists, feminists, environmentalists and many others.

On one level, Huston saw postmodernism as simply more modernism, given that it relied exclusively on the same methods of proof and knowing, all based on pure reason, and wouldn't consider other tools such as aesthetic knowing, mystical knowing or intuitive knowing via the *intellectus*. Consequently, when he later wrote about postmodernism, Huston sometimes hyphenated the term as "post-modernism," suggesting that it was mostly old wine in new bottles, though he actually saw it as even more dangerous than modernism. "If modernity rejected the traditional multi-storied worldview, postmodernism rejects all worldviews," he wrote in 1989, adding:

> Instead it offers us reality as kaleidoscopic. With every turn of the wheel of time and place, the kaleidoscope revolves and its pieces gestalt anew. Beyond these endlessly shifting gestalts there is no appeal, and as far as we can tell, nothing. . . . Call it historicism, call it constructivism, call it socio-linguistic holism, call it neo-

pragmatism, this is what postmodernity comes down to. It is ambiguity elevated to the level of apotheosis.[14]

Huston saw this as an enormous problem, since postmodernism was offering no purpose for our existence other than that we should watch out for other people's attempts to find a purpose. He began to speak out against it. In 1984, he published his third most important book, *Beyond the Postmodern Mind* (updated with two additional essays in 1989, after giving a lecture against postmodernism at the "Revisioning Philosophy" conference at Cambridge, England, that August). The book was dedicated to his grandchildren, about whose future he was deeply concerned.[15] In this book, Huston aired his arguments against postmodernism and two positions stand out from the rest. First, "to level the sharpest charge possible," he argued that the postmodernist tendency to constantly harp on the issue of relativism was, in the final analysis naïve, since,

> Relativism sets out to reduce every kind of absoluteness to a relativity while making an illogical exception for its own case. In effect, it declares it to be true that there is no such thing as truth; that it is absolutely true that only the relatively true exists. This is like saying that language doesn't exist, or writing that there is no such thing as script. Total relativism is an incoherent position. Its absurdity lies in its claim to be unique in escaping, as if by enchantment, from a relativity that is declared alone to be possible.
>
> Relativism holds that one can never escape human subjectivity. If that were true, the statement itself would have no objective value; it would fall by its own verdict.[16]

Deconstruction and *decentering* have philosophical utility, he maintained, if they lead us beyond cultural chauvinism toward a more universal or more tolerant viewpoint, and Huston applauded postmodernism in this regard. But what if we assume that there is always a one-to-one correlation between "centering" and totalitarianism, and that any attempt to find or espouse "truth" is inherently oppressive? Then we fall subject to the totalitarianism of their absolute relativism. "If we could see Deconstruction as an eternally important office of culture," Huston commented, "the office of ombudsman whose job is to prevent the oppression of minorities by majorities without opposing majorities in principle, this would distinguish it from postmodernism's lack of an overview, which lack could then be addressed."[17]

## CAR TROUBLE IN TANZANIA

The other primary reason for Huston's dissatisfaction with postmodernism had to do with the premise that all human experience is mediated by concepts, thoughts and language. In brief, postmodernists believed (and many still do) there is no such thing as a human experience uninfluenced by cultural conditioning. Sometimes this postmodern viewpoint is termed *contextualism*, since it maintains that all experience occurs inside a concept matrix, but otherwise it's termed *holism*, deriving from Saussure's view that words mean what they do via their relationships with other words in a specific language, rather than because of their relationship to a reality existing beyond language. "Practical holism," Huston noted, "goes on from there to argue that, because thinking invariably proceeds in social contexts and against a backdrop of social practices, meaning derives from, roots down into and draws its life from, those backgrounds and contexts. In considering an idea, not only must we take into account the conceptual gestalt of which it is a part [i.e., language]; we must also consider Wittgenstein's 'forms of life,' and Heidegger's historical horizons and ways of being-in-the-world, whose 'micro-practices' (Foucault) give those gestalts their final meaning."[18]

To summarize this abstraction, contextualists argued that no one ever, even for a moment, escapes human subjectivity or cultural conditioning, which Huston believed often caused the postmodernists to draw too deep a divide between words and things; between one individual and another; between one culture and another; and between the human race and the physical world. "Worldviews did not come to attention until global shoulder-rubbing confronted people with alternative versions thereof," he wrote in an article from this period.[19] "But if human history opened with only the world (views of it having not yet come to light), and if for an interval both sides of the polarity were acknowledged (the world and views thereof), with postmodernism the world vanishes. Only views remain. No world." Huston agreed that there *is* a separation between us and the world, between our culture and those of others, between one person and another, but this separation is certainly more porous than postmodernists generally allowed—and, as he said, even their own work would hold no value if there is no 'outside' truth to which it applies.

Discussing postmodernism with Michael Toms on New Dimensions radio shortly before the release of *Beyond the Postmodern Mind*, Huston offered that, "There is one move in philosophy today to argue that we're all caught up like silk worms in cocoons in our cultural and linguistic frame of reference. And it's true we're prisoners of that to some extent, but I don't think that's a stopping point." Later that same year, in a newspaper interview, Huston related a story to illustrate why not.[20] To make his point that whether or not we are deeply influenced by our conditioning we still access and interrelate with an exterior world, Huston talked about a time in the late 1960s when he was in Tanzania for a conference. He hadn't wanted to leave the country without seeing some of its spectacular wildlife, so after the conference he rented a "rickety jalopy" and drove out to the Serengeti Plain. Unfortunately, he became lost and ran out of gas.

"When we rent a car here," Huston told the reporter, "we assume the tank to be full. Not there. They give you about enough to get out of the lot, but I didn't know that and hadn't checked. At a total standstill, I could not think of a thing to do. The car was too hot to sit in, and there were no trees to shade me from the blistering sun." But just at that moment, two figures appeared dimly on the horizon and Huston started toward them. "They were disconcertingly large and wore nothing but spears taller than themselves and flapping cloths over their shoulders to ward off the sun somewhat." Making contact with two Masai hunters, but with no common language between them, Huston tried to communicate his predicament. At first he had no luck, but the men sensed his distress and tried to figure out his problem. Indicating the car, Huston endeavored to explain that it was out of gas and wouldn't move. Again, grasping only the outlines of the situation, and not able to understand why anyone wouldn't feel at home on the Serengeti, the Masai were baffled. But then Huston demonstrated that the car wouldn't roll. Finally, a light came on and one of the men set off across the plains, while his friend, whose arm Huston held tightly, remained behind to console the foreigner.

"In about an hour, the man returned with ten adult cohorts," Huston related to the reporter, "and the sun set that evening on as bizarre a scene (I feel sure) as the Serengeti

Plain had ever staged: a white man, seated in state at the wheel of his car steering, while twelve Masai warriors pushed him across the sands. My propellers were taking the experience as a great lark. Laughing and all talking simultaneously, they sounded like a flock of happy birds." After depositing Huston at an outpost near the Olduvai Gorge, where a decade or so earlier Louis and Mary Leakey had discovered the tooth that "set the human race back a million years," the Masai waved goodbye to Huston and walked away with no desire for a reward. "That encounter left me with a profound sense of human connectedness," Huston reminisced. "There we were, as different in every way—ethnically, linguistically, culturally—as any two groups on our planet. Yet without a single word in common, we connected." The Masai understood Huston's problem well enough to respond, and so he had learned, as he told his interviewer, that postmodernists must, "Beware of the differences that blind us to the unity that binds us."

Huston argued in *Beyond the Postmodern Mind* that our worldviews, however distinct, are indeed permeable, and this is important to consider:

> We would not honor the otherness of the Other if we did not also recognize her identity with us. However different she may be, she is identical with us in having idiosyncratic needs that are as entitled as are our own. Where is the place for Piaget's 'decentration' to balance Postmodernism's incessant (and usually appropriate) plea for differences? *Decentration* is the process of gradually becoming able to take a more and more universal standpoint, giving up a particular egocentric or sociocentric way of understanding, and acting and moving towards the "universal communications community." [21]

In the summer of 1989 when Huston wrote those words, the Cold War with the Soviets was moving to its close. After more than forty years of hatred and conflict, and during that autumn, after several weeks of civil unrest, all citizens of East Germany were finally allowed to visit West Germany, resulting in crowds of people crossing the wall or climbing over it. With the fall of the Berlin Wall, one might say that 'decentration' was in the air, and soon the Soviet president, Mikhail Gorbachev, called for new policies to guide world actions. Huston seemed to be right on track. Soon after this, he was invited to several of Gorbachev's World Forums, and while attending one in San Francisco, met a new author named Deepak Chopra. "I don't think he knew who I was," Chopra recalled, "but he was gracious and humble, and kind enough to answer my questions as we walked around the city one day. Huston had been a hero of mine and now he was offering ideas that everyone wanted to hear."

## HAVING RIDDEN AN ELEPHANT

After the release of the updated version of *Beyond the Postmodern Mind* in 1989, Huston was again asked to give the Plenary Address at the annual conference of the Academy of Religion—this time in Anaheim, California. There he outlined an article, "Postmodernism's Impact on the Study of Religion," he had written for the Academy's journal earlier that year, explaining that religions generally posit a higher reality, and quoting William James that religion says that the best things are the "more eternal things." [22] Asking his audience to keep an open mind, Huston commented that he was probably headed for trouble with postmodernists, "for 'things' [and especially 'best' and 'eternal' things] sound suspiciously like 'essences' and talk about them sounds suspiciously 'referential'—words postmodernism is not fond of."

Continuing his lecture and clearly looking for a fight, Huston aired his view that postmodernism had over-emphasized deconstruction, taking modernism apart but offering no new position. "Substantively, modernism is the outlook that accepted the scientific worldview as definitive, while postmodernism is that scientistic worldview adjourned but not replaced."[23] Derrida, Huston recognized, had argued that no view could ever grasp reality perfectly, with which Huston agreed, but that did not mean reality doesn't exist or that it can't be grasped with some degree of clarity. Consequently, he told his colleagues that Derrida's "strength lies in his reminder that there is a surd in every woodpile, no socio-linguistic construct can pull everything together. This sounds promising in suggesting that there is something beyond constructs that stands judgment on them. But if we pick up on that point and try to ask seriously what that something is, we are advised that every answer will be a (deconstructable) construct, which sucks us back into holism's Black Hole."[24]

Huston also criticized postmodernism for making the same mistake as modernism, that is, for assuming from the outset that since nothing metaphysical can be proven by science, nothing metaphysical can exist. "The problem with the modern study of religion," Huston observed, "is that it unfolds with a *modern* view of reality that is, in principle, hostile to the truth known in religion."[25]

Phil Novak, Huston's former graduate student at Syracuse, but now a professor, was in the audience that night at Anaheim, and shared details of what happened:

> Huston really had a fire in his belly, and he was gunning for the postmodernists. He was a well-known figure and he was well liked and intellectually respected. Within academia he was known as a generalist, but he was a generalist who could put together a damned good AAR article and really stand toe to toe with some of those philosophers of religion. He wasn't just a persona and a great storyteller; he was brilliant and could really argue a point. So he delivered this talk about Derrida and the postmodernists, and how they never made their position clear enough, so you could never really respond to it—since they didn't construct. Anyway, it was a brilliant talk. I mean, seven or eight hundred people—scholars of the highest order—were in his hand. You could hear a pin drop in the place.

Huston ended with comments about how the postmodernists had missed the point that religion ultimately deals with an Infinite that is beyond all words, worlds and cultures, and to suggest that because no words can grasp it is proof that it doesn't exist is not only assumptive but unsatisfying to those who have experienced the Divine. "I have felt the swaying of the elephant's shoulders," Huston remarked, quoting Mirabai, a Hindu mystic poet of the fifteenth century, "and now you want me to climb on a jackass? Try to be serious."[26]

"Right after that," Novak continued, "Huston played a tape of the Gyuto monks of Tibet doing their chanting, full blast in a huge auditorium for like three minutes straight, as if to say, 'this is either going to take you to another place or at least indicate to the most flat-footed, flat-headed, flatlanders of you that there's something here you're missing.' In my direct first-hand experience of Huston, that was one of his finest hours."

Huston had thrown down the gauntlet. It was inevitable that someone would pick it up, and that someone was a young scholar at Dartmouth named Steven Katz.

# Car Trouble in Tanzania

## GOING TOE TO TOE

On one level, postmodernism was dismissing all religion as bunk, since no religion, it argued, could claim ultimate Truth. On another level postmodernism could also be interpreted as allowing all forms of truth, with each religion claiming its own choices as equally valid to those of any other. However, even when there arose a cadre of "postmodern believers" (a term that John Horgan, a former editor at *Scientific American*, has rightly termed something of an oxymoron),[27] these scholars still disliked the theory of a perennial philosophy, seeing it as just another attempt to create an overarching Truth to which all other truths would be subjugated. Where perennialists saw mystical insight as an alternative and complementary means of apprehending reality, which might restore the Truth that science had eroded (and thereby create a true form of postmodernism), conventional postmodernists saw only its potential for marginalizing disparate viewpoints. And in the late 1970s and early 1980s, this became the received viewpoint on the perennial philosophy in religious studies.

In 1978, while teaching at Dartmouth, Katz had edited a book, *Mysticism and Philosophical Analysis*, in which he accused perennialists of being evangelists rather than scholars, because they begin with an *a priori* assumption of a Divine Ground and then marshal their thoughts to be consistent with its supposed existence. John Horgan has called Katz's book "an all-out assault on the perennial philosophy"[28] and indeed he begins his essay with the contention that, "There is no *philosophia perennis*, Huxley and many others notwithstanding."[29] To defend his position, Katz argued that there are three distinguishable forms of the perennial philosophy, ranging from weakest to least weak, but each is wrong-minded. The weakest position ("Thesis I") came from those perennialists who believed that all mystical experiences are essentially the same; the second weakest position ("Thesis II") was that all mystical experiences are the same but descriptions of them vary due to the different cultural backgrounds of the mystics involved; and the strongest-though-still-weak position was that there are several types of mystical experience but they are described differently in different cultures.

Katz was convinced that Huxley's viewpoint falls into Thesis I, that, "All mystical experiences are the same [and] even their descriptions reflect an underlying similarity which transcends cultural or religious diversity,"[30] though he offered no quotes from Huxley to support his position, and Huxley was actually saying that only all experiences of the Divine Ground are the same. Katz argued that all three theses are erroneous because each depends upon the existence of something that doesn't exist, an unmediated experience of something transcendental. All experiences, Katz contended, are mediated, meaning that the vagaries of a particular mystic's culture and personality always color whatever experience he or she is having, making a universal mystical experience entirely impossible. "To flesh this out, straightforwardly," Katz wrote, "what is being argued is that, for example, the Hindu mystic does not have an experience of *x* which he then describes in his familiar language and symbols of Hinduism, but rather he has a Hindu experience . . ."[31] Consequently, for Katz, all experience is fundamentally subjective. Because no experience is ever free of cultural biases, it is useless to compare experiences across the cultural divides, for in every case we are comparing apples to oranges.

Katz's essay, comprising 52 pages of small print, is more of a short book than an essay, and yet he had still more to say, following up his first diatribe against perennialism with a second in 1983, titled *Mysticism and Religious Traditions*. Enlisting his department chair at Dartmouth, the renowned scholar Hans Penner, to help him out, Katz and his colleagues basically review the same positions they had discussed earlier. For instance, in Penner's essay, "The Mystical Illusion," we are told: "The basic assumption of this essay is that there are no direct experiences of the world, or 'between individuals except through the social relations which "mediate" them.' Once this principle has been granted, it does not make much sense to speak of states of 'pure consciousness' or experiences not constituted from within a linguistic framework."[32] In brief, Penner argued that mysticism is "an illusion, unreal, a false category," because accounts of 'mystical experience' are culture-specific and no 'pure' experience is possible.

For Katz, Penner and their colleagues, this view liberated the religions from each other. Where perennialists had hoped to bring people together by saying that every religion contains the same unitive knowledge of the Divine Ground, whether it places a premium on that experience or not, Katz argued that perennialists were mostly marginalizing people who think differently. For Katz, it was better to isolate the religions in their respective silos than to subsume them into a false mix. Each religion deserved the right to claim its own truth, since truth, after all, cannot be other than culture-specific, and to do otherwise was to establish a hegemony of absolutism. For him, perennialism was a meta-narrative that brought all faiths under the umbrella of its universalist viewpoint. He hoped to liberate the religions, allowing them to hold onto their differences as well as their uniqueness.

For Huston also, the differences between the religions were important; furthermore, he, like Huxley, didn't conceive of the perennial philosophy as a variety of universalism because it didn't dictate to the religions what was most important about their teachings (nor did it try to set up a Church). Huston believed, and would argue, that Katz and his colleagues were really the ones who had made *a priori* assumptions that skewed their conclusions in a biased direction.

Beginning with his 1987 essay, "Is there a perennial philosophy?",[33] and continuing after his presentation at Anaheim, Huston opened a debate with Katz that reached a crescendo in the spring issue of the *Journal of the American Academy of Religion*.[34] There Huston explained that Robert K.C. Forman [in *The Problem of Pure Consciousness*] had not only given strong arguments in support of the unitive knowledge as unmediated but also pointed out that though "Katz claims that his approach makes no 'a priori assumptions,' just the opposite is true [since] once he has assumed that language enters and in part shapes and constructs all experiences, the remaining 39 pages of [of his essay] provides virtually no further argumentation [for this assumption]." Turning to the essay itself, it's difficult to disagree with either Huston or Forman; Katz indeed offers no arguments for his axiomatic assumption that "cultural solipsism"[35] (Huston's term) can never be escaped.

In 2003, John Horgan, while reviewing the debate between Huston and Katz, made several astute observations, giving credit to Huston for having a more defensible position. First, Horgan agreed that Katz had been wrong to assume that there are no transpersonal or universal experiences, writing:

> Smith's point is well taken. We must share certain universal experiences in spite of our circumstantial differences, if only because we share the same biology. Descriptions of hunger and thirst and sexual desire may vary from person to person and

culture to culture, but does that mean these basic biological drives are products of our social conditioning? Certain aspects of the external world, too, transcend context. If Aristotle's descriptions of the moon differ from those of Carl Sagan, does that mean they didn't see the same thing? Katz's contextualism implies as much.[36]

But then Horgan also offers a comment on mystical experience that favors Huston's view—even when it criticizes some overly zealous perennialists:

> Mysticism is stranger and more complicated than perennial philosophers often imply; scholars like Katz and McGinn have made this point convincingly. But their stance—whether called postmodernism or contextualism—is also too indiscriminating. They argue, in effect, that all mystical revelations are unprovable, hence they cannot be distilled into a single, coherent worldview such as the perennial philosophy. All mystical visions may be unprovable in an absolute sense, but surely some are more demonstrably false—and potentially harmful—than others.[37]

## POSITING A TRULY POSTMODERN POSTMODERNISM

During his debate with Katz, Huston argued that the perennial philosophy is derived, in the final analysis, from a direct experience of the Divine Ground rather than from a comparison of mystical experiences among the traditions; consequently, it is something more trans-cultural than pan-cultural, or pan-cultural because it's trans-cultural, rather than the least common denominator of comparative analysis between religious texts. Huston was positing a truly new form of postmodernism in which a unique method of gaining insight (the Unitive Knowledge) would be considered as both plausible and useful. Furthermore, in *Beyond the Postmodern Mind*, he had added that the metaphysical intuitions of the *intellectus* should also be taken seriously, and to defend his position he began by pointing out that this wasn't something new: "Romantic philosophers and poets followed Blake in proposing an active imagination that in important respects resembles the Intellect proper," he wrote, "and Heidegger came to extol '[meditative] thinking' over reasoning of the calculative sort."[38] Continuing, he added that, "Plato discovered an organ of knowledge which, because it 'outshines ten thousand eyes,' he called the Eye of the Soul." Using this Eye of the Intellect, Huston proposed, new visions of reality were discernable and should be considered, adding:

> Whether the time is ripe to consider the possibility of an innate faculty in the human self that extends *through* cultural-linguistic wholes to the heart of Reality itself, fulfilling thereby our deepest wish to ultimately belong, I do not know; I present it simply as the most promising prospect I see. . . .
>
> Writing this concluding paragraph on the day that I learn of the death of a great Tibetan teacher, Kalu Rimpoche, I think of something he once said. 'Reason tells me I am nothing. Love tells me I am everything. Between these poles, my life unfolds." . . . So too, do our lives unfold between the poles of the Postmodern world and its sequel that is struggling to be born.[39]

The year that Huston gave his unorthodox, landmark presentation to the AAR in Anaheim, he also co-wrote with David Ray Griffin a book to explore new conceptions of postmodernism, titled *Primordial Truth and Postmodern Theology*,[40] and though the authors didn't share the same viewpoint, they were both opposed to the hegemony of modernist/post-modernist ideas in the academy, arguing for new directions. Offering specifics, Huston explained that he had "no quarrel with E=MC² as a basic scientific truth, and the modern concern for human rights is not a detail,"[41] but he wished, as was his constant inclination, for a reappraisal of metaphysics, and in this pursuit he thought science could actually help given that his new form of postmodernism drew "on natural science itself as a witness against the adequacy of the modern worldview."[42]

In summary, Huston was working in the late 1980s to stem the negative effects of postmodernism in two ways: by pointing out its shortcomings while also suggesting mystical experience as a possible antidote. "There is a way things are," he wrote in "Is Onto-theology Passe? Or can Religion Endure the Death of Metaphysics?", an essay published in the journal, *Religion and Intellectual Life* (1986), "which people perceive to varying degrees [depending on their ontic sensitivity]." Here he was referencing the unitive knowledge and asking his colleagues to weigh its virtues. "Such metaphysical realism runs counter to major currents in philosophy that tell us that it is no longer possible to talk this way," he continued, but then added, "The direct retort to that proscription might be, 'Excuse me, but I just did.'"[43]

# Chapter Twenty-Three:
# Peyote in Mazatlan

The first "people of life", as I prefer to call the primitive, had a lively sense of what we would call soul, and feared the loss of it as the greatest calamity that could befall them. . . . [For] hundreds of years now all understanding of the spirit has been narrowed and restricted to what can be rationally expressed about "the spirit." The spirit is no longer seen as a gift that we hold in trust from life but as something that is narrowed to a conscious, willful, rational egoism. The spirit is not only reason—although it includes reason; it is not only feeling—and of course it includes feeling as well; but it is for me, above all, intuition, which is a profound compass, bearing on our origin and our destination. And this is ultimately what religion is about: "origin and destination." The result has been that the spirit has lost, for the moment, what made it one of the greatest of all human passions. So it has abandoned the human being in his narrowed rational state, indulging the greatest pastime and specialty of our time, which is finding first-rate reasons for doing partial and wrong things.

Sir Laurens Jan van der Post

In May of 1989, Huston attended a conference in Beijing, titled, "Chinese Religion: Past and Present" and co-sponsored by the International Academy of Chinese Culture and the New Ecumenical Research Association in New York. This was a rare chance for Huston to go to China and speak about religious tolerance for the Chinese people, though attendees had been asked—even before leaving home—to pledge they would not mention Tibet. Ten professors traveled from the West to meet with their Chinese counterparts, and all hoped for some softening of the Communist Party's position on religion; however, on May 20th, the day after their inaugural meeting, the delegates learned that pro-democracy demonstrations by students in the city had caused martial law to be declared, so no softening would take place. "Legally our conference should have been closed [after the demonstrations began]," Huston wrote later in "Beijing Byline," a section of his travel journal, "since there was a ban on all meetings, . . . [b]ut like the rest of the city, we ignored the decree as unenforceable."

When Huston learned what had happened, he and some colleagues decided they would like to help the demonstrators, perceiving the cause of democracy as consummate with the cause of religious freedom. With enthusiastic support from their hotel staff, they set off to meet the protestors, their taxi plastered with slogans reading 'Foreign Visitors Support Students' Efforts.' The gesture paid off, for as they approached the action in the city center, students who were controlling the traffic flow waved them into the heart of Tiananmen Square, cheering wildly. And when the students learned that several of the scholars actually spoke Chinese, they pressed for one of them to make an address. Standing on the roof of the car, one of Huston's colleagues exclaimed at the climax of his talk that democracy was not only for China, not only for America, but for the whole world. "The students' cheers knew no bounds!" Huston recalled.

After the talk and despite the frenzy of the throng, a lane miraculously opened up and the group was able to make its way back to the hotel. Huston was impressed with the students' level of self-control, writing in his journal that evening, "though determined, they were not angry, and were admirably organized and disciplined." Ambulances had been allowed into the crowd to ferry away some of the 3,000 hunger strikers who had finally reached their limit, and Huston interpreted the students' self-control as an attempt to challenge the Communist Party without either soliciting or resorting to violence. Using the media as a way to get their message to the public, they had made three specific demands: that the Party allow more freedom of the press; that there be greater democratic access to the Party's ranks; and that there be an end to the rampant corruption of Party officials. And though their demands weren't met, at least publicly, the students gained the attention of the world (who can forget that television image of the young man stymieing the movements of an armored tank?), which eventually caused some softening of government policy, though Huston believed not nearly enough.

After the conference and before returning home, Huston celebrated his 70th birthday by visiting his old haunts in Shanghai, including the church he had attended in his student days. To his delight, several people there remembered Huston's family and the Smiths' many years of service in China, but there were also painful memories that were shared. "In the China I knew [as a boy]," Huston wrote several years later, "if you asked people what Church they belonged to, the typical answer would be, 'The great Church (*tai chao*), of course'—a federation of Confucianism, Taoism and Buddhism woven together like strands in a single rope."[1] Furthermore, in those days of a more tolerant China, even foreign religions were not objects of ridicule. But the Cultural Revolution changed all that. Parishioners at Huston's church were dragged out into the street and made to kneel with dunces' caps on their heads. They were characterized as buffoons and foreign sympathizers, forcing them to worship in secret, away from the bullying of the police and the gangs of zealous Communist youth.

Hearing these stories, Huston realized it hadn't only been his parents or the Tibetan people who wished for more religious freedom in China; it had been many of the Chinese themselves. "We all know about the suppression of the student protest in Tiananmen Square, but for a moment while I was in China during that time," Huston remembered, summarizing his trip, "it really did seem to everyone like things were about to change. If only that had been true, and if only the Chinese could have demanded of their leaders that religious freedom be accepted as a basic human right."

## THE CULMINATION OF A CAREER

As Huston moved into his eighth decade, he hit a comfortable stride. His mature viewpoint was well in place and he felt confident expressing it to his colleagues as a viable position. Audiences on the lecture circuit boosted his confidence even further by telling him how valuable his ideas had been to their lives. Even academics were coming forward to express their gratitude. "In his fearless challenge of the common [academic] wisdom he has been clear, imaginative and wise," Leroy Rouner, Professor of Philosophical Theology at Boston University, wrote in *On Community* (1991), a book of essays dedicated to Huston: "He and his work have made the forgotten truths of the perennial philosophy effective bearers of relevance and new meaning for our time."[2] In fact, so many scholars wished to express their admiration and gratitude to Huston that Arvind Sharma of McGill University decided to compile a *festschrift* of essays celebrating his career.

"He was totally free from any sense of being pompous," Sharma recounted. "It took me some time to convince Huston that he deserved such an honor, even though he had influenced so many scholars—both inside the Traditionalist camp and out." When asked why Huston had been significant, Sharma only paused a moment before claiming: "He actually made the study of religion possible. What I mean to say is when you read his book you realize why somebody would be a follower of Hinduism or Buddhism or Islam. You understand why somebody would follow that tradition. That, I think, for me, is the primary or fundamental purpose of the study of religion. To make people aware of why somebody would be somebody."

When the *festschrift* came out, late in 1991, titled *Fragments of Infinity*, it contained testimonials about Huston's importance and serious academic arguments for the need to accept metaphysical theories into the academic study of religion, at least, if a true postmodernism was ever to emerge. There were 19 essays in all, including those of the Christian theologian Marcus Borg and James B. Wiggins, the Executive Director of the American Academy of Religion. Also included were a host of scholars arguing the Traditionalist perspective, including Huston's old Sufi friends, Seyyed Hossein Nasr and Victor Danner, the scholar who had gone around the world with him on the IHP trip in 1975. "Huston didn't care about big names," Sharma explained to me. "He wanted the book to salute the work of his Traditionalist friends, whom he believed were often judged too harshly." Notoriety had come to Huston and he hoped to use it for a noble purpose; his friends had wanted to salute him, and true to his innate humility Huston returned the honor by hosting their controversial essays. "In Huston," Marilyn Gustin wrote at the end of her own tribute, "greatness is honesty of person, penetrating sensitivity, but above all, his flowing kindness."[3]

And so the 1990s was a decade of summing up and receiving honors, some highlights of which were that Huston updated *The Religions of Man* as *The World's Religions* (to avoid gender-biased language, and to add new chapters on Tibetan Buddhism, Sufism and Native American religion); gave featured lectures at conferences in Paris and Seoul (1991); delivered the plenary address a third time at the American Academy of Religion (1994); spent three days in Berlin with his old friend Ram Dass to help launch the International Peace University (1995); received an honorary doctorate and celebrated the establishment of the Huston Smith Archives at Syracuse University (1996); presented a series of lectures at the prestigious and innovative Chatauqua Institute in upstate New York (1997); was interviewed twice on the Public Television series, "Thinking Allowed" with Jeffrey Mishlove (1998); made two public appearances at UCLA with his friend the Dalai Lama (in April of 1991 and June of 1997); received two more honorary Ph.D.s, from St. Mary's College and the California Institute of Integral Studies (1997); accepted the Open Center Award for "facilitating religious understanding" (1998); accepted a fellowship in 1998 from the Rockefeller Center in Bellagio, Italy, to work on several writing projects (and afterward toured Europe with Kendra); and last but not least, was featured in a five-part series of interviews with Bill Moyers for Public Television in 1996. Titled "The Wisdom of Faith, with Huston Smith," the series outlined the religions of the world and Huston's personal views on them, and garnered an Emmy nomination. "America's religious landscape is changing," Moyers observed during the first broadcast, "and no one has done more to prepare us for the new religious reality than Huston Smith."

Philip Goldberg called the Moyer's series, "the culmination of Smith's celebrity."[4] High praise also came from the travel writer Pico Iyer, who commented to *Shambhala Sun* magazine in 2003 that the video collection of that series is "one of the only possessions I always keep in my two-room apartment in rural Japan." James Cutsinger, Professor of Religion at the University of South Carolina, enumerated the elements that made that series popular:

> Huston is superb as an interviewee. He's able to walk some kind of fine line between complicated scholarship, that would put off many listeners or television viewers, on the one hand, and really good sound-byte stuff on the other hand. He can come up with a really, really brilliant image or a really, really *apropos* way to communicate something profound in fairly accessible language very quickly, and he can do it again and again. There's the compassion, the human kindness, the person, but there's also the capacity to convey and communicate simply but profoundly. During that series, he really caught people's imagination.

Not everyone saw the show as a success and some scholars disagreed with Huston point for point, even publishing rejoinders after the series aired. Watching those programs today, one appreciates the pursuit of serious inquiry, and one is glad to find something that isn't fluffy, preachy or overly sentimental. Moyers is clearly reverent during his interviews but also asks difficult questions. Why does religion matter? What does it do? Why did Huston believe we're 'in good hands'? The program's tone is that of a visit to a wise old grandfather who allows us to make up our own mind, as Christopher McQuain has pointed out in his essay for "Online Review":

> For his part, Moyers is intent on making the series a conduit from Smith's expansive mind to us, but he is never afraid to ask the expert to clarify or re-explain himself as necessary. In the final episode, in which Smith makes a claim for faith vs. atheism and the feasibility of a pluralistic implementation of multiple faiths at the same time, Moyers asks him some rather tough, even critical questions, to which Smith provides his best, most honest, and most well-considered answers, leaving us to decide how convincing they are for Moyers or for us.

The show reached a huge audience and had a great impact, partially because it was a follow-up to an enormously popular series Moyers had done with Joseph Campbell, "The Power of Myth," in 1988. The success of that earlier show, along with the success of the book that followed (published at Doubleday with the help of an enthusiastic editor named Jackie Onassis)[5] had encouraged Moyers to go further with his exploration of our spiritual heritage, and Huston had been, of course, the logical choice.

These celebrations of Huston's life marked the culmination of a career. But Huston was hardly finished working. His passion for illuminating the public about world religions, along with his desire to open the minds of dogmatists too set in their ways, had never burned brighter. Maybe some day he would go fishing or collect stamps, but for now he had books to write and battles to fight. The 1990s would mark his most passionate cause ever, and this time in defense of religious freedom for Native Americans.

## "The Employment Division of Oregon vs. Alfred Leo Smith"

In 1990, Huston learned that he didn't have to go as far away as China to witness the suppression of religious freedom, for that's when the U.S. Supreme Court decided that the Bill of Rights, specifically the "free exercise of religion" clause in the First Amendment to the Constitution, did not apply to the Native American Church, due to its sacramental use of Peyote.[6]

Alfred Leo Smith, a member of the Klamath tribe of Oregon, was raised on a reservation until he was eight, after which he was taken from his parents and put into a Catholic parochial school for all of his formal education.[7] In young adulthood, Smith suffered from alcoholism and a sense of lost identity. By 36 he had recovered, thanks to Alcoholics Anonymous and his participation in the Native American Church, which, at that time included about a quarter million members.[8]

Having turned his life around, Smith decided to help others to do the same, taking jobs in several programs to help other Native Americans with alcohol and drug treatment. In 1984, the director of the program where he was working learned that Smith was a member of the Native American Church and attending peyote ceremonies from time to time. He told Smith that if he didn't stop he would be fired, and that's exactly what happened. After his dismissal, Smith applied for unemployment compensation but was denied, resulting in a six-year court battle that eventually moved all the way to the U.S. Supreme Court. The Court then not only denied Smith his benefits but, based on his case, also limited the rights of the Native American Church. Since peyote was, and is, listed as a controlled substance "of great danger" under American law, the Court decided to revoke its use even as a religious sacrament, removing any claim that Smith might have had to an infringement of his Constitutional rights.

The standing legal precedent for such cases as Smith's had been that unless a state could prove why a particular Native American practice was harmful to state interests, the state should not intervene. This precedent was labeled the test of "compelling state interest," but in Smith's case, the Supreme Court overturned it. "To support its retreat from this well entrenched legal precedent," James Botsford, a Native American attorney working on the case, wrote at the time:

> Justice [Antonin] Scalia argued that America's religious diversity had become a "luxury" that a pluralistic society could no longer "afford," and that the "compelling state interest" test had to be withdrawn. In addition, the Court removed from First Amendment protection an entire body of law—specifically, criminal law—so that, in effect, the First Amendment was being rewritten to mean that, "Congress shall make no laws *except criminal laws* that prohibit the free exercise of religion."[9]

When the case was heard before the Court, Justice Harry Blackmun dissented from the majority opinion, observing: "I do not believe the Founders thought their dearly bought freedom from religious persecution was a 'luxury,' but an essential element of liberty—and they could not have thought religious intolerance 'unavoidable' [as Scalia had maintained was inevitable in so diverse a society] for they drafted the Religion

Clauses precisely in order to avoid that intolerance."[10] However, regardless of Blackmun's views, the decision held, and on April 17,1990, the Court ruled that the "free exercise of religion" clause in the First Amendment did not extend to the Native American Church's use of peyote.

"The *Smith* decision was devastating to the Native American Church," Huston wrote later. "For four and a half years that decision forced it underground in a way reminiscent of the catacombs. Arrests were on the minds of its members as they lived like criminals fearing the knock on the door. It was as if Columbus had been right: Indians had no religion—none worth protecting by law."[11]

Having grown used to such treatment, many Native Americans felt like giving up, but a few decided to fight back, and key among these was Reuben Snake, a 70-year-old elder of the Winnebago tribe. With the endorsement of elected church officials, Reuben created what Huston has called "the strongest coalition in Native American Church history," dubbing themselves the Native American Religious Freedom Project and established to deal directly with Washington. "At the outset, his [Reuben's] project appeared impossible," Huston observed, "[to] overturn the highest court of the land without a dime in his coffers! When he was asked how he proposed to accomplish the task he replied, 'With a frequent flyer coupon and a prayer.'"[12]

Reuben Snake had long black hair and high cheekbones. He had been named Kikawunga by his great-grandfather, a name that means "To Rise Up," and he came to see his name as a sacred commission, an obligation to resurrect the heritage of his people, including their sacramental use of peyote.[13]

"Five hundred years ago," Reuben wrote, "the people on this continent had the same worldview. They saw themselves set within (and an integral part of) something great and wonderful that drew them compellingly to live in accord with its beauty and harmony. This was true all the way from the Bering Strait to Tierra del Fuego." Continuing, he pointed out, "This is the way our ancestors lived for countless generations. They put the Creator first, and we try to follow them in that. We try to respect and honor our families and friends; we try to have compassion for our fellow men, for that's what our Creator tells us to do." And for Reuben and his people, peyote was integral to that sacred mission, giving them the vision and inspiration needed to see it through. "The outlook I have been describing comes to us through a sacred herb, one that is sacred because it is, in fact, divine. We call it Peyote, but more often, because of what it does for us, we call it our Medicine."[14]

Peyote was considered a gift of the Creator, a way for the people to feel the love of God, "the love that God is, not that God has," which, they believed was inside of each person if he or she would open to it. And if they did? "From there it overflows in compassion for human beings and all other kinds of creatures," Rueben maintained. Through the peyote's teaching, Reuben's people learned the *wosh-kun*, the "Way [or] way to be" in this world, a disposition toward one's life that is free of pride and jealousy, or as another elder, Johnny White Cloud, once summarized the "peyote road," it teaches a way of life that "promotes family stability, sobriety, self-sufficiency and brotherly love."[15]

With such a noble tradition behind him, Reuben Snake sought the help of people who could support the cause, and among the first to volunteer were the filmmakers Gary Rhine and Phil Cousineau.

"I got a phone call," Cousineau remembered, "from my dearly departed film partner, Gary Rhine—rest his soul [Rhine died a few years later in a plane crash]. 'Rhino' says to me, 'There's just been this terribly destructive decision by Justice Scalia and the Supreme Court to rule peyote as a drug and not a religious sacrament. We need to respond to this. We need to make a film!'" Cousineau agreed immediately, and learned from Rhine that he had already contacted Huston Smith, who in turn had already heard about the Court's decision from James Botsford, an attorney who worked on Native American causes. (As it turned out, Botsford had been a student of Huston's at Syracuse.) "So," Cousineau continued, "Rhino told me that he and Huston were flying down to Santa Fe the next day to attend a meeting of Native American elders—so they could decide what to do—and he asked if I was 'in.' I dropped everything and got on that plane."

When they arrived in Santa Fe, Huston, Cousineau and Rhine were met at the airport by Reuben, who greeted them with an extended hand, saying with a wry smile, "Hello, I'm Reuben Snake, your humble serpent." Next he explained that he only had ten thousand dollars to respond to the United States Supreme Court, but could they help him with a documentary film about the case? Together they reached the decision that it made the most sense to use the shoe-string budget to focus on documenting the peyote religion and its benefits, and to do so, they further decided to film an actual peyote ceremony, with Huston Smith, the well-known scholar of religion, participating. The ceremony would be held in Mazatlan, Mexico, and Huston would have to spend four nights in a peyote trance at the age of 73. "It was terrible," Huston recalled, "and absolutely wonderful."

## MAZATLAN

Huston hadn't ingested a psychedelic drug for many years, and the last time he did, it hadn't gone so well. It took some courage to go through the experience again. "I had to keep remembering why I was there," he reminisced, "and why this was so important. Peyote was being classified as a Schedule One drug—just like heroin—and that's where the mistake begins. Peyote is a harmless cactus and addiction to it is impossible. Also, there has never been a recorded case of a crime committed on the substance, unlike alcohol, which has caused so many crimes, so the whole thing was absurd. The Supreme Court had no problem with alcohol as a divine sacrament, but peyote was the sacrament of the 'other,' and that was the problem. To call peyote a 'drug,' which is what the Supreme Court was doing, was like calling the Catholic sacrament of wine at Mass, 'booooooooze.'"

Once in Mazatlan, the group was driven by jeep for four hours over dusty roads into the mountains where the peyote ceremony would take place. Campsites were set up and tents were erected, including the large tent for the ceremony itself, where Reuben Snake would preside. "It is attention to details that preserves the sanctity of our traditions," Reuben wrote later, speaking of the ritual. All details were carefully followed.[16] That first evening, the group was led into the teepee, "the womb of the mother." There they encircled a fireplace, as all things in nature also circle and gyrate, and sat on the ground to make contact, physically and spiritually, with the earth. Prayers were sung to call upon the Great Spirit to guide them and bring their hearts together in one voice. Peyote, in the form of a tea, was passed around the circle, with each person taking an amount considered appropriate.[17]

Reuben, as the "Road Man," acted as the officiant of the ceremony, overseeing all activities, while the Cedar Man added cedar to the fire regularly for purification, and passed the peyote around clockwise. The Drum Chief, sitting on Reuben's right, accompanied the prayers with his hypnotic rhythms, while each person turned his attention to the fire. Huston was told that in the White Man's church, people look at the back of each other's necks during the service, but in the teepee, each person looks directly at God, whose tongue is the flames of the fire that talks to them if they will only listen. Together and individually, they were seeking guidance about what they should do, and Reuben felt certain that if what they asked for were worthy, it would be given.

"This was one hell of an adventure," Cousineau reported. "The elders wanted to chronicle this event as a tool to change the law, and they knew that Huston could champion their cause. So they created a kind of village up in the mountains with the help of the local Huichol, inviting elders from Canada, the U.S., Mexico and Central America. The idea was that Huston would actually experience what happened during the peyote ceremony to prepare him for his testimony before Congress."

Huston had recently been operated on for prostate cancer and wasn't feeling as fit as he would have liked, but, Cousineau related, he sat "ramrod straight" during the ceremony, barely moving as the peyote took effect and the chanting continued. "It's hard to sit for that long but the man never moved. We had one or two hours of sleep for those four days. We went in there at dusk and sat for ten or twelve hours until morning, and Huston was able to do that, despite being sick several times." Johnny White Cloud, who was also at the ceremony and seated near Huston, told Huston that if he felt sick, he could go outside but that he should remember that the "Indian people" had been struggling for a long time and he could offer up his pain to Wakan Tanka, the Great Spirit.

When asked if the peyote experience had been challenging," Huston answered, "Very!" He provided details:

> You had these successive all-night vigils. Sleep during the day on your sleeping pad and then in the tepee from dark to dawn. And there would be a fire in the middle and there would be a Fireman who would rake the coals and so on, and Reuben Snake would sing all night long. And then the peyote buttons and the tea would just circulate, which made several of us sick. You could go outside but it was thought better to use 'the can.' There was this Hills Brothers Coffee can and the first time I felt it coming, I yelled out, 'Can! I need the can!' but it didn't get to me in time, so I vomited all over the dirt floor. But the Fireman had no problem with that. He just raked dirt over it and a bit later shoveled it up and took it outside. It was part of his job.
>
> Another time I had to pee, so I went outside and, my legs in that cramped position, it felt so good to stretch them out. It was a beautiful night and I found myself, under the influence of the peyote, enthralled by the stars in the sky. I was just taking my time, but the next thing I knew an elder came to retrieve me. "All right, you're taking a leak," he said, "but you're also leaking energy from the tepee." So I went back inside with him and rejoined the group.

During the deep hours of those four nights, confessions often erupted, and a mood of humility and compassion became palpable, but there was never any shame or judgment from the group if someone broke down and began to weep; the Road Man commended the person for speaking with sincerity, praising their sweet words of regret. "Laying defenses aside," Reuben once explained the practice, "we can bare our souls to one another, confessing our mistakes and asking for God's, and our neighbor's, forgiveness."[18]

Each morning, the Water Woman, who is the embodiment of the Peyote Woman, brought water into the teepee to signal the end of that day's ceremony, and a ritual breakfast was enjoyed. On the last day, there came a time when several elders spoke, giving thanks to the Great Spirit for the visions they had received. Huston was asked to give an address also, and so he thanked the elders for inviting him and assured them that he would do his best to convey the depth and sincerity of their spirituality—from which he also drew inspiration—to Congress. Cousineau related that Huston said in his address that he had been all over the world "but couldn't remember ever encountering anything as searingly honest and profound as what he had encountered with them." As for Cousineau himself, Reuben Snake told him during their first night in the teepee that, "Everything you need to know is in that fire," and despite being sick several times, Cousineau came to see that, "he was exactly right."

## RESUMING THE FIGHT

Once back in the United States, Cousineau and Rhine began working on the documentary film, newly titled *The Peyote Road*, to clarify the character and purpose of the Native American Church in the public mind. They created different versions of the film, to accommodate specific venues and attention spans, while Reuben Snake and others set up opportunities to show the film to U.S. senators and congressmen. Inspired by the message of the film, the public and the press quickly came onboard, and eventually Senator Daniel K. Inouye of Hawaii, Chairman of the Senate Committee on Indian Affairs, and Congressman Bill Richardson from Arizona, provided Congressional leadership. Inouye sponsored a new bill to restore the Native American Church's right to resume their ceremonial use of peyote.

After Inouye had collected information from hearing held throughout Indian country, Richardson introduced II.R.4230, the "Religious Freedom Restoration Act," in the House of Representatives, where it passed by unanimous vote on August 8,1994. The next step was for Inouye to bring the bill before the Senate, which he did with the help of Senator John McCain, and again after some deliberation, the bill was passed unanimously. On October 6, 1994, President Bill Clinton signed into law "The Religious Freedom Restoration Act." The details of the case were later recorded in a book that Huston compiled with Reuben Snake, *One Nation Under God: the Triumph of the Native American Church* (1996). In Huston's twenty-page chapter outlining the case, only one important figure goes unacknowledged: Huston Smith.

"Huston's testimony before Congress had a tremendous impact on their decision," Cousineau maintained, as one who had followed the case closely. "Here was this famous scholar of religion and he was saying the peyote ceremony was a beautiful and valuable practice, important to the mission of the religion itself. They couldn't help but take him seriously." According to Cousineau, on the day of Huston's testimony, Huston was asked by the elders to take a small amount of peyote before he spoke before Congress, tuning himself into the Sacred in order to speak most clearly. "It's deeply moving to me," Cousineau added, "that he actually felt compelled to take some on his tongue that day. The equivalent would be that he was about to write on Christianity, so he goes to Mass on Sunday and takes the Eucharist. This is why he cottoned to the Native American elders. You're not allowed to speak with authority among them unless they see that you've experienced something for yourself. Huston saw the wisdom in that."

Reuben Snake died in 1993 and did not live to see the passage of the Act, nor the publication of the book that he helped write, but Huston honored him with a special chapter, titled "The Death of a Roadman." He was also able to secure a foreword for the book from Senator Inouye, who then offered a benediction for both Reuben and the Native Americans' struggle for religious freedom:

> As recently as the 1960s the goal of federal Indian policy was the forced "termination" of the official existence of all Indian tribes.
>
> It is within this repressive climate and historical context that the struggles of the Native American Church and the unflagging efforts of one of its great leaders, Mr. Reuben Snake, must be understood.
>
> Centuries before there was an environmental movement in the United States, the native people of this country expressed their reverence for the earth and all of its creatures on a daily basis. The conservation and preservation of natural resources were an unquestioned and integral part of everyday life. It is only in modern times that we as a nation have begun to realize how much we have to learn from the First Americans.[19]

Reflecting on his part in the court case, Huston observed, "I never felt more proud. My only wish is that Reuben had been there to see it."

## CLEANSING THE DOOR OF PERCEPTION

The Religious Freedom Restoration Act did not hold for very long. Three years later, in 1997, the U.S. Supreme Court ruled (in the Flores Case) that the Congress had overstepped its constitutional authority by passing it, since, as Justice Sandra Day O'Connor explained, it went against the Eleventh Amendment to the Constitution on the grounds that it afforded the Native American Church special rights and protections that weren't extended to nonreligious groups or other religions. The result was that laws for and against the use of peyote were left up to the various states, as they had been prior, and different states today have different laws, some more lenient than others. None, according to Huston, is liberal enough:

> When the separation of Church and State was originally built into the First Constitutional Amendment, the intent of the framers was to protect religions from the tyranny of state-run religions. The authors of the First Amendment had come out of centuries of religious oppression in Europe, and they were concerned that the establishment of a state religion would result in the oppressing of the other religions.[20]

By returning the decision to the state level, the Supreme Court intended to return state power, but with it came the power of the state to abuse and censor. And states have used it liberally.

Regarding the subject of psychedelic experience, wasn't Huston's belief in the value of peyote a contradiction of his view that, "once you've gotten the message, hang up the phone?" He replied, apparently thinking out loud.

"Let's try this out and see how it sounds. I've always felt that people put too much attention on altered states and not enough on altered traits, but for the Native Americans, they seem already to understand that the altered states have no value if they don't result in compassionate actions, so they have a cultural safeguard that allows them more leeway to repeat the practice. And certainly I wouldn't want to suggest that they shouldn't do so, since it's been part of their spirituality for centuries."

Several years earlier, in a newspaper interview, Huston had described psychedelic experience as acting like a "moral compass." When the interviewer had asked "in what sense," Huston responded:

> Say you were in the presence of Mother Teresa. Can you imagine following her for a day and then going off in the evening and getting drunk or doing abominable acts? Well, these visions lay the same foundation—when we see human life in a broader, and a more true, a more *veridical* light, we see ourselves as more than we had thought we were. And that 'more' never leads in the direction of evil or sin.[21]

When quizzed if this wasn't how the Native American Church used states to lead to traits, Huston answered, "Exactly! They find themselves in the presence of the Great Spirit, and this causes them to feel a need to clean up their act. Furthermore, having felt the love of God, they want to share it. It's a beautiful and wise tradition."

But Huston believed that even outside of Native American society there could be a value to psychedelic experience. "You must have seen accounts of the Johns Hopkins' study," he wrote a few years later to Tim Casady, his former student at MIT. "The study shows that psychedelics can occasion powerful mystical experiences." And here Huston referred to the research of Roland Griffin and his colleagues at Johns Hopkins, who had administered psilocybin to 36 middle-aged people, after which, as reported in *Scientific American Mind*, two-thirds maintained that, "the trip was among the most profound spiritual events in their life."[22] Huston saw the study as a validation of the Good Friday Experiment he had participated in with Walter Pahnke, and again it seemed that psychological research was catching up to him.

During the late 1990s and first years of the 21st Century, Huston quietly endorsed psychedelic experience on several occasions, though, as John Horgan has pointed out, he never brought it up during his interviews with Bill Moyers, probably to avoid alienating the conservative members of his audience. Huston's viewpoint on psychedelics came to include several interesting nuances, and these were richly explored in several interviews and publications: in Timothy White's interview for the magazine *Shaman's Drum* (1998); in Jeffery Mishlove's interview for the television series, "Thinking Allowed" (1998); in a preface to *The Road to Eleusis* (1998), a book by Gordon Wasson, Carl Ruck and Albert Hofmann, purported to prove conclusively that *kykeon,* the substance used in the Greek mystery cults, was a psychedelic; Robert Forte's interview for his book *Timothy Leary: Outside Looking In* (1999); a very interesting interview with journalist Richard Scheinin, published in the *San Jose Mercury News* on November 4, 2000, and in a preface for *Zig Zag Zen: Buddhism and Psychedelics* (2002), edited by Allan Hunt Badiner and the artist, Alex Grey. However, Huston's primary discussion and endorsement of psychedelics and his most complete work on the subject came out as a book.

In 2000, Huston published a collection of essays he had written over a forty-year period, with updated comments, dealing with psychedelics and their relationship to religion and spiritual experience. Since the book was meant to complement and update Huxley's seminal work, Huston titled it, *Cleansing the Doors of Perception*. The book is dedicated to Walter Pahnke, Huston's late friend and colleague, along with Pahnke's wife, Eva, and their three children, whose lives had been jolted when Pahnke drowned in a scuba-diving accident in Maine in 1971. The book begins with a short essay titled "Empirical Metaphysics," and continues with reprints of his landmark articles, including: "Do Drugs have Religious Import?" from *The Journal of Philosophy*; his article on Wasson's theory of Soma being derived from a psychedelic mushroom for JAAR; and his discussions of Stanislav Grof's research (originally published in *Forgotten Truth*), the Good Friday Experiment and the Native American Church's use of peyote. The message of the book is that when we accept the fact that psychedelics can trigger mystical experiences, we can move on to explore the implications of that fact.

Huston's interviews and publications during this period reveal that he continued to consider the drugs a tool that could be used or misused, a catalyst that could trigger awakening (as do fasting, sweat lodges, yoga, breathing exercises, meditation, devotional practices and Sufi dancing), but not guarantee it. The experience, he believed, could also be subsumed by the ego to produce an effect that is the opposite of awakening, driving oneself further into selfish and delusional behavior. We may use yoga only to boost our physical attractiveness; we may go to sweat lodges only to socialize; we may attend church and pray so that people will think we're pious or to content ourselves with being 'saved,' and likewise, we may participate in the peyote or ayahuasca rituals only to be perceived as hip. Like Galileo's telescope, Huston believed we could use psychedelic tools for purposes other than those best suited to the search for knowledge and insight.

When *Cleansing the Doors of Perception* came out, Huston remarked in an interview with Richard Scheinin: "I still do not know whether the public is ready. . . . If anyone, just seeing the cover of this book and my name, took it as a come-on for taking drugs, I will be very sorry that I published it. Because there are risks in taking any kind of mind-altering substance, including the entheogens. Many drug experiences are just cacophony and may be delusory. [But] The corollary is that there can also be gains."[23] And the gains were, as he said in the next moment, "the possibility of having a foretaste of that [which] can give something precious to the religious seeker—can boost their confidence so that they do not simply take these teachings of the religions as hearsay or on faith." Here he was echoing Huxley, who also believed psychedelics, though a "gratuitous grace," could give a glimpse of eternity, inspiring the seeker to continue the search.

While promoting his new book, Huston offered that mainstream America might consider using something like a structured program for administering the drugs. This is what the Native American Church provided for Native Americans, and this, presumably, is what the Eleusinian Mystery cults had provided for the ancient Greeks. Could there be a legitimate way to apply the psychedelics responsibly? When this question came up with Scheinin, Huston indicated that he was a historian of religions and a philosopher, not a program director, but then he added an endorsement: "The practical problem I delegate to a group, right here in the Bay Area, that calls itself the Council on Spiritual Practices. Can we devise the equivalent, for the entheogens, of seat belts in automobiles? The council is working on that."[24]

Huston's views of the drugs and their uses hadn't changed much over the years, but science and the study of psychology had somewhat caught up to him. This shift in public opinion felt like something of a validation and vindication to him, and Huston celebrated it from time to time when he bumped into Paul Lee, Ralph Metzner, Ram Dass or one or other of their gang from the IFIF days. Even Timothy Leary sometimes showed up, making clear yet again that though he was sincere about the value of psychedelics, Leary was still a huckster. This was proof to Huston that he hadn't yet sorted out the 'traits over states' issue. Yet Huston felt a fondness toward Leary nonetheless, and gratitude also.

"In the end it was hard to know what he [Leary] stood for other than getting attention," Huston told Robert Forte in 1999, explaining that,

> When I introduced him for his final book reading at Cody's Books in Berkeley [in 1995]—his early books were riveting, but that last one was a paste-up hodge-podge [to make money]. . . . I am left looking back on his life with gratitude, and also with sadness. Gratitude not only for the doors to my psyche that he opened but also for the friendship, fun, and excitement he provided during those Harvard years. Sadness for the way his life went downhill. . . . His spirit remained unbroken, however.[25]

### A LIFE OF NORMAL JOYS AND DEFEATS

The 1990s was overall a decade of triumph for Huston. But there was tragedy also. In most ways, his personal life was stable and fulfilling, nourished in 1993 when Kim, his youngest daughter, gave birth to a grandson, Antonio. That same year, Karen, his eldest daughter, was diagnosed with cancer. Huston had faced challenges in his life to his conviction that "we are in good hands," but none was so soul shaking as this event.

Karen had just turned 49, and as the mother of two healthy children, Sierra and Isaiah, was looking forward to the years ahead. "The best time of her life, she felt, was beginning," Huston wrote later in his memoir, *Tales of Wonder*. "She had a hysterectomy scheduled, but after hysterectomies women lead full lives, and Karen intended living hers to the fullest."[26] However, the surgery revealed a rare form of sarcoma, which had begun in her abdomen and spread to her vital organs, and the doctor informed her that she had only a short time to live.

The prognosis was that she would last two months—four with chemotherapy—and she should put her affairs in order. Huston found himself falling into despair, but comfort and strength came, and they came from Karen herself.

"Karen lived her remaining time heroically," Huston remarked, "Her life had had its normal joys and defeats, but the spiritual work that she accomplished in those thirty or so weeks of dying was more than enough for a lifetime."[27] Consequently, Huston found himself drawing comfort from his daughter's courage. How could he be sad if she was not? "It was as if shards of perfection pierced my sobs through the heroic way our daughter and her immediate family rose to her death. These experiences gave me the conviction that her death was not the last word."

In *Tales of Wonder*, Huston described his immediate reaction to Karen's passing:

> The night she died, after Kendra and Gael washed her body, we remained at her bedside. As one by one people drifted out of the room to catch some sleep, I sat there alone with my daughter's body. I would sob uncontrollably, crying in an-

guish, and then suddenly I would feel completely calm.  She's here, I sensed, not just her corpse, but *her*.  The sensation was so palpable I almost turned around, expecting to see her.

After such a night, life cannot go on, but it does go on.[28]

*****

Struggling with a broken heart, Huston tried to deal with Karen's death.  He turned to the desert, hoping to find the inspiration that Huxley had found there.  The result was that there came a night when he felt a spiritual sense working inside him with exceptional force: "My wife and I were spending a week in the dead of winter in Death Valley, California, and on the full-moon night that we were there I awoke around two A.M. to a call that seemed to come from the night itself, a call so compelling that it was almost audible."[29]  Heeding the call, Huston hurried into some clothes and went out to see a sky filled with brilliant stars, and for half an hour he walked along a road, looking up at the stars without a thought in his head.

"It may have been as close as I have ever come to the empty mind that Buddhists work toward for years," he wrote later.[30]  Feeling a strong sense of peace and tranquility, mixed with a sense of beauty, wonder and awe, he found that the experience was both replenishing and beyond words.  A year or so later he stumbled upon a poem by Giacomo Leopardi, that he recognized as "giving words to the night in question."  In that poem, a nomadic shepherd in Asia poses questions to the moon—"questions," Huston wrote, "whose horizons are themselves infinite:"[31]

> *And when I gaze upon you,*
> *Who mutely stand above the desert plains*
> *Which heaven with its far circle but confines,*
> *Or often, when I see you*
> *Following step by step my flock and me,*
> *Or watch the stars that shine there in the sky,*
> *Musing, I say within me:*
> *'Wherefore those many lights,*
> *That boundless atmosphere,*
> *And infinite calm sky?  And what the meaning*
> *Of this vast solitude?  And what am I?*

# Chapter Twenty-Four:
# Why Religion Matters

Bent on *control*, the West has lost sight of the virtues of *surrender*. Bent on changing the world, it has seen comparatively less to be gained by changing oneself.

Huston Smith

Terrorism is not a new weapon. Throughout history it has been used by those who could not prevail either by persuasion or example. But inevitably they fail, either because men are not afraid to die for life worth living, or because the terrorists themselves come to realize that free men cannot be frightened by threats.

John F. Kennedy

Huston enjoyed that his grandson Antonio, born when Huston's daughter Kim was 43 years old, could be a willful little fellow. Kendra said that, "A desk has been almost as much a part of Huston's life as his arms, but Antonio didn't enjoy it when his grandfather became too engrossed in his work." Consequently, one day while Huston was out of his office for a moment, Antonio went in and pushed all the books off the bottom shelf onto the floor. Returning to a mess, Huston accepted that he'd probably been too distracted that day and patted the boy on the head with a smile. After that, Huston purposefully kept books on the lowest shelf that were of no consequence, encouraging Antonio to have a go at it. This helped form a connection between them, with Huston giving the boy license to disrupt his work for more important things whenever necessary.

As the twentieth century turned into the twenty-first, Huston, in his eighties, was dealing with the infirmities that come with age. He had had surgery for prostate cancer in 1993 and in 2001 also had a hip replacement, which put him into a wheelchair for several months. His hearing was going (he would eventually have a Cochlear implant) and he was suffering the first stages of osteoporosis. He would soon require a walker. But his spirits were strong and he continued to be a lively speaker and writer. In 2001, he published *Why Religion Matters*, which won him the Wilbur Award from the Religion Communicators Council. He also delivered the Ingersoll Lecture at Harvard Divinity School (2001); he published an introduction to Buddhism with his friend Philip Novak (2003); he co-wrote two books with Phil Cousineau, including *The Way Things Are* (2003), a collection of interviews; and then he wrote *The Soul of Christianity* (2005), an attempt to reclaim his boyhood religion from the fanatic fringe that had begun to threaten it.

Huston's litany of publications and awards also included the Martin E. Marty Award from the American Academy of Religion in 2004, for "forwarding the public understanding of religion." In November of 2006, he was celebrated at Esalen with a short documentary film about his life. And on March 30, 2007, the Chaplaincy Institute co-hosted an interfaith event with Grace Cathedral Episcopal Church in San Francisco, "Honoring the Life of Huston Smith, A Living Treasure of World Religions." As part of that ceremony, "Professor Smith" received the Courage of Conscience Award, previously presented to the Dalai Lama, Rosa Parks, Martin Luther King Jr., Julia Butterfly Hill and others who have "dedicated their lives to peace, justice and service." Of all these honors, along with those that came before and after, none touched Huston so deeply as a letter written in his name for the Esalen event, coming from a friend who could not attend. Dated October 21, 2006, the testimonial was sent by Tenzin Gyatso, the Fourteenth Dalai Lama:

> I am very happy to know that the Esalen Institute, Big Sur, is planning to pay tribute to my old friend Huston Smith in recognition of his many achievements over the last sixty years or so. He is an outstanding authority on the world's religions, not only because of his far reaching knowledge of their teachings and scriptures, but also because he has put so many of them into practice, and as we say in Tibetan Buddhism, discovered their real taste. Huston seems to have an intuitive grasp of the spirit that animates the religious life that it is about kindness and transforming our attitude and conduct in order to make our lives more meaningful. I know of few other people who have done so much to bring about the tolerance, religious harmony and mutual respect that we so urgently need today.
>
> I have had the great pleasure of meeting Huston on many occasions. I have vivid memories of these meetings, not only because of the warmth of his welcome, but also because of the gentle kindness and strength of character he always exhibits. The many conversations we have had over the years have regularly served to reaffirm my conviction in the importance of inter-religious dialogue and the essential role that all major world religions can play in promoting basic human good qualities such as love, compassion, tolerance, and forgiveness in the modern world.
>
> Besides his work to promote the general cause of religious harmony and understanding, I have been touched to note that for forty years or more Huston has shown a special sympathy for Tibetan Buddhism and the difficulties we Tibetans have faced. He has been a staunch friend and I would like to take this opportunity to thank him for his unflinching fellowship. I pray that Huston's already long and fruitful life may continue for may more years to come to be a source of joy to him, his family and his many friends.

This letter came forty years after Huston first met His Holiness and affirmed Huston's journey as no other could. Huston held profound respect for the Dalai Lama's level of insight and commitment to world peace, which had been honored in 1989 with the Nobel Prize and in 2007 with the Congressional Gold Medal, presented to him by President George W. Bush, who, coincidentally, shares the same birthday as His Holiness.

Huston's work during this period focused increasingly on illuminating what the world's religions have in common, and in this case he wasn't talking only about their "transcendent unity." He was investigating the overlaps in ethics, values and outlooks of the religions. There had been a practical bent in Huston's viewpoint all his life, so it made sense to him to emphasize how Spirit functions in the world of lives and consequences. He saw utilitarian value in Tibetan Buddhism, for instance, since whether it was ultimately 'right' or not, it promoted compassion for all creatures. Additionally, he valued Native American religion because it promoted harmony with the natural world. And in all the religions he recognized resources for Earth's people to find identity, community, meaning and purpose.

Religions are different at the exoteric level, and those differences must be noted, but are the religions *entirely* different? That was the question. Huston, like his friend the Dalai Lama, didn't think so.[1] Huston, talking in 1993 with Jeffrey Kane about the universal overlaps among the religions, offered a first set of principles, suggesting that two levels first needed to be identified. "The one which is the more explicit is what we should do, but beyond that is the question of the kind of person we should try to become."[2] On the first level, regarding ethical behavior, Huston identified four areas of human activity that religion was designed to address: "violence, wealth, the spoken word and sex." For him, the moral precepts of every religion were devised to secure life-sustaining behaviors in each of them; furthermore, the religions' edicts were remarkably uniform across the cultures: Do not murder, do not steal, do not lie, do not commit adultery. "These," Huston contended, "are the basic guidelines concerning human behavior."

As for the kind of person we should try to become, Huston believed the virtues point the way. In the West, these are commonly identified as humility, charity and truthfulness, but Huston was careful to add that Hinduism and Buddhism also contain these virtues. Describing them to some extent "by the back door," they speak in terms of the "three poisons," the negative traits that keep the virtues from flourishing. "The three are greed (the opposite of humility), hatred (the opposite of charity) and delusion (the opposite of veracity)," Huston continued. "To the extent that we expunge these three poisons, the virtues will flood our lives automatically. The convergence of East and West in these areas is remarkable."[3]

Over the next fifteen years, Huston kept revisiting his list of exoteric overlaps among the religions' ethics and values, adding a third level of common characteristics in an interview with radio host Michael Toms in 1999:

> And then finally, after ethics and the virtues, what is common to them all is their vision of reality. And there the three things they all say is that things are more unified/integrated than we normally realize; second they are better than we normally perceive, because we normally see little dribs and drabs and do not see the whole picture; and the last is they're more mysterious than we normally suppose.[4]

After the turn of the new century, Huston's theories about how the religions' overlap came to be couched in terms that he borrowed from Noam Chomsky, his former colleague back at MIT. Chomsky, a linguist, had theorized that humanity's common biology expressed itself in shared social and psychological tendencies, generating a "universal grammar of human language" that could be detected at the root of all languages. Huston began to wonder: could there also be a Universal Grammar of Religion? Huston's close friend, Jon Monday, may have first suggested to Huston this connection with Chomsky's work, but whatever the case, Huston found the idea stuck his head. Eventually, he worked out a list of 14 common characteristics of his 'grammar' that are, in many ways, an extension and elaboration of Huxley's "minimum working hypothesis," since they begin and end with Huxley's position that there is a Transcendent Reality from which our psyches spring, and to which they should conform.

In 2008, Huston's list was published in a small book titled *Is There a Universal Grammar of Religion?* This book derived from a series of conversations he had with Henry Rosemont Jr., a scholar of Chinese religion who co-wrote the book. Huston, a year later, wished the book had never been released. "These were ideas I had been thinking about for a very long time, and I think there's some truth to them, but I didn't want to suggest to anyone I was attempting to draft a systematic philosophy, and I worried the list might do that." Like Huxley, Huston had always pointed to noticeable tendencies and patterns in the religions, but had never tried to work out a detailed system. In fact, he faulted others, including Ken Wilber, for doing so. Referencing the last of Huston's three points concerning the nature of reality (which he agreed were in every religion), he sometimes described the third point as that the universe is "perfect."[5] It is mysterious in its perfection, functioning even on the exoteric level in ways that are, by nature, impossible to map perfectly, and yet perfection is there. While describing the last of his 14 common characteristics, Huston makes two points: first that, "The world is perfect, and the human opportunity is to see that and conform to that fact"; however, he adds that we should also remember that reality is ultimately ineffable, and so to some extent, "we are born in mystery, and we die in mystery."[6]

In the interview with Toms, Huston returned to his position that the religions have utilitarian value, and this was the overall point he wished to make. And when Toms asked him about religious dogma, Huston remarked: "Religious dogma and doctrine help orient us in life, they are the crystallizations of these truths about the nature of life and reality and I hold them in very high regard. They are the winnowed wisdom of the human race." He did acknowledge that doctrines have sometimes been used for wrong purposes, though these transgressions were more the fault of people than religion. "The bottom line [of what is included in dogma] that should never be lost sight of is the respect for other people," Huston observed, "and this is ingrained deeply in all the enduring traditions." The most heinous use of dogma is using it as an excuse to impose one's views on others, and Huston argued that prohibitions against doing so are another characteristic of the religions. "I'm tempted to say this is the cardinal sin, the thing most to be avoided. . . . A line from the Koran says it nicely: 'There can be no compulsion in religion.'"

## WHY RELIGION MATTERS

Huston had backed off from framing a systematic view of what the religions hold in common, but he lost no steam in forwarding their interests. In his next book, *Why Religion Matters*, he went at that project with hammer and tongs. Talking about the book just after it was released, Huston told an interviewer he was stirred up and "coming out swinging," because of decades of frustration over Scientism's hold on academia and society's unwillingness to think another way. "I've tried to turn a pleasing, smiling face toward the public," Huston explained, "But you cannot live in this pigsty of a world without bumping into things that just annoy the *daylights* out of you!"[7]

The book, subtitled, "The Fate of the Human Spirit in an Age of Disbelief," grew out of Huston's desire to describe the possibilities for religion in the twenty-first century,[8] but he focused mainly on his many arguments against scientific materialism. He began by sharing the Allegory of Plato's Cave, describing it as the realm of ignorance, where nobody understands the value of the "Great Outdoors." Then he extended this metaphor by elongating the cave into a tunnel. The limited view of Scientism, which has, he contended, mesmerized our society and kept us locked in the dark; however, Huston wished to pose a question: Is there light at the end of the tunnel? On the philosophical level, he answered 'yes,' and the second half of the book is a shorter version of the perennial philosophy (almost exactly as he described it earlier in *Forgotten Truth*). Yet if we try to answer the question on the historical level, or relative to the contemporary situation, his answer was not so straightforward. Who knows where the twenty-first century will lead us? Who knows where we will lead the twenty-first century?

Huston described the cave/tunnel with two walls, a floor and a ceiling—each having been set in place by Scientism. The tunnel's floor is the outlook of Scientism, while the tunnel's left wall, right wall, and ceiling reflect the effects of Scientism on various aspects of our culture—higher education, the Law and the media, respectively. Much of the content of *Why Religion Matters* is a review of Huston's objections to Scientism, conjoined with fresh examples of how it has influenced our world. Huston's real hope for the book was to make one more plea for contemporary society to consider a splice between science and religion. His epilogue was entitled, "We Could Be Siblings Yet."

"I suggest that you try to understand where we believers are coming from," Huston wrote, addressing Richard Dawkins, E.O. Wilson and other scientific materialists. "The polemical among you are not good at doing that." Huston argued that his shelf of books on science-for-the-laity was as long as those for each of the major world religions, but he doubted the materialists could say as much from their side. Their standard criticisms of religion sounded "so much like satires of third-grade Sunday school teachings that they make me want to ask when you last read a theological treatise and what its title was."[9] Huston was clear that he had no problem with science itself, only with those who become dogmatic in its application. Antithetical to those with such poor habits, he offered examples of scientists who tried to create a splice. "Schrodinger's trilogy of small books for the general public ends with the Upanishads' resounding refrain, 'Atman is Brahman.' Niels Bohr credited Soren Kierkegaard's writings with sparking his doctrine of *complementarity*. Robert Oppenheimer read the Bhagavad Gita in Sanskrit...."[10]

Huston made clear that more listening needed to take place on both sides, but the key for splicing science with religion—or exploring the possibility of doing so—could only come if those in power, namely the scientists, would stop dismissing religion out-of-hand. As a capstone comment, he argued:

> Another problem I have with E.O. Wilson is that I don't like the way he positions science and religion as combatants. There's a lot of combativeness going on, as each side has vested interests it wants to protect. . . . It is my hope and a major point in *Why Religion Matters* that they can settle down as partners, each respecting its own capabilities in certain areas and recognizing its limitations in others, and agree that there are areas where it does not have competence and look on its neighbor as a partner and ally rather than an antagonist.[11]

Would strict materialists listen? Huston hoped so. Sadly, just a few weeks after *Why Religion Matters* was released, the chance for a splice became entirely moot, along with Huston's hopes for it. The tragedies of 9/11 shook the world. Did religion matter?

'Yes,' the scientific community, and everyone else, seemed to say. 'But only because it's so dangerous!'

# 9/11

On Tuesday, September 11th, 2001, a series of four coordinated terrorist attacks was launched upon the United States by the Islamic terrorist group al-Qaeda. Four passenger airliners were hijacked by 19 terrorists in several cities in order to fly them into the two World Trade Center buildings in New York City and the Pentagon in Washington. Two of the flights, United Flight 175 and American Airlines flight 11, crashed into the south and north towers of the Trade Center respectively; the third flight, American Airlines flight 77, crashed into the Pentagon; and the fourth flight, United Airlines flight 93, also targeted for Washington, crashed in a field in Pennsylvania, when passengers tried to overwhelm their hijackers. Altogether, almost 3,000 people died that day, including all of the hijackers and passengers (227 people), along with many firefighters, in what would become the deadliest incident for firefighters in American history. This was the first attack of a foreign power on U.S. soil since the American revolution.

Huston, who was doing his best to establish a new attitude toward religion and spirituality for the twenty-first century, felt stymied and depressed by the events of 9/11. Now his anger turned toward religious extremists as well as materialists. He had spent a lifetime defending the integrity of the religions but, over and over again, fanatics commandeering media attention were undoing his efforts. During the next five years, Huston would be asked to comment on the 9/11 tragedy numerous times, in articles for newspapers and magazines, including *Newsday* (for the Christmas after 9/11). There were requests for lectures on the subject from Harvard Divinity School (just five weeks after the tragedy), UCLA (for the "The Future of Religion" conference in 2003), San Francisco (for a conference featuring talks by the Dalai Lama, Imam Mehdi Khorasani and himself, in 2006), the University of South Carolina (for "A Gathering of Hearts Illuminating Compassion," with the Dalai Lama and a group of prominent religious scholars); and McGill University in Montreal, with Deepak Chopra and others for the "Revisiting Religion Post 9/11," also in 2006. What did Huston have to say? Were the events of 9/11 the death knell for religion? Had it run its course? Or perhaps the cause was somehow with Islam. Was Islam inherently violent?

The secularists wanted to pin blame on religion itself, but Huston would have none of it. Atrocities are not always committed in the name of religion. And to those who disagree? "I would try to get them to think about this monstrous twentieth century that we lived through that witnessed more destruction than the innumerable centuries that preceded it."[12] Huston reminded his audiences that the Nazis, the Soviets (with their Museum of Atheism) and the Maoists had, in total, killed 70 million of their own people. Why did no one advance the notion that secularism was inherently malicious? Extremism and dogmatic ideology were the problem, not religion in and of itself.

But wasn't it true that Islam is inherently an ideology of violence and conquest, less peaceful than other religions? "No, again," Huston said. "The very name of Islam means 'peace,' and there have been great spokesmen for the religion throughout history who have preached the message of peace." Just after 9/11, Huston published a short introduction to Islam[13] in the hope of educating people about peace as an ideal of the religion. In it he discussed the issue of violence, citing Norman Daniel's historical analysis that revealed, "Islam has resorted to violence no more than has Christianity," while adding, frankly, that, to say Christianity is just as *bad* is not to say it's good or to give much support for Islam.[14]

Exploring the use of force in Islam, Huston noted that Muhammad was driven to violence by those who wished him dead and his mission destroyed. Yet even then,     he "introduced chivalry" into warfare, setting specific limitations for how Muslims were allowed to behave.[15] Huston pointed out that there is "no scorched earth policy or leveling of Hindu temples or destruction of Buddhist statues in authentic Islam." For the true Muslim, brute force is justified for defense, not aggression, and the Koran makes this clear. Huston noted in his *Newsday* article that Allah's mercy and compassion are mentioned 192 times in the Koran, compared with 17 references to his vengeance and wrath. Huston concluded the piece, "Hear this, bin Laden!"

If the root causes of 9/11 were not religion or Islam, what were they? Huston responded like an Old Testament prophet, pointing an accusing finger at forces in our world that he believed were leading us down the road to ruin. First, he identified politicians and religious extremists who commandeer religion for their own selfish interests, demonizing those who disagree with their policies, disallowing any grounds for discussion or negotiation. "We live in a politically divided world in which each half shouts: 'We are on God's side.' The flip side of that is believing your opponents are the devil, the evil axis, the empire of evil. The rhetoric is exactly the same. The vicious cycle of religious or political blame games leads to the dehumanizing of entire peoples...."[16]

During speaking engagements, Huston sometimes singled out President George W. Bush, who characterized Iraq as part of the "axis of evil," and his war on Iraq as a "crusade." He also chastised fanatics of al-Qaeda, who referred to the United States as the "Great Satan" and had declared Jihad on America without the consent of the Ulema, the clerics of Islam who interpret Islamic law and who must be consulted. Huston called out America and the West for policies, both economic and political, which drive people in the Third World to violent action. Huston pleaded with us to do some soul-searching around whether or not we were completely free of blame for what had happened.

"It was a completely inexcusable act," Huston said, referring to destruction of the Trade Center. "However, it was not completely unprovoked." Huston believed that if we tried to pin all the blame on religious extremism or religious differences, we were missing a chance to learn from our mistakes. "In the fifteenth century, Islam was the most flourishing and advanced civilization in the world," he has written elsewhere. "Progressively, beginning with colonialism, we have reduced them to a condition of poverty, relative to the rest of the world, and despair."[17] Shouldn't this be noted, he wondered?

In his talks and articles, Huston explained that Islamic fundamentalism has arisen mostly as a reaction to feeling threatened, and is largely a regional phenomenon centered in the Middle East with ripples in Indonesia and Africa. He argued:

> The reason it is powerful in Middle Eastern Islam is that 80 percent of the Muslims there are traditional in their outlook and way of life, while the 20 percent who rule them have been educated in the West and are modern in outlook and lifestyle. It takes no great feat of imagination to sense the threat the traditional majority feels

from the ruling minority, and it causes them to dig in their heels. Two worlds, the old and the new, are in sharp collision.

Huston suggested that Middle Eastern militancy wasn't always about religion but sometimes more focused on defending a traditional way of life. "The figures are that one percent of the world's population owns about 80 percent of the wealth," he explained. "Well, what can we expect? That other people of the world will grin and bear it and not object to this inequity?" Huston was referring to globalization and its erosion of traditional cultures. He brought up Reinhold Niebuhr, who had argued all his life for solving the problem of world poverty. "With the inequality between the haves and the have nots," Huston related, "and starvation rampant throughout the world, and here we are eating our healthy meals. What do we expect them to do? Not try to call it to our attention that we've got to change our ways? If we're self-reflective that's the lesson to be learned from that dastardly act of the Twin Towers. I must say that sounds a little glib but the words are right."

## THE WAY THINGS ARE

In his reaction to and analysis of 9/11, Huston argued that on balance religion matters for the good. "We would lose if we throw the baby out with the bathwater," he explained to Cousineau in an interview in 2003, as they discussed 9/11 for Huston's book, *The Way Things Are*. "The bathwater is there. It's dirty and should be discarded, but it would be an incalculable loss if we threw out the baby with it. What is the baby a metaphor for here? In a word, religion, but what makes it precious is its insistence that there is a reality other than the materialistic universe in which we live."[18]

As Huston weighed the world situation (and suffered over causes and solutions), he wasn't willing to let religion off the hook entirely. He was reticent to criticize religion, since popular views were eager to do so, but finally he came out with some recommendations for religion in an interview for the magazine titled *What is enlightenment?*, in 2003. The editors were putting together an issue titled, "Can God handle the 21st Century?" and wanted to know Huston's views on the subject. Huston, to their surprise, said they might not like what he had to say. "My personal judgment," he told them, "is that my perspective differs so markedly from the mind-set of your readers that you would do better to bypass me on this one...."[19] That comment only made the editors more eager to hear Huston's thoughts. His comments offered the position that "the traditions may help us *hope* for a good outcome, but they may not be equipped to actually help us manifest it." And here Huston was sharing conclusions he had reached after serious and bitter reflection on 9/11. Their value for us is that they give us the pulse of Huston's viewpoint in the first decade of the new century.

In the article, Huston explained that the traditional religions arose during times when "people were isolated, living by themselves, and they did not realize that institutional structures are man-made."[20] They confused their laws for natural laws, attributing to God what they themselves had created, and thereby making those laws seem absolute. This assumption caused problems later when the traditions began to rub shoulders, since other societies had other values and institutional structures they beieved to be absolute. Conflict ensued as each society found it difficult, or sacrilegious, to think of its God-given views as provisional or culture-specific. The compassion that each society, based on its religious beliefs, taught within its respective fold was not extended to the 'Other' who lived elsewhere.

Huston further expounded that even within the respective societies of the early religions, as with the societies of the world today, there is an added problem: as societies recognized their views were essentially human constructs (which, he observed, "occurred emphatically in the sixteenth and seventeenth centuries"), they also became aware they were responsible for social injustices or inequalities they had been attributing to God. If a society, over a long span of time, had come to mistake their laws for natural laws but now understood better, wouldn't they be obligated to review such practices as the caste system, ill-treatment of women and slavery? "So that introduced a change in religion because suddenly we were responsible not just for our neighbor but also for these social and institutional structures [in our own society]."

Huston observed that, sadly, there was rarely evidence of change, and he attributed this immutability not only to the fact that social conventions gain momentum over time, but because "societies are constitutionally incapable of sacrificing themselves." Here Huston was referring to an idea borrowed from Reinhold Niebuhr's *Moral Man and Immoral Society*, that individuals may do things to help others, as a person may give a piece of bread to a starving man, but collectively governments and societies are conservative, selfishly protecting the *status quo* of their institutions. To make his point, he offered an example:

> Today, there are economic structures and class structures in which those of us who are more well-off, who have savings and stocks and bonds, can prosper just by doing nothing. We reap the benefits of our consumerism, while at the same time, no family receiving the minimum wage—the marginal people—can live on what they make. But are we compassionate enough to change that? No....
>
> I mean, what chances would President Bush have for re-election if he said, "We have to lower our standard of living in order to increase foreign aid." He wouldn't survive. What faction of society would voluntarily lower its income to raise the income of the destitute?[21]

For Huston, this societal tendency presented the religions with the specific task of reshaping themselves in order to "cross over into justice, and then into love." But how would they do so and what changes would be needed to bring justice and love to our planet? Huston offered some advice:

> In the foundation of all the traditions, compassion is the bottom line. But . . . we do need for them to move that compassion over into the social and ecological spheres. If they do not make this move from face-to-face charity and compassion to concern for justice—and in that justice I'm talking about social relations, as well as our effect on the biosphere . . . then they will be inadequate.

The interviewer then posed the question: Would the religions do so? Huston's answer was "probably not." The historical record seemed to indicate otherwise, as Niebuhr had pointed out. But didn't the religions still have an obligation to try? "Oh, of course," Huston answered. "They have a responsibility—but good luck. *The New Yorker* magazine used to have a little quip in every issue, 'Neatest trick of the week.' Well, if the traditions could succeed, that would be the neatest trick in human history—changing, redeeming human nature—because that's too tall an order for any institution or combination thereof."[22]

As the interview moved to its conclusion, Huston seemed to fall into a dark mood, having arrived at a hopeless position. Like John Lennon's famous billboard in Times Square, which advertised during the Vietnam War that, "War is Over if you want it," Huston was accusing both religion and society of being so sclerotic in their habits of greed, ignorance and pride that they didn't recognize their own ability to produce change. The problems of social injustice, world hunger, environmental degradation, religious extremism, fanatical patriotism and economic destitution could all be dealt with, 'if you want it.' On the level of the singular 'you,' many people did want this, but at the level of the plural, Niebuhr had had it right.

So why work for change at all? Huston offered because change does sometimes happen—as it did with the civil rights movement and the women's rights movement. But if it's so rare, the interviewer wondered, how can one be optimistic that change will come? Huston answered by noting a distinction between optimism and hope. He recalled Czech president Vaclav Havel saying that "optimism" suggests that we think things will turn out well, while "hope" is a force that motivates us toward right action whether we believe things will turn out well or not. And it was out of hope that Huston found motivation to keep working for change. We must, Huston argued, be like the doctors who fight to end disease whether or not they believe they will ever succeed. "The fulfillment comes through doing what one can, not in wasting time predicting outcomes."[23]

The interviewer wondered if the "happy ending" or final salvation religions predict could actually happen and could there be a "second coming?" Huston speculated that though most societies believe they want such a thing, they really don't. The prophecies tell us that a second coming or the arrival of Maitreya Buddha or the Islamist Madhi would bring dramatic change, and societies, as he had argued, don't like change. But if God does not intervene, Huston added, that doesn't mean a happy ending isn't possible for the individual. "If it doesn't happen here, that doesn't mean that it's not going to happen, as the Tibetans would say, on some other *bardo* or some other plane."

And what would that other plane be like? "Eternal bliss," Huston offered, concluding his comments. "Try to imagine that in any way you wish and as far as your imagination can carry you."[24]

## *KALI'S CHILD*

For over half a century, Huston had posited that if individuals and societies wanted to respect their different perspectives on life and morality, the foundation for doing so would be to understand each other's perspectives. Consequently, Huston believed that informed scholars, working in conjunction with religious liberals, had a responsibility to lead the global discourse in order that the "culture wars" being referenced in the press could be reframed in a more generous light. And he worried that without the concerted efforts of such people, the fanatics of the various religions, including those who embrace the secular ideology of Scientism, would take over the conversation, reducing it to little more than a shouting match. Huston lost a measure of confidence in academia's role in the defusing process when, in 1995, Jeffrey Kripal, a Ph.D. candidate from Huston's *alma mater*, The University of Chicago, published *Kali's Child*, a book that many viewed as a slanderous attack on the nineteenth century Hindu holy man, Sri Ramakrishna.

In *Kali's Child,* Kripal employed a methodology based on psychological theory, partially informed by the work of Sudhir Kakar and Gananath Obeyesekere, and used it to dissect the mind and actions of the revered Bengali saint. Kripal's project, as he viewed it, was a straightforward act of scholarship, analyzing an historical figure through a specific theoretical lens until he arrived at a rationally defensible set of conclusions. The conclusions *were* defensible, which is why the book won the American Academy of Religion's "History of Religion Award," for 1996. The subtitle of the book was "The Mystical and the Erotic in the Life and Teachings of Ramakrishna," and among Kripal's conclusions was the assumption that the saint had engaged in homoerotic behavior. Though Kripal contended that he had meant no disrespect, and had only reported what his analysis suggested, disrespect was taken. Eventually the Indian Government becames involved, disclaiming Kripal's work.

What might have been a small academic issue turned into a full-blown controversy in January of 1997, when Narasingha Sil, an Indian professor teaching in the United States, published a full-page review of *Kali's Child* in *The Statesman,* Calcutta's leading English-language newspaper. As a result, the book was pulled out of one context (academia) and set into another (international relations), with incendiary effect. A flurry of angry letters poured into the offices of *The Statesman.* Though the book had only sold a few thousand copies worldwide, and though most of its detractors had likely never read it, there was a moment when it seemed that everyone was talking about it. *Kali's Child* became a battleground in what author Philip Goldberg has termed "a name-calling standoff," with critics of Kripal's work labeled homophobes, Hindu extremists, ultra-nationalists and prudes, while his supporters were called Hinduphobes, cultural imperialists and sex-obsessed Freudians.[25]

Huston stayed out of the fray for three years, but jumped in when, in 2000, Kripal published an article defending his work in the *Harvard Divinity Bulletin,* titled, "Secret Talk: The Politics of Scholarship in Hindu Tantrism."[26] Professionally, Huston objected to the methodology and tone of *Kali's Child.* He was also personally affronted because so many of his friends in the Vedanta Society had taken offense, given that Ramakrishna had been the guru of the Society's founder, Swami Vivekananda. Huston drafted a rejoinder and submitted it to the *Bulletin,* where it was published in the next issue, along with fresh comments from Kripal. "I doubt that any other book," Huston began, pulling no punches, "not even those of early, polemical, poorly informed, and bigoted missionaries—has offended Hindu sensibilities so grossly. And understandably, for despite Kripal's protestations to the contrary, . . . *Kali's Child* is colonialism updated."[27]

Kripal cried foul, arguing that the book was mostly disturbing to readers who rejected Ramakrishna's "homosexualities" (Kripal's term) as morally wrong, and not to those who were more open-minded, many of whom had found the book a sympathetic portrait. For Kripal, his findings were only scandalous if homosexuality was somehow implicitly scandalous, and why should it be? But Huston wasn't buying Kripal's position, believing that Kripal had gone too far, feigning naiveté about the ruckus his work would cause, while also transgressing the boundaries of propriety. Many college professors had come out in support of Kripal, arguing that when scholars are doing their work, they shouldn't need to tip-toe around the 'sacred cows' of religious dogma or sensibility; however, Huston argued back that the offending bits in *Kali's Child* were more about inter-cultural insensitivity than academic freedom. How were the people of the world ever going to get along with each other if they, and their intellectuals, didn't show proper courtesy towards each other's values?

Huston wrote in the *Bulletin* that he agreed homosexuality isn't implicitly offensive, and that societies should work "to alleviate the suffering of those whose sexual orientations differ from those of the majority." The question was how to proceed in doing so. For him, it wasn't by offending people, as Kripal had done. Social views and values needed to be massaged slowly and respectfully, not blatantly challenged or subsumed. "Cultures accord sex very different meanings," he commented in the *Bulletin*, and so, "we do well to proceed cautiously when venturing on foreign soil." [28]

Huston then offered Kripal some advice, saying that the whole mess could have been avoided if Kripal had vetted his manuscript with the "community of believers" before sending it off to press, as Huston himself had done with *The Religions of Man*. Kripal disagreed, writing later in his third book, *The Serpent's Gift* (2007), that he didn't "accept the notion that the religions should set the ground rules for the practice of scholarship." [29] Kripal believed people had misread his intentions and overemphasized just one aspect of his research (which was certainly true). The two scholars reached an *em passé*, with neither one giving ground, and both finding some consternation with that fact. It irked Huston that academia still seemed to 'have it out' for religion, and Kripal, on the other hand, was bothered that Huston felt this way, given that he had always admired Huston's work and claimed no animosity toward Hinduism.

"That exchange was my closest contact with Huston," Kripal revealed. "And it was quite painful because I had read his work for years, appreciated it and also taught it for most of a decade. What hurt me most—of all the attacks that came my way over *Kali's Child*—was Huston calling me a neo-colonialist." One consequence of this was that Kripal visited Huston at his home in Berkeley and tried to state his case more clearly. But there was no reconciliation, despite the fact that both men had listened carefully to each other's positions.

Regarding the fate of *Kali's Child* and the strength of its arguments, several attempts have been made either to discredit or buttress Kripal's view of Ramakrishna, and the debate continued[30]—though mostly without the participation of Kripal or Huston. Appraising the dispute in retrospect, one irony that jumps out is that Huston and Kripal were in some sense natural allies. Each had indentified the dangers of scientific materialism in the academic study of religion, and both defended metaphysical viewpoints (including the perennial philosophy) in their work, though they held opposite views of organized religion.

Kripal became the J. Newton Rayzor Professor and Chair of Religious Studies at Rice University, and as Huston had been for decades, a leading defender in academia of the legitimacy and relevance of mystical experience. Kripal argued that consciousness is expandable and that we should strive to expand it. This view led him to become a board member of the Esalen Institute, where Huston taught many times. Kripal also argued, again in accordance with Huston, that discussion of altered states of consciousness has been reduced to inaccurate homilies by both religious fundamentalists and the advocates of Scientism. One can almost hear Huston's voice when Kripal writes, as he did in *The Serpent's Gift,* that "at least some of what we do and who we are is fundamentally and irreducibly anomalous, inexplicable, uncanny." [31] The dispute over *Kali's Child* must have provided satisfaction to those academics who denigrated both men for their interests in mysticism and metaphysics, while it also prevented a natural alliance.

# Chapter Twenty-Five:
# No Wasted Journey

What the religions say is that there is a happy ending that blossoms from the difficulties that must be surmounted. I think these intellectual difficulties with seeing transcendence and perfection are part of the necessary groping and grappling and overcoming. Again, because then we have a part in the achievement. It isn't just handed to us.

Huston Smith

When you came into this world, you cried and everyone else smiled. You should so live your life that when you leave, everyone else will cry, but you will be smiling.

Paramahansa Yogananda

Huston in his eighties still maintained a daily regimen of spiritual exercises. For many years, the form of those practices was that he would begin each morning with Islamic prayers he had learned as an observing Sufi, followed by a session of hatha yoga and meditation, and closed with a period of reading and reflection from one of the world's sacred texts. Sessions were missed, mostly while traveling, but Huston was fastidious about his practice. Into his nineties, he continued to spend mornings reading scriptures in his living room, which, with the help of his Tibetan caretakers, had come to look more like a Buddhist shrine chamber.

Huston became renowned as a scholar who embraced the gravity of the world's religions in his personal life, and as such was often asked how he was dealing with old age and the inevitability of death. The deaths of his parents, his brother and his daughter had most assuredly tested him, so he had experience to draw upon. But nothing that came before prepared him for the loss of his granddaughter, Serena, which added, as it was, to his misery over the events of 9/11.

## LOST AT SEA

In 2002, Serena, who had once lived with her mother on the first floor of Huston and Kendra's house, turned 30 years old and had blossomed into a beautiful young woman. Huston has written, "modeling-agency reps stopped her on the street."[1] But Serena wasn't just a pretty face. "Emotionally she was lovelier yet," Huston continued, "young or old, acclaimed or unknown, rich or poor made no difference to her, as she drew everyone out and made them feel better."[2]

Serena had recently begun a romance with a professional basketball player named Bison Dele, who had played for the Chicago Bulls in 1997, earning himself an NBA championship ring. Dele then did something unexpected; with five years remaining on his contract, he abruptly decided he'd had enough. There were other things he wanted to do, and so, according to Tim Keown of ESPN Sports, he just walked away "from more than $30 million dollars."[3]

Sparks flew between Serena and Dele when they met, but their timing was off. Dele had adventures he wished to undertake and Serena wasn't yet ready to settle down with anyone. She had been apprenticing as a make-up artist in Los Angeles but moved to New York when an old family friend invited Serena to join her selling real estate. "Serena soon became a top seller, selling more than anyone else in the agency," Kendra recalled. "She began to study for her broker's license, which she eventually got." In 2001, Serena was selling high-priced real estate in Manhattan and living happily, when suddenly the events of 9/11 occurred. She was relieved to get a call from Dele, who had been watching the news from Australia aboard his 55-foot catamaran, the "Hakuna Matata." Dele was sailing around the world to fulfill one of his dreams, and now, with the catastrophe in New York, he invited Serena to take a break and sail along with him. She agreed. She wasn't certain her life would be with him, but this was a chance to find out.

Serena joined Dele when he reached Tahiti, and they began enjoying their time together. Things were going along well until Dele's brother suddenly arrived. Kevin Williams, also known as Miles Dabord, was a known drug addict living in Palo Alto with no steady employment. In early July, Dabord came to Tahiti to borrow money from Dele; however, Dele refused, telling Dabord it was time to stand on his own two feet. Dabord seems to have accepted the refusal at first, since on July 4th he sailed with his brother, Serena and the boat's captain, Bertrand Saldo, when they left Tahiti for Honolulu. However, the boat never reached Hawaii.

"Serena's last phone calls to Gael and me were in early July," Kendra recalled. "She said they would be sailing to Honolulu and would not be able to call for a while." But by late July, when there still was no word from Serena, her mother grew concerned and reached out to Serena's father, Stuart Karlan, for emotional support. Huston, Kendra, Kim and other family members soon joined them in Colorado in a quiet vigil—or what they had wished to be a quiet vigil. "In the following weeks," Huston wrote in *Tales of Wonder*, "major news organizations from *America's Most Wanted* to CNN and *60 Minutes* pursued the story of the disappearance of the athletic star Bison Dele. Our sorrow and fear were thus lived out in the midst of a media circus."[4]

Police investigations revealed that Dele's boat had been returned to Tahiti, where it was docked in a private slip with its hull repainted and renamed. Witnesses said they had seen a man fitting Dabord's description docking the empty boat on July 15th, but Dabord had left the island two days later, eluding capture. Dabord was finally tracked down on September 14th, comatose on a beach in Tijuana, Mexico, after an apparent insulin overdose. Dabord was flown to San Diego but never recovered, and though it's assumed he had murdered his brother, Serena and Saldo, the bodies were never recovered and there was no resolution in the case, except that Serena, Dele and the boat's captain were gone.

"The grief we felt for Serena was multiplied by our feeling Gael's grief as well," Huston wrote later. "At Karen's funeral both Kendra and I had spoken; at Serena's service we fell mute, in a stony realm beyond words."[5]

When Karen died, Huston found solace in a trip to the desert, which, as Huxley had pointed out, can be a metaphor for the undifferentiated vastness of the Divine Ground. With Serena's death, the desert was only a metaphor for the emptiness he felt. "There are desert periods of the spirit," Huston told Bill Moyers in 1996. Now Huston was in one, a wasteland of suffering that tempers the soul.

As a public figure, Huston wasn't allowed to suffer and grieve in private. People wanted to know how he was weathering it, and in *Tales of Wonder*, he wrote that a reporter asked if his tragedies hadn't shaken his faith in God:

> I thought it a ridiculous question. What about the Holocaust and all the other catastrophes we know as history? They did not make my own loss less but kept me from imagining that I had suffered a unique vengeance that impugned the idea of God instead of making God more necessary.[6]

Serena's death did not break him, as it didn't break either Kendra or Gael, but it measured them all, and in the months ahead the wounds would be slow to heal. Huston believed he, and we also, must face what life throws at us. In his own exemplary way, he faced his loss. Pico Iyer observed of Huston in an article for *Shambhala Sun* (Nov., 2003): "The other thing that gives him a special authority, and the natural authority of one graced with a very special humility, is that he has suffered, as much as any of those he writes about; his is not the innocence that comes before experience but the one that comes after."

## THE BERKSHIRE

During the mid-2000s, Huston, with his back bent by osteoporosis, relied so much on Kendra to take care of him that she was having difficulties taking care of herself. After a few failed attempts to find a suitable housekeeper/nurse, it became clear Huston must go to a managed care facility. In the spring of 2008 he moved into The Berkshire, near downtown Berkeley. Trying to make the best of things, Huston flew Tibetan prayer flags from his small balcony, hung pictures on the walls, and settled into his small room with an attached bath. "People go to nursing homes, I've heard it said, to die," he related. "But I came to this assisted-living residence, it seems, to cheer people up." When asked what he meant, Huston shared that he had added a fourth practice to his daily regimen of prayers, yoga and meditation: "Mentally I take a census of the other residents here, and as each appears in my imagination, I ask how I might improve his or her day." Sometimes he did favors for the residents or brought them small gifts; at other times he consoled them or made them laugh. "We have a music night every Wednesday," he explained, "and I never miss it. Someone plays the piano and we all sing along. I love to sing old songs, and I love to get everyone else singing too."

Preparing to go downstairs for lunch in the dining hall, Huston spoke about how he didn't have time to feel sorry for himself. Life hadn't selected him for any special punishment, and for a man pushing 90 he was actually doing quite well. Later he would write in *Tales of Wonder*, which he finished while at The Berkshire, "I could obsess about my ailments and be an old man in misery. Instead I forget them and wonder how I came to be so fortunate and what I am even doing in an assisted-living home."[7]

Huston was delighting in small graces, including bird songs at his window, and had accepted the circumstances of his life as an opportunity to consider its ephemerality. Stepping into the elevator to go downstairs, Huston remarked, as a word of warning, "Do you know how medieval monks sometimes kept a skull on their dining table to remind themselves of their mortality? Well, when we get downstairs, you're going to see a lot of skulls!" It seemed Huston was using his fellow residents as objects of reflection.

## THE DAZZLING DARKNESS

Huston was never morose when he talked about death. In the years just prior to his entering The Berkshire, he was asked about it frequently, and even agreed to do film interviews on the subject with his friend Gray Henry in 2006,[8] and the gerontologist, Ken Dychtwald in 2009.[9] One reason for the curiosity about Huston's views on the subject was obvious: he was old and wise, but on another level Huston was puzzled and amused by the attention, writing in his memoirs:

> People ask me, the professor of religion, 'What happens when we die?' Every time, I think of the student who approached the Zen master.
>
>> Student: What happens when we die?
>> Zen Master: I don't know.
>> Student: But you're a Zen master!
>> Zen Master: True. Quite true. But I am not a dead Zen master.[10]

When urged to offer a guess, Huston would sometimes speculate. In *Why Religion Matters*, he wrote:

> Stated in the first-person singular, my extravagantly explicit scenario is this: After I shed my body, I will continue to be conscious of the life I have lived and the people who remain on earth. Sooner or later, however, there will come a time when no one alive will have heard of Huston Smith, let alone have known him, whereupon there ceases to be any point in my hanging around. Echoing John Chrysostom's reported farewell, 'Thanks, thanks, for everything; praise, praise, for it all,' I will then turn my back on planet earth and attend to what is more interesting, the beatific vision. As long as I continue to be involved with my individuality, I will retain the awareness that it is I, Huston Smith, who is enjoying that vision; and as long as I want to continue in that awareness I will be able to do so. For me, though—mystic that I am by temperament, though here below not by attainment—after oscillating back and forth between enjoying the sunset and enjoying Huston-Smith-enjoying-the-sunset, I expect to find the uncompromised sunset more absorbing. The string will have been cut. The bird will be free.[11]

When asked for further details, Huston made clear to his interviewers he couldn't say.

Exactly what would be on the other side is a mystery that has never been answered to everyone's satisfaction, nor, Huston believed, could it be.

Life, Huston said often, confronts us like a Rorschach inkblot test. We must each make of it what we will. Yet Huston saw the mystery in a positive light: "We are born in mystery, we live in mystery, and we die in mystery," he reflected one evening. "But it is not a dead mystery that bogs down in befuddlement. Religious mystery invites; it glows, lures, and excites, impelling us to enter its dazzling darkness ever more deeply."

The great religions do more to celebrate the mystery than they do to solve it or explain it away, functioning like fingers pointing at the moon while the 'moon' itself escapes their grasp. Huston believed the essence of the Great Mystery of Life and Death can be experienced in the unitive knowledge, but that experience, though it infuses one's spirit with complete meaning, cannot be fully approximated in concepts. John Horgan relates in *Rational Mysticism* that Huston once told him he was "convictionally impaired,"[12] but as Horgan understood Huston meant by this only that no particular 'finger' can entirely grasp the 'moon.' He was not being wishy-washy about the value of religion, but speaking as a postmodernist, heeding the warning that we must be careful of making ideas and concepts too real. Truth, after all, is experiential.

Some audiences might have considered Huston a Pollyanna, comforting himself (as Freud argued all religious believers do) with pretty dreams to ease his worries about death. But Huston didn't worry about death, nor did he hide from it. He was never a person to choose what was comfortable over what was true. Once, while discussing the many ways life can be interpreted, Huston stated this clearly. Having commented that though life is inscrutable, he had faith in it—defining faith as "the choice of the most meaningful hypothesis."[13] To which the interviewer rejoined: "That sounds a little like William James's pragmatism, which would have us believe things because of their positive effects on us." But Huston disagreed, taking the opportunity to clarify his stance:

> I'm not a pragmatist; I do not believe in believing in things because of their beneficial effects on us. I reject the argument that says, 'Here is this mysterious Rorschach blot, *life*. Let's interpret it optimistically because that energizes us and makes us feel good.' To hell with that line of thought! The question isn't what revs us up and makes us feel good, but what is true.[14]

Others in Huston's audiences understood what he meant about life and the afterlife, understanding the import of his reasoning and taking inspiration from it. Huston's optimism and insight affected a wide variety of readers and fans, as letters in his archives at Syracuse University attest. To give but one example, John Densmore, former drummer for The Doors, once wrote him a letter of appreciation.

Huston had met Densmore one night in 2003, after a talk at the Lobero Theatre in Santa Barbara. Soon afterwards Densmore wrote his letter. "You have helped me immensely," he told Huston, "not only as an example of living a long vibrant life, but recently with this *The Way Things Are* book. I'm a budding mentor, and examples such as you are rare and cherished. When you said, 'either we settle for it (the world) not making sense, or we press to the hilt the possibility that it is the way it should be,' I had an epiphany. Thank you for furthering my search." Many of the letters in Huston's archives made this same point, testimony to the fact that few writers on spiritual matters have left such a footprint of hope on so many people as Huston Smith.

In 2011, while reflecting on the "Bridge-Builder Award" he had received from Loyola Marymount University, Huston related that he had drawn inspiration for his attitude towards life from a 4th century Christian saint. The saint had run afoul of a despotic noblewoman because he stood up for the poor and denounced her extravagence. As punishment for crossing the woman, the saint was dragged behind a chariot until he was dead. "And as he died," Huston explained, "he is reputed to have said, 'Praise, praise for everything . . . thanks, thanks for all.'" This was the mindset of gratitude that

Goto Roshi had recommended to Huston so many years before and that he had thus far maintained. From the perspective of the Big Picture everything is as it should be and we should be grateful for it. "Not always easy!" Huston admitted. "But if circumstances permit, I hope those words of the saint can be my last words as well."[15]

## REFLECTIONS ON A LEGACY

In 2009, Huston's life took a happy turn when he was able to leave the retirement facility and move home with Kendra. Kendra had been coming to see him almost daily, but he missed his regular life with her, along with the company of their two dogs, Bobby and Chuki. The Smiths had worked out an arrangement with the Tibetan family living in their guesthouse (a renovated garage): Kendra would let them live in the big house with Huston while she moved into the smaller accommodations of the guesthouse. Dolma and Ngodup Gyalten, along with their daughter, son-in-law and two grandchildren, moved into the main house, tending Huston's needs and sharing a spiritual life with him. Kendra, who had for many years been what Huston called a "Buddhist Unitarian," came over each evening for dinner. Their relationship continued after more than 65 years of marriage.

*****

Asked about his legacy as an author and lecturer, Huston was dismissive of the idea he had made much impact, as he was when Phil Goldberg once asked him the same question, answering: "I like the Vedantic statement that the impact of any human being has on history is like putting a finger in a glass of water and taking it out again."[16] But, Goldberg observed, "Some fingers make a bigger splash than others."

Assessing and summarizing Huston's career, we can say he was the first and only person outside of fiction (Yann Martel's novel, *The Life of Pi*, comes to mind) who lived all of the world's major religious traditions. That alone is significant. Furthermore, he brought us along on his quest for insight. Huston tried to make world citizens of his readers by broadening their comprehension of the human experience. And he was doing this for a practical reason. "We have come to the point in history," Huston wrote more than 50 years ago in his introduction to *The Religions of Man*, "when anyone who is only a Japanese or only an American, only an Oriental or only a Westerner, is but half human; the other half of his being which beats with the pulse of all mankind has yet to be born."[17] If we, as individuals and societies, wish to have peace in the world, Huston argued that we must make peace with the world, and history has shown that this is wise advice. Looking back at the Earth from the moon, Edgar Mitchell reached the same conclusion, realizing that there can no longer be 'us and them' on so small a planet with so many people. There is only 'us,' and Huston was one of the first to insist we open our eyes to that fact.

Appraising Huston's general posture towards religion, it's interesting to note he was more liberal than his conservative fans (e.g., among the Traditionalists) often realized, given that he advocated the value of psychedelic drugs and endorsed the free-inquiry going on at Esalen and elsewhere. But, enigmatically, Huston was also more conservative than many of his liberal fans realized, arguing as he did against a New Age approach to religion or the possibility of perfect enlightenment. Though he advocated studying religions beyond one's own, he did so mostly to help us understand the views of others, not because we should take a 'let me try them all' approach to religion. On a spiritual level, any insights we gain by investigating the world's religions were, in many ways, a 'gratuitous grace' for Huston, as Huxley had termed the insights gained from psychedelics, unnecessary for a full religious life. Where religious liberals often cite Max Muller's comment that, "To know one religion is to know no religion," since we then have no basis for comparison, Huston argued that, "To know one religion is to know all religion," since each path is, as he often said, "sufficient to salvation."

Huston believed every religion is completely adequate, in that serving as a finger pointing at the moon it directs our attention from the transient world to what lies beyond it. This is what makes Huston so beloved by religious liberals from all the faith traditions and beyond them: his steadfast emphasis on the need to connect with the Divine and his open-mindedness about how to get there. John Horgan once wrote: "Given the enormous diversity of the religious beliefs, how should we choose among them? Smith's response was that of a grandfather confronted with grandchildren demanding to know whom he loves most: I love you all! he replied, so sincerely that everyone can go away happy."[18]

Reviewing Huston's legacy further, two contributions come to mind. First, he has been a great champion of the Infinite, like Friedrich Schelling, Ralph Waldo Emerson and Aldous Huxley before him, advocating that we return metaphysics to philosophy and renew our attention to the wisdom of the past. "I am not an original thinker, I am simply a lover of the ancients," Huston once remarked to Phil Cousineau. "Confucius again put it succinctly: 'Heaven and Earth. Only Heaven is great.' It's the ancients' right-minded regard for transcendence that I love, and I have tried to use the ounces of my strength to get it to the general public, to share that love."[19] And so in an epoch when Scientism has ruled the roost, Huston was a steady voice for the benefits of thinking otherwise.

Huston's second major contribution is that he taught so many people the value of listening to others. In 1958, Huston ended *The Religions of Man* with a rumination on listening that expressed his reasons for why it's so important. Today, in a time when terrorist attacks reveal the dangers of not listening to each other attentively, his words have as much relevance as they did then:

> Daily the world grows smaller, leaving understanding the only place where peace can find a home. [And yet] we are not prepared for the annihilation of distance that science has effected. Who today stands ready to accept the solemn equality of peoples? Who does not have to fight an unconscious tendency to equate foreign with inferior? Some of us have survived the bloodiest of centuries; but if its ordeals are to be birth pangs rather than death throes, the century's scientific advances must be matched by comparable advances in human relations. Those who listen work for peace, a peace built not on ecclesiastical or political hegemonies but on understanding and mutual concern. . . .
>
> So we must listen to understand, but we must also listen to put into play the compassion that the wisdom traditions all enjoin, for it is impossible to love another without hearing that other. If we are to be true to these religions, we must attend to others as deeply and as alertly as we hope that they will attend to us; Thomas Merton made this point by saying that God speaks to us in three places: in scripture, in our deepest selves and in the voice of the stranger. We must have the

graciousness to receive as well as to give, for there is no greater way to depersonal-ize another than to speak without also listening.

Said Jesus, blessed be his name, "Do unto others as you would they should do unto you," Said Buddha, blessed be his name as well, "He who would, may reach the utmost height—but he must be eager to learn." If we do not quote the other religions on these points, it is because their words would be redundant.[20]

## WISDOMKEEPER

Beyond what has already been said about the significance of Huston's career, he was the leading flag carrier in the past half century for the perennial philosophy. The pe-rennial philosophy states that the omega experience (not the description, but the ac-tual experience of union with the Divine) is identical in all the mystical branches of all the world's religions. This has implications for how we should live our lives, which Huxley succinctly laid out in his Minimum Working Hypothesis:

*That there is a Godhead, Divine Ground of Being, or Brahman that our reality
   depends upon for its existence.
*That this Ground both transcends the world and is imminent as the world.
*That it is possible for human beings to love, know and, from virtually, to become
   actually identical with the Divine Ground.
*That to achieve this unitive knowledge is the ultimate end and purpose of
   human existence.
*That there is a Way or Dharma that must be obeyed if people are to achieve their
   final end, and this Way is a way of peace, love, humility and compassion.

Huston believed the perennial philosophy is the esoteric essence of all spirituality and the inspiration of all religion, but more than this, his life has been an expression of the efficacy of this position. Huston's life has provided an example of what can be achieved by embracing the mystical heart of all religions, though he recommends that we reach it by sticking with just one. His kindness toward others; his willingness to listen and learn; his determined embrace of his own soul; his humility before the mystery of life; and his gratitude towards life, have not only supplied proof that his viewpoint has virtue but have served as an inspiration to others who have embraced that viewpoint. Huston's contribution has been not only to carry the flag of the perennial philosophy, but personally to dive into the mystical branches of the world's religions as a means of confirming that they do end in the same place of Divine Peace, Love and Understand-ing. This is what radiated from Huston to those who have known him and what has made Huston Smith a spiritual giant of the twenty-first century.

## EPILOGUE: A FINAL WORD ON THE PERENNIAL PHILOSOPHY

Huston argued the validity of the perennial philosophy for most of his career. How does it fare today? Some scholars see Huston's endorsement as outdated, while others see it as timeless. Some see the perennial philosophy as extinct, while others see it thriving as never before. When *Tales of Wonder* came out in 2009, *Newsweek* magazine ran a story on Huston that included a very one-sided appraisal of his impact, coming as it did from one of his critics rather than a friend. "Smith and others have led us down a rabbit hole of nonreality that we are now trying to climb back out of," Stephen Prothero, author of *God is Not One* (2010), claimed,[21] expressing his worry over the supposed homogenizing influence of the perennial philosophy on religion. "Is Islam the same as Christianity?" he asked. "To con ourselves into thinking they're the same is to believe in something false." Prothero added that Huston's work had value in the past, when we were "more parochial," but now, "It's time to move on."

Weighing the point, it's Prothero's position that sounds more parochial and hidebound. These criticisms of Huston Smith stem from thirty years ago, when Prothero's colleague at Boston University, Steven Katz, first raised them. Academics never went down a "rabbit hole of nonreality," for when was the perennial philosophy ever the leading opinion in the academy? And if we're dealing with concepts of reality, what proof does Prothero offer as conclusive evidence in eliminating Huston's position? None that any scholar can't easily dispute, and that Robert K.C. Forman hasn't already deconstructed.[22] Prothero doesn't understand Huston's position, as his comments testify. Huston did not say that the religions aren't different, nor did he privilege the esoteric perspective in religion over the exoteric perspective. In fact, Huston said repeatedly that those who follow the strictures of exoteric religion would do well to ignore any deconstructive or heretical tendencies offered to them by mystics. Only on the esoteric level do the religions merge into the unitive knowledge.

Few people today recognize the term 'perennial philosophy,' and there are scholars who argue that the theory has now faded in importance and credibility. But perennialism has actually become so entrenched in the contemporary mindset that we often can't see the forest for the trees. To emphasize how prevalent the view actually is in the self-help area, Ken Wilber's "integral spirituality" and Deepak Chopra's "quantum spirituality" are, intentionally or unintentionally, iterations and extensions of Huxley's original viewpoint. In transpersonal psychology from Maslow and Stanislav Grof to the present, the guiding principle of "self-actualization"—the fulfillment of a secular and therefore scientifically more acceptable description of enlightenment—is again highly suggestive of and mostly derived from perennialism. When Andrew Weil, Dean Ornish and Dean Radin, the well-known doctors and authors, discuss health and wellness, they often echo and build off of Huxley's viewpoint—or one indistinguishable from it. Even researchers in the field of psychedelic studies present theories that fit perfectly with Huxley's viewpoint. For instance, Dr. Rick Strassman, in his book *DMT: The Spirit Molecule* (2001), explains that psychedelics can induce "firsthand knowledge of the sublime," and adds that this "may help develop a more broad-minded and universal approach to the spiritual."[23] Again, Huxley's theory of spiritual awakening as the core of religion and the goal of our lives is so prevalent today that we have trouble recognizing it.

If we take Huxley's "minimum working hypothesis" that there is an Absolute metaphysical reality that we can and should experience directly and look at the course catalogs for Esalen, the Institute of Noetic Sciences, the Omega Institute, the Kripalu Institute, the California Institute of Integral Studies and scores of other such facilities, and if we take the pulse of what is taught by the tens of thousands of yoga instructors and meditation teachers in America, we find that the perennial philosophy is alive and well. Huston Smith has brought a tremendous influence in spreading the word, not only about the nature of the viewpoint but that it exists as a pattern in many religions and worldviews.

Many people today who are repulsed by religion and religious institutions do believe in an underlying Godhead—something beyond this universe—and most of them might even apply the word spiritual to their belief system so long as it's not tied to any single religion. In this loose system of belief, the perennial philosophy is more acceptable to them than any established religion or religious institution. Many others are comfortable inside their traditional religions and enjoy the benefits of organized religion, yet also believe that other faiths have their value and are inspired from the same source of spirit that animates their own. (Evidence that this is becoming an accepted viewpoint is found in the growing movement of interfaith chaplains who minister across the wisdom traditions.) Huston's lessons on the perennial philosophy have given solace and inspiration to both groups, and these groups are growing stronger with every day that passes.

# Notes

## Chapter One: A Middle Child of the Middle Kingdom

1. All quotes attributed to Huston and Kendra Smith that are not given a separate citation are taken from interviews I conducted with them during many days spent at their home in Berkeley between 2007 and 2011.

2. Huston Smith, "The Long Way Home," in *Paths of the Heart*, ed. James S. Cutsinger (Bloomington, IN: World Wisdom, 2002), 256.

3. Huston Smith with Jeffery Paine, *Tales of Wonder* (New York: HarperCollins, 2009), 8.

4. Huston Smith, "My Christmas as a Child in China," in *On Faith*, 2007.

5. This last remembrance is from chapter one, "Saving the Moon," of a rough and unpaginated manuscript for a forthcoming book by Huston to be titled *And Live Rejoicing*, sent to me by Huston in 2011.

6. Huston Smith, *Why Religion Matters* (New York: HarperCollins, 2001), 35-36.

7. Huston Smith, "The Battle for the Human Mind," an interview with Richard Gazdayka, in *The Way Things Are*, ed. Phil Cousineau (Berkeley: University of California Press, 2003), 149-150.

8. Huston Smith, *The Way*, 20.

9. Huston Smith, "The Long Way Home," in *Paths*, ed. Cutsinger, 257.

10. Philip Novak, "The Chun-tzu," in The Syracuse Alumni Bulletin, 8.

11. John Horgan, *Rational Mysticism* (New York: Houghton Mifflin, 2003), 19.

## Chapter Two: The Night of Fire

1. Don Lattin, *Following our Bliss* (New York: HarperCollins, 2003), 160.

2. David Ray Griffin and Huston Smith, *Primordial Truth and Postmodern Theology* (Albany: State University of New York Press, 1989), 8.

3. Lattin, *Bliss*, 160.

4. Griffin and Smith, *Primordial*, 8.

5. Ibid., 8-9.

6. Huston Smith, *The World's Religions* (New York: HarperCollins, 1991), xi.

7. Huston Smith interviewed by Phil Cousineau, "Why Fundamentalism Matters," in *Parabola*, winter, 2005, 55-56.

8. Huston Smith interviewed by Phil Cousineau for Monday Media DVD, "The Roots of Fundamentalism," 2005.

9. See Huston Smith, *The Soul of Christianity* (New York: HarperCollins, 2005), 17-24.

10. Huston Smith, *Soul*, xii.

11. Huston Smith, *The Way*, 76.

12. Huston Smith, *Why Religion Matters*, 74.

13. Griffin and Smith, *Primordial*, 9.

14. Ibid.

15. Ibid.

16. Huston Smith, *Tales*, 34.

17. Griffin and Smith, *Primordial*, 9.

## Chapter Three: Deepening the Search

1. Huston Smith, *Why Religion Matters*, 74.
2. Huston Smith, *Cleansing the Doors of Perception* (Boulder, CO: Sentient Publications, 2003), 3.
3. Huston Smith, *Tales*, 35.
4. Huston Smith, "Empiricism Revisited," in *The Empirical Theology of Henry Nelson Wieman,* ed. Robert W. Bretall (New York: Macmillian, 1963), 244.
5. Huston Smith, *Why Religion Matters,* 76.
6. Huston Smith, *Tales*, 81.
7. Kendra Smith in private correspondence with the author, but also in Huston's *Tales,* 83.
8. Ibid.
9. Huston Smith, "The Operational View of God," in *The Journal of Religion*, Vol. 31, No. 2, Apri., 1951, 94-113.

## Chapter Four: The Best Kept Secret of the 20th Century

1. Griffin and Smith, *Primordial*, 10.
2. Smith, *The Way*, 81.
3. For a close view of their relationship, see Isherwood's *My Guru and His Disciple*.
4. Aldous Huxley, *The Perennial Philosophy* (New York: Harper & Row, 1970), 14.

## Chapter Five: Hitchhiking to California

1. This reference was drawn from a biographical note in Huston's first professional article, "The Operational View of God," in *The Journal of Religion*, Vol.31, No.2 (Apr.,1951), 94, an excerpt from his Ph.D. thesis.
2. Griffin and Smith, *Primordial*, 11.
3. Gerald Heard, *Pain, Sex and Time* (Rhinebeck, NY: Monkfish, 2004), xxvii-xxviiii.
4. Ibid., viii.
5. Ibid., xxii.
6. Ibid., 243-244.
7. M. Darrol Bryant ed., *Huston Smith: Essays on World Religion* ((New York: Paragon, 1992), xx.
8. Huston Smith, *The Way*, 81.
9. Huston Smith, "Remembering Aldous Huxley," in *LA Times*, 11/20/1988. Related to Huston's comment, Huxley wrote a very good essay on the desert as a "natural symbol of the divine," called simply "The Desert," in *Adonis and the Alphabet* (New York: Harper, 1956).
10. Huston tells us in *Tales of Wonder*, page 48, that it was Huxley who recommended Swami Satprakashananda to him, but note that elsewhere he has attributed both the recommendation and the remark about a "very good swami" to Heard. For instance, in Griffin and Smith, *Primordial*, 11, he says "On seeing me off for my return journey, Heard remarked: 'So you're moving to St. Louis. There's a very good swami there.'"

## Chapter Six: The Journey Within

1. Huston Smith, *The Way*, 263.
2. Bryant, *Essays*, 29.
3. Swami Satprakashananda, *Vedanta for All* (Chennai, India: Sri Ramakrishna Math, 2001, 62.
4. Aldous Huxley, *Island* (New York: Harper & Row, 1962), 179.
5. Huston Smith, *The Way*, 47.
6. Satprakashananda, *Vedanta*, 75.
7. Pico Iyer, in *Living Wisdom: Vedanta in the West* (Hollywood, CA: Vedanta Press, 1998), 150-151.

8. Satprakashananda, *Vedanta*, 59.

9. Huston Smith, *The Way*, 32.

## Chapter Seven: The Human Venture

1. Huston Smith, *Tales*, 114.

2. Gerald Heard, *The Eternal Gospel* (New York: Harper and Brothers, 1946, xi.

3. As Hal Bridges correctly observed in his book *American Mysticism* (New York: Harper & Row, 1970): "Emergent evolution, so fascinating to his friend Gerald Heard, is not one of Huxley's major themes," 88.

4. Huston Smith, *Why Religion Matters*, 24.

5. Huston says he went to California to be with Heard in the summer of 1953 but John Roger Barrie, caretaker of the Gerald Heard Archives, believes it was the summer of 1954. To further confuse the issue, Kendra remembers it as the summer of 1952.

6. In Huston's first endnote of that article (reprinted in Bryant, *Essays*, 14), he writes: "I am also indebted to Gerald Heard, whose lecture series at Washington University during the autumn of 1951 first suggested to the writer a number of ideas here elaborated."

7. Barrie writes (in Heard, *Pain*, xv): "Heard received a two-year fellowship grant from the Bollingen Foundation (1955-56) under the auspices of Washington University's Department of Philosophy, then headed by Professor Huston Smith [note however that Huston was never department head during his time at WU]. This enabled him to undertake the research that resulted in 1963's *The Five Ages of Man*. . . . "

8. In a letter about the IHP trip she took with her father, Kim's says that this trip to Mexico was in 1951, and Kendra remembered it as 1953, but the family took more than one trip to Mexico and 1954 makes the most sense in the chronology of Huston's life and Heard's career.

9. This story was taken from my notes but some of it also appears in Huston's *Tales*, 52-53.

10. Huston Smith, *Tales*, p.54.

11. Huston Smith, *The Purposes of Higher Education* (New York: Harper and Brothers, 1955), 69.

12. Ibid.

13. Ibid., 138-9.

14. Ibid.

15. Ibid., 130.

16. Huston Smith, *Why Religion Matters*, 155.

17. Huston Smith, *Tales*, 50.

18. Ibid., 69.

## Chapter Eight: Finding His Niche as a Philosopher

1. Huston Smith, *Tales*, 85.

2. From Jon Monday's tribute film about Huston for Esalen, 2006.

3. Huston Smith, *The Way*, 20.

4. Huston Smith, *Forgotten Truth* (New York: HarperCollins, 1992), vii.

5. Huston Smith, *The Religions of Man*, x.

6. Huxley, *Island*, 113.

7. Stephen Prothero, "A Dangerous Belief," in the *Wall Street Journal*, April, 2010: "When I was a student in college in the 1970s and 1980s I was told repeatedly that all religions are one. . . . From this perspective, popularized by 'perennial philosophers' such as Aldous Huxley, Joseph Campbell and Huston Smith, all religions are beautiful and all are true."

8. For example, see Harry Oldmeadow, *Journeys East* (Bloomington, IN: World Wisdom, 2004), 81.

9. Henry Nelson Wieman, in ed. Robert W. Bretall, *The Empirical Theology of Henry Nelson Wieman* (New York: Macmillan, 1963), 2.

10. Huston Smith, "Empiricism Revisited," in Bretall, *The Empiricism*, 253.

11. Huston Smith, "The Death and Rebirth of Metaphysics," in eds. William L. Reese and Eugene Freeman, *Process and Divinity, the Hartshorne Festschrift* (LaSalle, IL, Open Court Publishing, 1964), 37-47.

12. Herbert W. Richardson and Donald R. Cutler, eds., *Transcendence* (Boston: Beacon Press, 1969). Note that this volume contains essays by other important scholars of that time, including Harvey Cox and Robert N. Bellah, but also an essay by Michael Murphy, one of the founders of the Esalen Institute and later a close friend of Huston's.

13. Huston Smith, "The Reach and the Grasp: Transcendence Today," in ibid, 9.

14. Henry Nelson Wieman, "Transcendence and 'Cosmic Consciousness,'" in ibid., 154.

15. Ibid., 155.

16. Satprakashananda, *Vedanta*, 47.

17. Ibid., 12.

## Chapter Nine: The Religions of Man

1. Huston Smith, *The World's Religions*, xi.

2. Huston Smith, *The Religions of Man*, ix.

3. Huston Smith, *The Way*, 85.

4. Philip Goldberg, *American Veda* (New York: Harmony Books, 2010), 104-105.

5. Ibid., 106.

6. Huston Smith, The *Religions,* 313.

7. Huston Smith, *Tales,* 59.

8. Ibid., 60.

9. Huston Smith, *The Way*, 45.

10. John B. Noss, *Man's Religions* (New York: Macmillan, 1949), 209.

11. Ibid., 208.

12. Ibid., 126.

13. Ibid., 127.

14. Huston Smith, *Tales,* xiii.

15. Huston Smith, *The Religions*, 310.

16. Ibid.

17. Ibid., 311.

18. Griffin and Smith, *Primordial*, 12.

## Chapter Ten: Temple of the Marvelous Mind

1. Huston Smith, *The Religions*, 8.

2. Ibid., 9.

3. Huston Smith, "Accents of the World's Philosophies," reprinted in Bryant, *Essays*, 4.

4. Bridges, *American Mysticism*, 114.

5. Alan Watts, *In My Own Way* (New York: Pantheon, 1972), 126-135.

6. Griffin and Smith, Primordial, 13.

7. Bridges, *American Mysticism*, 107.

8. Ibid., 108.

9. Watts, *In My Own Way*, 119.

10. Philip Kapleau, *The Three Pillars of Zen* (Boston: Beacon Press, 1965), xi.

11. Watts, *In My Own Way*, 78.

12. An abridged version of the interview appears in James Nelson ed. *Wisdom for Our Time* (New York: W.W. Norton, 1961), beginning on page 137, with the citation on 140.

13. Ibid., 141.

14. Bridges, *American Mysticism*, 104.

15. See Huston's *Tales*, 124. However, note that this passage suggests it was this meeting with Suzuki, at the interview, that inspired him to visit Kyoto's Myoshin-ji temple to study Zen, which would be problematic, given that he talked about his training at Myoshin-ji during that interview. My guess is that an earlier meeting with Suzuki had inspired his visit to Japan.

16. Huston Smith and Philip Novak, *Buddhism, a Concise Introduction* (New York: HarperCollins, 2003), 208, but also see Huston's *Tales,* 130.

17. Huston Smith, *Tales*, 128.

18. Huston Smith, *The Way*, 31-32.

19. Huston Smith, *Tales*, 131.

20. Ibid., 132.

21. Ibid., 133.

22. Bryant, *Essays*, 259-260.

## Chapter Eleven: The Search for America

1. Watts, *In My Own Way*, 277-8.

2. Huston Smith, *Tales*, 123.

3. He said it to me and he seems to have passed it along to Pico Iyer, who shared it in his introduction to Huston's *Tales*, xii.

4. Watts, *In My Own Way*, 181.

5. Huston Smith, *Tales,* 123.

6. Huston Smith ed., *The Search for America* (Englewood Cliffs, NJ: Prentice-Hall, 1959), 131.

7. Ibid., 145.

8. Ibid., 169.

9. Kapleau, *Three Pillars*, xiii.

10. Huston Smith, *The Search*, 174. Note also that Tillich had read widely in Zen and had acknowledged that it influenced his views.

11. Bryant, *Essays*, 71.

12. Alan Watts, *The Joyous Cosmology* (New York: Vintage, 1962).

13. These lectures at were taken from a course Huxley had taught at UCSB in 1959, collected and published posthumously as *The Human Situation*.

14. Robert Forte ed., *Timothy Leary: Outside Looking In* (Rochester, VT: Park Street Press, 1999), 255.

15. Cutsinger, *Paths to the Heart*, 255.

16. Ronald Clark, *The Huxleys* (New York: McGraw-Hill, 1968), 348.

17. Aldous Huxley, *The Doors of Perception* (New York: Harper, 1954), 22-23.

18. For a longer account of Huxley's experiences with psychedelics, see my book, *Aldous Huxley, A Biography* (New York: Crossroad, 2002), and for the best book of Huxley's own writings on psychedelics, see Michael Horowitz and Cynthia Palmer's excellent anthology, entitled appropriately, *Moksha*.

19. Leary's first trip is described in detail in Robert Greenfield, *Timothy Leary, A Biography* (Orlando, FL: Harcourt, 2006), 110-114.

20. Timothy Leary, *Flashbacks* (New York: Putnam, 1990), 33.

21. Ibid., 38.

22. Forte, *Outside Looking In*, 157.

23. Ibid., 246.

24. Michael Horowitz, Leary's archivist and friend, gave me a copy of this letter during one of my several visits to his home.

25. Huston Smith, *Cleansing*, 7.

## Chapter Twelve: Into the Fire

1. Leary, *Flashbacks,* 36.

2. Huston insinuates in *Cleansing,* page 10, that he and Kendra each took two capsules, but note that Greenfield, in *Timothy Leary,* page 131, says Kendra took three, which agrees with what Kendra told me about that day at Leary's.

3. Huston Smith, *Cleansing,* 10.

4. Huston Smith, *The Way,* 223, but note also that on page 250 of Forte, *Outside,* there is a reprint of Huston's four-page session report for that first trip, which Forte obtained compliments of Michael Horowitz, Leary's archivist.

5. Huston Smith, 'Wasson's *Soma,*' in the *Journal of The American Academy of Religion* XL:4, p.481, note 2(9), December, 1972.

6. Forte, *Outside,* 252.

7. Huston Smith, *Tales,* 174, and also Greenfield, 131, who gives a good report on this part of the trip.)

8. Huston Smith, "The Incredible Assumption," in *The Pulpit* 32, no.2, Feb. 1961, reprinted in *Beyond the Postmodern Mind* (New York: Crossroads, 1989), 262.

9. Huxley, *Island,* 67.

10. Michael Horowitz, Leary's archivist, gave me copies of Huston's session reports.

11. Don Lattin, *The Harvard Psychedelic Club* (New York: HarperCollins, 2010), 69, and Jay Stevens, *Storming Heaven,* 161.

12. Leary, *Flashbacks,* 101.

13. See Huston's description in *Cleansing,* 99-105, and in Lattin, *Havard,* 69-77.

14. Greenfield, 181.

15. Forte, *Outside,*157.

16. Ibid., 257.

17. W.T. Stace, *Mysticism and Philosophy* (Los Angeles: Tarcher, 1987), 44.

18 Walter Houston Clark, *Chemical Ecstasy* (New York: Sheed and Ward, 1969), 78.

19. Greenfield, 159.

20. Stevens, *Storming,* 160.

21. Ibid., 163.

## Chapter Thirteen: IF Squared

1. Watts had been inspired by the spiritual changes he saw in his friends Huxley and Heard after they had tried psychedelics, so he underwent experiments of his own with Keith Ditman, a psychiatrist at UCLA. For example, see Greenfield, 155, and Watts, *In My Own Way,* 342-3.

2. Forte, *Outside,* 186.

3. Huston Smith, *Cleansing,* 16.

4. Horowitz gave me a copy of IFIF's Statement of Purpose but it also appears in Forte, *Outside,* 11.

5. Greenfield, 193.

6. Forte, *Outside,* 260.

7. Ibid., 189.

8. Greenfield, 195, and see also Stevens, *Storming,* 163.

9. For Weil's part in all this, see Latin, *Harvard,* 82-83 and 90-92, and also Forte's interview with Weil in Forte, *Outside,* 305-318.

10. Greenfield, p.197.

11. Lattin, *Harvard,* 90.

12. Andrew Weil, *The Natural Mind,* (New York: Houghton Mifflin, 2004), 8-9.

# Notes

13. Greenfield, 211.

14. Forte, *Outside*, 261-2.

15. Clark, *Chemical Ecstasy*, 46.

16. Forte, *Outside*, 254.

17. Stevens, *Storming*, 196.

18. Lattin, *Harvard,* 109.

19. Greenfield, 206.

20 Forte, *Outside*, 260-261.

21. Leary quoted in Stevens, *Storming*, 192.

22. Huston Smith, *Cleansing,* 30.

23. Ibid., 16.

24. Huston Smith, *Cleansing,* p.30.

25. Greenfield, 279.

26. Ibid., 280.

27. Ibid.

28. Lattin cites the same quote in *Harvard,* 139.

29. Huston Smith, "The Reach and the Grasp, Transcendence Today," in *Transcendence*, 13.

30. Stace, *Mysticism*, 31.

31. Huston sometimes attributes this quote to Ram Dass, e.g., in *Tales*, page 175, but at other times he says it was Watts. To my mind it was most likely Watts, e.g., see Watts' *In My Own Way*, page 347: "My retrospective attitude to LSD is that when one has received the message, one hangs up the phone."

## Chapter Fourteen: Trying to Count at MIT

1. Forte, *Outside*, 46 and see also Leary, *Flashbacks*, 109.

2. Huston Smith, *The Way,* 269.

3. Huston Smith, *Tales,* 67.

4. Quoted in Stanislav Grof, *The Cosmic Game* (Albany, NY: SUNY Press, 1998), 227.

5. Quoted in Simon Blackburn, *The Oxford Dictionary of Philosophy* (Oxford: Oxford University Press, 1994), 344.

6. Huston Smith, "Technology and Human Values: The American Moment," in ed. Cameron P. Hall, *Human Values and Advancing Technology* (New York: Friendship Press, 1967), 19.

7. Ibid., 24.

8. Ibid., 27.

9. Huston Smith, *Beyond*, 86-87.

10. Horgan, *Rational Mysticism*, 24.

11. Huston Smith, *Tales*, 67.

12. Huston Smith, *Why Religion Matters* (New York: HarperCollins, 2001), 237.

13. Huston Smith, *Condemned to Meaning*, 39.

14. Ibid., 28.

15. Peter Berger, *Sacred Canopy* (New York: Doubleday, 1967).

16. Like Huston, J.D. Salinger kept a long-term relationship with the Vedanta Society, though in his case at the Boston offices, and many of its ideas filter into his novels and stories.

## Chapter Fifteen: Teaching Science to the Dalai Lama

1. Huston Smith, *The Way,* 86.

2. Huston gave the Charles Strong lectures in Australia, in 1961 (See Bryant, *Essays*, 18), so he either visited Blofeld in 1961 or he made a second trip, which I doubt and he can't remember.

3. Huston Smith, *Why Religion Matters,* 269.

4. John Blofeld, *The Wheel of Life* (Berkeley: Shambhala, 1972), 236.

5 Harry Oldmeadow, *Journeys East* (Bloomington, IN: World Wisdom, 2004), 141.

6. Greenfield, *Leary*, 228-229.

7. Forte, *Outside*, 259.

8. Bryant, 167.

9. Ibid.

10. Ibid.

11. Quoted by Marsha Newman in Huston Smith, *The Way*, 168.

12. Huston Smith, *The Way*, 271.

13. Ibid.

14. Huston Smith, *The Way*, 71.

15. Ibid.

16. Dalai Lama, *The Universe in a single Atom* (NY: Morgan Road Books, 2005), 26-27.

17. For a similar treatment of this story, see Huston Smith, *Forgotten Truth*, 123.

18. Michael Toms, "The Wisdom of Huston Smith" (Ukiah, CA: New Dimensions Radio, 1998).

## Chapter Sixteen: Leaving MIT

1. Bryant, 69.

2. Huston Smith, *Tales*, 108.

3. Bryant, 227.

4. Huston Smith, *Tales*, 108.

5. Huston has often remarked that it was *he* who went north to meet the Dalai Lama. For example, he said in an interview in 1992, reported in *The Way*, 69: ""We ended the week by flying together from Calcutta to Delhi. I was going up to the Tibetans in northern India at Dharamsala, and he was going down to Thailand to his death." However, most of this is not correct. Huston was not on sabbatical, so it is likely he had to get back to work. Furthermore, Merton's detailed biography by Thomas Mott and the one by Monica Furlong, both say that he went north to Dharamsala at that time, after which he went to Darjeeling, before leaving India for Sri Lanka, and then, finally, Bangkok.

6. Huston Smith, *Tales*, 62.

7. Ibid., 63.

8. See Huston Smith, *The Way*, 103, but note that Phil Cousineau follows Huston's note on the reprint that the interview occurred in April of 1972, but the reprint itself says that it took place on March 8, 1973. This seems more likely.

9. Ibid., 106.

10. Ibid.

11. "Henry Nelson Wieman" on the website for the "Dictionary of Unitarian & UniversalistBiography",(http://www25.uua.org/uuhs/duub/articles/henrynelsonwieman.html)

12. Ibid.

13. This interview is easy to find online, e.g., watch it at (http://www.youtube.com/watch?v=o8ppwpRkUdA)

14. For example, see Philip Goldberg, *American Veda*, 161.

15. Huston Smith, *The Way*, 65.

16. Ibid., 110.

17. Robert Bellah, *Habits of the Heart* (Berkeley, CA: UC Press, 1985), 228.

18. Huston Smith, *The Way*, 152.

19. Huston Smith in Seyyed Hossein Nasr, *Ideals and Realities of Islam* (Boston: Beacon Press, 1972), xiv.

20. For example, in *The Way*, 53, Huston says: "The Koran itself had seemed to me the least accessible scripture in the world."

## Chapter Seventeen: Becoming a Sufi

1. See almost this same exact comment from Huston in Martin Lings, *A Return to the Spirit* (Louisville, KY: Fons Vitae, 2005), xii.

2. Note that Huston says in *Tales of Wonder*, on page144, that he read Schuon's books as he traveled around the world in 1974, but in several other places (e.g., in *Transcendent Unity*, p.x, and *The Way*, p.xix) he says it was the 1969 trip, which is what he told me.

3. Huston Smith in Fritjof Schuon, *The Transcendent Unity of Religions* (Wheaton, IL: Quest Books, 1984), p.x.

4. Ibid.

5. Seyyed Hossein Nasr, ed., *The Essential Frithjof Schuon* (Bloomington, IN: World Wisdom, 2005), 149.

6. Schuon, *Transcendent*, 10.

7. René Guénon's *The Multiple States of the Being* (Hilldale, NY: Sophis Perennis, 2001), 83.

8. In the years ahead he would launch scathing diatribes against the Western world, and as Jacob Needleman has noted in his excellent introduction to Traditionalist philosophy, *The Sword of Gnosis* (p.11): "Many of Guénon's books, notably *The Reign of Quantity*, are such potent and detailed metaphysical attacks on the downward drift of Western civilization as to make all other contemporary critiques—be they sociological, psychological or moralistic—seem half-hearted by comparison."

9. Jacob Needleman, *The Sword of Gnosis* (Baltimore, MD: Penguin, 1974), 14.

10. Ibid.

11. Huston Smith, *The Way*, 157.

12. Mark Sedgwick, *Against the Modern World* (Oxford: Oxford University Press, 2004), 89, and note that Sedgwick describes the controversy in detail on 88 to 92.

13. Huston Smith, *Tales*, 144.

14. Lings, *A Return*, 11.

15. Huston was very clear when I quizzed him that he had not been initiated or named by Schuon, but note that he says otherwise in *Tales*, 145. Also, I feel compelled to add, Huston shared his Muslim name with me but made me promise not to reveal it while he was alive, which is why it doesn't appear here.

16. Huston in Nasr, *Ideals*, v.

17. Greenfield, *Leary*, 438-439.

## Chapter Eighteen: Forgotten Truth

1. S.H. Nasr, ed., *The Essential Frithjof Schuon* (Bloomington IN: World Wisdom, 2005), 68. (Here Schuon is paraphrasing a well-known saying by St. Irenaeus.) For another very good, short introduction to the Traditionalists' form of perennialism, see Jacob Nedleman, ed., *The Sword of Gnosis*.

2. James S. Cutsinger, *Advice to the Serious Seeker: Meditations on the Teachings of Frithjof Schuon* (Albany, NY: SUNY Press, 1997), 28. Note that his quote is from Schuon himself.

3. Ibid, 189.

4. Smith, *The Way*, 7.

5. Mark Sedgwick, *Against the Modern World* (New York: Oxford University Press, 2004), 167.

6. According to Huston (See *Forgotten Truth*, 153), Ellsberg actually proofread his manuscript for *Forgotten Truth*, making comments and suggestions.

7. See also Ken Wilber, *No Boundary* (Boston Shambhala, 2001), 124, and Ken Wilber, *One Taste* (Boston: Shambhala, 2000), 53: "Aldous Huxley, of course, wrote a famous book, *The Perennial*

*Philosophy*, which is about the universal core of the world's great wisdom traditions. Huston Smith's *Forgotten Truth* is still its best introduction."

8. Bryant, 113.

9. Ibid. 114-115.

10. Huston Smith, "Frithjof Schuon's *The Transcendent Unity of Religions*: Pro," JAAR XLIV, 4, Dec.1976, pp.721-725.

11. Ibid., 722.

12. Or as Huston put it in *Forgotten Truth*: ". . . neither can such terms be avoided. Insofar as we think, spatial images are inevitable, for thought proceeds through language, and language is forged in our encounter with the spatio-temporal world." (20)

13. Smith, *JAAR*, 1976, 723.

14. Ibid., 724.

15. Danner actually lead the branch of Schuon's group in Bloomington, where Huston was initiated.

16. From my interview with Philip Novak, who reported these words of Danner.

17. Smith, *Why Religion Matters*, 252.

18. Smith, *Tales*, 121.

19. Ibid., 122.

## Chapter Nineteen: Stan and Joe

1. Bryant, 91.

2. Saul Bellow, quoted in Smith, *Cleansing*, 68.

3. Stanislav Grof, *The Cosmic Game*, xxxiii-xxxiv.

4. Jeffrey J. Kripal, *Esalen: America and the Religion of No Religion* (Chicago: University of Chicago Press, 2007), 255.

5. Grof, *Cosmic Game*, 3.

6. Stanislav Grof, *The Holotropic Mind* (New York: HarperCollins, 1993), 21.

7. Smith, *Forgotten Truth*, 155-6.

8. Grof, *Cosmic Game*, 3.

9. Smith, *Cleansing*, 20.

10. Ibid., 23.

11. Ibid.

12. R.C. Zaehner, *Zen, Drugs & Mysticism* (New York: Vintage Books, 1972), 79.

13. Ibid, 109-110.

14. Huston Smith, "Wasson's SOMA, a Review Article," *JAAR*, IL, 4 (Dec., 1972): 480-499. See also Smith, *Cleansing*, 45-63.

15. Philip Goldberg, *American Veda* (New York: Random House, 2010), 106.

16. Watts, *In My Own Way*, 231.

17. Joseph Campbell with Bill Moyers, *The Power of Myth* (New York: Doubleday, 1988), xvi.

18. Ibid., xv.

19. Ibid., xi.

20. For another telling of this story, see Huston Smith, *And Live Rejoicing!* (Novato, CA: New World Library, 2012), 174-175.

21. Stanislav Grof, *When the Impossible Happens* (Boulder CO: Sounds True, 2006), 21.

22. Ibid.

23. Grof, *Cosmic Game*, 248.

24. Huston Smith, *Tales*, 13, but note that in actuality Campbell was raised a Catholic and not exposed to Calvinism, a mistake on Huston's part.

# Notes

## Chapter Twenty: Esalen

1. Kripal, *Esalen*, 6.

2. Ibid., see for a description of Huxley and Heard's influence on Esalen, 85-92.

3. Maslow's lists are given on p.25 of *The Third Force* by Frank Goble (New York: Simon & Schuster, 1971), and it's interesting to note how similar they are in criteria to those of Maurice Bucke, who, in his book *Cosmic Consciousness* (1900), also made lists of self-realized people.

4. Grof, *Impossible*, 187.

5. While Huston and I were discussing Campbell's view that the content of myth can be applied meaningfully to the issues of daily life, Huston remarked, "But that was it. He didn't have any real interest in other traditional techniques of awakening. He didn't meditate or anything like that." At the time, I simply filed the comment away, but the point came up again when I read Kripal's history of Esalen. Kripal relates that after Campbell died, Huston wrote a short piece about Campbell for the Esalen catalog which contained an addenda to what Huston told me. It seems that Huston and Joe were at the Menniger Foundation, attending a conference on traditional techniques of awakening, and Campbell was exhibiting more energy than any of the yogis, gurus, and psychics in the room, so he was quizzed about this. As Huston explained it in the catalog: "When asked about his 'yoga,' Campbell denied that he had one, other than 'reading books.' He then thought for a moment: 'Actually, I do have a yoga,' he said. 'It consists of rare roast beef, good Irish whiskey, and forty laps in the pool every day—in twenty minutes.'" (Kripal, *Esalen*, 192.)

6. Huston had published an essay, "Empirical Metaphysics," in Ralph Metzner, ed., *The Ecstatic Adventure* (New York: Macmillan, 1968), and often used the term in his later work.

7. Smith, *The Way*, 254.

8. See "The Sacred Unconscious," in Huston's book *Beyond the Postmodern Mind* (New York: Quest Books, 1996), 247-256, for a detailed description of his new position on enlightenment.

9. Smith, *Forgotten Truth*, 113.

10. See Novak's own article on enlightenment as an asymptote in *ReVision*, Summer 1989 (vol.12,no.1), 45.

11. Bryant, 97.

12. Smith, *The Way*, 97. This quote comes in Chapter 6, "Encountering God," a three-page chapter in which Huston confesses his own inability to hold onto the ultimate perspective: "But I cannot hold onto it. When those grace-filled moments arrive, it does not seem strange to be so happy, but in retrospect I wonder how such gold of Eden could have been mine."

## Chapter Twenty-One: Wisdomkeepers

1. Huston went to Kyoto in 1983 to attend an "International Symposium for Religious Philosophy," and in 1985 attended a conference on 'Religion and Science' in Bombay, where he gave a paper on "The Conceptual Crisis in the Modern West."

2. See Huston's essay, "Another World to Live in, or How I Teach the Introductory Course," in Bryant, 237, since this essay came from his first workshop.

3. From my phone interview with Robert Forte.

4. Huston's presentation didn't make it into the book, but in 2000, he released his own collection of essays about psychedelics, *Cleansing the Doors of Perception*, which included his comments, and is another of the books I most recommend on the subject.

5. Huston Smith and Phil Cousineau, *A Seat at Table* (Berkeley: University of California Press, 2006), 2.

6. Ibid.

7. Michael Toms, "The Wisdom of Huston Smith: in conversation with Michael Toms" (Santa Rosa, CA: New Dimensions Radio, 1999), four cassette tapes.

8. Huston Smith, *Philosophy East and West* 22, 4 (October 1972): 441-459.

9. Huston Smith, *A Seat*, 52.

10. Ibid., 163.

11. See another version of this story in Huston Smith, *The Way*, 208.

12. Smith, *The Way*, 209.

13. Smith and Cousineau, *A Seat,* 4.

14. Smith and Cousineau, *A Seat*, xvii.

15. Ibid., 169.

16. The Panchen Lama is the second highest ranking lama in the Geluk sect of Tibetan Buddhism, and as such must grant legitimacy to the choice made by those selecting the new Dalai Lama after the old one dies.

17. This is all from Serena's dad's (Stuart Karlan's) description of her disappearance in the *San Francisco Chronicle*.

## Chapter Twenty-Two: Car Trouble in Tanzania

1. We find Huston telling pretty much the same story in *Why Religion Matters*, 189.

2. From Dena Kleiman, "'Tunnel Vision' Termed a Threat," *The New York Times*, June 24, 1980.

3. Huston Smith, *The Way*, 125.

4. For the development, in 1926, of what is commonly called "Schrodinger's wave equation," based on his studies of photons in the use of X-rays.

5. Erwin Schrodinger, *Was ist Leben?*, trans. L. Mazurczak, Bern, 1946,128, but translated into English in Lothar Fietz, "At the Crossroads of Science, Metaphysics and Religion," *Aldous Huxley Annual*, vol.7, 2007, Munster, Germany, 224.

6. Ibid., 230.

7. Huston Smith, "Excluded Knowledge," *Teachers College Record*, vol.80, 3 November, l979.

8. Huston Smith, *Beyond the Postmodern Mind* (New York: Crossroads Publishing, 1989), 84.

9. Ibid.

10. Ibid., 137.

11. Ibid., 85.

12. Huston Smith, in Bryant, *Essays*, 270.

13. Simon Blackburn, *The Oxford Dictionary of Philosophy*, 295.

14. Huston Smith, in Bryant, *Essays*, 270.

15. *Beyond the Postmodern Mind* was dedicated to Huston's grandchildren: Serena, Gael's daughter, and Sierra and Isaiah, Karen's daughter and son. Another grandchild, Kim's son Antonio, was not yet born.

16. Huston Smith, *Beyond*, 217-218.

17. Ibid., 240.

18. Huston Smith, in Bryant, *Essays*, 271.

19. Ibid., 270.

20. Huston Smith, *The Way,* 34-35.

21. Huston Smith, *Beyond*, 239.

22. Huston Smith, in Bryant, *Essays*, 263, and in *JAAR* LVIII/4 (1990), 653-670.

23. Ibid., 262.

24. Huston Smith, in Bryant, *Essays*, 274.

25. Ibid., 269.

26. Ibid., 270-271.

27. Horgan, 40.

28. Ibid., 41.

29. Steven T. Katz, "Language, Epistemology, and Mysticism," in Steven T. Katz, ed., *Mysticism and Philosophical Analysis* (New York: Oxford University Press, 1978), 24.

30. Ibid., 24.

31. Ibid., 26.

32. Hans Penner, "The Mystical Illusion," in Steven T. Katz, ed., *Mysticism and Religious Traditions* (New York: Oxford University Press, 1983), 89.

33. Huston Smith, "Is There a Perennial Philosophy?", *JAAR*, vol.55,No.3, (Autumn, 1987), 553-566.

34. Steven T. Katz, *JAAR* LVIII/4 (1990), 653-670, and in the same issue, Huston on pp.757-759.

35. Huston Smith, in Horgan, 48.

36. Ibid.

37. Ibid., 48-49.

38. Huston Smith, *Beyond*, 244.

39. Ibid., 245.

40. David Ray Griffin and Huston Smith, *Primordial Truth and Postmodern Theology* (Ablany:SUNY Press: 1989).

41. Huston Smith, in David Ray Griffin and Huston Smith, *Primordial Truth and Postmodern Theology* (Albany: SUNY Press, 1989), 74.

42. Ibid., xiv.

43. Huston Smith, "Is Onto-theology Passe? Or can Religion Endure the Death of Metaphysics?," in the Journal *Religion and Intellectual Life*, III, 3 (Spring,1986), 9.

## Chapter Twenty-Three: Peyote in Mazatlan

1. Huston Smith, *Why Religion Matters* (New York: HarperCollins, 2001), 207-208.

2. Leroy S. Rouner, ed., *On Community* (Notre Dame, ID: University of Notre Dame Press, 1991). This was a book dedicated to Huston Smith, who had worked on several other book projects with Rouner, including *On Nature* (1984) and *On Freedom* (1989).

3. Marilyn Gustin, in Arvind Sharma, ed., *Fragments of Infinity* (Bridport, England: Prism Press, 1991), 13.

4. Philip Goldberg, *American Veda*, 28.

5. Betty Sue Flowers, in her "Editor's Note" to Joseph Campbell, *The Power of Myth* (New York: Doubleday, 1988), xi.

6. Huston Smith and Reuben Snake, *One Nation Under God* (Santa Fe, NM: Clear Light Publishers, 1996), 10.

7. Huston Smith, *Why Religion Matters*, 124.

8. Huston Smith, *One Nation*, 9.

9. Ibid.,136, but note that Alfred Smith tells his own story of the court case in the same book, beginning on page 68, and see also the description of the case by Frank Dayish Jr. (then President of the Native American Church) in Huston Smith, *A Seat at the Table* (Berkeley: UC Press, 2006), 102-112.

10. Ibid. 137.

11. Ibid., 138.

12. Ibid., 140.

13. Ibid., 15.

14. Ibid., 18.

15. Ibid., 84.

16. Ibid., 22.

17. Beginning on page 75 of *One Nation* there is an excellent description of the Peyote ritual by Phil Cousineau and Gary Rhine.

18. Ibid., 21.

19. Ibid., 8.

20. Huston Smith, *The Way*, 239.

21. Ibid., 222.

22. Jamie Talan, reporting in *Scientific American Mind*, Oct. 4, 2006, 7.

23. Huston Smith, *The Way*, 223-224.

24. Ibid., 224.

25. Forte, *Outside Looking In*, 265.

26. Huston Smith, *Tales*, 89.

27. Huston Smith, *The Way*, 25-26.

28. Huston Smith, *Tales*, 90-91.

29. Huston Smith, *Why Religion Matters*, 276.

30. Ibid.

31. Ibid.

## Chapter Twenty-Four: Why Religion Matters

1. For instance, the Dalai Lama wrote in *The Essence of the Heart Sutra* (Boston, 2002), 10: "Although the world's religions differ widely in terms of metaphysics and philosophy, the conclusions these differing philosophies arrive at—that is, their ethical teachings—show a high degree of convergence. In this sense we can say that regardless of whatever metaphysical explanations religious traditions employ, they all reach similar conclusions. In some form or other, the philosophies of all world religions emphasize love, compassion, tolerance, forgiveness, and the importance of self-discipline. Though interfaith and interpersonal communication, sharing, and respect, we can learn to appreciate the valuable qualities taught by all religions, and the ways in which all religions can benefit humanity."

2. Huston Smith, *The Way*, 205.

3. Ibid.

4. Note that two years later, in 2001, he shared these same points in an interview with Phil Cousineau: "First, reality is more unified than it appears. Second, reality is better than it ordinarily seems to us. Third, reality is more mysterious than it looks."

5. Huston Smith, *The Way*, 185.

6. Huston gives his universal grammar in an appendix to *Tales of Wonder*, and in Henry Rosemont Jr and Huston Smith, *Is There a Universal Grammar of Religion?*, Peru, IL: Open Court Publishing, 2008.) Huston's list of the 14 common characteristics of the world's religions is as follows: (1) Reality is Infinite: (2) The infinite includes the finite, "or we would be left with infinite plus finite and the Infinite would not be what it claims to be"; (3) The contents of finitude are ordered in a hierarchical arrangement, "from the meagerest kind of existence through every possible grade, up to boundless Infinite"; (4) Causation is from the top down (so consciousness produces the world, rather than vice versa); (5) "In descending to finitude, the singularity of the Infinite splays into multiplicity, the One becomes the many." And so, "The parts of the many are virtues" and the "foundational virtue is existence; to be more than figments of the imagination, virtues must exist." And here he lists the Indian "virtues" as consciousness and bliss, and the "West's ternary is the good, the true, and the beautiful," and all of these open out into "creativity, compassion, and love until we arrive at Islam's Ninety-nine Beautiful Names of God." And the last of these virtues, he tells us, is mystery itself; (6) As we ascend the causal ladder, all things, including the virtues, merge toward Oneness and lose their individual identities. "Flannery O'Connor titled one of her short stories *Everything That Rises Must Converge* and this is so"; (7) viewed from the top of the ladder, "absolute perfection reigns"; (8) What is highest above us is also what is deepest within us, and so from one perspective we are half-way up the

Ladder of Being but from another we are the entire Ladder in microcosm, having both finite and infinite characteristics in each degree (see Huston's diagram of this point in *Beyond the Post-modern Mind*, 68); (9) "Human beings cannot fully know the Infinite." And "if we are to know it confidently, the Infinite must take the initiative and show itself to us in the way nature takes the initiative in instilling the universal grammar of languages in the human mind"; (10) "intimations of the Infinite have to be interpreted," and they do so through four progressively higher "steps of ascending importance: literal, ethical, allegorical, and anagogic, the text's capacity to inspire us"; (11) "Religion's technical language is symbolism . . . [and] more fully, it is myth, metaphor, parable, figures of speech, and story:" (12)"there are two distinct and complementing ways of knowing: the rational and the intuitive," and here he means by "intuitive" the application of *intellectus*; (13) "Walnuts have shells that house kernels, and religions likewise have outsides and insides; outer, exoteric forms that house inner, esoteric cores"; (14)"we are born in mystery, and we die in mystery."  He ends his 'grammar' by adding: "In a single sentence: The world is perfect, and the human opportunity is to see that and conform to that fact."

7. Huston Smith, *The Way*, 181.

8. Huston Smith, *Why Religion Matters*, xiv, where Huston tells us his working title for the book had been, "The Human Spirit in the Third Millennium."

9. Ibid., 273.

10. Ibid.

11. Ibid., 180.

12. Huston Smith, *The Way*, 259.

13. Huston Smith, *Islam, a Concise Introduction* (New York: HarperCollins, 2001), and note that this book is mostly a reprint of his chapter on Islam from *The World's Religions*.

14. Ibid., viii.

15. Ibid., viii-ix.

16. From the 2005 Parabola article with Phil Cousineau, "Why Fundamentalism matters," 62.

17. Huston Smith, *The Way*, 265.

18. Ibid., 260.

19. Huston Smith, with Jessica Roemischer, "Can Religion Save us?," in *What is Enlightenment?* (Spring/Summer 2003), 72.

20. Ibid., 74.

21. Ibid.

22. Ibid., 75.

23. Ibid., 76.

24. Ibid.

25. Goldberg, 241.

26. Jeffrey J. Kripal, "Secret Talk: The Politics of Scholarship in Hindu Tantrism."). *Harvard Divinity Bulletin*, vol.29, no.4, winter 2000/2001, 14-17.

27. Huston Smith, in *Harvard Divinity Bulletin*, vol.30, no.1, spring 2001, 2.

28. Ibid.s

29. Jeffrey J. Kripal, *The Serpent's Gift* (Chicago: University of Chicago Press, 2007), 17.

30. The most denigrating criticism of *Kali's Child* came from Swami Tyagananda (a monk of the Vedanta Order, who is also the Hindu chaplain at both MIT and Harvard) and Pravrajika Vrajaprana (a nun of the Ramakrishna Order living in Santa Barbara), in their book *Interpreting Ramakrishna: Kali's Child Revisited* (Motilal Banarsidass, July 2010), and the most exhaustive analysis of the dispute, which for the most part sided with Kripal, came from Rajagopal Chattopadhyaya, an Indian scholar, in *Ramakrishna: Kali's Child and Lover* (San Jose, CA: Vyasdeb Chatterjee, 2010).

31. Kripal, *Serpent's Gift*, 18.

Chapter Twenty-Five: No Wasted Journey

1. Huston Smith, *Tales*, 91.

2. Ibid.

3. (From the ESPN website, transcript from Show 131 of the weekly "Outside the Lines" with Tim Keown reporting on "The mystery of Bison Dele," which aired on September 29th (http://espn.go.com/page2/tvlistings/show131transcript.html). For further details, see also Chris Ballard, "Lost Soul." *Sports Illustrated* (October 21, 2013).

4. Huston Smith, *Tales,* 92.

5. Ibid., 92-93.

6. Ibid., 94.

7. Ibid., 181.

8. Gray Henry, film interview with Huston Smith, "Death and Transformation" (2006), available from Fons Vitae Press (www.fonsvitae.com)

9. Film of Ken Dychtwald interview with Huston Smith, "The Arc of Life" (2009), available from Gems Tone (www.mondayMEDIA.com)

10. Huston Smith, *Tales*, 185.

11. Huston Smith, *Why Religion Matters*, 270-271.

12. Horgan, 233.

13. Huston Smith, *The Way*, 26.

14. Ibid.

15. Note that Huston makes a very similar comment in *And Live Rejoicing!,* 194, and gets the details correct. Huston often attributed the story of being pulled behind a chariot to the life of John Chrysostom, but Chrysostom died after a forced march had exhausted his aged body. What matters is the that Chrysostom's last words were indeed words of gratitude.

16. Goldberg, 106.

17. Huston Smith, *The Religions of Man*, 7.

18. Horgan, 18.

19. Huston Smith, *The Way*, 276.

20. Huston Smith, *The World's Religions,* 390-391.

21. Stephen Prothero comment in Lisa Miller, "Huston Smith's Wonderful Life," *Newsweek* (May 11, 2009), 49.

22. See especially Robert K.C. Forman, *Mysticism, Mind, Consciousness* (Albany: SUNY Press, 1999). Though Forman criticizes the perennialists in certain regards, his defense of the viability of Pure Consciousness, which Huxley termed the unitive knowledge, strongly supports their general thesis.

23. Rick Strassman, *DMT: The Spirit Molecule* (Rochester, VT: Park Street Press, 2001), 341.

# Index

# Index

# Index